Residential Mortgage Lending

5th Edition

Principles and Practices

THOMSON

SOUTH-WESTERN

Residential Mortgage Lending: Principles and Practices, 5th Edition
By Marshall W. Dennis and Thomas J. Pinkowish

Vice President/Editorial Director
Jack Calhoun

Vice President/Editor-in-Chief
Dave Shaut

Director of Publishing, Real Estate, and Professional Certification
Scott Person

Developmental Editor
Sara Froelicher

Production Manager
Tricia Matthews Boies

Production Editor
Tim Bailey

Marketing Manager
Mark Linton

Design Project Manager
Bethany Casey

Manufacturing Coordinator
Charlene Taylor

Cover Designer
Bethany Casey

Production
Argosy Publishing
(Waltham, MA)

Printer
RR Donnelley
(Crawfordsville, IN)

Residential Mortgage Lending

5th Edition

Principles and Practices

Marshall W. Dennis
President, REMOC ASSOCIATES, LTD

Thomas J. Pinkowish
President, Community Lending Associates

THOMSON

SOUTH-WESTERN

Australia · Canada · Mexico · Singapore · Spain · United Kingdom · United States

Contents

Chapter 16   Compliance

Chapter 17   Construction Lending

Chapter 18   Home Equity Loans

List of Figures

Preface

The basic purpose of this textbook remains the same as prior editions: to identify and explain the fundamentals of residential mortgage lending in as simple and concise a manner as possible. The textbook is designed for both employees of mortgage lenders and college students studying real estate finance who want to supplement that study with practical residential mortgage-lending principles and practices. Unlike many real estate finance textbooks published recently, which spend an inordinate amount of space on mathematical formulas, this textbook will actually help the reader learn how to make a residential mortgage loan.

A new employee of any mortgage lender probably needs at least the first six months to understand both the specific job requirements and some of the fundamentals of residential mortgage lending. This textbook is for that individual, whether the employing mortgage lender is a mortgage banker, commercial bank, savings and loan institution, credit union, or savings bank.

The backgrounds of those entering the mortgage-lending field today range from those with solid real estate finance training to those with no formal academic training. Whatever their experience or training, all of these students can and will succeed if they have the ability to learn and apply what they have learned. No prior knowledge of finance or any part of mortgage lending is assumed in this textbook. The reader is assumed to possess only the ability and willingness to learn.

This textbook discusses each topic beginning with the fundamentals and develops them to the point at which it is hoped the reader has a basic understanding of that topic. Not all topics are applicable to every mortgage lender, nor will they be of interest at the time to all readers, but to understand the basics of modern residential mortgage lending, each subject included needs to be comprehensively understood. Changes occur so rapidly in this segment of the economy that an area in which a particular mortgage lender is not involved today may be where the growth and profit potential are tomorrow. All mortgage lenders should prepare for this growth and change by either employing suitably educated personnel or providing that education.

While explaining the fundamentals of residential mortgage lending, this textbook also examines the similarities and differences that exist among mortgage lenders. Basically, therefore, this book is designed to fulfill the need of all mortgage lenders for a basic textbook to prepare new employees for the important job of helping to finance the growing housing needs of the United States.

Finally, with this edition, I am pleased to introduce Thomas J. Pinkowish as coauthor. Tom is an accomplished third-party underwriter of mortgage loans for many different classifications of mortgage lenders and is the director of the Community Lending Institute. His mortgage-lending experience is extensive and includes running the loan administration department of a savings bank. Tom worked on the chapters covering processing, underwriting, appraisal, mortgage insurance, and construction lending. I'm honored to have Tom as coauthor.

Acknowledgments

Both Tom and I are deeply indebted to a number of experts for their valuable advice and assistance in preparing this textbook. These individuals were most generous with their time and shared their many years of experience in mortgage lending.

John P. Brady, executive vice president, Staten Island Savings Bank, Staten Island, New York, assisted in reviewing conventional lending practices.

Dr. Jack Brick, president, Brick and Associates, East Lansing, Michigan, reviewed material in the chapter on the role of mortgage lending in the economy.

Jeffrey L. Briggs, senior vice president, Centerbank, Waterbury, Connecticut, contributed to the discussion on loan servicing.

Louis Capobianco, vice president, Credit Bureau of Connecticut, Rocky Hill, Connecticut, provided the credit report and instructions on how it is to be read.

Doug Duncan, chief economist, Mortgage Bankers Association of America, Washington, D.C., provided valuable insight into loan servicing.

Stephen A. J. Eisenberg, general counsel, Pentagon Federal Credit Union, Alexandria, Virginia, reviewed the chapter on real estate law and made many valuable suggestions.

Robert Halpin, executive vice president, and David Zamary, vice president, First County Bank, Stamford, Connecticut, were very helpful in providing residential mortgage loan documents.

Joseph F. Lynch, Northeast regional sales manager, Sound Software, Shelton, Connecticut, provided examples of documents for a first-mortgage loan when the need was great.

Denise M. Ouellette, vice president—secondary markets, Mortgage Department, Navy Federal Credit Union, Vienna, Virginia, assisted with the two chapters on the secondary mortgage market.

Michael J. Robertson, branch manager, Wells Fargo Wholesale Lending, Madison, Wisconsin, and a licensed appraiser reviewed and made valuable comments on the appraisal chapter. Mike was the coauthor of the fourth edition of this book.

Griff Straw, CMB, regional sales director, United Guaranty Residential Insurance Company, Fairfax, Virginia, an old friend and former student whose knowledge far exceeds his professor, provided valuable assistance in writing this book.

David W. Stokes, executive vice president, Integrated Loan Services, Rocky Hill, Connecticut, was very generous with various loan documents.

Barry Stricklin, vice president, Pentagon Federal Credit Union, Alexandria, Virginia, provided information on VA loans.

Wayne Walker, senior vice president; Kathleen Zembrzuski, vice president; and Ava Bonardi, delivery systems manager, all of People's Bank, Bridgeport, Connecticut, were very generous in providing various conventional loan documents.

Marina Walsh, manager of economics and research, Mortgage Bankers Association of American, Washington, D.C., provided recent information and guidance on the costs of servicing residential loans.

Heidi Yanavich, assistant to the president, McCue Mortgage Company, New Britain, Connecticut, provided current information dealing with government programs and wrote part of Chapter 8.

We'd also like to thank the associates of CFT, Center for Financial Training, and in particular Michael Mackay, Frank J. Pidgeon, and J. T. Turner, for their invaluable input on the manuscript.

Finally, a special thank you to my wife, Marilyn, for her many hours of tedious reading of the chapter drafts.

Marshall W. Dennis
Monroe, Connecticut

Dedication

After nearly thirty years, she is still there—hard to believe with what she has to put up with. To my patient wife, Marilyn, with love.

And a special dedication to my daughter Lisa, who shares a birthday and many traits with me!

—Marshall W. Dennis

To my wife, Mary, who provided support and understanding and who was behind me all the way. To my parents, Alex and Juddie, from whom I always received help, guidance, and love.

—Thomas J. Pinkowish

History of Mortgage Lending

Introduction

Today's student or practitioner of residential mortgage lending may be hard pressed to keep pace with this rapidly changing business. This is a segment of our society and economy that indeed changes from year to year, if not month to month. The extent of the recent changes in residential mortgage lending is breathtaking and is reflected in the following events:

- $2 trillion per year (2001 and 2002) of total residential mortgage **originations**
- Lowest interest rates for 30-year **fixed-rate mortgage** (5.50 percent in first quarter 2003) in decades
- Homeownership at a historical high of 68.1 percent (2002)
- Extensive use of automated underwriting systems and other technological changes
- Dramatic growth in the use of **mortgage-backed securities (MBSs)**
- Evolution of alternative types of mortgage instruments
- Ever-increasing dominance of the **mortgage banking** strategy
- Expansion of online mortgage origination

These developments could lead one to assume that all meaningful changes have occurred in only the past couple of years or so. That assumption would be wrong. Residential mortgage lending is, and always has been, a constantly changing part of our economic life and history.

The basic concepts of mortgage lending have developed over centuries, and the use of **mortgages** can be traced to the beginning of recorded history. Many of the complexities of today's residential mortgage lending system are the result of problems that existed not only half a century ago but hundreds of years ago as well. To truly understand how and why residential mortgage lending works today, an understanding of this history is essential.

The Beginning

The underlying product in all real estate activities is land. Sociologists have claimed that the use of land, the desire to acquire it, and the need to regulate its transfer were among the fundamental reasons for the development of governments and laws. As government developed, laws were formulated to govern the ownership and use of land.

Because of the importance of land in an agrarian society, it was soon being used as security to assure the performance of such obligations as debt repayment and the fulfillment of military service.

Evidence of transactions involving land as security has been uncovered in such ancient civilizations as Babylonia and Egypt. Many of the basic principles of mortgage lending—including the essential elements of naming the borrower, naming the lender, and describing the property—were developed in these early civilizations. For example, there is evidence that the Egyptians were the first to use surveys to describe mortgaged land. The annual flooding of the Nile River, which often obliterated property markers, undoubtedly necessitated this practice.

During the period when Greek civilization was at its peak, temple leaders often loaned money with real estate as security. In fact, throughout history, organized religion has taken a strong interest in real estate and related activities.

Roman Law

The Roman Empire developed mortgage lending to a high level of sophistication, beginning with the *fiducia*. This transaction was an actual transfer of possession and **title** to land. It was subject to an additional agreement that stated that if the borrower fulfilled the obligation, a reconveyance would occur. As Roman government became stronger and the law more clearly defined, a new concept of security called the *pignus* was developed. No title transfer occurred. Instead, the land was "pawned." According to this concept, title and possession remained with the borrower, but the lender could take possession of the property at any time if it was deemed that a possibility of **default** existed.

The most important Roman development regarding mortgages, however, was the *hypotheca*, which was a pledge. The *hypotheca* is similar to the **lien** theory (described later) that exists in most states in this country today. The title remained with the borrower, who was also allowed to retain possession of the property. Only when an actual default occurred (a failure to perform on the part of the borrower) was the lender entitled to take possession of the land and its title.

As the Roman Empire receded in Europe during the Dark Ages, Germanic law introduced a new concept. A borrower was given the choice of fulfilling an obligation or losing the security. If the **mortgagor** defaulted, the **mortgagee** had to look exclusively to the property itself. This security system was called a *gage* in Germanic law: something was deposited for the performance of an agreement. As the Dark Ages continued and the governmental authority of Rome weakened to such a degree that lenders were not sure they would have support from central authorities in securing their debts, the *hypotheca* system decayed and died, and the more primitive concept of the *fiducia* returned.

English Developments

Later, in Europe, a new system of government and social structure—the feudal system—became widespread. The essential characteristic of the feudal system was the totality of the king's control. He was the owner of all lands, and he granted their use to certain lords in return for the lords' military fealty. Lords given the use of the land were permitted to continue on the land as long as they fulfilled their military obligation to the king. If this obligation was not fulfilled, or if the lord died, the use of the land was revoked and given to others. In this situation, land served as a security for the performance of an obligation—military service.

Along with the feudal system of land tenure, in 1066, William of Normandy introduced the Germanic system of the *gage* into early English law, following his successful invasion of England. The word *mortgage*, not found in English literature until after the Norman invasion, derives from the French words *mort*, meaning "dead" (the land was dead, since the mortgagor could not use or derive income from it), and *gage*, meaning "pledge." During the years after the Norman invasion, the Catholic Church established civil law in England. Church policy at this time stated that charging interest for money loaned was usury.

As the common law evolved in England, there occurred a gradual shift from a concept of favoritism or protection of the mortgagee to favoritism or protection of the mortgagor. Finally, the common law reached a more balanced position. The initial concept of mortgagee favoritism was dictated by the realities of the economic and legal systems that existed at this early stage of mortgage development.

Mortgage lending was not a common occurrence during this period for two reasons: first, there was very little need for it; and second, no incentive to lend existed without the ability to collect interest. The mortgage lending that did occur was not for the purpose of providing funds to purchase real estate, but was usually provided to finance large purchases (such as a new mill or livestock) or perhaps to prepare a dowry for a daughter. Since lenders could not collect interest on these **loans**, they would take both title and possession of a designated portion of the borrower's land and thus be entitled to all rents and profits from it. When the obligation was fulfilled, title was reconveyed to the mortgagor. If the mortgagor defaulted, the mortgagee would permanently retain title and possession of the mortgaged land. The mortgagee was still entitled to expect performance of the underlying obligation also.

During the fifteenth century, courts of **equity** allowed the mortgagor to perform the obligation, even after the required date, and redeem the property. This concept was expanded, and by 1625, nearly all existing mortgage lending practices ended because a mortgagee never knew when a mortgagor might perform and thus redeem the property. To alleviate this problem, mortgagees petitioned the court for a decree requiring mortgagors to redeem the property within six months or lose the right to do so.

American Developments

Land development banks, borrowing primarily in Europe to finance their land purchases in the developing West, financed westward expansion in America following the Revolutionary War. Much of this land acquisition was speculative and eventually culminated in the bankruptcy of nearly all the land development banks. Thereafter, little, if any, real estate financing was done on an organized basis until after the Civil War.

During the first 75 years of this country's history, most of the population lived on small farms whose ownership was passed down through families. Little need existed for mortgage lending in this society except for an occasional purchase of new land or for seed money. Primarily, family and friends provided the small amount of mortgage lending that did occur during this period. It is important to realize that until the 1920s, the largest category of mortgage lenders in the United States was composed of individuals, not financial institutions.

Thrift Institutions

The birth of various thrift institutions provided an opportunity for change in mortgage lending. The first thrift institution formed was a mutual savings bank, the Philadelphia Savings Fund Society, which was established in 1816. Of greater long-term importance to mortgage lending was the organization of the first building society in the United States. Modeled after societies that had existed in England and Scotland for 50 years, the Oxford Provident Building Association was organized in 1831 in Frankfort, Pennsylvania. This association, like the ones that soon followed, was intended to exist only long enough for all the organizers to obtain funds to purchase homes. Ironically, the first loan made by this association became delinquent and another member of the association assumed the debt and took possession of the house. Later, other associations were formed, providing a popular means of financing home purchases across the United States.

Even with these new financial institutions, mortgage lending was still not an important part of the economy in the first half of the nineteenth century. Most families still lived on farms, which met basically all their requirements. No urgent need for savings existed. Away from the farm there were few employment opportunities with which excess cash could be accumulated for savings. In fact, the concept of saving was still new, and the number of active savers was very small. Then, as now, the impetus for mortgage lending was the inflow of savings to the institutions that would lend funds; thus, mortgage lending was not frequent.

Mortgage Companies

After the Civil War, the nation's expansion continued and developments in mortgage lending resumed. Starting with a new westward expansion, which opened virgin lands for farming, a regular farm mortgage business developed in the predominantly rural Midwest. The Midwest is an area where many mortgage companies began, and it still has one of the heaviest concentrations of mortgage companies.

These companies did not originate mortgage loans for their own **portfolios**, as did the thrift institutions. Rather, these loans were for direct sale to wealthy individuals or to institutional investors such as life insurance companies. Most of these individual and institutional **investors** were located on the East Coast and needed local mortgage companies to originate loans for them. This need developed into the mortgage loan correspondent system.

The bulk of the mortgage business consisted of financing farms, usually with a prevailing loan-to-value ratio of 40 percent. An occasional 50 percent loan might be made on a farm in a well-developed area. The term of the loan was short (less than five years), with interest payable semiannually and the **principal** paid at the end of the term. By 1900, outstanding farm mortgages originated by these mortgage companies totaled more than $4 billion.

During this period of time, the population movement to urban areas began to increase, swelled by the ever-mounting numbers of immigrants. In 1892, the United States League of Savings Associations, a trade organization, was founded in response to the expanding savings and loan industry. These institutions provided urban residents a place to save money and a source of funds to use in purchasing homes. Some of these mortgages made by savings and loan associations were repaid on an installment basis, not at the expiration of the term, as were mortgages from other types of lenders.

Commercial Banks

Commercial banks made few real estate loans until the Civil War, when a sudden demand for loans to finance new farmsteads encouraged state-chartered commercial banks to make low-ratio farm mortgages. Except for a brief period of time, federally chartered commercial banks could not make real estate loans.

This competition from state-chartered banks eventually forced a change in federal banking law. In 1913, the Federal Reserve Act authorized federally chartered banks to lend money on real estate. This initial authorization limited mortgage loans to improved farms for a five-year term with the loan-to-value ratio of 50 percent. This authorization was extended in 1916 to include one-year loans on urban real estate.

Many changes have occurred in both state and federal laws relating to the types and terms of mortgage loans made by commercial banks. These changes have tended to lag behind advances made by other mortgage lenders. However, the contribution made by commercial banks to mortgage lending has been meaningful, especially in those areas of the country where they function as the principal mortgage lender.

Turn of the Century

During the period from 1870 to the early 1900s, a few **mortgage companies** in or near urban areas began to make loans on single-family houses. Initially, such loans constituted a very small percentage of their business, but they gradually grew to account for more and more total origination volume. The Farm Mortgage Bankers Association, a trade organization formed in 1914, changed its name in 1923 to the Mortgage Bankers Association of America in order to reflect the increasing emphasis on residential lending.

In the first two decades of the twentieth century, the typical loan made by a mortgage company on a single-family dwelling called for no more than a 50 percent loan-to-value ratio, with a three- to five-year mortgage term. There were no provisions for **amortization** of the loan, and interest was generally payable semiannually. The majority of these mortgages were renewed upon maturity, since few families had the money to retire the debt. The mortgage companies originating these mortgages charged the borrower from 1 to 3 percent of the amount of the loan as a fee. Upon renewal, an additional 1 percent fee was charged.

As the twentieth century progressed, thrift institutions—especially savings and loan associations—continued to expand. Savings banks, which had their greatest growth after the Civil War, remained principally in the New England states, but savings and loan institutions continued to grow and spread across the country. During this time, thrift institutions were originating short-term mortgage loans for their own portfolios.

All mortgage lenders participated in the real estate boom years of the 1920s. This was a period of unrestrained optimism. Most Americans believed growth and prosperity would continue forever. Real estate prices appreciated as much as 25 to 50 percent per year during the first half of the decade. Many lenders forgot their **underwriting** standards, believing that inflating prices would bail out any bad loan. As with any speculative period, the end came, and along with it, many personal fortunes dissipated.

Depression Era

The real estate boom of the 1920s began to show signs of weakening long before the stock market crash. By 1927, real estate values that had appreciated excessively in the early 1920s began to decline dramatically. Following the disastrous dive of the stock market in 1929, the entire economy of the United States was in danger of collapse. Real estate values plunged to less than half the level of the year before. The ability of both the individual borrower and the income-property mortgagor to meet quarterly or semi-annual interest payments was reduced by the large-scale unemployment that followed the collapse of the stock market and the loss of economic vitality throughout the nation.

Because periodic amortization of mortgages was not common, a six-month lag often occurred before an institutional investor realized a mortgage was in trouble. In addition, the various financial institutions were faced with a severe liquidity crisis that required them to sell vast real estate and mortgage holdings under very unfavorable conditions. This need to sell real estate holdings to obtain cash, coupled with a rise in **foreclosures** and tax sales, severely depressed an already crumbling real estate market. Many individual homeowners were threatened with property loss even if they retained their jobs because when their five-year mortgages expired, many were unable to refinance their mortgages: lenders were caught in the liquidity crisis and did not have the funds to lend.

Thrift institutions also experienced problems during this period even though some of their mortgagors had installment-type mortgages. As many workers lost their jobs and unemployment reached 25 percent, the savings inflow to thrifts diminished drastically. All types of financial institutions began to fail, and as a result savers withdrew funds and the liquidity crisis worsened for all lenders. In the early 1930s, many commercial banks and savings and loan institutions failed due to massive withdrawals of savings and the high foreclosure rate. By 1935, 20 percent of all mortgage assets were in the "real estate owned" category.

Second and third mortgagees, who needed to foreclose immediately in order to protect what little security they had, made the vast majority of all foreclosures during the 1930s. The highest number of foreclosures occurred from 1931 to 1935, averaging 250,000 each year. The increasing number of foreclosures, especially on family farms in the Midwest, forced the beginning of compulsory moratoria. In the Midwest, where economic deterioration was aggravated by the dust bowl storms, the cry for a moratorium reached the stage of near rebellion, and some violence occurred. Reacting to the hysteria sweeping the farm belt and some of the larger cities, many mortgagees voluntarily instituted **forbearance**, some for as long as two years. The first law requiring a mortgage moratorium became effective in Iowa in February 1933. Over the next 18 months, 27 states enacted legislation suspending nearly all foreclosures. Most of the moratorium laws enacted during this period were intended to last for two years or less, although many were reenacted and allowed to continue as law until the early 1940s.

It is important to note that during the period when these laws were in effect, some foreclosures did occur. The determining factor on whether to grant relief was the soundness of a debtor's fundamental economic position. If it was determined that a debtor would eventually lose the land anyway, postponing the foreclosure or granting a moratorium was considered a waste of time and an injustice to the creditor. The moratoria of the early 1930s did not provide an actual solution to the underlying economic problems, but they did provide a respite during which public unrest could be soothed and the federal government could introduce some economic remedies.

Government Intervention

In the early 1930s, the federal government realized that the drop in real estate values would continue to add to the growing depression of the entire economy, preventing its revitalization. Therefore, the government instituted a series of programs designed to help stabilize real estate values and, it was hoped, the entire economy. This marked the beginning of a drastic reversal in previous governmental political philosophy, which had been generally laissez-faire.

Federal Legislation

Beginning in the last year of the Hoover administration, federal legislation usurped, in large measure, control over real estate and mortgage-lending activities that previously had been left to the states.

The first legislation designed to meet the threat of the Depression created the Reconstruction Finance Corporation (RFC) in 1932, which, among other things, provided liquidity to commercial banks. Shortly thereafter, the Federal Home Loan Bank (FHLB) was created to provide a central credit facility to home finance institutions, primarily savings and loan institutions. The next major legislation was the Home Owners Loan Act (HOLA) in 1933. This act provided for federal charters for savings and loan institutions and created the Home Owners Loan Corporation (HOLC), which was designed to provide emergency relief to homeowners by refinancing or purchasing defaulted mortgages. This program kept many tens of thousands of families from losing their homes in the 1930s.

One of the most far-reaching enactments of this period was the National Housing Act (1934), which created the **Federal Housing Administration (FHA)** and the Federal Savings and Loan Insurance Corporation (FSLIC). FSLIC and the Federal Deposit Insurance Corporation (FDIC) were instrumental in encouraging depositors to return desperately needed deposits to financial institutions. FHA has provided the framework and the impetus necessary for the development of a true national mortgage market. FHA has also been credited with either initiating or making popular many innovations in mortgage lending, such as **mortgage insurance (MI)** and the long-term, self-amortizing mortgage.

The Growth Era

A minimal amount of single-family housing construction occurred from 1926 to 1946 as a result of the Depression and World War II. At the end of the war, however, 5 million servicemen returned home, and a tremendous demand for housing was created. The government, as part of its responsibility to returning veterans, as well as a way of stimulating housing, passed the Servicemen's Readjustment Act (1944). One of the major features of this act was a guaranty program that provided a desirable way of financing homes for veterans. The most distinguishing characteristic of this guaranty program (then and now) is the lack of a **down payment** requirement for eligible veterans. Under this program, no mortgage insurance **premiums** are collected from veterans; instead, the government absorbs the cost of the mortgage guaranty.

The highly liquid position of financial institutions was the second great impetus to the rapid expansion of single-family housing construction following World War II. In 1945, more than half of the assets of financial institutions were tied up in the no-risk but low-yielding government securities that institutions were obligated to purchase during World War II. At the end of the war, these bonds could be sold and the cash converted into mortgages, which provided a higher **yield**.

The greatest boom in housing construction in the history of this country, and possibly the world, occurred from 1945 to 1955. The two government housing programs (FHA and the Veterans Administration, VA), the built-up demand for housing, and the liquid position of lenders were instrumental in this dramatic growth in housing. Since the end of World War II, mortgages have been the largest user of long-term credit in the entire U.S. economy.

Housing Act of 1949

The Housing Act of 1949 is one of the most important pieces of social legislation passed in the last half of the twentieth century because of the national commitment made to provide "a decent home and suitable living environment for every American family." Much of the legislative action in the housing and mortgage-lending field since then has been an attempt to fulfill this commendable but probably unrealistic goal.

The 1950s and early 1960s were a period of national optimism, economic growth, and, as far as mortgage lending is concerned, relative quiet in the legislative arena. This period of tranquility soon dissipated in the face of an onslaught of such national crises as political assassinations, civil rights demonstrations, urban blight, and the war in Vietnam.

Department of Housing and Urban Development

The lack of adequate housing, a situation often associated with poverty, was partially addressed in 1965 by the consolidation of the many federal housing agencies into a new cabinet-level department, the Department of Housing and Urban Development (HUD). HUD was to be the focal point of much of the new legislation in the years to come as it assumed a dominant position in regulating real estate and mortgage lending.

The avalanche of legislation and regulation that was to so change mortgage lending began a few years after HUD was created, when the Housing and Urban Development Act (1968) was enacted. This was the first major legislation passed in the mortgage-lending field in over a decade. The act committed the government to a goal of 26 million new housing starts in the next decade. At the time, many argued that this goal was impractical on fiscal and political grounds. However, the act introduced a new concept in government programs for residential real estate by adopting the principle of subsidizing interest rates.

These government subsidy programs, combined with national economic growth, stimulated housing production in 1972 to more than 3 million units—the highest ever. With political pressure to increase housing production, the inevitable problems developed almost immediately. Report of possible scandals in subsidized housing began to appear in 1971, involving FHA officials and some mortgage lenders. These scandals were followed by congressional investigations, which spotlighted the unforeseen high costs of these programs.

In January of 1973, President Richard Nixon ordered a freeze on all subsidy programs. This was partially lifted later, but only after a thorough review of government programs by a special task force created by HUD. This task force reviewed the history of government involvement in real estate and analyzed the impact of the various subsidy programs on housing. The task force concluded that the goal of providing homeownership for everyone was neither practical nor desirable when weighed against the cost.

The government's concept changed from subsidizing homeownership to subsidizing rent. The Housing and Community Development Act (1974) formalized this change with the Section 8 program. This program allows low- and moderate-income families to choose the rental unit in the community in which they want to live, with the government subsidizing the amount of fair market rent that is in excess of 25 percent of the family's monthly income. This program provides assistance both to families who cannot afford the minimal housing expenses stipulated in prior programs and families whose incomes are just over the maximum income limit to qualify for assistance in home purchasing.

Consumer Protection

The way residential mortgage lending is conducted today is controlled to a great extent by a series of federal laws and regulations. The Consumer Protection Act of 1968 was the first in a series of legislative acts that redefined the concept of consumer protection regarding mortgage lending, thus changing forever the way in which residential mortgage lending is conducted. Through the next three decades, the federal government strove to remove all inequities from residential mortgage lending. These actions have met with mostly good results, but occasionally inequities still appear. The various pieces of federal legislation are discussed in detail throughout this book.

Role of Government

The government's role in the management of the nation's economy in general, and mortgage lending in particular, is one that has been analyzed and debated many times—and undoubtedly it will continue to be debated in the future. There seems to be little argument that government, regardless of whether it is federal, state, or local, has an obligation to its citizens to provide adequate shelter for all—even if people cannot afford it themselves. There are many arguments, though, regarding how to provide this basic necessity. In the last decade, the federal government tried helping people in need of shelter in a variety of ways, first by providing rent assistance, then mortgage assistance so people could purchase rather than rent, and, finally, by returning to subsidizing rent payments.

Recently, some commentators have suggested that excessive governmental interference has resulted in fewer families being able to afford the average-priced home. That may be true, but most governmental laws and regulations have had a commendable impact on real estate and mortgage lending. The Interstate Land Sales Full Disclosure Act (1968), which helped to prevent fraudulent land sales, is an obvious example. Many of these new laws and regulations were necessitated by excesses and failures on the part of the lending community. The contribution of some of these laws cannot be overstated. In fact, one governmental creation, the Federal Housing Administration, has provided the framework for a modern, vibrant mortgage-lending system that has made this the best-housed nation in the world.

Following is a list of the more important federal legislative acts that impact residential mortgage lending.

1913—**Federal Reserve Act.** Established the Federal Reserve system and authorized federally chartered commercial banks to make real estate loans.

1916—**Federal Farm Loan Act.** Provided for the formation of Federal Land Bank Associations as units of the Federal Land Bank system, which was given authority to generate funds for loans to farmers by the sale of bonds.

1932—**Reconstruction Finance Act.** Created the Reconstruction Finance Corporation that was designed, among other things, to provide liquidity to commercial banks.

1932—**Federal Home Loan Bank Act.** Established the Federal Home Loan Bank Board and 12 regional banks to provide central credit facilities for home finance institutions that were members of the FHLB.

1932—**Home Owners Loan Act.** This act produced two results: (1) created the Home Owners Loan Corporation with authority to purchase defaulted home mortgages and to refinance as many as prudently feasible; (2) provided the basic lending authority for federally chartered savings and loan associations.

1934—**National Housing Act.** Authorized the creation of the Federal Housing Administration and Federal Savings and Loan Insurance Corporation.

1938—**National Mortgage Association of Washington.** This governmental agency, soon renamed **Federal National Mortgage Association (FNMA)**, was authorized to provide **secondary mortgage market** support for FHA mortgages.

1944—**Servicemen's Readjustment Act.** Established within the Veterans Administration a mortgage guarantee program for qualified veterans.

1949—**Housing Act.** Stated that the national housing goal was to provide "a decent home and suitable living environment for every American family." Consolidated past lending programs of the Farmers Home Administration.

1961—**Consolidated Farmers Home Administration Act.** Extended authority for the agency to make mortgage loans to nonfarmers in rural areas.

1965—**Housing and Urban Development Act.** Consolidated many federal housing agencies into the new Department of Housing and Urban Development, which was given expanded authority.

1966—**Interest Rate Adjustment Act**. Authorized the setting of maximum savings rates and the creation of a differential between the savings rates of commercial banks and thrift institutions.

1968—**Fair Housing Act.** Prohibited discrimination in real estate sales and mortgage lending based on race, color, national origin, and religion.

1968—**Interstate Land Sales Full Disclosure Act.** Required complete and full disclosure of all facts regarding interstate sale of real estate.

1968—**Consumer Credit Protection Act.** Contained Title I, better known as truth-in-lending, which authorized the Federal Reserve Board to formulate regulations (Regulation Z) requiring advance disclosure of the amount and type of finance charge and a calculation of the **Annual Percentage Rate**. Title VI, better known as the Fair Credit Reporting Act, established disclosure requirements regarding the nature of credit information used in determining whether to grant a loan.

1968—**Housing and Urban Development Act.** This act put the existing Federal National Mortgage Association (FNMA) in private hands and authorized it to continue secondary mortgage market support. The act created a new governmental agency, the **Government National Mortgage Association (GNMA)**, and authorized it to continue the FNMA special assistance function and guarantee mortgage-backed securities.

1969—**National Environmental Policy Act.** Required the preparation of an Environmental Impact Statement for the Council on Environmental Quality in order to determine the environmental impact of real estate development.

1970—**Emergency Home Finance Act.** Created a new secondary mortgage market participant, the **Federal Home Loan Mortgage Corporation (FHLMC)**, which had as its stated objective providing secondary mortgage support for conventional mortgages originated by thrift institutions. The act also gave FNMA authority to purchase conventional mortgages in addition to FHA/VA.

1974—**Flood Disaster Protection Act.** Effective in 1975, mortgage loans could not be made in a flood hazard area unless flood insurance had been purchased.

1974—**Real Estate Settlement Procedures Act (RESPA)** (as amended in 1976 and 1992). This act as amended required mortgage lenders to provide mortgage borrowers with an advance disclosure of loan settlement costs and charges. Further, this act prohibited kickbacks to any person for referring business. The 1976 amendment required lenders to provide applicants with a Good Faith Estimate of Settlement Costs and a HUD booklet. A Uniform Settlement Statement (HUD-1) must be furnished to the borrower before or at the settlement. The 1992 amendment extended RESPA to subordinate financing, effective 1993.

1974—**Equal Credit Opportunity Act (ECOA)** (as amended in 1976). This act as amended prohibited discrimination in lending on the basis of sex, marital status, age, race, color, national origin, religion, good faith reliance on consumer protection laws, or the fact that a borrower receives public assistance. In addition, if an application is rejected, the borrower must be notified within 30 days of the reason for rejection.

1975—Home Mortgage Disclosure Act (HMDA) (as amended in 1992). This act required disclosure by most mortgage lenders of geographic distribution of loans in metropolitan statistical areas. The purpose was to establish lending patterns of lenders.

1976—RESPA amendment (*see* 1974).

1976—ECOA amendment (*see* 1974).

1978—Fair Lending Practices Regulations. These FHLB regulations required members to develop written underwriting standards, keep a loan registry, not deny loans because of age of dwelling or condition of neighborhood, and to direct advertising to all segments of the community.

1978—Community Reinvestment Act. This act required FSLIC-insured institutions to adopt a community reinvestment statement, which delineates the community in which they will invest; maintain a public comment file; and post a Community Reinvestment Act (CRA) notice.

1979—Housing and Community Development Amendments. This legislation exempted FHA-insured mortgages from state and local usury ceilings. (Other concurrent legislation exempted VA and conventional mortgages.)

1980—Depository Institutions Deregulation and Monetary Control Act. Congress extended the savings interest rate control and thrift institution's one-quarter of 1 percent differential for six years. The act also extended the federal override of state usury ceilings on certain mortgages. Other changes included simplified truth-in-lending standards, eased lending restrictions, including geographical limitations, loan-to-value ratios, and treatment of one-family loans exceeding specified dollar amounts.

1980—Omnibus Reconciliation Act. Limited the issuance of tax-exempt housing mortgage revenue bonds.

1982—Garn–St. Germain Depository Institutions Act. Preempted state due-on-sale loan restrictions; mandated phaseout of interest rate differential by January 1, 1984; provided FSLIC and FDIC assistance for institutions with deficient net worth; and allowed S&Ls to make consumer, commercial, and agricultural loans.

1984—Deficit Reduction Act. Extended the tax exemption for qualified mortgage subsidy bonds; created new reporting procedures for mortgage interest.

1986—Tax Reform Act. Reduced top corporate tax rate from 46 to 34 percent; reduced taxable income bad debt deduction from 40 to 8 percent; provided for three-year carrybacks and 15-year carryforwards for savings institution net operating losses.

1987—Competitive Equality Banking Act. Set the FSLIC $10.8 billion recapitalization in motion, kept intact Savings Bank Life Insurance, and gave thrifts flexibility to form different types of holding companies.

1987—**Housing and Community Development Act.** Notice of availability of counseling must be given within 45 days of **delinquency** on single-family primary residence.

1989—**Financial Institutions Reform, Recovery and Enforcement Act (FIRREA).** Restructured the regulatory framework by eliminating FHLBB and FSLIC; created the Office of Thrift Supervision (OTS) under the Treasury Department; enhanced FDIC to supervise safety and soundness of financial institutions, the Savings Institutions Insurance Fund, and the Bank Insurance Fund; created the Resolution Trust Corporation (RTC) to dispose of failed savings and loans; established new capital standards for thrifts.

1992—**RESPA amendment** (*see* 1974). Coverage of RESPA is extended to subordinate financing.

1992—**HMDA amendment** (*see* 1975). Mortgage companies and other nondepository institutions required to comply with HMDA.

1994—**Home Ownership and Equity Protection Act (HOEPA).** Designed to provide protection to consumers from abusive practices involving high-cost home loans. Applies to so-called Section 32 loans.

1994—The **Veterans Administration** guarantees its 14 millionth home mortgage.

1997—**Taxpayer Relief Act of 1997.** Exempts gains of up to $500,000 on the sale of home from capital gains taxation. It also reduces the top tax rate on capital gains from 28 to 20 percent.

1998—**Homeowners Protection Act.** Effective July 1999, this federal law is designed to protect people who buy homes using **private mortgage insurance (PMI).** It allows for the cancellation of PMI in certain circumstances and ensures that borrowers are duly notified by the lenders of their right to cancel it when certain requirements have been met.

Recent Residential Mortgage Lending

The most productive boom in real estate construction and financing in the United States has occurred during the past 30 years. More housing units and other types of buildings have been constructed during this period than in all the years since this country was founded. This boom can be credited to the availability of capital at a reasonable rate and the corresponding creation of the secondary mortgage market. For example, **Fannie Mae** (Federal National Mortgage Association) was given expanded purchasing authority in 1970 and was joined by **Freddie Mac** (Federal Home Loan Mortgage Corporation) in that year to provide secondary market facilities for conventional mortgages originated by savings and loan institutions. While the housing boom changed the landscape of the American countryside, new office buildings, apartment complexes, and shopping centers provided the amenities and services needed by the families in these new homes.

In the 1970s, providing or stimulating housing for low- and moderate-income families was not the exclusive province of government at the federal level. Before 1960, the state of New York had the only state housing agency, but by 1975, nearly all states had some type of housing agency. Although some states have used tax-exempt bonds to raise revenue to lend to homebuyers at below-market interest rates, many have fulfilled their social responsibility by providing financing for multifamily units.

The 1980s: The Decade of Historic Change

The decade of the 1980s will be remembered as the time when the economy went through startling changes and, as a result, changed residential mortgage lending and mortgage lenders. This period witnessed positive developments such as the rapid growth of mortgage-backed securities, the evolution of alternative mortgage instruments, and, in general, more sources of needed capital. All of these positive developments combined with much lower interest rates resulted in 1–4 family originations of nearly $500 billion in both 1986 and 1987.

However, the decade also witnessed double-digit inflation, a major recession, a record high for the Dow Jones Industrial Average, and then a crash exceeding that of 1929. The decade ended with the near total collapse of the savings and loan industry and the related taxpayer bailout of the Federal Savings and Loan Insurance Corporation (FSLIC). All of these events produced drastic changes for the nation's economy in general and for mortgage lending in particular.

Federal Reserve and the Money Supply

The 1980s began with the nation's economy clearly running out of control. The Federal Reserve, responsible for managing and regulating interest rates and monetary supply, was forced in the fall of 1979 to bring about some order to the economy. Its fundamental decision was to stop attempting to regulate short-term interest rates and, instead, to exercise control over growth in the money supply. The theory was that control of the money supply would help reduce inflation, and that this in turn would decrease upward pressure on interest rates as investors decreased their need for inflation protection.

Prime Rate at $21^1/_2$ Percent

The immediate result of this action was sharply higher interest rates. The most visible rate, the so-called prime rate, peaked at $21^1/_2$ percent in 1981. Interest rates did come down fairly rapidly after that peak, partially as a result of the Federal Reserve action but primarily because of a serious recession that followed this action. The recession that followed, the worst since the Great Depression, resulted in unemployment reaching over 10 percent. This recession and the action of the Federal Reserve deflated the inflation balloon to the point at which inflation in the mid-1980s fell to about 1 percent per year before turning up modestly at the end of the decade. As a reaction to control over inflation, the prime interest rate dropped sharply to $7^1/_2$ percent by the spring of 1987 before turning up slightly.

With inflation under control and interest rates declining, the stock market rocketed to levels only dreamed of by the most optimistic of market watchers as the Dow Jones Industrial Average hit a record of 2722. Some market watchers were calling for 3000 by the end of the year, but what happened instead was a crash that exceeded (in **points**, but not percentage) the 1929 crash. A 508-point drop in the Dow Jones Industrial Average shocked Wall Street on October 19, 1987. A week later, the market dropped another 175. The sound heard around the world was the hard landing of other stock exchanges as they followed the lead of Wall Street.

The reasons for the crash of 1987 are many and varied, but the two principal ones are that the market was simply overvalued and that investors in the United States and abroad had lost faith in the ability of the U.S. government to control its huge deficit. The federal deficits for the second half of the 1980s averaged approximately $150 billion a year. These huge deficits have turned the United States into the world's largest debtor nation, which owes hundreds of billions of dollars to foreigners. The impact of the crash of 1987 and the 1990–1991 recession chilled the home-purchasing plans of many Americans, and originations trailed off for the rest of the decade from the record years of 1986–1987.

Financial Institutions Reform, Recovery and Enforcement Act (FIRREA)

By 1988, the problems of the savings and loan industry, which had been festering since the late 1970s, reached a climax. Speculative lending, negative earnings, low capital, and poor management characterized many savings and loan associations in the 1980s. These problems eventually culminated in the failure of many of these savings and loan associations and the insolvency of the Federal Savings and Loan Insurance Corporation (FSLIC)—the deposit insurance fund for savings and loan associations.

The failure of FSLIC precipitated a massive federal bailout of the insurance fund and the closing of hundreds of failed savings and loans. The 1989 law that mandated these changes was called the Financial Institutions Reform, Recovery and Enforcement Act (FIRREA). The cost of this federal bailout is projected to be as high as $400 billion to $500 billion over the life of the bonds sold to finance it.

The 1990s: Boom Years

The 1990s began with a recession that purged much of the spending excesses of the 1980s from the U.S. economy. Unemployment reached a little over 7 percent throughout the United States, but in some areas, especially New England and California, unemployment exceeded 10 percent. As the Cold War ended with the fall of Communism throughout Europe, the American defense budget was cut and cut again, resulting in tens of thousands of Americans losing their jobs in the defense-related industries. With the economy in trouble and unemployment up, consumers stopped spending. This change in consumer attitudes toward spending, when combined with a drop in inflation, convinced the Federal Reserve to lower interest rates in the hope this would stimulate business to expand and hire more workers.

At first, this drop in interest rates had another benefit: Americans jumped to refinance their home mortgages at the new low interest rates. This wave of refinancing during 1991 to 1993 allowed millions of Americans to refinance their home mortgages at interest rates that were the lowest in 20 years. During one period late in 1993, 30-year fixed-rate mortgages declined below 7 percent. It is estimated that American homeowners, as a result of these refinancings, will annually save tens of billions of dollars in mortgage payments. Much of the money saved from the lower mortgage payments will be used to purchase consumer goods, thus helping to stimulate the economy in general. In 1993, 1–4 family first-mortgage originations reached the staggering level of $1.1 trillion! Of that amount, approximately 55 percent was from refinancing of existing mortgages. This was the first time ever that refinancing exceeded purchase money mortgages for a whole year. An interesting sidebar to the story of the surge in refinancing is that the overall quality of loans serviced improved as delinquencies hit a 20-year low in 1993.

New Administration and Deficit Reduction

After the success of Desert Storm, it appeared President George H. Bush would have little trouble with reelection, but the economy continued to deteriorate and other politicians entered the race for the presidency. In a three-way race, Governor William Clinton, a Democrat from Arkansas, was elected president.

During President Clinton's first year in office, an agreement was reached between the president and Congress on a deficit reduction package that, if not later modified by Congress, could help reduce the federal budget deficit gradually over a number of years. The financial markets reacted positively to the fact that Congress finally was reaching some closure on deficit reduction, and, as a result, interest rates continued to decline throughout 1993. Interest rates bottomed in late 1993 at 20-year lows and began a modest turn upward in 1994, led by Federal Reserve action designed to keep a lid on inflation.

First Decade of the Twenty-First Century

The new century started out with the largest dollar amount of mortgage originations ever. A historically high $2 trillion in 1–4 family mortgage loans were originated in 2001 and 2002. The reason nearly one out of three mortgages outstanding were refinanced in these two years was decade-low interest rates. With many Americans refinancing their homes to lower rates, others refinanced to pull equity out. The consumer greatly reduced the impact of the modest recession of 2001–2002 by spending the money obtained by pulling equity out from homes. One very positive result of the generally healthy economy and low interest rates was the increase in the U.S. homeownership rate to a record high of 68 percent.

Although mortgage **originators** profited greatly with the millions of mortgages that refinanced during the early years of the new century, many mortgage servicers were hurt badly by the refinancings. These servicers had expected the loans, which refinanced, to remain on their books for a long enough period of time to make a profit on **servicing** those loans. This expectation was not borne out as some consumers refinanced their mortgages two and three times within a three-year period. On the other hand, mortgage servicers may eventually benefit from these refinanced loans since the new loans at lower rates may have longer lives than normal. These servicers probably will enjoy a longer stream of servicing income; thus, the value of servicing the mortgages that refinanced has increased.

Need for Additional Funds for Housing

The two major secondary mortgage market players, Fannie Mae and Freddie Mac, project that the following factors will lead to a need for increased mortgage financing in the first decade of the new century:

- 13 to 15 million more households in the first decade
- Homeownership rate increasing from 68 to 71 percent
- 14 million additional homeowners in the decade
- Homeownership growth for minorities (who trail the ownership rate for whites by 25 percent)
- 16 million new houses
- $16 trillion more in home loans (an average of $1.6 trillion each year)

Evolving Mortgage Lending
Issues in the New Century

One of the more far-reaching issues being debated in the first decade of the new century is the potential redefinition of the primary and secondary mortgage markets. The major players in the primary market are concerned about the separation of the two markets and the possibility that the players in the secondary market will absorb some of their functions and maybe replace them completely. For example, underwriting was once considered a function of the primary market until automated underwriting at the secondary-market level made it a function of the secondary market. (Of course, Freddie Mac started out underwriting loans offered for sale before delegating the underwriting function to lenders.) **Automated valuations** (**AVs**) are another example, plus some of the marketing that secondary market players are doing in the marketplace (for example, kiosks at McDonalds explaining mortgage finance to consumers). Also mortgage originators are concerned about the secondary market players and their direct contacts with real estate agents and brokers.

The growth of online mortgage originations is another evolving issue in the new century. Some experts are suggesting that online mortgage originations may soon reach 25 percent of all loans originated. Technology will certainly continue to change the way residential mortgage lending is done from origination to closing. An example of the continuing change is the digital signature bill enacted by Congress in 2000 that authorizes the usage of digital signatures as legally enforceable signatures.

Discussion Points

1. Examine how the concept of private ownership of land has evolved since the days of the Egyptians.

2. How has the involvement of the federal government in real estate and mortgage lending allowed for growth in homeownership?

3. The Great Depression was the beginning of modern residential mortgage lending. Examine the changes that occurred during this period and their importance to modern mortgage lending.

4. The 1960–1970 period witnessed the enactment of many major consumer protection laws/regulations. How have these federal enactments changed the way residential mortgage lending is conducted?

5. What is the difference between the *title theory* and *lien theory* of mortgage lending? Which exists in your state?

Role of Residential Mortgage Lending in the Economy

Introduction

The importance of housing, and therefore residential mortgage lending, to the nation's economic health is unquestionable. Economic commentators have contended from the time of the Great Depression that housing construction and related sectors (e.g., real estate sales, financing, home furnishing, taxes) are among the most important integrals of the engine that powers the economy of the United States. Economists have concluded that housing and related sectors account for about 21 percent of the gross domestic product (GDP)—a measure of the nation's total output of goods and services. See Chapter 17, "Construction Lending" for additional discussion of housing and GDP.

Examples of the economic importance of housing, and therefore residential mortgage financing, comes from the National Association of Home Builders (NAHB, **www.nahb.com**), which estimates that housing construction, sales, and financing account for 1 out of every 12 jobs in the United States. The NAHB calculated in 2002 that the economic impact of the construction of 1,000 single-family houses created nearly 1,800 man-years of employment, over $80 million in wages, and more than $42 million in federal, state, and local tax revenues. This economic stimulus was then and is now vital for a strong national economy.

Residential Mortgage Debt

At the end of 2002, outstanding residential debt in the United States exceeded $6 trillion. This figure is larger than the $3 trillion of marketable Treasury securities and the $2.7 trillion of U.S. corporate debt outstanding. Residential mortgage debt is expected to grow at a 10 percent rate during the first decade of the twenty-first century. Many economists expect that total outstanding residential debt in 2010 will be near $12 trillion.

Economic Stimulus

This economic stimulus is generated by the following factors:

- Consumption of raw materials for construction of the home
- Wages earned by home builders that are spent on food, clothing, cars, furniture, and schooling, in addition to many other products and services

- Federal, state, and local taxes
- Fees earned by real estate professionals when the home is sold
- Interest earned by financial intermediaries on mortgage loans financing the construction and purchase of the home

As is generally accepted, the ripple effect of a healthy home-building industry stimulates the entire economy. Obviously, there cannot be a healthy home-building industry without mortgage lending.

The sharp drop in housing construction in 1989 and 1990 certainly contributed to the recession experienced in that time frame. Likewise, the substantial increase in housing construction in 1993–1994 contributed significantly to the economic revival of the mid-1990s. More recently, the strength of the housing sector during the recession of 2001–2002 is given much of the credit for that recession being shorter and less severe than other recessions.

Effect of Low Interest Rates

The low interest rates during this period (30-year rates reached a low of 5.75 in 2002) allowed record originations of over $2 trillion in 2002. These low interest rates allowed more people to become homeowners, as witnessed by the homeownership rate, which reached an all-time high of 68 percent in 2002. Low rates also allowed these home-buyers to purchase more-expensive homes than they might otherwise have been able to afford. This housing and mortgage-lending activity stimulates the economy directly through the sales transaction and indirectly through related purchases and expenditures that ripple through the economy after the sale.

Although over half of the 2002 record volume was for refinancing, nearly $1 trillion was for home purchases. This home purchase figure is important because it is estimated that homebuyers spend on average around $9,000 on home-related items within a year of purchase. According to Fannie Mae, purchasers of older homes spend nearly $7,000 in the first year as they make improvements. These expenditures help the overall economy by providing many jobs as well as tax receipts.

These same low interest rates also provide homeowners the opportunity to reduce their mortgage payments by refinancing and to gain access to accumulated equity in their homes. In turn, this process pours money directly into the economy since it frees up consumers' resources for discretionary spending.

Figure 2-1   Spending by New Home Buyers in the First Year after Purchase

Property alterations	$3,194
Home furnishings	3,632
Appliances	2,079
Total Spending	8,905

Source: Housing: The Key to Economic Recovery, *NABH Economics, 2002, p.4, from NAHB, Bureau of Labor Statistics Consumer Expenditure Survey.*

Demographic Forces

Demographic forces are contributing to continued strength in housing demand. Couples reaching their home-buying years, new immigrants, and certain minority groups are creating demand for housing. These groups are forming new households at a rate of more than 1 million per year. This rate of growth in new households is expected to continue for the next decade. Financing this demand for housing will challenge the housing finance system but will also provide an opportunity for tremendous growth in residential mortgage lending for mortgage lenders.

The National Association of Realtors (NAR, **www.realtor.com**) reports that 5.25 million existing homes were sold in 2001. Combined with new single-family home construction of 1 million, home sales were over 6 million. These combined home sales could only have occurred with a dynamic housing-financing system.

Value of Housing

According to calculations of the National Association of Homebuilders, the market value of homes owned by U.S. households now stands at an astonishing $12 trillion. The market value of housing has increased by 50 percent over the past five years. This increase in market value reflects a large volume of housing production during this period of time. Existing homes have also appreciated strongly during this period. Perhaps more important, housing equity (market value less mortgage debt) increased by the same proportion over this time frame and is about $7 trillion.

Other Economic Benefits of Residential Mortgage Lending

Another economic benefit derived from residential mortgage lending is that it provides a means whereby an attractive return on savings can be generated for those individuals who are in the saving cycle of their lives. Residential mortgage lending could not

New Households Fuel Demand for Housing: Projected Number of Households, 2003–2010	TABLE 2-1

Year	Number of Households
2003	108,800,265
2004	109,907,037
2005	111,052,797
2006	112,216,108
2007	113,396,397
2008	114,596,986
2009	115,802,105
2010	117,059,577

Source: Housing: The Key to Economic Recovery, *NABH Economics, 2002 from Bureau of the Census, 1996 projections updated with 2000 Census results.*

New and Existing Home Sales 1990–2001		TABLE 2-2
	New Homes	Existing Homes
1990	534,000	3,219,600
1991	509,000	3,186,000
1992	610,000	3,479,000
1993	666,000	3,786,000
1994	670,000	3,916,000
1995	667,000	3,888,000
1996	757,000	4,196,000
1997	804,000	4,382,000
1998	886,000	4,970,000
1999	907,000	5,205,000
2000	907,000	5,123,000
2001	950,000	5,258,000

Source: New home sales: U.S. Census Bureau, National Association of Home Builders; existing home sales: National Association of Realtors.

How Household Wealth Is Divided	TABLE 2-3
Description	Percentage of Wealth
Real estate	28
Life insurance/Pension fund reserves	19
Equities/Mutual funds	17
Deposits	10
Unincorporated businesses	10
Consumer durables	6
Credit market instruments	4
Other assets	6

Source: Federal Reserve Flow-of-Funds Accounts, fourth quarter of 2001.

provide these many economic benefits without the many and varied types of mortgage lenders. These lenders are discussed in detail in Chapter 3, "The Mortgage Lenders."

Residential mortgage lending, in addition to being an important part of our nation's economy, also allows for the fulfillment of certain sociological demands, principal among them obtaining the "American Dream"—owning a home. As previously mentioned, as a result of low interest rates, homeownership reached a historic high of 68 percent in 2002, but many minority groups have ownership rates 25 percent lower. These groups will demand more housing, and it will be through mortgage financing that this will occur. Our society will benefit from higher homeownership by all groups of people. People who have their own home have a more substantial stake in their community and our nation's society, with many resulting benefits.

Availability of Credit

The health of the home-building and the real estate industry is often controlled by the availability of credit for home financing and by its cost. The demand for credit for housing grows every year. It is estimated that housing will require $2 trillion a year from the **capital markets** in the first decade of the twenty-first century in order to meet the projected housing demands of consumers. This chapter examines how this money for housing is created and then made available to homebuyers.

Importance of Savings to Housing

The common requisite for all residential mortgage lenders, whether depository institutions or not, is the accumulation of sufficient savings to produce the capital needed for mortgage loans. Unless financial intermediaries have access to sufficient savings, capital shortages result and credit restraints occur that affect all mortgage lenders, often with disastrous results. This has been the situation periodically in U.S. economic history, and, as a result, during those periods, housing starts and sales of existing homes have dropped dramatically. Secondary mortgage markets can assist housing somewhat during these periods of credit restraint by tapping the capital markets, but they cannot solve the basic problem of a lack of savings inflow to mortgage lenders.

Shortage of capital is not always the reason for falloffs in housing starts. The dramatic falloff in housing starts in 1989 to 1991 was not the result of a shortage of capital for housing, but rather a sharp drop in consumer confidence because of the Gulf War and a spreading recession.

Capital Formation

The funds required for capital formation are derived primarily from the savings of individuals and businesses. This process of capital formation produces most of the capital used by the various segments of our economy. *Business savings* are defined as retained earnings and capital consumption allowances. They exceed personal savings by a substantial amount. However, the savings generated by individuals—either as deposits at financial institutions or as reserves in whole life insurance policies— account for approximately 90 percent of the funds used for residential mortgage lending.

Savings Rates

The importance of personal savings to residential mortgage lending cannot be overemphasized. Since the end of World War II, the personal savings rate has ranged from the current low of about 0 to a high of about 9 percent of disposable income. These savings have permitted (except for brief periods of disintermediation) borrowers to obtain needed funds at reasonable rates. Through this process, the percentage of Americans who own the home in which they live has reached an all-time high and should continue to increase in the first decade of the twenty-first century.

Savings inflows are not constant, and the savings function must compete with food, shelter, clothing, transportation, recreation, and other real or perceived demands for an individual's after-tax income. Those individuals who do save are usually motivated by such desires as accumulating funds for retirement, future security, and major purchases such as a home or a college education.

Decline in the Savings Rate

The reasons for declines in the savings rate include the low interest paid on passbook savings and the fact that the interest received is subject to federal, state, and (in some situations) city income taxes. Another reason for previous declines in savings rates has been inflation psychology. During the high inflation period of the early 1980s, many sophisticated individuals realized it was more prudent to borrow than to save. They rationalized it made sense to borrow money now for immediate consumption and then pay back the money later with deflated dollars. That psychology, as it spread to many Americans in the early 1980s, led to a period of *disintermediation*—withdrawal from financial intermediaries of more money than was being deposited. During this period, capital was very short, and, as a result, interest rates were very high for residential mortgage loans.

Many potential savers believe that today's society offers fewer reasons for people to save than in the past. Many individuals believe, for example, that they can rely on company pensions, or Social Security, or both for retirement, thus they don't need to save. Others believe they need not accumulate additional saving because inflation has dramatically increased the equity in their home.

Recently, for a number of reasons, the savings rate for the average American has decreased to nearly zero. One important reason for this decrease in savings is that many Americans feel financially comfortable because of gains in the value of their stock portfolio or the equity in their home.

This lack of savings may reverse itself in the new century because of the following factors:

- An aging population that normally saves more and borrows less
- An erosion of confidence in the economy
- Lack of alternatives (e.g., stock market too volatile)

Changes in the economy directly influence savings in many ways. For example, if the business cycle is down and unemployment increases, individuals may increase savings because of uncertainty about their employment. The result could be a savings inflow, which theoretically should cause interest rates to decline as more dollars chase less demand. On the other hand, with a downturn in the business cycle and an increase in unemployment, those who are unemployed may have to withdraw savings for living expenses. If the economy is expanding, savings may also accumulate since the demand for funds could reach a point at which high interest rates attract more savings.

For a period of time during the late 1970s and early 1980s, depository institutions could not attract savings during periods of high interest because limits were placed on the amount of interest that could be paid to savers. This is not the case now, since lim-

		1–4 Family				Multifamily		
Year	Total Residential	Total	FHA	VA	Conv.	Total	FHA	Conv.
1985	$1,738	$1,533	$153	$131	$1,249	$205	$40	$185
1990	2,932	2,647	313	155	2,179	286	47	239
1995	3,784	3,511	352	182	2,977	274	47	227
2000	5,602	5,192	500	218	4,474	410	54	356

Residential Mortgage Debt Outstanding by Property Type (in billions of dollars) — TABLE 2-4

Source: *HUD, Federal Reserve Board, VA, FHA.*

its on interest rates on savings have been deregulated and the rates now move with the market. This change in itself will have a major impact on future availability of funds for residential mortgage lending.

Mortgage Markets

In our economy, the total financial market consists of the capital markets and the money markets. These two markets compete with each other for funds. The basic difference between the two markets is the maturity of the financial instruments. Money market instruments (U.S. Treasury bills, corporate commercial paper, etc.) mature in less than one year. Capital markets, on the other hand, are markets for long-term obligations. The mortgage market is only part of the complete capital market. Within the capital market, a specific demand for funds (e.g., mortgages) must compete with other instruments, such as corporate bonds. The competition is determined by the price a user of funds is willing to pay. The price of money is stated as the interest rate.

Users of Credit

In today's economic environment, the demand for credit is derived from three factors:

- Business demand
- Consumer demand
- Government demand

Businesses demand credit for financing inventory, accounts receivable, plant expansion and modernization, and occasionally for research and development. The magnitude of business loan demand is normally tied to the economic cycle. Business normally looks to commercial banks to provide needed capital usually at the prime rate (or lower in some cases). If a business's credit rating is high enough, that business may look to sell commercial paper.

Consumer demand is also impacted by the economic cycle and employment. When interest rates are high, many consumers cannot qualify for a loan, thus demand falls off. Further, when unemployment increases, consumers become concerned for their employment; thus, they tend to decrease borrowing. Consumer credit is used to purchase automobiles, furniture, clothing, and other durable and nondurable goods. In addition, consumer credit includes funds to purchase residential real estate (or to refinance existing home mortgages).

Finally, all levels of government have experienced insatiable appetites for borrowed funds from the late 1970s to the present time. These borrowed funds have been used primarily to finance the federal government's deficits, in addition to other local needs such as mortgage revenue bonds. The amount of borrowing by the federal government is controlled by the government's fiscal policy, which establishes spending and taxing levels. Regrettably, for all users of credit, the fiscal policy of the federal government has been to continue to spend more money than it collects.

Interest Rates

If the demand for available funds is high, the price for these funds (the interest rate) will probably be high as well. Therefore, the price of money is subject to supply and demand like any other commodity. For example, if the federal government is borrowing extensively to fund its deficits, the greater the demand for funds, and thus the higher mortgage interest rates will be.

Competition for Funds

As a general rule, any users of credit can obtain needed funds if they are willing to pay the price (interest rate) for those funds. But, when all users of credit are competing for funds at the same time, some users are in an unfavorable position. For example, if business demand for credit is high and business is willing to pay a price equal to that offered by mortgages, funds would generally flow to bonds to the detriment of mortgage lending.

The explanation for this preference for corporate debt lies in the unique characteristics of mortgage debt. Mortgage debt requires a higher yield because of the longer maturity, lack of uniformity in real estate laws, lower liquidity, and the problems and delays of foreclosure. Although inflation and supply and demand for funds are the most important factors in the rise and fall of interest rates, the degree of risk inherent in a mortgage loan or a bond offering also is influential. Of course, if the other major consumers of capital—the various levels of government—are also active in the capital markets, they will take all they need.

Public Debt versus Private Debt

When any government—federal, state, or local—spends more money than it collects, it must borrow in the same markets in which other users of credit borrow. This includes issuers of corporate bonds and homebuyers. In this manner, government competes with other users of credit for the limited capital available. The federal government in particular has been in a severe deficit position for the past couple of decades, a condition that many economists believe was the basic cause of the persistent inflation of the early 1980s. This inflation and the continuing credit demands of the federal government resulted in high interest rates, which played havoc in both the money markets and the capital markets. As a result, all users of credit suffered during this period.

			Interest Rate			
Mortgage Amount	**6.0%**	**6.5%**	**7.0%**	**7.5%**	**8.0%**	**8.5%**
$ 50,000	$ 300.00	$ 316.00	$ 332.50	$ 349.61	$ 367.00	$ 384.45
100,000	600.00	632.00	665.00	699.00	734.00	768.90
150,000	900.00	948.00	997.50	1,048.50	1,101.00	1,153.35
200,000	1,200.00	1,264.00	1,330.00	1,398.00	1,468.00	1,537.80
250,000	1,500.00	1,580.00	1,662.50	1,747.50	1,835.00	1,922.25
300,000	1,800.00	1,896.00	1,995.00	2,097.00	2,202.00	2,306.70
350,000	2,100.00	2,212.00	2,327.50	2,446.50	2,569.00	2,691.15

TABLE 2-5 Lower Interest Rates Make Housing More Affordable: Monthly Principal and Interest Payment on a 30-Year Mortgage

The reason why the federal government's borrowing has such a negative impact on other borrowers is that the federal government will always get as much money as it needs because of its unquestioned credit. Therefore, unless available credit is expanding at a rate that allows for the accommodation of all users of credit, excessive federal borrowing will have a crowding-out effect on less creditworthy borrowers.

For a brief couple of years in the late 1990s and early 2000s, the federal government actually ran a surplus. The result of this rare surplus was that interest rates in general plummeted and long-term residential mortgage rates reached levels not seen in decades.

Monetary Policy and Interest Rates

Another important element in determining interest rates is monetary policy. *Monetary policy* (as implemented by the Federal Reserve) is when the supply of money is controlled rather than interest rates. Thus, when the Federal Reserve wants to stimulate the economy, it increases the supply of money. The fiscal policy of the federal government often forces the Federal Reserve to act in an attempt to moderate the impact of federal borrowing on the nation's economy.

The Federal Reserve

In addition to its banking functions, the Federal Reserve is responsible for controlling the nation's credit system through financial institutions. The Federal Reserve has several methods of implementing this control:

- *Reserve requirements.* By increasing the amount of money a member institution must have in its reserve account, less money is available to be loaned. Conversely, if the Federal Reserve policy is to increase the amount of money in order to make credit easier to obtain, it can lower the reserve requirement.
- *Open-market operations.* This commonly used method allows the Federal Reserve to decrease the supply of money by selling Treasury securities on the

open market. The securities are paid for by checks drawn on commercial banks. This decreases the banks' reserves, therefore reducing the amount of funds that can be loaned. If the Federal Reserve intends to increase the supply of money, it buys the securities by issuing a check drawn upon itself.

- *Fed funds target—Intended federal funds rate.* Open-market operations (purchases and sales of U.S. Treasury and federal agency securities) are the Federal Reserve's principal tool for implementing monetary policy. The short-term objective for open-market operations is specified by the Federal Open Market Committee (FOMC). This objective can be a desired quantity of reserves or a desired price (the federal funds rate). The *federal funds rate* is the overnight interest rate at which depository institutions lend balances at the Federal Reserve to other depository institutions.

- *Discount rate.* The Federal Reserve operates a service of discounting (paying less than **par**) commercial paper from member institutions. By discounting, the Federal Reserve provides funds that can be loaned. If the *discount rate* (considered to be the interest rate that a member institution pays the Federal Reserve) is increased, it becomes more difficult for an institution to borrow to obtain necessary reserves. Consequently, the interest rate a member institution must then charge a borrower increases. If the discount rate is lowered, borrowing is easier for a financial institution and the interest rate charged to a borrower could be lowered. Although the discount window was long ago superseded by open-market operations as the most important tool of monetary policy, it still has a complementary role in the day-to-day implementation of policy. The discount window functions as a safety valve in relieving pressures in reserve markets; in circumstances in which extensions of credit can help relieve liquidity strains in the banking system, the window also helps to assure the basic stability of financial markets more generally.

The ability of the Federal Reserve to influence the economy was very evident during the first two years of the new century. During 2001 and 2002, the Federal Reserve cut the fed funds target rate twelve times, trying to stimulate an economy slowed by the twin forces of recession and the terrorist attacks of September 11, 2001. The last reduction, in November 2002, took the fed funds target rate to 1.25 percent, the lowest since 1961.

Countercyclical Nature of Real Estate

During periods of high demand for credit (normally, the apex of an economic cycle), the capital markets are usually unable to satisfy the combined demands for credit of individuals, government, and business. Mortgage lending usually suffers during such periods because the price of money, as indicated by the interest rate, is too high for most homebuyers to qualify for a mortgage. In some situations in the past, mortgage interest rates have been forced up against a state's usury ceiling. Because real estate in general and mortgage lending in particular are the losers in a credit crunch, they have often been classified as countercyclical. The development of the secondary mortgage market has eased this situation by being able to provide funds from the capital markets for housing during periods of high credit demand.

	Federal Funds Target Rate		TABLE 2-6

| | Change (basis points) | | |
Date	Increase	Decrease	Level (percent)
2001			
December 11	—	25	1.75 %
November 6	—	50	2.00
October 2	—	50	2.50
September 17	—	50	3.00
August 21	—	25	3.50
June 27	—	25	3.75
May 15	—	50	4.00
April 18	—	50	4.50
March 20	—	50	5.00
January 31	—	50	5.50
January 3	—	50	6.00
2000			
May 16	50	—	6.50
March 21	25	—	6.00
February 2	25	—	5.75

Source: Federal Reserve.

The countercyclicality of real estate means that real estate activity, and consequently mortgage lending, usually expands when the general business cycle is down and credit demand is low. The normal situation when the economic cycle is down is lower interest rates in general, which allow more borrowers to qualify for a mortgage loan. Conversely, as the economy begins to improve and demand for credit from other users increases, real estate activity begins to slow down as interest rates increase. This somewhat simplified explanation demonstrates the direct relationship between the availability of credit and real estate activity.

Financial Intermediaries

The more modern and clearly more descriptive term, *financial intermediaries*, describes that classification of economic units previously called financial institutions. Their principal economic function is to serve as the middleman—the intermediary— between the saver and the borrower. Both saver and borrower benefit from this arrangement. The saver, as is explained later, is able to earn a higher return on savings, while the borrower can obtain needed funds at a more reasonable rate.

The term *financial intermediaries* includes these major economic units, among others:

- Commercial banks
- Savings and loan institutions
- Mortgage companies
- Credit unions
- Mutual savings banks
- Life insurance companies
- Finance companies
- Investment companies
- Pension funds
- Money market funds
- Stockbrokers

Financial intermediaries are essential to the entire economy but are especially crucial to mortgage lending, since they lend much of the funds required by homebuyers, and those funds are accumulated almost exclusively from individual savers. The characteristics of these lenders are examined later, but let us first examine how savers benefit from using these intermediaries.

How Savers Benefit

When dealing with financial intermediaries, many of the benefits to savers are obvious, such as higher yield, safety, and diversification. Others, such as economies of scale, variety of maturities, and specialization, are not. Higher yields result from the increased level of knowledge and experience intermediaries have over the average saver. The experts know where, how, and when to make safe, profitable investments. Safety is derived both from federal deposit insurance and from the informed investment decisions of the experts. Diversification is also an element of safety that, for a smaller saver, can be reached without sacrificing yield only through the use of an intermediary.

Exhibit 2-1	United States Housing Stock					
Total	115,904,650		Total	115,904,650	
1 unit, detached	69,696,206	60.1%	Built 1999 or later	2,074,556	1.8%
1 unit attached	6,463,097	5.6%	Built 1995 to 1998	8,536,191	7.4%
2 units	5,348,994	4.6%	Built 1990 to 1994	8,480,468	7.3%
3 or 4 units	5,618,388	4.8%	Built 1980 to 1989	18,274,758	15.8%
5 to 9	5,966,119	5.1%	Built 1970 to 1979	21,154,043	18.3%
10 to 19	5,042,714	4.4%	Built 1960 to 1969	15,376,686	13.3%
20 or more	9,071,115	7.8%	Built 1940 to 1959	23,127,371	20.0%
Mobile	8,604,733	7.4%	Built 1939 or earlier	18,880,577	16.3%
Boat, RV van etc.	93,284	0.1%			

Source: U.S. Census Bureau, 2000 Census.

How Mortgage Borrowers Benefit

The cost to a consumer in need of a mortgage loan is made lower by dealing with an intermediary. Instead of having to solicit many savers for funds, this mortgage borrower need only deal with one financial intermediary, which has been able to pool the funds of many savers. The benefit to savers in this arrangement is a higher yield, since a part of the saved cost of borrowing can be passed on to them while borrowers also benefit from this economy of scale. Each saver has different objectives in mind for savings deposited. Since financial intermediaries can also lend to borrowers with differing needs and for differing maturities, the match is beneficial to both parties. Finally, since many financial intermediaries specialize in a selected type of lending, they can provide that type of lending more cheaply than competitors, with a resulting benefit to both saver and borrower. An example of this type of specialization is thrift institutions and single-family mortgage lending.

Gross Profit Spread

Financial intermediaries are able to fulfill their important economic function by operating on a spread between their cost of funds (generally, the interest on savings of individuals) and their portfolio yield (the interest earned on loans outstanding). As a general rule, savings institutions require a gross profit spread of 2 or 3 percent (200 or 300 **basis points**). As an example, if the average interest rate paid by a savings bank on all savings deposits is 5 percent; the average portfolio yield must be between 7 and 8 percent for that institution to be profitable.

Interest Rate Risk

The primary economic danger to financial intermediaries that are portfolio lenders, such as some credit unions and savings institutions, is that interest rates will begin a rapid increase. The financial institution would have to match the rising rates on savings deposits in order to retain its deposits. It could then lend these funds out at what should be an increased mortgage rate. The problem is that even with the increased interest rate on current mortgage production, the entire mortgage portfolio may not have a sufficient yield to generate a profitable spread. Thus, even though an institution is currently lending at 200 to 300 basis points above its cost of funds, the portfolio yield may not be sufficient for a profitable spread; in fact, it may even be negative, as it was for savings institutions during the high interest rate period of 1981 to 1983.

Mortgage Lenders and the Primary Mortgage Market

The primary economic function of a residential mortgage lender is to lend money for the purchase or refinancing of residences of all types in the **primary mortgage market**. This would include single-family detached, **condominiums**, cooperative housing, and 2–4 family housing. These loans are secured by either a first or second mortgage. The primary mortgage market is that market in which funds are loaned (credit extended) directly to a borrower. This market differs from the secondary mortgage market, in which mortgages originated in the primary market are bought and sold. The secondary mortgage market is discussed in detail in Chapter 11, "Secondary Mortgage Market."

Financial intermediaries usually involved in the residential primary mortgage market include the following:

- **Mortgage bankers**
- **Mortgage brokers**
- Commercial banks
- Savings and loan institutions
- Savings banks
- Credit unions
- Housing finance agencies

These mortgage lenders, along with a few nontraditional mortgage lenders (such as General Electric and General Motors Acceptance Corporation), originate nearly all residential mortgage loans each year. Some of these mortgage lenders also hold mortgages in their own portfolio. Others, such as mortgage bankers, sell all of their originations to other lenders or into the secondary mortgage market. Some of these same lenders are also very active in commercial mortgage lending.

Mortgage Debt

Residential mortgage debt, originated by any of the lenders mentioned previously, has increased every year since the Federal Reserve began tracking it in 1953. Over the past 30 years, mortgage debt growth has averaged about 10 percent a year, more than 2 percent higher that the gross domestic product. Fannie Mae projects that during the first decade of the twenty-first century, growth in residential mortgage debt will average about 10 percent per year.

Lenders obtain the money for residential mortgage loans from the following sources:

- Funds deposited by savers
- Funds borrowed from other financial intermediaries
- Sale of commercial paper (short-term **promissory note**)
- Proceeds from the sale of mortgage loans

Normally, all of the residential mortgage lenders are active on a day-to-day basis in the primary market, but during some stages of the economic cycle, one or more may temporarily drop out. When this occurs, it is usually because of the high cost of funds to lend. By bringing together borrowers and savers from different economic sectors and geographic locations, mortgage lenders as financial intermediaries contribute to a more efficient allocation of the economy's resources. The mortgage lenders are discussed individually in detail in Chapter 3, "The Mortgage Lenders."

Mortgage Investors

In addition to mortgage lenders that hold mortgage debt in their own portfolios, a number of other financial intermediaries are important holders of mortgage debt. These intermediaries hold only residential mortgage debt (either individual loans or mortgage-backed securities); they do not originate any loans. Classified as mortgage investors, they include the following:

- Federal National Mortgage Association (Fannie Mae)
- Federal Home Loan Mortgage Corporation (Freddie Mac)
- Federal Home Loan banks
- Retirement and pension funds
- Other federal agencies
- State housing agencies
- Life insurance companies
- Individuals

These investors acquire the mortgage debt they hold either directly from the mortgage lenders that originated them or through the operation of the secondary mortgage market. Some participants in the primary mortgage market will, on occasion, also buy loans from other originators because they believe they can acquire mortgage loans and/or servicing rights cheaper this way. For a discussion of the secondary mortgage market, see Chapter 11, "Secondary Mortgage Market."

Recent Trends in Mortgage Lending

Residential mortgage lending continues to evolve rapidly. More changes are occurring now than at any other time since the 1930s. These changes affect the following factors:

- Who the lenders are in the primary market
- How residential loans are originated
- How technology is used to enhance profits
- How funds for mortgages are generated
- How interest rates are calculated
- How mortgages are sold and securitized
- How mortgages are serviced and by whom
- How borrowers are qualified
- Who the mortgage investors are in the secondary markets

Some of these changes are discussed in this text. Others, such as who the lenders of tomorrow will be, are beyond the scope of a text of this type. The most meaningful changes in residential mortgage lending over the past 10 years include the following:

- Demise of thrifts as the dominant originator of residential debt and the rise of the mortgage banker
- Widespread use of mortgage-backed securities to access the capital markets for additional funds for residential loans
- Adoption of alternative mortgage instruments by financial intermediaries to spread the risk of mortgage lending
- Explosion of refinancings in 1998 and 2001 because of low interest rates and the resulting runoff of servicing

These subjects are discussed in detail in later chapters.

Mortgage Revenue Bonds (MRBs)

Prior to 1978, state housing finance agencies were the only government entities using tax-exempt MRBs to provide financing for mortgage borrowers. Their normal method of financing was to borrow money and then provide below-market-rate loans to low- and moderate-income groups.

The concept behind using tax-exempt MRBs for financing is quite simple. An issuer, whether state or city, is able to sell its tax-exempt bonds in the capital market with an interest rate substantially below taxable bonds because of the tax savings to investors. This money is then channeled through various mortgage lenders to mortgage borrowers. As a result of this low-cost borrowing, mortgagors often can obtain a loan two or three percentage points below the conventional market rate.

The various state programs in past years caused little reaction as they attempted to help the low- and moderate-income groups, but when new programs developed that were designed to assist middle-income groups, the concern of many segments of society was vocalized. The Mortgage Subsidy Bond Act (1981) resulted from this rising concern. This act severely restricts the use of tax-exempt MRBs issued by state and local housing authorities. It limits eligibility of buyers and imposes purchase price ceilings and limitations on states' annual volumes.

Mortgage Credit Certificates (MCCs)

The law extending authority for mortgage revenue bonds also provided state and local governments with an alternative to MRBs with which to assist first-time homebuyers. This alternative provides for the issuance of MCCs to qualified homebuyers, allowing them a nonrefundable tax credit of from 10 to 50 percent (as determined by the state or local government) of the interest paid on home mortgage indebtedness. MCCs are limited to first-time homebuyers having a joint income below the local area median income and to the purchase of homes whose **acquisition costs** do not exceed 90 percent of the local average purchase price. The MCC concept is an attempt to ensure that the entire amount of the subsidy, in the form of tax credits, flows directly to first-time homebuyers and not partially to others. Congress perceived that MRBs had a part of the subsidy flowing to tax-exempt investors and intermediaries, in addition to the homebuyer. The MCC provides the same subsidy or more as the MRB to first-time homebuyers and at a reduced revenue loss to the federal tax coffers. This subsidy is meant to complement the mortgage interest deduction that provides greater benefits to higher-income home-buyers and little or no benefit to low- and middle-income taxpayers.

Under the law, state and local governments have the choice of issuing MRBs or MCCs or a combination of both. The aggregate annual amount of MCCs issued by a state may not exceed 20 percent of the authorized MRB volume for the state. The state's MRB volume is determined by an average of originations over the past three years or $200 million, whichever is greater.

Builder Bonds

Builder bonds are being used frequently today as a means whereby builders can access the capital markets directly in order to obtain the funds needed by the purchasers of their homes. To builders, the obvious benefit of this financing technique is that they can sell more houses than they could otherwise. This is true even during those periods of the economic cycle when some of the traditional lenders are out of the market because of a lack of savings inflow. A builder (or group of builders) will use a mortgage banker or a similar organization to take local applications, underwrite the loan, and provide loan servicing.

As important as this direct access to the capital market is, another aspect is more important to some builders. The use of builder bonds to finance the purchase of houses allows a builder to report house sales on an installment basis for tax purposes and thus be able to defer most of the income tax until later years. The reason is that since the mortgage payments are spread out over 20 years or more, the house is paid for over that same period. Taxes are paid according to the amount of profit earned each year.

Builder bonds are mortgage-backed securities that are backed either by the individual mortgages on houses sold or by Government National Mortgage Association or Ginnie Mae certificates purchased for the purpose of serving as collateral for a builder bond. For an extensive discussion of mortgage-backed securities, see Chapter 11, "Secondary Mortgage Market."

Discussion Points

1. Real estate and mortgage lending are a major part of the American economy. Examine and explain the magnitude of their involvement in the economy.

2. Real estate and mortgage lending are significantly impacted by changes in the economy, especially interest rates. What was the impact on mortgage lending of the dramatic drop in interest rates in 2001–2002? Why did interest rates drop so much?

3. What is the difference between *financial intermediaries*, *mortgage lenders*, and *mortgage investors*?

4. How does "the Fed" attempt to manage the economy? What tools are most important?

5. As a general rule, from where does the money for residential mortgage lending come?

6. How do demographic forces impact real estate and the mortgage markets?

The Mortgage Lenders

Introduction

The objective of this chapter is to examine those financial intermediaries—the mortgage lenders—that originate residential mortgage loans in the primary mortgage market. Care should be taken to understand that *originators* of mortgage debt are not necessarily *holders* of mortgage debt. Some mortgage lenders, such as credit unions, hold in their portfolios most of the mortgage debt they originate. On the other hand, mortgage bankers must sell all of the loans they originate.

The term *financial intermediary* is applied to all residential mortgage originators even though not all mortgage lenders are depository institutions. For example, mortgage bankers, who annually originate about half of all residential mortgage loans, are not depository institutions (i.e., they do not take deposits from savers). Mortgage bankers obtain funds for residential mortgage lending by borrowing from other financial institutions or through the sale of commercial paper.

Holders of Residential Debt

Before the Great Depression, wealthy individuals made up the largest classification of holders of residential debt. In today's highly sophisticated and segmented residential mortgage lending market, holders of mortgage debt are the financial intermediaries that originated residential mortgage loans and retained them in their own portfolios. If, on the other hand, the originating lender sells mortgage loans to other financial institutions or the secondary market, the purchaser of the loans or the mortgage-backed security itself is classified as the holder of residential mortgage debt. Although individuals today still hold billions of dollars of residential debt, their percentage of the total residential mortgage debt is very small. This chapter focuses on a discussion of the major residential lenders in order of their origination volume, starting with mortgage bankers.

Mortgage Bankers and Mortgage Brokers

A discussion of residential mortgage lenders must start with mortgage bankers and mortgage brokers since they originate approximately 60 percent of all residential mortgage loans each year. In addition, mortgage bankers service approximately 70 percent of the nearly $6 trillion in outstanding residential mortgage debt. Both of these figures represent major growth in the 1990s and early 2000s.

	Savings Inst.	Commercial Banks	FNMA/ FHLMC	Credit Unions	Finance Cos.	Mortgage Pools	All Others*	Total
Holders of 1–4 Family Mortgage Debt (in billions of dollars)								**TABLE 3-1**
1990	$692	$ 466	$127	$ 50	$ 39	$1,076	$482	$2,932
1995	544	689	223	67	45	1,807	409	3,784
2000	656	1,043	214	127	111	3,041	410	5,603

*All Others includes state and local credit agencies, FHLBs' mortgage portfolios, REITs, individuals, and life insurance companies.

Source: Federal Reserve Board.

A mortgage company is usually identified as a mortgage banker but may actually be a mortgage broker. The term *mortgage banker* is somewhat misleading since it implies that this lender is a depository for savings like other financial intermediaries are. Mortgage bankers are not depositories for savings but are classified as intermediaries since they serve as a financial bridge between borrowers and lenders. As mentioned, mortgage bankers obtain the money they lend to homebuyers by either borrowing the money from another intermediary (usually a commercial bank) or by the sale of commercial paper.

Mortgage Brokers (Not to Be Confused with Mortgage Bankers)

The 30,000 mortgage brokers active in the United States today are major producers of residential mortgage loans in the marketplace. In a typical mortgage transaction involving a mortgage broker, the broker takes the application for a residential mortgage loan from a consumer and then sells that loan to another mortgage lender (often called a wholesale lender) before the loan is closed. After the unclosed loan is sold, the mortgage broker has no continuing responsibility in regard to the loan, and the loan is closed in the name of the purchasing mortgage lender. In some situations, the mortgage broker will close the loan in its own name but immediately sell it to a wholesale lender (and release the servicing to that lender also—see Chapter 14, "Mortgage Loan Servicing and Administration," for a discussion of this activity).

The mortgage broker acts as an independent contractor in providing such services as preparing the borrower's loan package, taking the loan application, ordering verifications, and counseling the borrower. With the mortgage broker fulfilling these functions, it allows wholesaler lenders to cut origination costs and thus improve profits. Viewed another way, mortgage brokers help consumers with lower loan rates due to their minimal overhead and setup costs. Mortgage brokers state that their mission is to find a loan that best suits the borrower's financial circumstances, needs, and goals. A mortgage broker does not earn a fee from the consumer until the loan closes. Thus, the broker has the ultimate incentive to provide the best possible customer service to the consumer.

Exhibit 3-1 / Mortgage Loan Origination Agreement

You, *Thomas Stavola/Susan Stavola* agree to enter into this Mortgage Loan Origination Agreement with **NORTHFIELD MORTGAGE COMPANY (NMC)** as an independent contractor to apply for a residential mortgage loan from a participating lender with which we from time to time contract upon such terms and conditions as you may request or a lender may require. You inquired into mortgage financing with **NMC** on June 18, 2003. We are licensed as a "**Mortgage Broker**" under the Laws of the State of Florida.

Section 1. Nature of Relationship. In connection with this mortgage loan:
- We are acting as an independent contractor and not as your agent.
- We will enter into separate independent contract agreements with various lenders.
- While we seek to assist you in meeting your financial needs, we do not distribute the products of all lenders or investors in the market and cannot guarantee the lowest price or best terms available in the market.

Section 2. Our Compensation. The lenders whose loan products we distribute generally provide their loan products to us at a wholesale rate.
- The retail price we offer you—your interest rate, total points, and fees—will include our compensation.
- In some cases, either you or the lender may pay us all of our compensation.
- Alternatively, both you and the lender may pay us a portion of our compensation. For example, in some cases, if you would rather pay a lower interest rate, you may pay higher upfront points and fees.
- Also, in some cases, if you would rather pay less upfront, you may be able to pay some or all of our compensation indirectly through a higher interest rate, in which case we will be paid directly by the lender.

We also may be paid by the lender based on (i) the value of the Mortgage Loan or related servicing rights in the market place, or (ii) other services, goods, or facilities performed or provided by us to the lender. By signing below, the mortgage loan originator and mortgage loan applicant(s) acknowledge receipt of a copy of this signed Agreement.

_____*Iamm Fiducia*_____ Date _6/18/03_   _____*Thomas Stavola*_____ Date _6/18/03_
Mortgage Loan Originator   **Applicant**

                                            _____*Susan Stavola*_____ Date _6/18/03_
                                            Applicant

Fees Charged by Mortgage Brokers

Mortgage brokers typically charge fees to the mortgage applicant and also receive fees from a wholesale lender. Is this legal? Federal law (RESPA—see Chapter 16, "Compliance") allows fees to be charged by service providers, as long as those fees are reasonable for services, goods, or facilities actually provided. Similar to retail mortgage originators (such as commercial banks or mortgage banks), mortgage brokers provide the same services to consumers for which an **origination fee** is often charged. These loan origination services include taking the loan application, ordering the **credit report** and **appraisal**, counseling the consumer on the loan process, and collecting the necessary documents.

Mortgage brokers may also receive a fee from the wholesale purchaser. This fee is earned because the broker provides separate and distinct services to wholesale lenders. These include marketing the lender's products and assembling and delivering the completed loan package. In addition to a fee for these services, wholesale lenders may pay mortgage brokers a premium (**yield spread premium** or *service release premium*—see Glossary), which may include compensation for the services and facilities, but which also represents payment for the intrinsic market value of the closed loan. For more information on mortgage brokers, see the National Association of Mortgage Brokers website at **www.namb.org**.

Mortgage Bankers (Not to Be Confused with Mortgage Brokers)

Mortgage bankers, on the other hand, sell all of the mortgages they originate (or purchase from others, such as mortgage brokers) and close the loan, but usually continue to service it after the sale. The number of independent mortgage bankers is actually quite small (only a few hundred), but many more financial institutions implementing the mortgage-banking strategy belong to the trade association, the Mortgage Bankers Association of America (MBA, **www.mbaa.org**). Today, either commercial banks or savings institutions own most of the largest 100 mortgage-banking companies. The majority of mortgage bankers is geographically located in traditional capital-deficit areas such as the South and West. These mortgage bankers continue to render a valuable service to both borrowers and mortgage investors by moving funds for mortgages

Originations of Residential Mortgage Loans by Lender (percentage of total originations)				TABLE 3-2
Year	Mortgage Companies	Savings Institutions	Commercial Banks	Others
1985	35%	41%	19%	5%
1990	34	30	34	2
1995	54	18	26	2
2000	57	17	24	2

Source: HUD.

Figure 3-1	Top 1–4 Family Mortgage Originators in 2001: All Channels of Origination* (billions of dollars)	
1.	Wells Fargo Home Mortgage	$196
2.	Chase Manhattan Mortgage	184
3.	Washington Mutual	166
4.	Countrywide Credit Industries	138
5.	Bank of America	86
	Total of Top Five	$769**

*All channels refer to: (a) retail, direct to consumer, (b) wholesale, through loan broker, and (c) correspondent, purchase of funded loan.
**Represents 38 percent of total originations for year.

Source: National Mortgage News.

from capital-surplus areas to areas where insufficient capital exists to meet the needs of homebuyers.

Not a Portfolio Lender

Unlike other mortgage lenders, a mortgage banker does not intentionally hold mortgages for its own benefit. Since a mortgage banker does not have a traditional portfolio like other intermediaries, all residential mortgage loans are originated with the intent of selling the loans to mortgage investors either directly or through the secondary mortgage market. On occasion, a mortgage banker may originate a "mistake" that cannot be sold as a conforming loan to an established investor. When this happens, the mortgage banker usually sells the loan to another investor at a **discount** rather than hold on to it.

Development of Mortgage Bankers

Mortgage companies, later called mortgage bankers, developed to fulfill a need for farm financing in the second half of the nineteenth century. Following the Civil War, the opening of new farmland in the Ohio Valley and further west required an infusion of credit from the capital-surplus areas of New England. Originally, a few real estate agents, attorneys, and some commercial bankers made the needed mortgage loan and then sold the loan to wealthy individuals or institutions in the East. This practice grew until farm mortgage lending specialists developed and formed the first mortgage companies. At the turn of the 20th century, approximately 200 mortgage companies existed. They originated farm mortgages with the following components: 50 percent loan-to-value, interest-only loans, with five-year maturities.

Following World War I, the migration from farms to the developing urban areas accelerated. At this time, a few of the more aggressive mortgage companies began to make single-family mortgage loans. This new type of loan was similar to the farm mortgages made by mortgage companies for the previous 50 years in regard to loan-to-value ratios and term. These nonamortized mortgages, which normally required refinancing at the expiration of the term, were the principal reason why such a large number of families lost their homes in the Depression of the 1930s. The reason for the lost homes was the liquidity crisis, which prevented financial institutions from refinancing mortgage loans as they rolled over.

Government Programs

In the early 1930s, officials of the federal government realized that some basic economic changes were needed to prevent more serious political changes from occurring. The first step taken toward stabilizing the economy was to put a floor under depreciating real estate values. Not only was demand for real estate at a low point at this time, the ever-increasing number of foreclosures was forcing real estate values down. The Federal Home Loan Bank System was begun in 1932 to help the savings and loan business, but, in 1933, the Home Owners Loan Corporation (HOLC) allowed all lenders, including mortgage bankers, to exchange defaulted mortgages for government bonds. This program helped save many family homes as HOLC restructured mortgages and put them on an amortized basis. It also helped stabilize real estate values, since foreclosed properties were no longer forcing down the market.

Beginning of Modern Mortgage-Lending Standards

The Federal Housing Administration (FHA), created in 1934, provided the main stimulus to the formation of the modern mortgage banker. FHA established minimum standards for both the borrower and the real estate before it would insure a mortgage loan. FHA minimum standards prompted life insurance companies to seek permission from state insurance commissioners to make out-of-state loans with higher loan-to-value ratios and longer terms. State regulatory authorities eventually agreed to the request, and mortgage bankers soon began originating FHA-insured mortgages for sale to life insurance companies.

FHA adopted the HOLC practice of amortizing mortgage loans to assist borrowers in budgeting mortgage payments. Amortized loans created a need for these loans to be serviced following their sale to investors. Servicing requires that the servicer collect the monthly principal and interest and forward the payment to an investor. This requirement for servicing was the linchpin that allowed mortgage bankers to become the dominant originators of FHA-insured mortgage loans. Their dominant position in regard to FHA-insured mortgage loans remains constant even to the present time.

After World War II, Congress created another type of mortgage loan with governmental involvement—the Veterans Administration (VA) guaranteed loan. The mortgage bankers quickly became the dominant originator of this type of loan also. Both the FHA-insured mortgages and the VA-guaranteed mortgages originated by mortgage bankers were sold to and serviced for the Federal National Mortgage Association (now called Fannie Mae), which bought only FHA and **VA mortgages** until the early 1970s.

Modern Mortgage Bankers

The evolution of mortgage bankers has produced a modern financial intermediary that is very capable of adapting to changes in economic and marketplace conditions. For instance, in 2001, the top five mortgage companies originated nearly 38 percent of 1–4 family mortgage loans produced either by direct origination, wholesale, or via their correspondent system. When viewed from the perspective of direct retail origination, these five major players originated about 13 percent of total 1–4 family originations.

The modern mortgage banker earns most of its revenue from four main sources:

- Origination fees charged to applicants
- **Servicing fees** paid by investors
- Marketing difference between interest rate on underlying mortgage and yield required by **commitment**
- **Warehousing** difference between interest rates on funds borrowed and loaned

Today, some mortgage bankers have dual capabilities—single-family housing and income property origination—while many companies have decided to specialize in only one type of property. The modern mortgage banker specializing in originating residential mortgage loans performs some or all of the following functions:

- Originates, processes, underwrites, and closes all types of residential mortgage loans
- Arranges construction financing
- Warehouses closed residential mortgage loans
- Sells residential loans, either as **whole loans** or participations
- Sells to private investors or secondary mortgage market
- Pools residential mortgages into mortgage-backed securities
- Services the loans after sale

Organization and Regulation

Unlike other mortgage lenders, mortgage bankers are not chartered by either a state or the federal government, but instead follow either the partnership or incorporation laws of the state in which they are located. Today, many states have passed laws specifically aimed at mortgage bankers and mortgage brokers, requiring them to be licensed by the states in which they want to originate mortgages. If a mortgage banker is domiciled in one state and wants to do business in another state, it usually has to register as a mortgage banker in the other state also. Mortgage bankers are also unique in that they are not subject to direct regulation or supervision by any federal agency.

If a mortgage banker is an FHA-approved lender, VA-approved lender, or an approved **seller/servicer** for Fannie Mae or Freddie Mac, it is subject to periodic audits by those entities. HUD has attempted to exercise some control over mortgage bankers by issuing regulations governing several areas of concern, among them the way a mortgagee handles delinquency problems with a mortgagor. During the early 1980s, when merger activity between commercial banks and mortgage bankers was common, the Federal Reserve exercised some control by requiring approval prior to an ownership change.

Financing the Mortgage Banker

Mortgage bankers finance their lending activity differently than most other residential mortgage lenders. The reason is, they have no funds deposited by savers to lend to mortgagors. A mortgage banker finances its residential mortgage lending activity by either the sale of commercial paper or by drawing on a line of credit with another lender—usually a commercial bank. Historically, the latter was the primary way of obtaining funds. Commercial paper is a short-term debt instrument with a maximum term of 180 to 270 days, which carries a fixed rate of interest for a fixed term. Mortgage bankers use this alternative during those periods in the economic cycle when the rate for commercial paper is lower than the prime rate.

Sale of Commercial Paper

In addition to a lower cost of borrowing, the use of commercial paper removes the need for *compensating balances*—funds left on deposit with a commercial bank to provide an additional incentive to lend funds. If a commercial bank lends its support to the commercial paper of a mortgage banker by backing it with an irrevocable letter of credit, the bank will require a fee and some compensating balances. On the other hand, if commercial paper is sold under the name of a holding company of a mortgage banker, no compensating balances are required. For this alternative to be used, the parent company must have an acceptable credit rating. The problem with selling commercial paper is the volatility of that market. During periods of tight money, only high-cost funds can be obtained and then only by those companies with the highest credit ratings.

Line of Credit and Warehousing

The second alternative used by mortgage bankers for obtaining funds to be loaned to residential mortgagors is by drawing on a line of credit with a commercial bank. This process is usually a part of a unique function performed by mortgage bankers—warehousing. *Warehousing* refers to when mortgage bankers hold mortgages in the "warehouse" on a short-term basis, pending sale to an investor. These first mortgage loans held in the warehouse also serve as security for the revolving line of credit at a commercial bank. This process finances the mortgage banker's loans to borrowers and the mortgage banker's **inventory** of closed residential loans. The loan from the commercial bank must be fully collateralized by closed mortgage loans retained by the mortgage banker until enough loans are grouped for sale to investors. The mortgage banker repays the commercial bank's line of credit from the proceeds of periodic sales of mortgages to investors. Warehousing aptly describes the flow of closed mortgages into a mortgage banker that is then used to secure the bank loan. The closed mortgages remain for 30 to 90 days in the warehouse until a group, or pool, of mortgages, typically in million-dollar units, is sold to an investor.

Commercial banks are attracted to this type of loan because it is short term and involves little risk. The risk is minimal because the residential mortgage loans serving as collateral are usually presold to an investor who is obligated to purchase by a commitment it has issued. Commercial banks usually require that compensating balances, typically 20 percent of the maximum line of credit, support this line of credit. These required compensating balances might consist of tax and insurance escrows collected by the mortgage banker and deposited with the lending bank until needed.

Mortgage Banking Today

Whether performed by an independent mortgage banker or another type of mortgage lender, the "mortgage-banking strategy" has become the predominant and preferred strategy for originating residential mortgage loans, minimizing risk, and growing a servicing portfolio. As mentioned, mortgage bankers originated (one way or another) over 50 percent of residential mortgage loans in recent years, and other lenders, such as commercial banks and savings institutions, also followed the same strategy of originating loans, selling them, and growing a servicing portfolio.

Commercial Banks

Commercial banks have the second largest (behind credit unions) number of institutions, about 8,000 banks (with 45,000 branches), and the greatest total assets ($6.5 trillion in 2002) of all financial institutions. The assets of all commercial banks are more than twice those of all savings and loans, savings banks, and credit unions combined. Commercial banks hold more 1–4 family mortgage loans—over $1 trillion—than any other classification of financial institution (only mortgage pools have a larger dollar amount of 1–4 family mortgage loans). In 2002, commercial banks were the second largest originators of 1–4 mortgages (about 25 percent) behind only mortgage bankers. They are also first in origination of income property loans and construction mortgages.

A *commercial bank* is a private financial institution organized to accumulate funds primarily through time and demand deposits and to make these funds available to finance the nation's commerce and industry. Over the past 20 years, commercial banks have expanded their real estate finance operations from what were mostly short-term mortgage loans to include many long-term mortgage loans.

Historical Development

Except for a one-year period following the enactment of the National Bank Act of 1863, federally chartered commercial banks were not allowed to make real estate loans until 1913. During the period from 1863 to 1913, state-chartered banks thrived, since they were able to make real estate loans. Then in 1913, the Federal Reserve Act provided the authorization for federally chartered commercial banks to make mortgage loans. The typical mortgage loan provided by banks during this early period was similar to those made by other lenders: a 50 percent loan-to-value ratio for a five-year term, with the principal payable at the end of the term and with interest payable semiannually.

Commercial banks in the 1930s were in a position similar to that of other financial institutions—lack of liquidity—and consequently many failed. (In fact, the number of commercial banks decreased during this period from more than 30,000 to about 16,000.) During the early months of President Franklin D. Roosevelt's first term, many new federal laws affecting the economy were enacted. The Federal Deposit Insurance Corporation (FDIC), authorized by the Banking Act of 1933, helped restore confidence in commercial banks and encouraged badly needed funds to flow back into bank vaults to provide liquidity for new loans. Currently, the Bank Insurance Fund (BIF), a part of FDIC, insures deposits in all commercial banks up to $100,000.

Organization and Regulation

Commercial banks are chartered either by the federal government (through the comptroller of the currency) or by a state banking agency. State-chartered banks outnumber federally chartered banks by about two to one, although more assets are in the federally chartered banks. State-chartered banks may be members of the Federal Reserve system, but only 1,000 (10 percent) are members. All federally chartered commercial banks must be members, however. This central banking system, comprising 12 Federal Reserve districts, provides many services to its members such as issuing currency, holding bank reserves, discounting loans, and serving as a check clearinghouse.

Commercial banks historically have been interested in maintaining a balance in the maturity of their source of funds and their loan portfolio. Bank funds are primarily short term and derived from passbook savings and deposits in checking accounts. Because of the maturity of their funds, long-term lending of any type is generally not attractive. Most commercial banks are interested in commercial and industrial loans that are normally short term and provide a better match between the maturity of assets (loans) and liabilities (deposits). When commercial loan demand is high, practically all commercial bank funds flow to meet that demand, and mortgage loans are neglected. During those periods in the business cycle when commercial loan demand is low, banks place excess funds in real estate.

Mortgage-Lending Activity

Larger commercial banks, as a general rule, are different from other major mortgage lenders in that they are not organized for, nor philosophically inclined toward, residential mortgage lending. On the other hand, banks located in smaller, more rural areas have a greater inclination toward residential mortgage lending. As a whole, banks increased their real estate lending activity (both residential and income property) by about 50 percent from 1984 to 1992. The growth since then has been nearly as strong. Part of the reason for this shift in emphasis is the capital requirements (50 percent risk weight) for single-family mortgage loans, which are half that required for commercial and industrial loans (100 percent risk weight). Put another way, a commercial bank needs twice the capital to make commercial and industrial loans as needed for single-family mortgage lending.

Real estate financing activity has been very profitable to banks during certain phases of the business cycle. But it has also been very damaging to banks at times because some of the mortgage loans that were made probably should not have been. In the second half of the 1980s, banks made a major move into real estate. For example, during 1988 to 1990, Citicorp was the largest originator of mortgage debt in this country. However, for some of the banks, this recent experience with real estate lending was not profitable. Many bank failures of the late 1980s and early 1990s, according to FDIC, were the result of poor real estate lending by the banks.

Currently, commercial banks make all types of mortgage loans, but **construction loans** on residential and income properties comprise a large percentage of mortgage financing activity. On the bank's books, these loans are normally classified as ordinary commercial loans, not real estate loans. The interest rate is generally two to five points above the prime rate, depending on the borrower. These loans are attractive to commercial banks because of the yield and because the loans are short term (6 to 36 months), making it similar to the term of the bank's source of funds.

Federal Reserve Regulations

The board of governors of the Federal Reserve system issues regulations affecting real estate lending activity by member banks. State-chartered banks are governed by the regulations of the responsible state agency. These regulations usually are similar to those of the Federal Reserve. Current Federal Reserve regulations allow loans up to 90 percent of value to be amortized up to 30 years with no limit on the loan amount, although they are subject to the maximum loan limit in the secondary market. A bank can lend up to 70 percent of its deposits or 100 percent of capital and surplus, whichever is greater. Commercial banks may have up to 10 percent of real estate loan units in a "basket," or nonconforming classification. Leasehold loans are allowed if the lease extends at least 10 years past the date of full amortization.

The mortgage-lending activity of commercial banks is more diverse than that of other lenders. Banks not only engage in both government and conventional residential mortgage lending, but also are the largest income-property lender. They are the largest mortgage lender for construction loans, and they help finance other lenders, especially mortgage bankers, by issuing lines of credit allowing for the warehousing of loans.

Commercial banks, like other mortgage lenders, originate residential mortgage loans for their own portfolio and for sale to others. Also, like other lenders, banks purchase mortgages originated by others.

Savings Institutions

The historical role of savings institutions (sometimes called thrift institutions) in the nation's economy is the pooling of savings of individuals for investment, primarily in residential mortgages. The term *savings institution* is used here to include both federal or state-chartered savings and loans (S&Ls) or savings banks (SBs) that are either stock or mutual associations. This financial intermediary is still fulfilling that role today, even though savings institutions have had great difficulty since the hyperinflation period of the early 1980s. Even with all of the problems facing savings institutions, in the first decade of the twenty-first century they are still originating about 20 percent of the first mortgage loans made each year. At year-end 2002, savings institutions held nearly $448 billion in 1–4 family mortgage debt. As large as the amount is, it is a substantial decline from $526 billion held at year-end 1988.

Although they may be called differently in some states (e.g., homestead associations, mutual savings bank, building and loan, cooperatives), their role remains the same. Savings institutions operate in all 50 states and numbered approximately 1,500 (with about 20,000 branches) at the end of 2000. Total assets for savings institutions at year-end 2000 were approximately $1.2 trillion, which is the same size as year-end 1985. The number of savings institutions has decreased rapidly since 1970, when about 4,700 existed. This decline in the number of savings institutions is expected to continue for a while longer. For example, in the year 2000, after adding in de novo and charter conversions, the total number of savings institutions declined by 35 for the year.

Savings institutions are no longer the largest private holder of residential mortgage debt (commercial banks overtook them in 1992), and they are no longer the largest originator of residential mortgage debt each year (mortgage bankers and commercial bankers are both larger).

Historical Development

From the founding of the first association in 1831 (Oxford Provident Building Association in Frankfort, Pennsylvania), S&Ls have spread across the United States, providing funds for the housing growth of the nation. For example, S&Ls provided much of the institutional financing of urban homes for middle-income Americans before the 1930s. Although the largest number of S&Ls was reached in 1927, when more than 12,000 were in existence, the contribution S&Ls have made to providing financing for housing has been critical ever since.

The 1930s were years of dramatic change for S&Ls. More than half of those in existence failed during this decade, and more than 25 percent of S&L mortgage assets were in default. In addition to the general economic depression, the major problem for all lenders during the 1930s was a lack of liquidity. This liquidity crisis was caused by the panic of the American public following the stock market crash and the failure of some banks, which precipitated a rush to withdraw savings from all financial institutions. To help alleviate this liquidity problem, Congress created the Federal Home Loan Bank (FHLB) system in July 1932. The FHLB provides liquidity during periods of credit restraint for member S&Ls and serves the industry in the way that the Federal Reserve system serves the needs of commercial banks. The law provided for the creation of 12 regional banks, one to serve each geographic area. Many of the functions of the FHLBs were stripped away with the enactment of the Financial Institutions Reform, Recovery and Enforcement Act (FIRREA) in 1989.

Another important step toward the development of the modern S&L occurred with the creation of the Federal Savings and Loan Insurance Corporation (FSLIC), as authorized by Title IV of the National Housing Act of 1934. This step was vital for the restoration of faith in the safety of deposits in S&Ls, and it paved the way for new deposits needed to make new mortgage loans. Today, as a result of changes mandated by FIRREA, deposits in savings institutions are insured up to $100,000 by a successor to FSLIC called the Savings Association Insurance Corporation (SAIF), which is a part of the Federal Deposit Insurance Corporation (FDIC).

An Institution in Trouble

The 20 years before the enactment of FIRREA (1989) contained periods of highs and lows for S&Ls. The 1970s witnessed steady growth in total assets and profitability, but during the 1980s, the S&L industry struggled for survival and many institutions didn't make it. The reasons for the collapse of many S&Ls and of their insurance fund (FSLIC) with the resulting federal bailout have been debated in many forums. The experts agree that the primary reason for the eventual collapse of S&Ls was the low-yielding, fixed-rate mortgages of the early 1980s, which, when combined with high inflation, created a negative spread between the cost of funds and the portfolio yield.

The S&L industry attempted to solve this problem by seeking and winning federal government/regulatory approval for deregulation of depository institutions, in addition to creative accounting changes that differed from GAAP (generally accepted accounting principles). Further, S&Ls lobbied for and received regulatory permission to expand their activity into high-yield/high-risk lending. All of these changes occurred without an increase in supervision. For a few years, these changes allowed S&Ls to improve their bottom line. But these changes proved to be the undoing of many struggling S&Ls. The Tax Reform Act of 1986 was most likely the beginning of the end. This act eliminated many of the tax benefits from real estate that had made real estate such an attractive investment. As a result of these tax law changes, builders and developers found they could not sell their properties, and many S&Ls that had financed these properties had to take them back. Earnings were once again under pressure, and regulators were starting to look very carefully at earnings and loan portfolios. What they saw was a disaster developing: the S&L industry lost $20 billion in 1989 alone.

The National Association of Realtors sums up the problem this way, "Deregulation and new investment powers made financial and managerial demands that most thrift executives had not contemplated. Speculative investments, a regulatory system which failed to exercise controls, basic mismanagement and an unprecedented level of fraud and abuse perpetrated by many thrift executives resulted in the inevitable legislative backlash." That legislative backlash was FIRREA, which is estimated to cost the American taxpayer up to $400 billion over the life of the bonds sold to finance the S&L bailout.

Organization and Regulation

Savings institutions may be chartered either by a state or by the federal government and can be either mutual or stock institutions. Recently, a fairly equal number were chartered by the states and by the federal government and an equal number were stock and mutual institutions. The enactment of FIRREA in 1989 completely changed the way savings institutions were regulated. FIRREA restructured the regulatory framework by abolishing the Federal Home Loan Bank Board (but not the Federal Home Loan Banks) and FSLIC. FSLIC insurance of deposits was replaced with the Savings Associations Insurance Fund (SAIF), a part of FDIC. The Office of Thrift Supervision (OTS), under the Treasury Department, replaced the role of the FHLBB as regulator. The Office of

	Non-OTS-Regulated Savings Institutions	OTS-Regulated Savings Institutions					Grand Total
		Federal Charter		State Charter		Total	
		Stock	Mutual	Stock	Mutual		
1985	352	385	1,364	710	815	3,274	3,626
1990	456	684	825	347	503	2,359	2,815
1995	593	744	431	101	161	1,437	2,030
2000	522	607	309	46	106	1,068	1,590

Thrift Institutions by Charter Type — **TABLE 3-3**

Source: OTS.

Thrift Supervision is the primary regulator of all federally chartered and many state-chartered thrift institutions, which include savings banks and savings and loan associations. OTS is funded by assessments and fees levied on the institutions it regulates.

Non-OTS-regulated savings institutions are savings banks that are chartered by state regulatory authority with the primary federal regulation provided by FDIC. FDIC was given extensive new powers to ensure the safety and soundness of financial institutions (but not credit unions) and was given the supervision of separate S&L (SAIF) and bank deposit insurance funds (BIF). Finally, FIRREA created the Resolution Trust Corporation (RTC) to dispose of failed S&Ls and their assets.

Savings Institutions Today

Over the years, savings institutions have loaned hundreds of billions of dollars to millions of borrowers at the prevailing market rate for the purchase of homes. During the past decade, as the problem at savings institutions multiplied, the share of originations has decreased. But, notwithstanding all of these problems, savings institutions are still a major source of mortgage money. The surviving institutions (approximately 1,500) will once again place greater emphasis on residential mortgage lending and less on commercial lending. The principal reason for this reliance on 1–4 family mortgage lending is that it requires less capital than other types of lending.

Today, many savings institutions are active in the secondary mortgage market, both as buyers and as sellers. Beginning in 1987, savings institutions had many years of being net sellers of mortgages in the secondary mortgage market. For example, in 2001, these institutions originated $398 billion in 1–4 family mortgage loans and sold $403 billion. This development is significant in that it demonstrates a change in lending philosophy from one dominated by local concerns to one affected and shaped by the nation's economy. Some savings institutions have even formed mortgage-banking subsidiaries to originate all types of loans for sale into the secondary mortgage market.

Because of their historical local focus and previously existing legal limitations on their lending area, many savings institutions did not become involved in either FHA-insured or VA-guaranteed mortgages. Instead, savings institution deposits were invested in local conventional mortgages originated either for savings institutions' own portfolios or for sale. Today, changes in the marketplace have forced many savings institutions to originate all types of residential loans, including second mortgages.

Savings Banks (SBs)

Savings banks have often been categorized as commercial banks and sometimes as savings institutions. Although a savings bank has some of the characteristics of both, it is actually a unique thrift institution.

Historical Development

Like the first savings and loan, the first savings bank was founded in Pennsylvania. The Philadelphia Savings Fund Society (now called Meritor Savings Bank), the nation's largest savings bank, began in 1816 and was followed in 1817 by the founding of the Provident Institute for Savings in Boston.

Unlike the early building societies, these institutions were organized to provide ongoing facilities to encourage savings by the small wage earner, who had been virtually ignored by the other financial institutions. Savings banks were well received and began to spread throughout the New England states. By 1875, the number of SBs had reached a peak of 674. The SB concept never spread far from its origins, though, most likely due to the development of S&Ls, which encouraged savings and housing, and the development of savings accounts at commercial banks. Today, most of the approximately 300 remaining savings banks are located in three states: Connecticut, Massachusetts, and New York.

Organization and Regulation

Until the early 1980s, all savings banks were mutual organizations and as such had no stockholders. Beginning in the early 1980s, many savings banks realized that they needed additional capital if they were going to be able to compete in the new, deregulated environment. Today, about half of the savings banks are stock institutions, and the trend appears to be in the direction of more mutuals converting to stock.

If an SB remains a mutual organization, all depositors share ownership and it is managed by a self-perpetuating board of trustees, usually made up of prominent local business leaders. If the SB is a stock organization, then a board of directors, representing the stockholders of the bank, manages it.

In 1979, changes in federal law allowed savings banks to be federally chartered. Before this time, all SBs were state chartered. The majority of SBs is still state chartered, but that may change as federal law evolves regarding capital requirements and portfolio structure. Since the vast majority of SBs is chartered by various states, the regulations that govern their operations vary from state to state. State regulations establish guidelines for deposits, reserves, and the extent of mortgage lending allowed, as well as maximum loan amounts, loan terms, and loan-to-value ratios. These limits are usually similar to those of S&Ls and are governed to a great extent by what the markets require, especially the secondary mortgage market. FDIC insures all SB deposits up to a $100,000 maximum.

Mortgage-Lending Activity

Savings banks differ somewhat from S&Ls in that they were never encouraged by regulators to invest a set amount of money in mortgages. At the end of 2001, SBs had 50 percent of their assets in mortgage loans. Savings banks have had the authority to make other types of loans longer than S&Ls, and today most make consumer loans and commercial loans. Other assets include corporate stocks and bonds, U.S. Treasury and federal agency obligations, and state and local debt obligations.

In the current mortgage market, SBs originate both conventional and FHA/VA mortgages for their own portfolios. Since the majority of SBs are located in capital-surplus areas, and therefore have more funds than are demanded locally, they often purchase low-risk FHA/VA and conventional mortgages from other mortgage lenders, particularly mortgage bankers, in capital-short areas of the country. Recently, much of this purchasing has been in the form of mortgage-backed securities.

Credit Unions

A *credit union* is a specialized thrift institution. Credit unions are one of the fastest-growing financial intermediaries in the U.S. economy. Currently, credit unions serve nearly one out of every four Americans. At the end of 2002, the approximately 10,000 credit unions had nearly $500 billion in assets and were becoming very sophisticated. Over 80 million Americans belong to a credit union, which normally represents a specific industry group or community—a common bond. The largest credit union is the Navy Federal Credit Union, with 2.1 million members and assets of $16 billion.

Historical Development

Credit unions began in Germany during the middle of the nineteenth century. The principal objective of the founders of the credit union movement was to combat usurious rates at banks and to provide consumers with an opportunity to borrow at reasonable rates. The first credit union in the United States was organized in New Hampshire in 1908. Credit unions were chartered under state law only until the Federal Credit Union Act was passed in 1934.

Slowly, the various states enacted enabling legislation until, in 1969, the number of credit unions in the United States peaked at 23,876. Since then, the number of credit unions has declined fairly rapidly to below 10,000, as many smaller credit unions merged into larger ones.

Credit unions operate somewhat differently than other thrift institutions. After providing for operating expenses and reserves, credit unions return their earnings to their members. Credit unions pay, on average, about 80 basis points more in dividends than competitors' savings products. This is one of the primary reasons for their popularity.

Organization and Regulation

All credit unions are mutual organizations and, as such, are directed by a board of directors elected by the membership. The members of the board are all volunteers except in situations in which one member from management serves on the board. The management (excluding the board) of credit unions consists of professionals who, as a general rule, are paid.

Approximately 50 percent of credit unions are chartered by the federal government and as a result are regulated by the National Credit Union Administration (NCUA). State-chartered credit unions are regulated by the state and usually have greater leeway in what they may do and how they do it. The National Credit Union Share Insurance Fund (NCUIF), with the amount of deposit insurance the same as FDIC deposit insurance, insures nearly all credit unions. A small percentage of credit unions is insured privately.

Many state-chartered credit unions have had the authority to make real estate loans since the early 1930s, but federally chartered credit unions acquired that right only in 1978. One recent problem credit unions have experienced is the decline in the percentage of the assets invested in consumer loans in general and automobile loans in particular. This decrease in consumer loans is the result of increased competition from automobile manufacturers and other financial intermediaries. In the face of this increased competition and the resulting sea of liquidity, credit unions turned to mort-

Credit Union Originations (in billions of dollars)			TABLE 3-4
	First Mortgages	Total Originations	Fixed-Rate (%)
1995	$ 9.80	$17.10	61%
1996	15.60	24.60	65
1997	17.00	28.10	65
1998	31.90	43.80	78
1999	28.00	51.00	77
2000	20.00	45.00	65
2001	46.00	60.00	75
2002	40.00 (est.)*	55.00 (est.) *	65 (est.)*

*REMOC ASSOCIATES, LTD. estimate.

Source: NCUA.

gage lending in earnest in the 1980s. Of course, the tax law changes introduced in 1986 encouraged still other credit unions to enter into mortgage lending.

Mortgage-Lending Activity

Residential mortgage originations at credit unions, both first and second loans, totaled over $60 billion in 2001. First-mortgage loans originated were approximately $47 billion, which represents about 2 percent of total first-mortgage originations. By the end of 2001, mortgage loans totaled 40 percent of credit union loans outstanding, up from 6.4 percent in 1984.

According to the data compiled by NCUA, 50 percent of all credit unions were offering first-mortgage loans at the end of 2001, and nearly all credit unions with assets over $50 million were offering these loans.

First Mortgage Originations at All Lenders, at Credit Unions, and Credit Unions' Market Share (in billions of dollars)			TABLE 3-5
	Total Originations	CU Originations	CU's Percentage of Total
1998	$1,507	$32	2.2%
1999	1,287	28	2.2
2000	1,024	20	2.0
2001	2,040	46	2.2
2002	1,600 (est.)*	35 (est.)*	2.2

*REMOC ASSOCIATES, LTD. estimate.

Source: Federal Housing Finance Board, NCUA, and CUNA.

2001 Year-End Totals for Federally Insured Credit Unions (in billions of dollars)		**TABLE 3-6**

Assets:	$500	Loans/Assets	65%
Total loans:	325	Capital/Assets	11%
Mortgage loans:	130		

Source: NCUA.

As with most new entrants to residential mortgage lending, credit unions originated most of the mortgages for their own portfolios. At the end of 2001, credit unions held about $55 billion in mortgage loans in their portfolios. Estimates are that credit unions sold about half the first mortgages they originated into the secondary mortgage market in 2001. Many credit unions didn't sell any loans, probably as a result of their liquidity problems. A major change for credit unions in the 1990s was that most of their mortgages were standardized mortgage products and were of the type easily sold to regular secondary market outlets or specialized ones, such as CUNA Mortgage, which purchase loans from credit unions only.

As credit unions continue to grow in total assets and in sophistication, they most likely will increase their mortgage-lending activities. These activities will naturally expand to increased sales of mortgages into the secondary mortgage market.

Discussion Points

1. Explain which mortgage lenders are most important in residential mortgage lending as originators and which as investors.

2. Discuss the major difference between mortgage brokers/bankers and portfolio lenders.

3. The mortgage broker is a major originator of residential mortgages. Examine the inherent conflict a mortgage broker faces when originating a mortgage loan.

4. Why are mortgage bankers tied so closely to commercial banks?

5. Which mortgage lender originates the majority of FHA/VA mortgage loans? Why is this the case?

Strategies for Generating Residential Loans

Introduction

The residential mortgage lending process begins with attracting potential borrowers to a mortgage lender, resulting, hopefully, in a completed application for a mortgage loan. Mortgage lenders refer to this activity as loan origination. Residential mortgage loans are originated in the primary mortgage market (i.e., that market wherein credit is extended to a borrower[s]). Put another way, a primary mortgage market activity occurs when a mortgage lender agrees to extend credit to a borrower(s). This market is contrasted with the secondary mortgage market in which mortgage loans already originated are bought and sold. (See Chapter 11, "Secondary Mortgage Market.")

Obviously, all mortgage lenders perform the origination function to one degree or another. They may use different methods or employ alternative strategies to originate loans according to their own unique sources of funds, portfolio possibilities, fee income needs, staff resources, or other considerations, but they all perform some or all of the origination functions. In some situations, a mortgage originator may only take the application before turning the applicant over to another mortgage lender who completes the transaction. In most situations, the originating lender performs all of the origination functions. Mortgage investors, on the other hand, hold only mortgages that they have purchased from one of the many types of mortgage lenders or from other investors.

The First Step

The first step in originating a residential mortgage loan is getting an applicant in the door. With increased competition for mortgage loans, this first step can be a real hurdle for some lenders. Identifying who the customer is and establishing how to attract that customer is discussed in this chapter. The way a customer is treated once in the lender's office can determine whether that customer will continue the origination process with the lender. This initial treatment of a customer (hopefully soon-to-be-applicant) is important to all mortgage lenders since it may be what decides whether the applicant comes back for another mortgage loan later or recommends the lender to another consumer.

Requirements for a Successful Mortgage-Lending Operation

For any residential mortgage lender to have a successful first-mortgage program, five elements must be in place:

- Loan demand
- Product offerings
- Trained personnel
- Specific marketing
- Competitive pricing

Loan Demand

Loan demand is one of the most important elements for a successful mortgage-lending operation and the one most affected by the local, state, and national economies. It is also the one factor that is predominately out of the control of mortgage lenders. Obviously, there is a direct correlation between employment levels, interest rates, job creation, and consumer confidence and residential mortgage originations. For example, in 2001 and 2002, when residential originations exceeded $2 trillion, the nation was experiencing the lowest unemployment rate since records began, interest rates were low, consumer confidence was high, and competition for employees was breathtaking. Our economy has witnessed this correlation before during 1993–1994 and again in 1998 when originations hit what were record highs at the time.

When the economy turns down, as it did immediately after the Gulf War in the early 1990s, originations fall off dramatically. When originations drop nationally, the only alternative a mortgage lender has is to increase market share in a declining market.

Product Offering

Product offerings refer to the variety and scope of residential mortgage loans available. A crucial part of a successful residential mortgage lending operation is offering the consumers what they want in mortgage loans. The most practical method for increasing the number of customers seeking a mortgage loan is to offer them the loan in which they have an interest. It is important that lenders remember that customer appetites for mortgage loan products are constantly changing—thus, a lender's mortgage offerings must also continue to change. A mortgage lender should not fall in love with its mortgage product offerings, but instead should constantly check the wind to see which way consumer sentiment is blowing.

Although many mortgage borrowers may actually prefer fixed-rate mortgages (FRMs) during most interest rate environments (2002 is an example), there are circumstances in which consumers will become much more interested in adjustable-rate mortgages (ARMs). When mortgage rates are expected to rise for many months and lenders offer discounted rates on their ARMs creating an attractive spread between the FRM rate and the ARM rate, the proportion of total ARM originations increases. Such conditions existed from 1984 to 1988, when ARM production was quite strong. (In fact, in 1988, nearly 70 percent of all first mortgages originated were ARMs.) When

Exhibit 4-1	Sample First Mortgage Loan Information Form

FAIRFIELD SAVINGS ASSOCIATION
FIRST MORTGAGE LOAN INFORMATION

What Happens After You Apply?

The time it takes to complete the loan process varies for each application. Here is a list of the stages required to process a mortgage. Remember that completing your application accurately and fully will help speed the process.

PROCESSING

After you apply, a loan processor will collect documents and verification to support your request for a loan. The time in processing will vary depending on the type of loan and how quickly the processor receives the documents needed. Much of processing involves help from other sources, such as:
Appraisal - An appraiser will judge the value of the property, generally based on the recent sales in your market. **Credit Verification** - We'll request a credit report through a credit reporting agency to verify your outstanding debts and payment history. **Income Verification** - In addition to the documents we request from you, we'll ask your employer to verify your income. **Asset Verification** - To confirm that you have the funds required to close your savings institution. **Previous Housing Verification** - We'll request the history of your rent or mortgage payments from your lender or landlord.

UNDERWRITING

Once the application is processed, your processor will submit the complete package for review. The Underwriter compares your loan request to the guidelines of the lender or its investors for the type of loan. Then the underwriter issues a decision on your application based on established investor guidelines.

CLOSING

Closing occurs when you sign the papers for your mortgage loan, and when the property is transferred, if your loan is for a home purchase. Most closings take place at a title company or real estate office, but the location procedures varies by state.

WHAT YOU NEED TO BRING!

Mortgage Application Checklist
Information required at application:

INCOME
- Signed copy of Agreement of Sale or copy of Deed - if refinance.
- Current pay stub & W2's for 2 years.
- Names & addresses of employers for past 2 years.
- Details of all other continuing income sources.

ASSETS
- Names, addresses, account numbers and balances for:
  - Checking Accts. - IRA's 401 & Keogh
  - Savings Accounts - Credit union
  - Investment & stock accounts.
- Gifts - complete details on all monetary gifts.

DEBTS
- Names, addresses, account numbers and balances for:
  - Charge Accounts - Personal Loans
  - Auto Loans - Student Loans
  - Current Mortgages
- Alimony and child support payment.

Self-Employed Borrowers

Additional information required for commissioned or self-employed persons:

- Signed copies of last 2 years Federal Tax Returns (1040's) - with all schedules.
- Copy of Partnership Return for 2 years. (if applicable)
- Copy of Corporate Return for 2 years. (if applicable)
- Current Balance Sheet
- Most recent Profit and Loss Statement (no more than 120 days old)

NOTE:
A Borrower who has an ownership interest of 25% or more in a business is considered to be self-employed.

mortgage rates are expected to fall for many months and the spread narrows between initial ARM rates and FRM rates, then ARM production dwindles. Such conditions existed throughout most of the 1990s.

Variable-rate mortgages (or ARMs) are important loan products to mortgage lenders that are portfolio lenders because of their obvious asset/liability management value. They are also valuable to mortgage lenders because they allow the lenders to serve the mortgage needs of more of their customers (e.g., first-time homebuyers).

In 2002, when mortgage rates hit 30-year lows, fixed-rate mortgages accounted for about 80 percent of all first mortgages originated, while ARMs were only 20 percent. Some lenders believe that the ratio of fixed to variable has always been high and always will be because borrowers prefer fixed-rate loans. Yet, there have been times over the past 15 years when ARMs accounted for nearly 70 percent of all home mortgages originated. Whether a lender or a mortgage loan officer personally agrees with what a customer wants in a mortgage loan, they should still offer it!

Trained Personnel

During boom times in mortgage lending, some mortgage lenders fail. The reason is usually that they have inexperienced or poorly trained personnel in key positions. These key positions are not just at the senior management level, they also include loan originators and processors. Poor decision making in pricing or selling loans can be very costly, but treating customers poorly or performing a function incorrectly can also lead to frustrated consumers, lost business, possible lawsuits, and often failure of the lender.

A successful mortgage lender understands this and attempts to hire qualified personnel for all functions. That is sometimes easier said than done—especially during boom periods for originations. During those periods, the successful mortgage lender is the one that has an ongoing, productive training program for the mortgage staff.

Specific Marketing

Mortgage lenders must realize that the marketing of mortgage loans is not the same as marketing other loans such as consumer loans. Marketing of mortgage loans must be clear, consistent, and continuous. The biggest mistake some mortgage lenders make in marketing mortgage loans is to do it only once or twice a year. It is hard to believe that a customer, seeking a mortgage loan, is going to remember an advertisement the lender ran six months ago. The marketing of these important loans must be continuous throughout the year.

In today's market, it is absolutely critical to market mortgage loans on the Web. In a few years it will be critical that mortgage lenders be able to take mortgage applications over the Internet.

The Most Effective "Tool" in Attracting Mortgage Applications

At first blush, many mortgage people believe that mortgage loan advertisements or brochures are most important in attracting customers. And other mortgage lenders completely accept the conventional wisdom that the Realtors steer most borrowers to certain lenders. Recent studies indicate that the reality may be quite different, at least for borrowers who are not moving into a new region of the country. These studies strongly establish the importance of word of mouth between customers. The study concludes that recommendations from friends and family members are most important to borrowers in selecting a lender. Of course, this does not hold true if the borrower has moved to a different part of the country. Eye-catching mailers or posters are important (and recommended), but they are not the most successful tools in attracting mortgage applicants. Treating mortgage applicants well is critical!

If a borrower has had a good experience with a lender, he or she will go to that lender again when they need another loan. But provide a bad experience and that person is gone forever and will tell everyone he or she knows how badly the lender's service was. Treating the customer well includes making the mortgage loan process *convenient* for customers. First impressions are very important to success in attracting and keeping the mortgage applicant. Over 50 percent of those borrowers surveyed obtained a loan from the first lender they contacted. The other 50 percent talked to three or more mortgage providers before deciding on a lender.

Competitive Pricing

Competitive pricing would appear to be an obvious strategy for a mortgage lender, but it is one of the most common mistakes small lenders make. Often they have no idea at what rate other lenders are offering mortgage loans. The first decision a mortgage lender must make is whether it will sell originated loans in the secondary mortgage market or whether the loans will be portfolioed. If the lender portfolios most or all of the loans it originates, pricing off the secondary market is not necessary. On the other hand, if all or most of the loans will be sold, then being aware of secondary market prices is a necessity.

An important step for a lender that wants to be competitive is to price mortgage loans logically. For example, in 2002, secondary market pricing forced large mortgage banking companies to offer 5- and 7-year ARMs at rates higher than a 15-year fixed-rate loan. This pricing makes no sense at all. Why do these sophisticated mortgage companies quote those rates? Because they must sell loans to others and must deliver the yields those investors want.

The normal practice of pricing first-mortgage loans has the interest rate increase as the term of the loan or the period for repricing gets longer. For example, a 30-year fixed-rate loan is the highest rate, the 15-year is about half of 1 percent less, the 5-year ARM is about one-quarter to three-eighths of 1 percent less than the 15-year, the 3-year ARM is one-eighth to one-quarter of 1 percent less than the 5-year ARM, and the 1-year ARM is one-half to three-quarters of 1 percent less than the 3-year ARM.

This logical progression of rates assists customers in understanding the advantage of the various loan products. The advantage of an ARM loan is clear (lower rate), and the advantage of the fixed-rate is also clear (high initial rate but set for the life of the loan).

Most mortgage lenders review their first-mortgage loan rates daily. Reviewing mortgage rates daily does not necessarily mean rates must be changed daily, but only that the rates of local competitors, national players, and others are reviewed.

Example of Logical Pricing of Mortgage Rates (no-point option)		TABLE 4-1
Loan Type	Interest Rate (%)	
30-year fixed	6.75%	
15-year fixed	6.25	
5-year ARM	6.00	
3-year ARM	5.75	
1-year ARM	5.00	

When a mortgage lender establishes rates for the various first-mortgage products, it should offer its customers point and no-point options. Only quoting to customers a no-point option makes a competitor's one- or two-point option look better. Why? Most consumers see the interest rate, not the APR.

Consumer Stress in Applying for a Mortgage Loan

Mortgage lenders must be sensitive to the stress that most applicants are under when they enter a mortgage lender's office. The stress comes from the applicants having found their Dream Home and their anxiety in now having to apply and wait for approval for the financing. Lenders need to understand this stress and that the process of applying for a residential loan is often an intimidating experience for many applicants. Consumers often look upon lenders as adversaries, and if the origination function is neither smooth nor explained clearly and fully, it can further alienate applicants. Lenders should understand that most applicants have either never applied for a mortgage loan before or have done so only infrequently. Applicants must be treated with care and understanding, and the reasons for the various verifications, appraisal, survey, insurance, and other documentation should be fully explained. In addition, applicants should be given an indication of the likely turnaround time for approval of their application.

Some lenders have the attitude that they are doing mortgage applicants a favor by considering them for a mortgage loan. The lenders who have been able to increase their market share over the past few years have been those who have recognized that a mortgage applicant is a customer and is entitled to be treated courteously and fairly. With the entry into the market of so many new residential mortgage originators. the ability to treat customers courteously and fairly will be an important factor in determining a lender's market share.

Convenience for the Applicant

A fairly recent innovation has been the willingness of some mortgage lenders, especially mortgage bankers or brokers, to meet with applicants at any time and place that is most convenient for the applicant. This often takes the form of an originator meeting at the applicant's home in the evening or at the applicant's workplace. This accommodating approach is greatly appreciated by the applicants and gets the attention of real estate salespeople, who often recommend lenders, as well. A related issue is whether a mortgage lender's origination personnel consider themselves "order takers" or "sales-people." Today's competitive residential lending market places a premium on sales-people, whereas order takers are a relic of the past.

Information Booklet

In real estate transactions, time is usually of the essence; any delay can destroy the transaction. This is equally true for financing of the transaction. Many lenders handle this timing issue by providing potential applicants with a marketing brochure, which

---

Exhibit 4-2 / Sample Loan Tracking Summary

LOAN TRACKING SUMMARY 03/15/04

AP NUMBER: 100101920		
BORROWER: Joseph F. Lynch Margaret J. Lynch	**PHONE**:	203-333-3990
LOAN TYPE: FIXED RATE PURCHASE		

APP DATE: 02/13/04	**EST CLS DT**: 05/27/04	**APPROVED**:	
PMI ORDERED:	**FILE RECD**:	**TITLE REC**:	
LOAN STATUS:	**ACTION DT**:	**APPRAISAL**:	
AMOUNT: 189000.00	**ORIG CODE**: 123	**LTV RATIO**: 90.00	
RATE: 6.000	**PROC CODE**: 323	**DTI RATIO**: 20.15	
TERM: 360	**PROD CODE**: 001	**HTI RATIO**: 16.19	
RE AGENT: CENTURY 21		**PHONE**: 222-8976	
CLS AGENT: SEDENSKY & MYERS		**PHONE**: 315-366-8900	

VERIFICATIONS ORDERED	REQ SENT	EXPECTED	REQ RECD
* VOD Century 21	02/27/04	03/05/04	
* VOD Bank of Fairfield	02/27/04	03/19/04	
* VOD Bank of Fairfield	02/27/04	03/19/04	
* VOL Peoples Bank	02/27/04	03/12/04	
* VOL Chase Auto Finance	02/27/04	03/19/04	
* VOL Fleet Bank	02/27/04	03/19/04	
* VOE General Electric Corp.	02/27/04	03/19/04	
* VOE Town of Fairfield	02/27/04	03/12/04	
* VOE Fairfield University	02/27/04	03/12/04	
* VOR Jean Body	02/27/04	04/16/04	

OTHER CHECKLIST ITEMS:	REQ SENT	EXPECTED	RECEIVED
* APPRAISAL	02/27/04	03/12/04	
* TAX RETURNS	02/27/04	03/19/04	
* CURRENT PAY STUBS	02/27/04	03/18/04	
* SALES CONTRACT	02/27/04	03/19/04	
* TERMITE REPORT	02/27/04	03/19/04	
* DOWN PAYMENT SOURCE OF FUNDS	02/27/04	03/19/04	

APPLICATION NOTES:

Wants to close before school is out.

explains what information (e.g., W-2s, tax returns, divorce decree, credit card numbers, employment history) should be brought to the lender's office to apply for a loan. Having all the required information ready ensures that both the lender and applicant are using their time in the best manner. A booklet of this type can also be used to explain about housing and debt-to-income ratios, loan-to-value ratios, and other pertinent information a potential applicant should be familiar with before completing an application. If the applicant has all or most of this information at application time, the process can move rapidly toward a decision—possibly immediately!

Tracing the Progress of the Application

Once an application has been completed, it is quite normal for an applicant to wonder about the progress of the application or to have other questions while the application is being processed. Some mortgage lenders advise the applicant to talk to the loan originator when questions develop. Other lenders designate a loan processor as the person with whom an applicant should discuss the mortgage loan. Neither approach is any better than the other; rather, it depends on how the origination function is organized and whose time can best be spent answering the applicant's questions courteously and knowledgeably.

What Attracts Consumers?

A few years ago, the Mortgage Bankers Association of America (MBA) conducted a survey of its membership to determine their opinion of what attracted consumers for a residential mortgage loan. The survey confirmed some old beliefs and introduced some new ideas. One of the old beliefs confirmed was the importance of the real estate agent in determining where an applicant would seek a purchase money mortgage (not important for refinancings). Of course, as already mentioned, the most important element is referrals from friends. But, if a person is new to an area, the real estate agent becomes very important.

The three attributes considered the most important by mortgage lenders in this survey in attracting consumers who are new to an area are as follows:

1. Referral by real estate sales agents

2. Low interest rates on loans

3. Good company reputation

The next five are of about equal importance:

4. Friendliness of loan officers

5. Previous experience with company/institution

6. Recognition of company/institution name

7. Availability of various loan products

8. Convenience of home or office application

Finally, this survey established the importance of attracting the potential applicant while the applicant is still "shopping around." Once an applicant has submitted an application elsewhere it is extremely difficult to get him or her to drop that application and apply with another lender.

How Loyal Are Mortgage Borrowers?

Over the past 10 years, the mortgage lending business has witnessed three major waves of refinancing activity (1993, 1998, and 2001–2002). For example, refinancing of existing loans produced 55 percent of all the loans processed in 2002. Normally, refinancings generate about 25 to 30 percent of loan originations. The MBA surveyed its members and found that homeowners had little loyalty when it came to refinancing their mortgages. According to this survey, three out of five borrowers took their business elsewhere when they refinanced. As a result of this survey and others like it, some mortgage lenders developed a strategy of sending a letter to all of their existing mortgagors asking them to "call us first" when the mortgagors began to consider refinancing their mortgage loan. Other mortgage lenders simply made sure that they were offering attractive interest rates, attentive service, and were doing effective marketing to let all potential borrowers, including existing borrowers, know their interest rates and procedures. To put the concepts for successfully attracting and retaining mortgage consumers into a nutshell, consumers are looking for a lender that

- has the right mortgage product offered at an attractive rate,
- handles the application in a timely manner, and
- gives quality service.

Methods of Origination

In today's rapidly evolving primary mortgage market, four strategies or methods of loan origination are used:

- Retail loan origination
- Wholesale loan origination
- Combination of retail and wholesale loan origination
- Online loan origination

Internet or online loan origination is rapidly becoming the fourth strategy, but at the present time only a small percentage of mortgage loans are actually originated using this strategy.

Recent data indicate that most mortgage lenders continue to follow the traditional retail strategy, a growing minority uses the wholesale strategy, and a few larger lenders use a combination of the two. This does not suggest that the majority of loans are originated using the retail strategy; they are not, but the majority of lenders do use the retail strategy. The fastest-growing method is, no surprise, use of the Internet.

These four strategies are discussed in some detail in the following sections, with particular emphasis placed on the advantages and disadvantages of each.

Retail Loan Origination

The retail method of loan origination occurs when a mortgage lender itself performs directly all of the steps or functions of the origination process. Most borrowers are familiar with retail loan origination. It is still the strategy or method used by most mortgage lenders today, especially smaller financial institutions. The majority of mortgage loans, however, are not produced by this method; larger lenders tend to have a more diverse approach.

Importance of the Real Estate Agent

The principal customer or client of most mortgage lenders is the local real estate agent (i.e., for purchase money mortgages). Ultimately, of course, the customer is the mortgage borrower, but initially the real estate agent is the one who directs most borrowers to a mortgage lender. For any retail lender, good relations with real estate agents are essential. The National Association of Realtors and others have estimated that 80 to 90 percent of homebuyers follow the recommendation of the real estate agent who sold them their homes as to which lender to use.

It is customary in today's competitive real estate sales market for real estate agents to routinely advise consumers about current home-financing options and to recommend lenders who can fulfill the consumer's financing needs. Real estate agents usually recommend only those mortgage lenders who act promptly and who treat applicants in a courteous and timely manner. Once a mortgage lender has developed a negative image within the real estate sales community, it is difficult to change that image and convince agents to

1–4 Family Mortgage Originations, 1990–2001 (billions of dollars)		TABLE 4-2
	Total Dollar Volume	Percentage of Total, Refinancings
1990	$ 458	13%
1991	562	30
1992	894	48
1993	1,020	55
1994	769	33
1995	640	25
1996	785	29
1997	840	31
1998	1,550	47
1999	1,214	36
2000	1,067	18
2001	2,036	56
2002	2,000 (est.)*	58 (est.)*

*Fannie Mae estimates.

Source: U.S. Department of Housing and Urban Development, Survey of Lending Activity.

send new applicants. Those mortgage lenders that provide quality service to the real estate agents, and ultimately to the consumer, are the lenders that will increase market share.

Except in small markets or in refinancing situations, borrowers seldom seek out or identify a lender on their own. For this reason, it is essential to a lender's market share that it maintain a good working relationship with local real estate salespeople.

During periods of increased refinancing activity, real estate salespeople are less important, but relationships must be maintained for the next cycle, when purchase money mortgages are important again. During the refinancing frenzy (e.g., 2001–2002), interest rates and reputations of mortgage lenders attracted the most business.

Commission Loan Agents

In today's highly competitive primary mortgage marketplace, most retail lenders employ commissioned loan officers or loan representatives to solicit business from real estate agents or, in some cases, builders. Mortgage bankers and brokers have traditionally used commissions as the way to both compensate and motivate their originators. Other lenders, primarily smaller thrifts and credit unions, pay their originators a salary only. Some lenders will use a combination of salary and commissions.

The commission normally given to a retail mortgage loan originator is half of 1 percent of the loan amount (or, as normally stated, 50 basis points). This commission is payable, of course, only if the loan can be made according to the policies and procedures of the lender and when it finally closes. Some lenders give a smaller commission per loan until a certain quota has been reached, and then they increase the commission to a higher amount, say, 60 basis points.

With the introduction of many new nontraditional mortgage lenders (e.g., GMAC and GE) into an already crowded marketplace, developing ways to meet the competition has become the backbone of all mortgage lenders' game plans. This concern for market share has forced many lenders to change their lending philosophy from being simply order takers to being aggressive sellers of their mortgage products. Lenders with commissioned loan agents logically seem to be the lenders who will succeed in holding on to their market share and who will probably grow at the expense of lenders with only salaried loan officers. Increased compensation is still the best reward for increased productivity and as an incentive for additional effort.

					TABLE 4-3
		1–4 Family Mortgage Originations Market Share by Lender Group			
	Mortgage Companies (%)	Commercial Banks (%)	Thrifts (%)	Credit Unions (%)	Others (%)
1980	22%	22%	50%	1%	5%
1985	38	20	40	1	1
1990	35	33	30	2	—
1995	56	24	19	1	—
2000	58	23	17	2	—

Source: Department of Housing and Urban Development.

Functions Performed by Retail Lenders

The retail mortgage lender directly performs the following origination functions:

- Completes application with borrower
- Verifies all employment, income, and deposits
- Orders appraisal
- Obtains a credit report
- Prepares loan for underwriting/automated underwriting
- Underwrites the loan application
- Approves or rejects the loan application
- Closes and funds approved loan
- Portfolios or warehouses/sells loan

Historically, the vast majority of residential mortgage loans has been originated in this manner. Today, smaller mortgage lenders, especially financial institutions, still use this method predominately. An obvious benefit to retail lenders in originating mortgage loans themselves is that they can establish a long-term relationship with mortgage borrowers, which can prove profitable in future transactions. These future transactions can be either mortgage loans or other consumer loans.

Origination Income

Most retail mortgage lenders charge an application fee or origination points or both to offset some or all of the expenses incurred in performing the various origination functions. If the lender charges an application fee, that fee is usually large enough to pay for the credit report, appraisal, and any other direct out-of-pocket expense a lender has in processing the loan application. The use of application fees has given way to charging origination points at most lenders, but some charge both. The marketplace will determine which fees are charged and how much they are.

Origination points are often used by lenders for revenue to accomplish the following:

- Offset personnel and office expenses
- Increase yield on mortgages to secondary market requirements
- Produce current income

Estimates for the cost of processing a residential mortgage loan (not including the 50 basis points paid to a loan originator) range from 60 to 120 basis points. Keeping these costs as low as possible is the goal of all mortgage lenders. As a general rule, increasing loan volume helps to drive down the cost of processing.

Some mortgage lenders have concluded that they can put loans on the books more cheaply by buying residential mortgage loans from brokers rather than incurring the expense of processing the loans themselves.

FASB # 91

In its Statement of Financial Accounting Standards (# 91), the Financial Accounting Standards Board (FASB) has ruled any origination points that are not offset by actual expenses incurred in originating the loan must be amortized over the loan contract period or, if it can be clearly established, the expected life of the loan. This ruling has changed the way many lenders look at origination points. Those lenders that sell loans immediately into the secondary mortgage market (e.g., mortgage bankers and others) are affected the least, since they can take any fee income into current income immediately after the sale of any loan. But portfolio lenders (e.g., thrifts and credit unions) must amortize much of that fee income over the expected life of the loan. This ruling may hurt thrifts in particular since many have become comfortable using these fees to boost current income.

Points and Interest Rate Trade-offs

The long-term result of this FASB ruling may be a return to the low- or no-point lending of the 1970s. No-point lending does not necessarily interfere with a lender's overall yield, since it can increase the interest rate to offset the loss of fee income. As a general rule, a 1 percent origination fee (or 1 point) equals an increase in yield of one-eighth of 1 percent; thus, a quote of 10 percent and 2 points is approximately the same to a borrower as a 10.25 percent quote with no points.

Retail Branch Offices

A retail mortgage lender is primarily interested in giving the best possible service to its customers—local Realtors and mortgage applicants. Having a convenient location for loan origination offices is probably the most basic "service" to applicants, but it can be one of the most important rendered. Location is also important to a retail lender in regard to walk-in business. Although the percentage of this type of business to total originations is generally small, walk-in business for a new mortgage and refinancing can be just the additional business that makes a branch profitable. Therefore, each branch origination office should be easily reached by automobile or public transportation and should be in a highly visible location, preferably on a ground floor.

Figure 4-1	Refinancing Costs Based on a $200,000 Loan with 2 Points	
	Points	$4,000
	Title insurance	906
	Settlement fee	450
	Tax stamps, recording fee	350
	Processing fee	300
	Appraisal fee	300
	Document preparation	150
	Notary fee	50
	Flood certificate fee	24
	Credit report	16
	Total	$6,546

Source: USA Today *research, November 16, 2001.*

	Diversification of Origination Channels		TABLE 4-4
Year	Origination Channel	Percentage of Originations	
1993	Retail	45%	
	Broker	29	
	Correspondent	26	
1995	Retail	43%	
	Broker	21	
	Correspondent	36	
1997	Retail	39%	
	Broker	26	
	Correspondent	35	
1999	Retail	42%	
	Broker	28	
	Correspondent	30	
2001	Retail	33%	
	Broker	29	
	Correspondent	38	

Source: Inside Mortgage Finance.

Depending on whether loan processing is centralized or not, a branch office houses the loan origination personnel and appropriate support staff. If loan processing is not centralized, loan processors are located at each branch office.

Expected Mortgage Loan Volume

Mortgage loan volume per retail office varies widely depending on many factors, including what type of lender is involved (mortgage banker, credit union, etc.). But certain benchmarks exist for residential loan production. Many lenders believe a valid goal is to produce 70 to 80 loans per production employee (including originators, loan processors, underwriters, closing personnel, etc.) per year. An office with a staff of nine—a branch manager who handles closing, a secretary, three loan originators, three loan processors, and one underwriter—should produce about 600 to 700 loans a year. At an average loan balance of $150,000, loan production for this office should be about $100 million. Some lenders will do more, others less, depending on loan demand, the economy, and personnel expertise.

Wholesale Loan Origination

Over the past 20 years or so, the natural cycle of mortgage lending has been magnified by a number of unpredictable factors. These factors have contributed to changes in the way many mortgage lenders approach residential mortgage origination.

These factors include, among others, the following:

- Greater volatility in mortgage interest rates (e.g., fixed rates that ranged from 9 percent in 1979 to 18 percent in l982 and back down to 6.5 percent in 2002)
- Massive swings in 1–4 family mortgage originations from year to year (e.g., ranging from $97 billion in l982, up to over a trillion dollars in l993, to an astonishing $2 trillion in 2001–2002)
- Increased geographical cycle of originations as one area then another became hot then cooled off
- New dynamic origination competition from traditional and nontraditional lenders
- Cheaper and more sophisticated technological support for mortgage lending
- Greater valuation of servicing rights

All of these factors, along with other factors unique to individual lenders, have contributed to the growth of wholesale mortgage lending by some mortgage lenders. This method of producing loans is sometimes referred to as "third-party origination," or TPO. In recent years, as much as 40 to 50 percent of residential mortgage loans have been originated using this strategy. These third-party originators have increased in numbers as the demand for their product has increased. The third-party originators are mortgage brokers and loan correspondents who sell mortgages they originate to acquiring mortgage lenders called wholesale lenders.

Mortgage Brokers and Loan Correspondents

This method or strategy of loan origination occurs when a mortgage lender acquires a loan processed to one degree or another from another lender who originated the loan. The primary reason for purchasing a mortgage loan originated by another lender is the purchasing mortgage lender's belief that it can originate mortgages (and/or servicing) cheaper that way. The other lender from whom loans are purchased is normally either a mortgage broker or a loan correspondent. The difference between these two lenders is that a mortgage broker usually has not begun either the processing or underwriting of the loan, while a loan correspondent typically has closed and funded the loan.

Functions Performed

The extent of loan processing by a broker varies depending on the needs of the originating lender and the acquiring lender. In many situations, the broker completes the application with the borrower and orders the various verifications. This material is then shipped to the acquiring lender (referred to as a wholesaler), who will then make the underwriting decision.

Table Funding

Loan correspondents, on the other hand, normally complete the loan processing and make an underwriting decision. The loan correspondent may or may not fund the loan. If the loan is funded by the acquiring lender, the transaction is called table funding. **Table funding** occurs when a broker closes a mortgage loan with funds belonging to an acquiring lender and immediately assigns the loan to that lender. This activity gives the originator the opportunity to say it is a direct lender, since it can close loans with its own funds. These originators believe that by funding the loan at closing, they acquire a marketing advantage over other brokers.

Upon purchase, the acquiring lender may reunderwrite the individual mortgage, or some or all of the mortgages, if in a package. The extent of underwriting by the acquiring lender depends to a great extent on the amount of business it has previously done with the loan correspondent.

If the loan is not closed before the correspondent sells the loan to the investor, the correspondent is most concerned with the turnaround time for an underwriting decision from the acquiring investor. The loan correspondent is normally looking for a 48-hour decision time. This is important to the originating lender since it may have to renegotiate with the applicant if the loan is declined as originally submitted. The ability of the wholesaler to fund quickly after the underwriting decision is also of great importance to the originating lender.

Yield Spread Premiums

Another tool used by mortgage brokers is to add a *yield premium* to the quoted yield requirement of an acquiring investor. For example, if an investor will buy conforming loans with a yield to the investor of 8 percent, the broker could close the loan to the consumer at 8.5 percent. This yield spread premium is not considered a violation of RESPA (Section 8, antikickback provisions) as long as the broker is providing a service to the borrower, the fees are reasonable, and the broker reveals the fee (the premium) to the borrower in the beginning of the application process.

What Motivates the Originating Lender?

The originating lender is not interested in holding the loans or in selling them into the secondary mortgage market. This lender has determined that it can operate more profitably by originating loans for other lenders without the inherent interest rate risk associated with holding mortgages for a short or long period of time. This lender will almost always be originating against commitments that have been obtained from those lenders who rely on them for production.

Fees and Premiums

The originating lender retains any application fee and will probably collect as large an origination fee as the market will bear. It is the originating lender's responsibility to pay the originating agent the 50-basis-point commission and also to have the staff necessary to process the loan. In addition to the fee income generated from the origination process, often an originating lender receives a fee called a *servicing release premium* from the acquiring lender. This fee is recognition that value (the value inherent in servicing a mortgage) is being transferred to the acquiring lender.

After the loans have been acquired and underwritten, the acquiring lender closes the loan in its own name and either puts the loan in its portfolio or sells it in the secondary mortgage market.

Affinity Groups

Another variation on the wholesale theme is the concept of one mortgage lender serving the mortgage-lending needs of an *affinity group*. This arrangement involves a mortgage lender who links up with a large corporation or membership group (such as a credit union) as the preferred provider of mortgage loans. The benefits of this type of arrangement are mutual: the sponsor (credit union) endorses the mortgage lender, and the borrowers usually are treated better than they would have been with an inexperienced lender and may get more attractive deals. Mortgage lenders are also interested in arrangements of this type because the new business is usually in addition to their own business; thus, the economies of scale become even more attractive. As a general rule, the arrangement between the mortgage lender and the affinity group contains provisions that prevent the lender from selling the servicing rights to another lender.

Advantages and Disadvantages of Wholesale Lending

As with most types of business strategies or methods of doing business, there are advantages and disadvantages for each. This is particularly true for the wholesale method of loan origination. The greatest advantage of wholesale loan origination to acquiring mortgage lenders is that it provides them with an inexpensive method of quickly originating a high volume of mortgage loans. This method is assumed by these lenders to be less expensive than retail lending for a number of reasons, including the ability to acquire loans without the need for a large loan-processing staff. Some experts indicate that from 60 to 70 percent of the cost of originating a mortgage loan involves personnel expenses. If the originating lender preforms some or all of the originating functions, the acquiring mortgage lender assumes it will enhance its own profitability.

An important item to be considered in determining which approach is most appropriate for a particular lender is the expected number of loans produced per production employee. The rule of thumb for retail mortgage lending is yearly production of approximately 60 to 70 loans per production employee, as already discussed. A recent study suggests that the direct cost of producing a mortgage loan using the retail strategy is approximately $1,700 per loan. For nonretail production, the direct cost per loan averaged approximately $500 per loan. The nonretail production figure is approximately 100 to 110 loans per production employee. This major difference in productivity occurs because retail lenders must have more employees to perform all of the origination functions, while a mortgage broker or loan correspondent performs only certain functions.

Another important advantage a wholesale lender has is the ability to move quickly into and out of markets that are changing. Since a wholesale lender does not have to be concerned with brick-and-mortar expenses or with acquiring personnel for a new office, it can quickly move into a geographical area that is attractive even if it is on the other side of the country. In addition, if a market deteriorates quickly, a wholesale lender can simply decide not to purchase any loans in that area; it does not have to be concerned with either selling its physical assets or relocating its personnel.

Unlike the retail lender, the wholesale lender does not have to be concerned with the attractiveness or the location of its offices. Not only will this lender need far fewer offices (each office can serve a very large geographical region), none are needed for direct face-to-face contact with applicants. As a result, offices can be less visible and thus less costly.

Wholesale lenders are usually quite interested in rapid growth in their servicing portfolio. These institutions desire large portfolios in order to obtain the economies of scale that can produce profits approaching 40 percent of servicing revenue. To these lenders, the quickest way to increase their servicing portfolios is to acquire large blocks of loans through the wholesale approach, sell the loans immediately into the secondary mortgage market, and strip off the servicing rights.

Quality Control

The strongest negative factor to wholesale lending is the issue of **quality control**. If a mortgage lender does not process or underwrite a mortgage loan, that lender's ability to control the quality of the loan is greatly reduced. Many wholesale lenders have addressed this issue by dealing only with well-established, reputable brokers or correspondents. Because the acquiring mortgage lender has these quality control problems, these lenders generally have higher underwriting and quality control expenses than retail lenders. They face the need of increased spot-checking of appraisals and verifications in order to manage quality. Since these loans are probably sold in the secondary mortgage market, the wholesale lender could see its servicing profits greatly diminished with increased servicing expenses if quality controls are not in place and strictly followed.

Unlike a retail lender, an acquiring lender does not receive any application or processing fee and normally receives none or just a small part of the origination points. This reduced fee is not a critical item to the wholesale lender since it does not have the expenses of a retail lender. The best example of an expense that an acquiring lender does not have to pay is the 50 basis points commission to an origination agent.

Internet Lending

In this computer and Internet era it should not be surprising that the use of the Internet for residential mortgage originations is rapidly growing. In addition to using the PC and Internet to underwrite, appraise, and obtain credit reports, many mortgage lenders are now using the Net to originate loans. Some of the major mortgage-banking companies report that as many as 30 percent of refinancing borrowers used the online services offered.

Practically all mortgage lenders today have a website on which they advertise mortgage rates, and many allow the borrower to begin the application process online. Although the majority of consumers still prefer the face-to-face method of applying for a mortgage loan, many younger people feel no hesitancy about completing the mortgage-lending process online.

	Online Mortgage Originations		TABLE 4-5
Year	Share of Total New Mortgages (%)	Share of Total Refinanced Mortgages (%)	Share of Total Annual Originations (%)
2000	5.1%	10.8%	6.3%
2001	6.0	13.0	9.2
2002	7.1	15.6	9.6
2003	8.3	18.7	10.6
2004	9.8	22.4	12.6
2005	11.6	26.9	15.0

2000–2002 actual; 2003–2005 projections.

Source: IDC Online Lending Consumer Survey, 2001.

Discussion Points

1. Discuss the five keys for a successful lending operation.

2. Identify the various methods of loan origination. Discuss the pros and cons of each method.

3. What functions are normally performed by a retail loan originator?

4. What features or attributes attract consumers to a particular mortgage lender?

5. Many mortgage lenders compensate their originators by commission. What is the typical commission for a loan officer and how is it calculated?

6. How do mortgage originators offset their expenses in producing a residential mortgage loan? What are the expenses in originating a residential loan?

Mortgage Instruments

Introduction

The recent explosive growth of the many types of alternative mortgage instruments is the result of fundamental changes in the way homes are financed. During the period between the Great Depression and the early 1980s, practically all residential real estate loan transactions were financed with the use of the standard fixed-rate mortgage. Today, residential real estate is financed by either the standard fixed-rate mortgage or by one of the various alternative mortgage instruments. Depending on interest rates, alternative mortgage instruments have been used for as many as 60 percent of all residential mortgage loans, or as low as 20 percent. Because residential mortgage interest rates were relatively low during the first half of the 1990s, fixed-rate mortgages once again were the product most consumers selected and continue to select. This can be expected to change if mortgage interest rates once again turn up meaningfully. If rates do move up significantly, consumers will again be interested in the various alternative mortgage instruments. Before reviewing these new instruments, a discussion of the standard fixed-rate mortgage is required.

Standard Fixed-Rate Mortgages

The standard fixed-rate mortgage was the product of an earlier financial upheaval, the Great Depression of the 1930s, which changed the way homes were financed at that time. Before this innovation, most homes were financed by a term mortgage with the entire principal due at the end (or term) of the loan. It was normal practice for one of these loans to be rolled over into another loan at the end of the term. However, as a result of this practice, many homeowners lost their homes during the economic emergency of the early 1930s because traditional lenders were unable to refinance these mortgages as they came due. This inability to refinance was the result of a severe national liquidity crisis.

The liquidity crisis was brought about by massive bank and thrift failures caused by a combination of bad loans and savers' panic withdrawals of their deposits. The resulting losses to depositors during this pre–depositor insurance period destroyed savers' confidence in financial institutions until deposit insurance arrived a few years later. As a means of addressing the national wave of foreclosures, the Home Owners Loan Corporation (HOLC), a federal agency, began exchanging government bonds for defaulted mortgages. If HOLC determined a loan it received was basically sound and in default only because of the liquidity crisis, that loan was reconstituted as a 20-year loan with a self-amortizing monthly payment of principal and interest. This became the standard fixed-rate mortgage, which was used almost exclusively until recently and which allowed this nation to have such a high ownership rate.

Direct Reduction Instrument

The standard fixed-rate mortgage is a monthly amortized, direct reduction instrument. This means that equal monthly payments for the term of the loan are used to directly reduce the amount owed by first paying interest due on the loan since the last payment and then using the remainder of the payment to reduce principal. This periodic reduction of principal combined with the fact that a borrower knows exactly how much is due each month are the two most important features of the standard fixed-rate mortgage.

The direct reduction of principal is also important for another reason. It allows for a considerable savings in the total amount of interest a borrower would have to pay if interest were calculated on the entire amount of principal, as occurs with a term loan. As noted earlier, term loans allow for no principal repayment during the term—only periodic interest payments, with the entire principal due at the end of the term. The savings to a borrower (before taxes) using an amortized loan as opposed to a term loan are seen in the following example.

Thus, with the standard fixed-rate mortgage, the monthly mortgage payment remains the same from the first payment until the next to last (the last could be slightly different), even though much of the first payment went to interest and practically all of the last payment went to principal. If the example were for a longer term, say 30 years, practically all of the first payment would go to interest.

This type of mortgage served both borrower and lender well from the 1930s until the middle 1970s. For those who obtained one of these mortgages in the early 1970s or earlier, the fixed nature of their monthly mortgage payment was obviously a beneficial feature during the high inflation period of the late 1970s and early 1980s. What was good

---

Figure 5-1   Example of Term Loan Repayment versus Amortized Loan

Example: $1,000 loan at 10 percent interest to be repaid in 5 years with annual year-end payments compared to the same loan repaid on an amortized basis.

	Term Loan				Amortized Loan		
Year	Interest	Principal	Total	Year	Interest	Principal	Total
1	$100.00	0	$100.00	1	$100.00	$163.80	$263.80
2	100.00	0	100.00	2	83.62	180.18	263.80
3	100.00	0	100.00	3	63.60	198.20	263.80
4	100.00	0	100.00	4	45.79	218.01	263.80
5	100.00	1,000.00	1,100.00	5	23.99	239.81	263.80
	$500.00	$1,000.00	$1,500.00		$319.00	$1,000.00	$1,319.00

for those fortunate borrowers was nearly ruinous for mortgage lenders after 1978. The billions of dollars in these fixed-rate mortgages was also a deterrent to new borrowers who had to pay higher interest rates in order to help offset low-yielding mortgages.

Mortgage Lenders' Dilemma

For those portfolio lenders active in residential lending, primarily savings and loans, savings banks, and some commercial banks, the path that eventually led to financial ruin for some was initially quite smooth and profitable. These institutions had served savers and borrowers well over the preceding 50 years as they borrowed money at 5 or 5.5 percent and loaned it out to homebuyers at 7 or 7.5 percent. The 150- to 250-basis-point spread between a lender's cost of funds and the yield on its portfolio covered all operating expenses and included an attractive profit. Through the process of financial intermediation, these institutions built up loan portfolios of 20- to 30-year mortgages worth hundreds of billions of dollars. It was this huge portfolio of low-yielding mortgages that became the nearly fatal characteristic of thrift institutions in the early 1980s.

Two events occurred during the late 1970s and early 1980s that changed how mortgage lenders operated: rapid increases in inflation and increased competition for depositors' savings. The result was a doubling of the cost of funds to lenders in just a period of months. Since thrifts were primarily mortgage lenders and did not have the benefit of a variable-rate asset structure, as did many commercial banks with commercial loans, they suffered greatly.

Annual Average of Monthly Mortgage Rates		TABLE 5-1
Year	Fixed Rate* (%)	Adjustable Rate** (%)
1985	12.42%	10.04%
1987	10.20	7.83
1990	10.13	8.36
1993	7.33	4.59
1995	7.96	6.06
1996	7.81	5.67
1997	7.60	5.61
1998	6.94	5.58
1999	7.43	5.98
2000	8.06	7.04

* Thirty-year conventional contract loan rate with 20 percent downpayment.

** One-year Treasury-indexed conventional contract loan rate with 20 percent downpayment.

Source: Federal Reserve Board and Freddie Mac.

Many portfolio lenders found themselves paying more for deposits than they were earning on their mortgage portfolios. Many lenders that normally worked with a positive spread of 200 to 250 basis points were now faced with a negative spread of over 100 basis points. As a direct result of these unforeseeable events, many lending institutions were forced to close their doors or to merge with other institutions. All mortgage lenders were forced to reexamine how they would lend on mortgages in the future.

As a consequence of this near disaster for those mortgage lenders portfolioing mortgage loans, many surviving mortgage lenders retreated from the standard fixed-rate mortgage to one of a number of alternative mortgage instruments. These alternative mortgage instruments were attractive because they allowed for some periodic adjustment to interest rates in a changing financial environment. Even those mortgage lenders that sold some or all of their production into the secondary mortgage market needed new mortgage instruments so that their investors would be protected from interest rate risk. The feature that lenders were looking for in these alternative mortgage instruments was a way of sharing with borrowers some of the risk of lending in an uncertain economic environment.

1990 to 2002: Return of the Fixed-Rate Mortgage

Although many lenders vowed they would never again originate and portfolio fixed-rate mortgages after the disaster of the early 1980s, these same lenders were forced to change their minds when long-term, fixed rates tumbled in the late 1980s and stayed low through the 1990s and into the new century. As rates on long-term, fixed-rate mortgages dropped to 20-year lows, consumers refinanced their existing mortgages, and over 80 percent of them selected fixed-rate mortgages of varying maturities.

10-, 15-, or 20-Year Mortgages

Until recently, most American homeowners had become conditioned to making monthly mortgage payments on a 30-year mortgage. However, over the last couple of years this situation has changed to the point that the 30-year mortgage at times makes up less than half the mortgages originated. Many homeowners refinanced their existing 30-year mortgages (as a result of the unprecedented drop in long-term mortgage rates) with 10-, 15-, or 20-year mortgages. These homeowners were paying out a certain dollar amount each month, and when they refinanced, they were willing to continue paying at that dollar amount. But, at the same dollar amount, loans would pay off sooner at the lower interest rates. The beneficial result to borrowers of the shorter-term mortgage is a substantial savings on total interest paid over the term of the mortgage loan.

Sharing the Risk

In order for residential mortgage lenders to remain active in the mortgage market on a daily basis, they must have ways of meeting interest rate shifts in a profitable manner. Some mortgage lenders have solved the problem of interest rate risk by selling some or all of the fixed-rate mortgages they originate. Other portfolio lenders have decided they can obtain a greater spread between their cost of funds and portfolio yield by retaining the fixed-rate mortgages with their higher initial yield in their mortgage portfolios.

During periods of interest rate volatility, mortgage lenders offer mortgage borrowers more variable-rate mortgages at attractive rates as those lenders move to protect themselves from interest rate risk. All mortgage lenders should develop strategies allowing future lending activity to produce a sufficient spread between their cost of funds and their portfolio yield to cover the following:

- Cost of funds/interest expenses
- Cost of loan processing
- Operating expenses
- Reasonable profit

In the past, many mortgage lenders borrowed short and loaned long by using market-sensitive savings to finance 20 to 30 year mortgages. Hopefully, with the bitter lesson of the 1980s behind them, lenders have become more sophisticated and have learned how better to match the maturity of their liabilities with their assets. The improvement in lenders' asset/liability management is evidenced by the increased use of certificates of deposit of longer maturity and by the use of alternative mortgage instruments. Many different types of alternative mortgage instruments have evolved since the first type was used in California in the early 1970s. The more common are discussed in the following sections.

Alternative Mortgage Instruments

Adjustable-Rate Mortgages (ARMs)

The most popular form of alternative mortgage instrument is the adjustable-rate mortgage (ARM), or as it sometimes called, a variable-rate mortgage loan. Over the past 10 years, the percentage of residential mortgage loans that were ARMs has been as high as 60 percent when interest rates were high, and as low as 15 percent when interest rates were low. An ARM is basically an alternative mortgage instrument that allows the interest rate to adjust periodically to some predetermined index, with the payment increasing or decreasing accordingly.

Alternative mortgage instruments, common around the world, were first used in this country in the early 1970s by state-chartered savings and loan institutions in California. These thrifts initially had only qualified success with these instruments. Many borrowers rejected the early ARMs because they were afraid that their interest rates would increase rapidly, and thus they continued to select fixed-rate mortgages. Only after mortgage lenders began putting caps on how far interest rates could adjust each year and over the life of the loan were borrowers willing to try these new instruments.

Mortgage interest rates are one of the most important factors affecting housing affordability. Typically, as interest rates decline, fewer people select adjustable-rate mortgages.

Structure of an ARM: Adjustment Period

The period of time in which the interest rate and payment can change is called the **adjustment period**. ARMs can have adjustment periods of varied length, but the most

Mortgage Interest Rates, 1984–2001			TABLE 5-2
Year	Fixed (1) (%)	Adjustable (2) (%)	ARM Share (3) (%)
1984	13.87%	11.51%	61%
1985	12.42	10.05	50
1986	10.18	8.42	31
1987	10.20	7.82	43
1988	10.33	7.90	58
1989	10.32	8.81	39
1990	10.13	8.36	28
1991	9.25	7.10	23
1992	8.40	5.63	20
1993	7.33	4.59	20
1994	8.36	5.34	39
1995	7.95	6.07	33
1996	7.81	5.67	27
1997	7.60	5.60	22
1998	6.94	5.58	12
1999	7.43	5.98	22
2000	8.06	7.05	25
2001	6.97	5.70	15

Source: (1) Federal Home Loan Mortgage Corporation (FHLMC) survey of major lenders of contract rates on commitments for fixed-rate, 80 percent loan-to-value mortgages. Does not incorporate points. (2) Effective closing rate for conventional adjustable-rate mortgages, as reported by the Federal Housing Finance Board. (3) Share of all home loans closed by all major lenders that are adjustable.

common are the one-year, three-year, and five-year adjustment periods. Therefore, an ARM with a one-year adjustment period is called a one-year ARM. The one-year ARM is often the most popular of the various ARMs offered today, but occasionally the three-year has more originations. One of the reasons for the popularity of the one-year ARM is that it usually has the lowest interest rate of all the various ARMs. As a general rule, the shorter the interval between adjustments, the lower the **initial interest rate**.

Index

The concept behind an ARM is that it will produce an interest rate that moves as interest rates in general move, thus providing the portfolio lender with some protection against interest rate risk. In order to accomplish this, the interest rate for the ARM is tied to an **index**. The index must be beyond the control of the lender; thus, it cannot be the lenders' cost of funds. As a general rule, the index is tied either to a general cost of funds (e.g., the 11th District of the Federal Home Loan Bank) or to a Treasury security with a similar period of maturity (e.g., a three-year ARM indexed to the three-year

Figure 5-2	Adjustable-Rate Mortgage Loan Adjustment Notice

Borrower: _John L. Lewis_   Date: _April 3, 2002_
                                   Loan Number: _#42668_
This notice is to inform you of:

__x__ An adjustment to your interest rate with a corresponding adjustment to your payment.
_____ An adjustment to your interest rate without a corresponding adjustment to your payment.
The interest rate on your loan with *First National Bank of Missoula* secured by a mortgage on property located at 53 Flathead St., Missoula, Montana is scheduled to be adjusted on May 1, 2002. The index on which your interest rate is based is "One year Treasury adjusted to a constant maturity" as found in Federal Reserve publication H-15.

You should be aware of the following interest rate adjustment information concerning your Adjustable Rate Mortgage Loan.

1. Your new interest rate will be _7.00%_ , which is based on an index value of _4.25%_.

2. Your previous rate was _6.75%,_ which was based on an index value of _4.00%._

3. Your loan has a _2%_ annual cap and a _6%_ lifetime cap. The initial interest rate on your loan was _5%_. The maximum interest rate on this loan can be _11%_.

4. Your new payment will be _$1,545.89._

5. Your new loan balance is _$135,989.90._

If you have any questions about this notice, please contact:

George Mitchell, Loan Officer
First National Bank of Missoula
_800-123-3456_

© REMOC ASSOCIATES, LTD.

Treasury). The most common index is the one-year Treasury bill (adjusted to a constant maturity). All of the indices can be tracked using the Federal Reserve Board's statistical release H.15 (found at **www.federalreserve.gov**).

Margin

In order to establish what the interest rate on an ARM will be, lenders add to the index rate another figure called the **margin**. The margin originally corresponded to a lender's

Figure 5-3   More About Indices

Treasury indices. Most ARM loans use one of the various Treasury indices. The *One-Year Treasury Index* is the most common index in the eastern United States. It is based on the "constant maturity" of all outstanding federal obligations with a year or less to maturity. The *Three-Year Treasury Index* (used for a 3/3 ARM) is based on all federal obligations with three years or less to maturity.

COFI—Cost of Funds Index. The Eleventh District Cost of Funds is the most prevalent index in the western United States. The COFI, which is a weighted monthly average, has been published since 1981 by the San Francisco Federal Home Loan Bank (the Eleventh District). This index is considered a trailing index since it measures existing liabilities at member institutions.

LIBOR—London Interbank Offered Rate. LIBOR is the rate on dollar-denominated deposits, also known as Eurodollars, traded between banks in London. The index is quoted for one-, three-, and six-month periods and, occasionally, for one-year periods.

operating expenses, but it is now market driven. Recently, margins have ranged between 200 and 300 basis points, with an average of about 275 basis points. This is an important number for a consumer to establish before entering into any ARM transaction. Once the margin is established, it is set for the life of the loan.

$$\text{Index Rate} + \text{Margin} = \text{ARM Interest Rate}$$

Interest Rate Caps

In addition to the requirement (truth-in-lending amendment) that all ARMs entered into after December 8, 1987, must have an interest rate ceiling, most ARMs today have other **caps**. *Interest rate caps* place a limit on the amount the interest rate can increase. The introduction of caps made the ARM acceptable to most consumers. Two types of interest rate caps are used today to make ARMs attractive to consumers:

- *Periodic cap*, which limits the interest rate increase (or decrease) from one adjustment period to the next—1 or 2 percent caps are the most common
- *Lifetime cap*, which limits the interest rate increase (or decrease) over the life of the loan—5 or 6 percent caps are the most common

A few ARMs have payment caps that limit the monthly payment increase at each adjustment period usually to a certain percentage of the previous payment. A payment cap that has been recently used is 7.5 percent, meaning that the payment cannot increase more than that amount each adjustment period. Payment caps are not very popular because they usually produce **negative amortization** (deferred interest). This occurs when the monthly mortgage payment isn't sufficient to pay all the interest due on the mortgage, thus the mortgage balance is increasing, not decreasing, as would be expected. These loans may not be saleable in the secondary mortgage market because of investors' concern that these mortgages have increased risk of delinquency.

Discounts

In order to make an ARM loan attractive to more consumers, most lenders lower the initial interest rate (and thus the payment rate) from what is called for by adding together the index and the margin. This initial rate is called a *discounted rate* and may be 200 basis points or more below the full indexed rate. If the rate is 300 basis points or more, the rate is called a *teaser rate*. Mortgage borrowers should be wary of teaser rates since they often require large loan fees or have larger than normal margins.

Mortgage lenders must be careful that they make the correct annual percentage rate (APR) disclosure when offering a discounted ARM. The correct annual percentage rate disclosure for a discounted ARM is a composite APR. A *composite APR* reflects the initial payment rate and the rate that would have resulted from the use of the full index (as it existed at closing) for the remaining term.

Spread

Offering a discounted ARM is important to a lender if that lender wants to originate ARMs. There must be enough of a difference between the rate at which the fixed-rate mortgage is offered and the rate for the ARM. If no meaningful difference exists, few borrowers would select an ARM because those borrowers would be taking on the risk of interest rates increasing. Therefore, lenders must compensate borrowers by making the initial payment rate of an ARM attractive as compared to the fixed-rate mortgage. This spread is usually from 200 to 300 basis points below that at which the fixed-rate mortgage is offered. As interest rates for all types of residential mortgages increase, the amount of spread between the fixed-rate and ARM rate necessary to attract borrowers decreases since consumers expect rates to drop in the future.

Sometimes a seller or builder will pay a lender money so a borrower can get a lower initial rate. A transaction of this type is called a **buydown** and is discussed in detail later in this chapter. The reason buydowns occur is so that the borrower can qualify for the mortgage at the payment rate rather than the FIAR (fully indexed accrual rate). The risk to a borrower with an ARM with a discounted rate is that the payment rate may still go up at the adjustment period even if the index does not.

Figure 5-4	Composite APR Example

Local Savings Bank offers its one-year ARM at an initial payment rate of 6.00 percent even though the full indexed accrual rate called for a rate of 8.00 percent. In order to correctly disclose the APR, the bank will use a composite APR that reflects the 6.00 percent rate for a year and the 8.00 percent rate for the remaining term.

Figure 5-5 / First Two Pages of Uniform ARM One-Year Note

Adjustable Rate Note
(1-Year Treasury Index — Rate Caps)

THIS NOTE CONTAINS PROVISIONS ALLOWING FOR CHANGES IN MY INTEREST RATE AND MY MONTHLY PAYMENT. THIS NOTE LIMITS THE AMOUNT MY INTEREST RATE CAN CHANGE AT ANY ONE TIME AND THE MAXIMUM RATE I MUST PAY.

February 25, 2003   Monroe,   Connecticut
[Date]   [City]   [State]

    53 Lazy Brook Rd
    Monroe, CT
[Property Address]

1. BORROWER'S PROMISE TO PAY

In return for a loan that I have received, I promise to pay U.S. **$100,000** (this amount is called "Principal"), plus interest, to the order of the Lender. The Lender is **Northland Mortgage**. I will make all payments under this Note in the form of cash, check or money order. I understand that the Lender may transfer this Note. The Lender or anyone who takes this Note by transfer and who is entitled to receive payments under this Note is called the "Note Holder."

2. INTEREST

Interest will be charged on unpaid principal until the full amount of Principal has been paid. I will pay interest at a yearly rate of **5.00%**. The interest rate I will pay will change in accordance with Section 4 of this Note.

The interest rate required by this Section 2 and Section 4 of this Note is the rate I will pay both before and after any default described in Section 7(B) of this Note.

3. PAYMENTS

(A) **Time and Place of Payments**

I will pay principal and interest by making a payment every month.

I will make my monthly payment on the first day of each month beginning on **April 1, 2003**.

I will make these payments every month until I have paid all of the principal and interest and any other charges described below that I may owe under this Note. Each monthly payment will be applied as of its scheduled due date and will be applied to interest before Principal. If, on March 1, 2033 , I still owe amounts under this Note, I will pay those amounts in full on that date, which is called the "Maturity Date."

I will make my monthly payments at **Northland Mortgage, 2001 Gerald, Monroe, CT** or at a different place if required by the Note Holder.

(B) **Amount of My Initial Monthly Payments**

Each of my initial monthly payments will be in the amount of U.S. **$438.78**. This amount may change.

(C) **Monthly Payment Changes**

Changes in my monthly payment will reflect changes in the unpaid principal of my loan and in the interest rate that I must pay. The Note Holder will determine my new interest rate and the changed amount of my monthly payment in accordance with Section 4 of this Note.

Figure 5-5 / First Two Pages of Uniform ARM One-Year Note (continued)

4. INTEREST RATE AND MONTHLY PAYMENT CHANGES

(A) Change Dates

The interest rate I will pay may change on the first day of **March 1, 2004**, and on that day every 12th month thereafter. Each date on which my interest rate could change is called a "Change Date."

(B) The Index

Beginning with the first Change Date, my interest rate will be based on an Index. The "Index" is the weekly average yield on United States Treasury securities adjusted to a constant maturity of one year, as made available by the Federal Reserve Board. The most recent Index figure available as of the date 45 days before each Change Date is called the "Current Index." If the Index is no longer available, the Note Holder will choose a new index which is based upon comparable information. The Note Holder will give me notice of this choice.

(C) Calculation of Changes

Before each Change Date, the Note Holder will calculate my new interest rate by adding **2.75** percentage points (%) to the Current Index. The Note Holder will then round the result of this addition to the nearest one-eighth of one percentage point (0.125%). Subject to the limits stated in Section 4(D) below, this rounded amount will be my new interest rate until the next Change Date.

The Note Holder will then determine the amount of the monthly payment that would be sufficient to repay the unpaid principal that I am expected to owe at the Change Date in full on the Maturity Date at my new interest rate in substantially equal payments. The result of this calculation will be the new amount of my monthly payment.

(D) Limits on Interest Rate Changes

The interest rate I am required to pay at the first Change Date will not be greater than **2%** or less than **2%**. Thereafter, my interest rate will never be increased or decreased on any single Change Date by more than two percentage points (2.0%) from the rate of interest I have been paying for the preceding 12 months. My interest rate will never be greater than **11%**.

(E) Effective Date of Changes

My new interest rate will become effective on each Change Date. I will pay the amount of my new monthly payment beginning on the first monthly payment date after the Change Date until the amount of my monthly payment changes again.

(F) Notice of Changes

The Note Holder will deliver or mail to me a notice of any changes in my interest rate and the amount of my monthly payment before the effective date of any change. The notice will include information required by law to be given to me and also the title and telephone number of a person who will answer any question I may have regarding the notice.

5. BORROWER'S RIGHT TO PREPAY

I have the right to make payments of Principal at any time before they are due. A payment of Principal only is known as a "Prepayment." When I make a Prepayment, I will tell the Note Holder in writing that I am doing so. I may not designate a payment as a Prepayment if I have not made all the monthly payments due under the Note.

I may make a full Prepayment or partial Prepayments without paying a Prepayment charge. The Note Holder will use my Prepayments to reduce the amount of Principal that I owe under this Note. However, the Note Holder may apply my Prepayment to the accrued and unpaid interest on the Prepayment amount, before applying my Prepayment to reduce the Principal amount of the Note. If I make a partial Prepayment, there will be no changes in the due dates of my monthly payment unless the Note Holder agrees in writing to those changes. My partial repayment may reduce the amount of my monthly payments after the first Change Date following my partial Prepayment. However, any reduction due to my partial Prepayment may be offset by an interest rate increase.

Figure 5-6	ARM Examples

Index	5.69%	Annual Adjustment Cap	2%
Margin	2.75%	Lifetime Adjustment Cap	6%
Discount	1.75%	30-Year Fixed Rate	7.85%

Example 1: Calculate the fully indexed rate:

Index	5.69%
+ Margin	2.75%
Fully Indexed Rate	8.44%

Example 2: Calculate the initial rate:

Index	5.69%
+ Margin	2.75%
– Discount	1.75%
Initial Rate	6.69%

Example 3: Calculate maximum rate after first adjustment:

Initial Rate	6.69%
Annual Adj. Cap	2.00%
Maximum Rate	8.69%

Example 4: Calculate the fully indexed rate when no change occurs from first year:

Index	5.69%
+ Margin	2.75%
Fully Indexed Rate	8.44%

Thus, payment rate could only increase to 8.44%.

Example 5: Calculate the maximum rate (lifetime) for this loan:

Initial Rate	6.69%
+ 6% Lifetime Cap	6.00%
Maximum Rate	12.69%

In order to protect consumers, Congress passed an amendment to Regulation Z (truth-in-lending) requiring lenders to provide the following information to consumers who apply for an ARM loan on the borrower's principal dwelling:

- The interest rate ceiling
- CHARM booklet (Consumer Handbook on Adjustable Rate Mortgages) explaining ARMs
- 15-year historical example of how rates would have changed with this loan
- Worst-case example assuming a $10,000 loan

Biweekly Mortgages

Developed during the middle of the 1980s, the biweekly mortgage is a popular instrument that some homeowners use for shortening the life of their mortgage debt and saving on the total interest paid over the life of the mortgage. A biweekly mortgage is a fixed-rate, level-payment, fully amortizing mortgage that requires the borrower to make payments every two weeks rather than monthly—for a total of 26 payments a year. Each biweekly payment is exactly half the amount that would be payable under a comparable monthly-payment mortgage. Thus, the 26 biweekly payments are equivalent to 13 monthly payments a year. The benefits to consumers of such a payment schedule are many. These benefits include the following:

- A payment schedule that fits the budget of those who are paid on a weekly or biweekly basis.
- More frequent payment schedule substantially reduces the total interest paid over the life of the loan.
- The life of the loan is meaningfully shortened.

The mortgage life is shortened and interest paid substantially decreased because with biweekly payments a borrower is paying off more of the mortgage principal in a year than would occur with monthly payments. The payment is calculated on a 30-year **amortization schedule** at the market rate that usually is at a 25- to 50-basis-point reduction from regular 30-year mortgages. The increased number of payments allows for more principal to be paid before the next scheduled payment, thus reducing the interest and the effective mortgage life. Because the principal is paid off faster, the loan matures in a shorter length of time.

The negative aspects of the biweekly mortgage are minor as far as the borrower is concerned. These negative aspects mainly center on coordinating the mortgage payment with the borrower's payday. Lenders have helped to make this easier for borrowers by setting up checking accounts that are debited every 14 days for the mortgage payment. Many borrowers have their paychecks deposited directly into these checking accounts, thus making the payment process even easier.

The major negative aspect as far as lenders are concerned is the increased cost associated with processing and calculating the increased number of payments; however, this may not remain an issue as lenders become more sophisticated with computer processing. Some lenders have calculated that it costs $10 to process each payment. Interest on biweekly mortgages is calculated using simple interest (365 rather than 360 days). A lender must have the capacity to reamortize the loan after each payment.

The underwriting requirements for a biweekly mortgage are the same as for any other mortgage except, to qualify borrowers, the biweekly principal and interest

Figure 5-7 Payment Terms for 30-Year Mortgage, Monthly Payment versus Biweekly Mortgage, Payment Every Two Weeks

Example: Assume a $100,000 mortgage at 8 percent for 30 years.

Loan Product	Periodic Payment	Term
30-year, monthly payment	$733.77	360 months
Biweekly payment	$366.89	272 months

Interest saved with the biweekly mortgage = $46,300.86

payment are adjusted to the equivalent monthly payment. Uniform biweekly notes and payment riders are available and should be used if a lender wants to be able to sell these mortgages. Fannie Mae buys 15- and 30-year biweekly mortgages through its Standard Commitment Window and will consider 10- and 20-year biweekly mortgages on a negotiated basis.

Buydowns

Buydowns became popular during the extremely high interest rate period of the early 1980s. This concept is designed to address the issue of affordability of housing and not the issue of protecting lenders' relative yields. Although market interest rates cannot be changed (the market dictates what they will be), the effective rate to a homebuyer can be changed by "buying down" the market rate to a rate that will allow a potential home-buyer to qualify for a loan. This buydown happens when a builder, home seller, parent of a buyer, or homebuyer prepays a portion of the interest a lender will earn over the life of the loan. This one-time nonrefundable payment is either paid directly to the lender in one lump sum or put into an interest-earning account that a lender debits monthly to subsidize the reduced monthly payment.

Through this method, mortgage payments can be bought down for a temporary period—usually 1 to 10 years—or permanently. The buydown can be structured in many ways; for example, a reduced monthly payment could remain constant over the life of the loan, increase yearly, or increase only once.

If a buydown is a permanent one, a homebuyer is qualified for the loan on the ability to make the established monthly payment. If the buydown is only temporary, as most are, the buyer is qualified on ability to make the initial lower payment rather than ability to meet the increased payment. This benefit allows many more families to qualify for a mortgage loan.

Convertible Mortgages

The main attraction of this mortgage is that it appears to combine the best features of the fixed-rate and the adjustable-rate mortgage. This mortgage, sometimes called a convertible ARM, allows a borrower to start out with the lower payment rate that makes ARMs attractive. Later, if it is to the borrower's advantage, the existing ARM can be converted to a fixed-rate mortgage.

The attractive features of any ARM include, as already discussed, an interest rate that is normally 200 to 300 basis points below the fixed-rate interest rate and yearly and lifetime caps on interest rate increases. As with most standard ARMs, borrowers using this mortgage are qualified at the lower ARM payment rate (usually with a certain minimum rate, e.g., 7 percent), which, of course, allows for more borrowers to qualify for a mortgage loan.

The one feature of a fixed-rate mortgage that makes this type of loan so attractive to consumers and that is missing with a standard ARM is the fact that the interest rate is capped at the rate set at closing. This attractive feature is normally found only in fixed-rate mortgages. Of course, if interest rates should drop, an ARM mortgagor is going to benefit from the drop in rates, while the fixed-rate holder would have to refinance to enjoy the interest rate drop.

Converting to a Fixed Rate

A convertible mortgage affords the borrower the opportunity, for a period of time, to convert the ARM to a fixed-rate mortgage in the future. The time frame within which to convert depends on the mortgage instrument, but most instruments allow the borrower to convert anytime after the 13th month and until the 60th month. The opportunity need only be used if the borrower decides it would be beneficial to convert. At first glance, the ability to convert may not appear to be of great value to a borrower since a borrower could always refinance the existing ARM and obtain a new fixed-rate mortgage. The problem with that strategy is the cost of refinancing. It is generally acknowledged that the cost of refinancing is from 2 to 4 percent of the outstanding balance. That can amount to many thousands of dollars.

With the convertible ARM, the borrower can convert and may have to pay only a fixed amount—say, $250 to $500. If the loan has been sold into the secondary mortgage market, an additional fee may be charged.

When would a borrower choose this convertible ARM over a normal ARM or a fixed-rate mortgage? It depends mostly on whether the borrower can qualify for a fixed-rate mortgage. In addition, a borrower must decide whether the spread between the mortgage alternatives makes one more attractive than another.

A convertible ARM usually has an interest rate 25 to 50 basis points more than a normal ARM. The convertible ARM makes sense to a borrower if the borrower expects interest rates to drop over the next couple of years. If that occurs, the borrower will benefit from the lower ARM interest rate initially and, after converting, will benefit by locking in the fixed-rate rate for the life of the mortgage.

Graduated Payment Mortgages (GPMs)

The GPM is an instrument that was specifically designed to provide borrowers with an opportunity to match their expected increase in income with a mortgage payment that is initially low but increases yearly. This instrument is not designed to address the issue of sheltering lenders from interest rate shifts. It does, however, help alleviate the problem of how to qualify more potential homeowners for mortgages. Many otherwise qualified potential homeowners are unable to qualify for a standard fixed-rate mortgage because their current income is not sufficient; however, if their conservatively estimated future income could be factored in, they could qualify.

With a GPM, the interest rate and the term of the loan are set, as with a standard fixed-rate mortgage. The difference is that the initial monthly payment begins at a lower level than it would with a standard mortgage. The result is monthly payments that are not sufficient to fully amortize the loan. Since the payments do not fully amortize the loan, the borrower, in effect, is borrowing the difference between the payment being made and the interest actually due. The amount of accrued but unpaid interest is added to the outstanding principal amount. Through this negative amortization, the outstanding principal balance actually increases for a period of time rather than decreases, as with a standard mortgage.

The following year the monthly payment increases to a predetermined rate, say, 7.5 percent, with additional increases occurring each year for a set number of years. Depending on the plan selected, as the yearly increases occur at some point, the monthly payments equal or exceed the payment under a standard mortgage. At that point, negative amortization stops, but the payment increases continue until they reach a level that fully amortizes the outstanding balance over the remaining years of the loan.

From the example, two important points emerge. First, the amount of family income to qualify for a GPM is substantially less, and therefore more families can qualify. Of course, if family income does not increase at the hoped-for rate, the burden of 7.5 percent mortgage payment increases may result in a default. The second point is that the total amount of interest paid is increased with a GPM. This is the result of the negative amortization during the early years of the mortgage when principal is increasing rather than decreasing as with a fully amortized mortgage.

In addition to conventional GPMs, the Department of Housing and Urban Development has an insured GPM (Sec. 245), which is basically the same as the GPM described.

Price Level Adjusted Mortgages (PLAMs)

A PLAM is one of the more recent alternative mortgage instruments and one that holds much promise, especially if a period of hyperinflation should reappear. The underlying concept of a PLAM is that the "real" mortgage payment remains constant over the life of the mortgage. This means that the rate at which interest is charged to a borrower is guaranteed to provide a lender with a "real" return above inflation.

Under a standard mortgage, the mortgage payment is at a level sufficient to return to the lender the following: principal plus interest plus an inflation premium to make up for the decrease in the value of the money repaid. This *inflation premium* adds several hundred basis points to a typical standard mortgage payment, possibly more during higher inflation periods.

The PLAM is designed to address this problem of real return and offers a solution that benefits both borrower and lender. A PLAM takes the expensive guesswork out of lending in an inflationary economy. The real return is guaranteed by increasing the monthly mortgage payment at the same rate as the increase in inflation (or stated differently, by the decrease in the value of money) as measured by an appropriate index such as the Consumer Price Index. The outstanding principal balance is also adjusted to constant dollars. The adjustments to both the monthly payments and the outstanding principal are on a yearly basis.

The basic assumption with a PLAM, as with many other alternative mortgage instruments, is that household income will increase at or near the inflation rate. Therefore, as the mortgage payment increases, the same percentage of monthly income will be used to meet that payment.

Two-Step, or Reset, Mortgages

This relatively new alternative mortgage instrument was developed after the convertible mortgage and shares some of the same features. This alternative provides a borrower with the certainty of a fixed-rate mortgage for a period of time (usually five or seven years), and then the rate adjusts to a new fixed rate (indexed to the 10-year Treasury, weekly average) with the payment remaining at that rate for the remaining 25 or 23 years. The advantage to the consumer is that this mortgage starts out low (lower than a 30-year fixed-rate mortgage) and remains at that low rate for five or seven years, with any increase in rates capped at 6 percent (Fannie Mae's program). A consumer may be planning to stay in the home for only that five or seven years, thus they benefit from the lower rate.

Reverse Annuity Mortgages (RAMs)

The RAM is designed to enable older retired homeowners who are likely to be on fixed income to use the equity in their homes (probably totally paid for) as a source of supplemental income while still retaining ownership. One of the many RAMs available today is Fannie Mae's Home Equity Conversion Mortgage, which is an FHA-insured reverse mortgage. This program is open to homeowners who are at least 62 years of age; who own their home free and clear or nearly so and who wish to use the equity in their homes to cover part of their living expenses after retirement. The loan is an ARM, with the rates adjusted either annually or monthly with caps on increases.

Other RAMs work as follows: a lender has the house appraised and then lends a certain percentage of the current value. The loan itself is to be paid to the homeowner in the form of a monthly annuity. This annuity comes from the mortgage lender directly or else the proceeds of the loan are used to purchase an annuity from a life insurance company. The annuity provides monthly payments for the life of the loan or the life of the annuitant(s), depending on how the RAM is structured. Throughout the time of the loan, the homeowner owns and lives in the house.

A lender's security for a RAM is the same as with a standard mortgage: the home itself. If the homeowner (or owners) dies before the term, the estate is liable for the debt. Of course, if the house is sold before death, the debt must be paid off.

If, when the loan comes to term, the homeowner (or owners) is still alive, a new RAM can be created, assuming that the property has appreciated. The proceeds from the new RAM first repay the old one, and the difference purchases a new annuity for the homeowner.

Although this mortgage concept has not been used much to date, it may become a necessary part of future mortgage lending as the American public grows older, especially if double-digit inflation returns.

Discussion Points

1. Discuss how the standard fixed-rate mortgage developed in the United States and why it was an important tool for reviving real estate and mortgage lending after the Great Depression.

2. Explain why a self-amortizing (direct reduction) mortgage can save a mortgage borrower a substantial amount of interest over a term loan.

3. Discuss the primary reason that adjustable-rate mortgages are used throughout the world with the exception being the United States.

4. Identify and discuss the components of an adjustable-rate mortgage.

5. What must a mortgage lender do to attract consumers to an adjustable-rate mortgage when fixed-rate mortgages are attractively priced?

Residential Mortgage Loan Origination and Processing

Introduction

The residential mortgage loan origination and processing functions include all actions and procedures that occur from the time a potential borrower has contact with the lender through the time the underwriter reviews the application for a decision to approve, deny, or counteroffer (explained in Chapter 7, "Underwriting the Residential Mortgage Loan"). The speedy, professional completion of this function is crucial to any mortgage lender and, along with the quality of loans originated, is the determining factor in the success and profitability of the residential mortgage-lending operation. As in all aspects of residential lending, the secondary market giants Fannie Mae and Freddie Mac continually set the industry standards. The majority of lenders nationwide follows their guidelines and uses their forms.

Loan processing remains the lengthiest step involved in producing a closed residential mortgage loan. Until the early 1990s, this step might easily have taken three weeks to 45 days. This is not acceptable in today's competitive marketplace. Now the trend is for faster loan processing—many mortgage lenders advertise that they will get an answer for the applicant within minutes. While not all lenders issue a loan decision within minutes (but many do), most lenders complete processing of a loan in a few days to a week, or maybe two weeks or more in times of increased refinance activity.

Another important change is in the approach to processing itself. Lenders no longer follow one universal procedure to process a mortgage application. How they process depends on the loan program. Additionally, the extent and type of processing documentation differs significantly from just 10 years ago.

A final but equally significant difference one sees today in the mortgage origination and processing area is a blurring of lines traditionally separating these functions. Prior to banking deregulation in 1978, loan officers were "order takers"—essentially they just completed the application for the single mortgage product offered and handed over the signed documents to the processor, who handled the application until it went to the weekly (or monthly!) loan committee meeting.

This passive role has evolved over the past 20 years, along with the mortgage marketplace. Today, loan officers counsel the consumer on the different loan products available, complete a significant amount of the processing at application, and maintain contact with the applicants until loan closing. This requires the loan officer to have additional skills and knowledge and can expose the lender to additional compliance risks, but both lender and consumer benefit tremendously from quicker approval times and higher approval rates.

Technology

These recent marketplace changes are a result of improvements in technology in practically all aspects of loan origination and processing affecting all lenders, from the largest to the smallest. The impact of technology on the mortgage industry cannot be overstated—an entire chapter and even a book can be devoted to this topic alone. Because the mortgage-lending industry relies so heavily on data management and cost efficiencies, significant improvements in technology have far-reaching effects and transform the way in which the industry operates.

Computer software programs designed for mortgage origination enable processors to accomplish work faster and manage more loans efficiently. These software programs greatly increase the capacity of a single processor. They allow processors to handle more functions, perform many calculations, accommodate more loan programs, save computer keystrokes, produce reports, and operate more reliably than when vendors first introduced them. With the click of one button, a processor (or even a loan officer at origination) now can simultaneously obtain a credit report, order an appraisal, produce disclosure documentation, and submit key information for financial management and compliance reporting.

As a result of increased computing capacity and speed, lenders now link one software program to others that handle underwriting, closing, secondary marketing, and servicing functions. This technique dramatically increases the efficiencies provided by better technology. Such lenders as Countrywide and Washington Mutual today accomplish in scope and complexity what was unthinkable 10 years ago. Small- and medium-sized lenders have experienced similar benefits. Consumers save more money when lenders increase efficiency, and they have more options when lenders offer more loan programs.

The Internet, improved technology, and proprietary software programs also allow secondary market investors to provide lenders with immediate confirmation of a loan's eligibility for sale and a list of *commitment conditions*—the processing documentation and underwriting conditions the lenders must obtain to complete this sale. This confirmation enables the lender to make a loan decision quickly and eliminates additional processing steps, reducing the time, effort, uncertainty, and stress for the consumer as well.

Interview

The first step in mortgage loan origination is the initial interview. The importance of this initial contact with the potential borrower(s) cannot be overemphasized. If handled correctly, the interview saves both consumer and mortgage lender considerable time and money. This contact can establish early on whether or not the potential borrower(s) can qualify for a mortgage loan. The person conducting this interview is most often called the loan officer. For purposes of clarity in this book, we refer only to the loan officer, but it is critical to remember that *any* employee, regardless of title, who interacts in this capacity with the consumer, formally or informally, intentionally or unintentionally, makes the lender responsible (and liable) for the completion of these functions in compliance with state and federal regulations.

Many initial interviews result in a completed (formal) application and then processing. However, the initial interview can have four outcomes:

- Counseling
- Prequalification—(not pre-approval)
- Formal application
- Credit decision

These potential outcomes reflect an increasing level of information exchanged between the potential borrower(s) and loan officer.

In the first three situations, the loan officer is *not* making a credit decision and should consciously and carefully avoid giving the consumer this impression. Here is a general description of what happens in these three outcomes:

> *Counseling*: The loan officer describes the various programs available, explains the general nature of the application process and the financial obligations inherent in a mortgage loan, and may recommend steps the potential borrower must take to prepare for a formal application.
>
> *Prequalification:* This process is mostly the same as counseling, but in addition the loan officer may "run the numbers" in more detail—apply the information to the potential borrower's (or borrowers') specific situation *but not convey an opinion on credit approval or denial.*
>
> *Formal application:* Usually contains the preceding steps, but is defined as when the potential borrower(s) actually completes a written application and pays any fees due at that time to the lender.

During counseling and prequalification, the loan officer does not complete a formal application or issue a credit decision. Still, the loan officer provides a valuable service by giving the potential borrower(s) specific information to help decide which of many loan products is best, or whether to apply at all. These types of initial interviews have become more common as consumers today are more likely to compare loan programs and shop around for rates from several different lenders.

A *credit decision* (loan approval, denial, or counteroffer) is the fourth outcome that may result from an initial interview. This may occur at the end of the initial interview if the lender has sufficient information and/or the technology and software discussed earlier. Usually, there are several conditions outstanding that must be met before the loan application is ready to close.

It is important to note that *all* initial interviews can be completed in the following way: face-to-face, by mail, by telephone, by fax, or over the Internet. Regardless of the outcome, each method of conducting an initial interview poses significant consumer compliance challenges for the lender and loan officer.

Formal Application

The following sections describe the formal application process.

Be Careful Not to Discourage a Formal Application

No lender can refuse a formal application from any potential borrower(s) who wants to submit one. After having the financial obligations of a mortgage loan explained to them in counseling or prequalification, most individuals will not apply for a mortgage loan if they realize they will not qualify. Regardless of the circumstances, a loan officer must be careful not to discourage potential borrower(s) from applying for a mortgage loan if they so desire.

Further, as mentioned, mortgage lenders must be careful that this initial interview does not imply a credit decision and it must not be explicitly represented as one. If a lender—even at this stage of the process—tells a potential applicant that, based upon the applicant's income, he or she does or does not qualify, the lender has made a credit decision. This requires a formal application, several disclosure and reporting requirements, and (depending on the case) a commitment letter or a notice of adverse action. There are serious consumer compliance issues if the lender improperly handles this situation.

The Uniform Residential Loan Application and Uniform Documentation

The mortgage application form is the most important document in the residential mortgage-lending process. Every step that follows is based on the information provided in the application. Numerous compliance and regulatory issues depend on its accurate completion. It is important to emphasize that all lenders should use the Fannie Mae/Freddie Mac Uniform Residential Loan Application (Fannie Mae Form 1003 or 1003[S] and Freddie Mac Form 65) and all other uniform processing and closing documentation—*regardless* of whether the lender intends to keep the loan in its portfolio or sell it on the secondary market to an investor. *Not* using this uniform documentation (also called standard or conforming documentation) makes selling those mortgages much more difficult and expensive.

Additionally, the use of a lender's own forms may place a lender (and subsequent investors, if the loan is sold) in violation of the various consumer protection laws if the forms are not drafted correctly. The Fannie Mae/Freddie Mac Uniform Application and additional uniform processing and closing documentation have been accepted as meeting all consumer protection requirements. (There is still a risk that uniform documentation may have an issue at the state level, but it is more likely that any potential problems have already been identified and addressed with these forms rather than with lender-produced forms.)

Once completed and signed by the applicant(s), the lender should not alter or discard the original application form. If the application is approved and is closing, the lender will generate a typed final application form for the borrower to sign at closing. This final application form contains the updated or verified information as a result of the lender's processing activities. The lender should always keep both the original and final application forms in the loan file.

Exhibit 6-1 | Sample Uniform Residential Loan Application

Uniform Residential Loan Application

This application is designed to be completed by the applicant(s) with the lender's assistance. Applicants should complete this form as "Borrower" or "Co-Borrower", as applicable. Co-Borrower information must also be provided (and the appropriate box checked) when [X] the income or assets of a person other than the "Borrower" (including the Borrower's spouse) will be used as a basis for loan qualification or [ ] the income or assets of the Borrower's spouse will not be used as a basis for loan qualification, but his or her liabilities must be considered because the Borrower resides in a community property state, the security property is located in a community property state, or the Borrower is relying on other property located in a community property state as a basis for repayment of the loan.

I. TYPE OF MORTGAGE AND TERMS OF LOAN

Mortgage Applied for:	[ ] VA [X] Conventional [ ] Other:		Agency Case Number		Lender Case No. 100101920
	[ ] FHA [ ] FmHA				

| Amount $ 189,000.00 | Interest Rate 6.000 % | No. of Months 360 | Amortization Type: [X] Fixed Rate [ ] GPM | Other (explain): [ ] ARM (type): |

II. PROPERTY INFORMATION AND PURPOSE OF LOAN

Subject Property Address (street, city, state, & zip code) 89 Harvester Road, Fairfield, CT 06825	No. of Units 1
Legal Description of Subject Property (attach description if necessary) single family ranch, detached garage one-half acre land	Year Built 1987

Purpose of Loan	[X] Purchase [ ] Construction [ ] Other (explain): [ ] Refinance [ ] Construction-Permanent	Property will be: [ ] Primary Residence [ ] Secondary Residence [ ] Investment

Complete this line if construction or construction-permanent loan.

Year Lot Acquired	Original Cost $	Amount Existing Liens $	(a) Present Value of Lot $	(b) Cost of Improvements $	Total (a + b) $

Complete this line if this is a refinance loan.

Year Acquired	Original Cost $	Amount Existing Liens $	Purpose of Refinance	Describe Improvements [ ] made [ ] to be made
				Cost: $

Title will be held in what Name(s) Joseph F. and Margaret J. Lynch	Manner in which Title will be held Joint	Estate will be held in: [X] Fee Simple
Source of Down Payment, Settlement Charges and/or Subordinate Financing (explain) Deposit on Sales Contract Savings		[ ] Leasehold (show expiration date)

III. BORROWER INFORMATION

	Borrower				Co-Borrower			
Borrower's Name (include Jr. or Sr. if applicable) Joseph F. Lynch				Co-Borrower's Name (include Jr. or Sr. if applicable) Margaret J. Lynch				
Social Security Number 123-45-6789	Home Phone (incl. area code) 203-333-3990	Age 50	Yrs. School 16	Social Security Number 987-65-4321	Home Phone (incl. area code) 203-333-3990	Age 47	Yrs. School 16	
[X] Married [ ] Unmarried (include single, divorced, widowed) [ ] Separated	Dependents (not listed by Co-Borrower) no. 3 ages 10, 13, 15			[X] Married [ ] Unmarried (include single, divorced, widowed) [ ] Separated	Dependents (not listed by Borrower) no. 3 ages 10, 13, 15			
Present Address (street, city, state, zip code) [X] Own [ ] Rent 1 No. Yrs. 384 Katona Drive Fairfield, CT 06824				Present Address (street, city, state, zip code) [X] Own [ ] Rent 1 No. Yrs. 384 Katona Drive Fairfield, CT 06824				

If residing at present address for less than two years, complete the following:

Former Address (street, city, state, zip code) [ ] Own [X] Rent 4 No. Yrs. 64 Merchant Street Bridgeport, CT 06606	Former Address (street, city, state, zip code) [ ] Own [X] Rent 4 No. Yrs. 64 Merchant Street Bridgeport, CT 06606
Former Address (street, city, state, zip code) [ ] Own [ ] Rent ___ No. Yrs.	Former Address (street, city, state, zip code) [ ] Own [ ] Rent ___ No. Yrs.

IV. EMPLOYMENT INFORMATION

	Borrower		Co-Borrower	
Name & Address of Employer General Electric Corp. 2645 Stratfield Road Fairfield, CT 06825	[ ] Self Employed	Yrs. on this job 4	Name & Address of Employer Town of Fairfield 100 Old Post Road Fairfield, CT 06824	[ ] Self Employed	Yrs. on this job 1
		Yrs. employed in this line of work/profession 6		Yrs. employed in this line of work/profession 6
Position/Title/Type of Business Accountant	Business Phone (incl. area code) 203-539-9755	Position/Title/Type of Business School Nurse	Business Phone (incl. area code) 203-939-5000

If employed in current position for less than two years or if currently employed in more than one position, complete the following:

Name & Address of Employer	[ ] Self Employed	Dates (from - to)	Name & Address of Employer Fairfield University 234 North Benson Road Fairfield, CT 06824	[ ] Self Employed	Dates (from - to) 1998 2001
		Monthly Income $			Monthly Income $ 3,600.00
Position/Title/Type of Business	Business Phone (incl. area code)	Position/Title/Type of Business School Nurse	Business Phone (incl. area code) 203-259-0900
Name & Address of Employer	[ ] Self Employed	Dates (from - to)	Name & Address of Employer	[ ] Self Employed	Dates (from - to)
		Monthly Income $			Monthly Income $
Position/Title/Type of Business	Business Phone (incl. area code)	Position/Title/Type of Business	Business Phone (incl. area code)

Freddie Mac Form 10/92	ITEM 7300L1 (9701)	Page 1 of 4 pages 100101920	*I/We acknowledge that the information provided on this page is true and correct JFL mjl	Fannie Mae Form 1003 10/92

GREATLAND ■
To Order Call: 1-800-530-9393 □ Fax 616-791-1131

Exhibit 6-1   Sample Uniform Residential Loan Application (continued)

V. MONTHLY INCOME AND COMBINED HOUSING EXPENSE INFORMATION

Gross Monthly Income	Borrower	Co-Borrower	Total	Combined Monthly Housing Expense	Present	Proposed
Base Empl. Income*	$ 5,000.00	$ 4,000.00	$ 9,000.00	Rent	$	
Overtime		200.00	200.00	First Mortgage (P&I)	679.06	$ 1,133.16
Bonuses				Other Financing (P&I)		
Commissions				Hazard Insurance		75.00
Dividends/Interest	50.00		50.00	Real Estate Taxes	200.00	250.00
Net Rental Income				Mortgage Insurance	50.00	39.38
OTHER (before completing, see the notice in "describe other income," below)				Homeowner Assn. Dues		
				Other:		
Total	$ 5,050.00	$ 4,200.00	$ 9,250.00	Total	$ 929.06	$ 1,497.54

*Self Employed Borrower(s) may be required to provide additional documentation such as tax returns and financial statements.

B/C	Describe Other Income	Notice: Alimony, child support, or separate maintenance income need not be revealed if the Borrower (B) or Co-Borrower (C) does not choose to have it considered for repaying this loan.	Monthly Amount
			$
			$
			$
			$

VI. ASSETS AND LIABILITIES

This Statement and any applicable supporting schedules may be completed jointly by both married and unmarried Co-Borrowers if their assets and liabilities are sufficiently joined so that the Statement can be meaningfully and fairly presented on a combined basis; otherwise separate Statements and Schedules are required. If the Co-Borrower section was completed about a spouse, this Statement and supporting schedules must be completed about that spouse also.

Completed [X] Jointly [ ] Not Jointly

ASSETS	Cash or Market Value	Liabilities and Pledged Assets. List the creditor's name, address and account number for all outstanding debts, including automobile loans, revolving charge accounts, real estate loans, alimony, child support, stock pledges, etc. Use continuation sheet, if necessary. Indicate by (*) those liabilities which will be satisfied upon sale of real estate owned or upon refinancing of the subject property.	Monthly Payt. & Mos. Left to Pay	Unpaid Balance
Description				
Cash deposit toward purchase held by Century 21	$ 2100.00	**LIABILITIES**		
		Name and address of Company Peoples Bank 180 Main Street Fairfield, CT 06824	$ Payt./Mos. 929.06 / 345	$ 234255.00
List checking and savings accounts below				
Name and address of Bank, S&L, or Credit Union Bank of Fairfield 532 Main Street Fairfield, CT 06824				
		Acct. no. 12-6896040		
		Name and address of Company Chase Auto Finance 3498 Hollis Tpke Long Island City, NY	$ Payt./Mos. 265.91 / 12	$ 3000.00
Acct. no. 123-4059	$ 3000.00			
Name and address of Bank, S&L, or Credit Union Bank of Fairfield 532 Main Street Fairfield, CT 06824		Acct. no. 1247950		
		Name and address of Company Fleet Bank 532 Main Street Fairfield, CT 06824	$ Payt./Mos. 100.00 / 7	$ 600.00
Acct. no. 12-59690	$ 5000.00			
Name and address of Bank, S&L, or Credit Union		Acct. no. 1234456934596		
		Name and address of Company	$ Payt./Mos.	$
Acct. no.	$			
Name and address of Bank, S&L, or Credit Union				
		Acct. no.		
		Name and address of Company	$ Payt./Mos.	$
Acct. no.	$			
Stocks & Bonds (Company name/number & description) GE	$ 10000.00			
		Acct. no.		
		Name and address of Company	$ Payt./Mos.	$
Life insurance net cash value				
Face amount: $200000.00	$ 2500.00			
Subtotal Liquid Assets	**$ 22600.00**			
Real estate owned (enter market value from schedule of real estate owned)	$ 265000.00	Acct. no.		
Vested interest in retirement fund	$ 15000.00	Name and address of Company	$ Payt./Mos.	$
Net worth of business(es) owned (attach financial statement)	$			
Automobiles owned (make and year) 97 Subaru 2000 Subaru	$ 3000.00 16000.00	Acct. no.		
		Alimony/Child Support/Separate Maintenance Payments Owed to:	$	
Other Assets (itemize) Furn/Prop Time Share - Aruba	$ 10000.00 12000.00	Job Related Expense (child care, union dues, etc.)	$	
		Total Monthly Payments	$ 365.91	
Total Assets a.	**$ 343600.00**	Net Worth (a minus b) ▶ $ 105745.00	Total Liabilities b.	$ 237855.00

Freddie Mac Form 65 10/92   ITEM 7300L2 (9701)   Page 2 of 4 pages   "I/We acknowledge that the information provided on this page is true and correct   *JEvgh*   Fannie Mae Form 1003 10/92

100101920

GREATLAND ■
To Order Call: 1-800-530-9393 ☐Fax 616-791-1131

Exhibit 6-1 Sample Uniform Residential Loan Application

VI. ASSETS AND LIABILITIES (cont.)

Schedule of Real Estate Owned (if additional properties are owned, use continuation sheet.)

Property Address (enter S if sold, PS if pending sale or R if rental being held for income)	Type of Property	Present Market Value	Amount of Mortgages & Liens	Gross Rental Income	Mortgage Payments	Insurance, Maintenance, Taxes & Misc.	Net Rental Income
384 Katona Drive Fairfield, CT 06824	Single P	$ 265,000.00	$ 234255.00	$	$ 679.06	$ 200.00	$
Totals		$ 265,000.00	$ 234255.00	$	$ 679.06	$ 200.00	$

List any additional names under which credit has previously been received and indicate appropriate creditor name(s) and account number(s):

Alternate Name	Creditor Name	Account Number

VII. DETAILS OF TRANSACTION

a. Purchase price	$ 210,000.00
b. Alterations, improvements, repairs	
c. Land (if acquired separately)	
d. Refinance (incl. debts to be paid off)	
e. Estimated prepaid items	916.26
f. Estimated closing costs	4,032.00
g. PMI, MIP, Funding Fee	472.50
h. Discount (if Borrower will pay)	1,890.00
i. Total costs (add items a through h)	217,310.76
j. Subordinate financing	
k. Borrower's closing costs paid by Seller	
l. Other Credits (explain)	
m. Loan amount (exclude PMI, MIP, Funding Fee financed)	189,000.00
n. PMI, MIP, Funding Fee financed	
o. Loan amount (add m & n)	189,000.00
p. Cash from/to Borrower (subtract j, k, l & o from i) From Borrower	28,310.76

VIII. DECLARATIONS

If you answer "yes" to any questions a through i, please use continuation sheet for explanation.

	Borrower Yes	Borrower No	Co-Borrower Yes	Co-Borrower No
a. Are there any outstanding judgments against you?		X		X
b. Have you been declared bankrupt within the past 7 years?		X		X
c. Have you had property foreclosed upon or given title or deed in lieu thereof in the last 7 years?		X		X
d. Are you a party to a lawsuit?		X		X
e. Have you directly or indirectly been obligated on any loan which resulted in foreclosure, transfer of title in lieu of foreclosure, or judgment? (This would include such loans as home mortgage loans, SBA loans, home improvement loans, educational loans, manufactured (mobile) home loans, any mortgage, financial obligation, bond, or loan guarantee. If "Yes," provide details, including date, name and address of Lender, FHA or VA case number, if any, and reasons for the action.)		X		X
f. Are you presently delinquent or in default on any Federal debt or any other loan, mortgage, financial obligation, bond, or loan guarantee? If "Yes," give details as described in the preceding question.		X		X
g. Are you obligated to pay alimony, child support, or separate maintenance?		X		X
h. Is any part of the down payment borrowed?		X		X
i. Are you a co-maker or endorser on a note?		X		X
j. Are you a U.S. citizen?	X		X	
k. Are you a permanent resident alien?		X		X
l. Do you intend to occupy the property as your primary residence? If "Yes," complete question m below.	X		X	
m. Have you had an ownership interest in a property in the last three years?	X			X
(1) What type of property did you own - principal residence (PR), second home (SH), or investment property (IP)?	PR		PR	
(2) How did you hold title to the home - solely by yourself (S), jointly with your spouse (SP), or jointly with another person (O)?	SP		SP	

IX. ACKNOWLEDGMENT AND AGREEMENT

The undersigned specifically acknowledge(s) and agree(s) that: (1) the loan requested by this application will be secured by a first mortgage or deed of trust on the property described herein; (2) the property will not be used for any illegal or prohibited purpose or use; (3) all statements made in this application are made for the purpose of obtaining the loan indicated herein; (4) occupation of the property will be as indicated above; (5) verification or reverification of any information contained in the application may be made at any time by the Lender, its agents, successors and assigns, either directly or through a credit reporting agency, from any source named in this application, and the original copy of this application will be retained by the Lender, even if the loan is not approved; (6) the Lender, its agents, successors and assigns will rely on the information contained in the application and I/we have a continuing obligation to amend and/or supplement the information provided in this application if any of the material facts which I/we have represented herein should change prior to closing; (7) in the event my/our payments on the loan indicated in this application become delinquent, the Lender, its agents, successors and assigns, may, in addition to all their other rights and remedies, report my/our name(s) and account information to a credit reporting agency; (8) ownership of the loan may be transferred to successor or assign of the Lender without notice to me and/or the administration of the loan account may be transferred to an agent, successor or assign of the Lender with prior notice to me; (9) the Lender, its agents, successors and assigns make no representations or warranties, expressed or implied, to the Borrower(s) regarding the property, the condition of the property, or the value of the property.

Certification: I/We certify that the information provided in this application is true and correct as of the date set forth opposite my/our signature(s) on this application and acknowledge my/our understanding that any intentional or negligent misrepresentation(s) of the information contained in this application may result in civil liability and/or criminal penalties including, but not limited to, fine or imprisonment or both under the provisions of Title 18, United States Code, Section 1001, et seq. and liability for monetary damages to the Lender, its agents, successors and assigns, insurers and any other person who may suffer any loss due to reliance upon any misrepresentation which I/we have made on this application.

Borrower's Signature	Date	Co-Borrower's Signature	Date
X *Joseph F. Lynch*	02/15/04	X *Margaret J Lynch*	02/5/04

X. INFORMATION FOR GOVERNMENT MONITORING PURPOSES

The following information is requested by the Federal Government for certain types of loans related to a dwelling, in order to monitor the Lender's compliance with equal credit opportunity, fair housing and home mortgage disclosure laws. You are not required to furnish this information, but are encouraged to do so. The law provides that a Lender may neither discriminate on the basis of this information, nor on whether you choose to furnish it. However, if you choose not to furnish it, under Federal regulations this Lender is required to note race and sex on the basis of visual observation or surname. If you do not wish to furnish the above information, please check the box below. (Lender must review the above material to assure that the disclosures satisfy all requirements to which the Lender is subject under applicable state law for the particular type of loan applied for.)

BORROWER ☐ I do not wish to furnish this information

Race/National Origin:	☐ American Indian or Alaskan Native	☐ Asian or Pacific Islander	X White, not of Hispanic origin
	☐ Black, not of Hispanic origin	☐ Hispanic	
	☐ Other (specify)		

Sex: ☐ Female X Male

CO-BORROWER ☐ I do not wish to furnish this information

Race/National Origin:	☐ American Indian or Alaskan Native	☐ Asian or Pacific Islander	X White, not of Hispanic origin
	☐ Black, not of Hispanic origin	☐ Hispanic	
	☐ Other (specify)		

Sex: X Female ☐ Male

To be Completed by Interviewer	Interviewer's Name (print or type)	Name and Address of Interviewer's Employer
This application was taken by:	William Lodovico	Fairfield Savings Association
X face-to-face interview	Interviewer's Signature Date	252 Main Street
☐ by mail	*Wilhm Lodovico* 2-15-04	Fairfield, CT 06824
☐ by telephone	Interviewer's Phone Number (incl. area code) 203-284-4591	

Freddie Mac Form 65 10/92   ITEM 7300L3 (9701)   Page 3 of 4 pages   Fannie Mae Form 1003 10/92

100101920

GREATLAND ■
To Order Call: 1-800-530-9393 ☐Fax 616-791-1131

Information Applicants Must Bring to Application

Most applicants, unless they have applied for mortgage loans before, have no idea of the amount of information they will be asked to provide a mortgage lender. In order to speed up processing, a lender should distribute to real estate brokers and/or applicants a brochure listing the information that applicants should bring to the application meeting. Many lenders and loan officers place this information on their websites or on the back of their business cards to assist potential applicants. Regardless, the information requested includes the following:

Nonfinancial information (for *all* applicants):

- Names in which title will be held and how title will be held (e.g., joint tenants) for the property being financed
- Address of property to be financed and, if available, its legal description (if the property is being purchased, include a copy of the contract of sale)
- Birth date and social security number of applicant(s) for use by credit bureau
- Principal residence address history of applicant(s) for previous two years

Financial information (for *all* applicants):

- Income history for the prior two years (verified in the form of original paycheck stubs covering the most recent month and original W-2s for the prior two years)
- Additional or supplemental income history (verified same as preceding)
- If self-employed, the most recent two years of signed, complete federal income tax returns and an accountant-prepared balance sheet and income statement for the current year
- Creditor and account number information: credit cards, revolving charges, leases, installment or automobile loans, current and past mortgages, and so forth
- Employment history for prior two years, including all names and addresses
- List of liquid assets and where they are held with account numbers and addresses (usually verified in the form of monthly statements for depository or mutual fund accounts)
- List of other investments and where they are held with account numbers and addresses

Please note that a lender should not discourage an application even if the applicants do not provide all of the preceding information at application. Sometimes it is impossible or less convenient for applicant(s) to apply in a face-to-face interview. Lending practices have become more customer-sensitive, so additional options exist for consumers who wish to apply for a mortgage but cannot meet with a loan officer: mail, telephone, and Internet applications. However, *for compliance, quality control, and customer service issues, it is strongly recommended that all mortgage loan applications be completed in a face-to-face interview.*

Applications Received by Mail

Circumstances sometimes require that an application be completed through the mail, usually when one or all out-of-town applicants cannot meet for a face-to-face interview. In these situations, a lending institution mails an application package containing several required documents. The lender should also include an instructional letter explaining the application process and providing specific directions on the following:

- Completing the application
- Requesting additional information
- Signing the various verifications
- Payment of application or other fees
- Returning the completed documentation
- Contacting the lender with questions

Upon receipt of the signed verifications contained in the completed package, the lender mails them out to the employers, depositories, and others identified on the application.

As with face-to-face applications, all of the federally mandated consumer compliance and protection regulations apply to mail-in applications. Even though the applicant completes the documentation, the lender is still responsible for compliance with these regulations and should review these applications quickly and carefully.

Internet Applications

Today, consumers have another option for submitting applications—the Internet. Internet applications comprised about 10 percent of all originations in 2002, up from only 2 percent in 1995. A lender's website is available across the nation. Lenders can reach many more consumers and become active in any geographic area of the country almost instantaneously and with minimal cost via a website. Think of the marketing opportunity this represents! Also, think about the impact it might have on a lenders' operation. While this method of origination may provide more business for the lender and additional convenience for the applicant, it also raises a number of security and compliance issues for the lender. Lenders must ensure this form of origination is consistent with their lending practices and policies and does not create compliance issues. For example, certain lenders have Community Reinvestment Act responsibilities, or may be restricted by charter (state, federal, or regulatory) and may lend only within a geographic area or to certain borrowers (e.g., credit unions can lend only to members). If Internet applications are not managed properly, the lender may lose control over who applies, what credit terms are requested, and how much application volume comes in. The result might be a net negative—the lender cannot meet the demand or spends too much time processing applications falling outside its lending area and its scope of operation, delaying service to viable applications.

Although some predictions forecast huge increases in Internet applications, a moderate but steady increase is more likely. Mortgage origination is still at its core a trust business. For most consumers, it is the largest personal financial transaction of their lives. Many applications are straightforward, but others require consultation with an informed lending expert. In order for the loan officer to provide the best advice, he or she must develop a professional relationship with the applicants in which they feel comfortable communicating their financial information and personal or family plans. Often these nonfinancial aspects have the greatest impact on what loan product is best suited to the consumer.

At present, the Internet application process cannot replicate many aspects of this important and effective personal relationship between the loan officer and consumer. For future Internet application volume to increase substantially, lenders must link together the convenience and efficiency the Internet provides with the art and skill the loan officer has in developing this relationship.

Qualifying an Applicant

The purpose of initially qualifying applicants is to provide them with the best information possible at that time. The loan officer must ask the consumer a number of general and specific follow-up questions to clarify the information disclosed and convert it into mortgage-lending use. At this stage, the purpose is not to make a credit decision, but to help the consumer and lender decide on how to proceed with the application process, if at all.

Although this is a preliminary stage, it still requires that the loan officer be familiar with all loan programs, policies and underwriting guidelines, and steps in the application process. The loan officer must then apply this information to the applicants' financial situation. When qualifying applicants, the loan officer wears three hats: business development, processor, and underwriter. The loan officer must view each situation creatively for its potential, request from the applicants the proper documentation needed to complete the transaction, and keep in mind the loan policy guidelines.

Many lenders structure their programs and policies to conform to secondary market standards. Portfolio lenders may have additional programs that provide the loan officer more flexibility and alternatives for the applicants. Secondary market agencies describe these transactions or programs as *conforming/nonconforming* or *eligible/ineligible* for the secondary market.

Areas of consideration when qualifying a mortgage applicant include loan transaction and program, debt/income ratios, credit history, collateral, and other compensating factors. This process by necessity involves a certain amount of what is traditionally called underwriting, but the information is not verified and, therefore, not final.

Qualifying an applicant involves many specific guidelines for a lender, but in its simplest form it involves addressing three main concerns: Does the proposed transaction conform to the lender's loan policy? Have the applicants demonstrated the ability and willingness to repay the proposed mortgage? Is the collateral sufficient to secure the proposed mortgage loan?

Lenders must qualify applicants fairly and in a consistent manner from loan application to loan application. Although a challenging task for lenders, the development of clear loan policies assists them in this step. These objective guidelines govern the lender's mortgage activities. They should explain how to handle the most common scenarios and should provide direction in more unusual circumstances.

The secondary market provides recommended guidelines detailing how to qualify an applicant. These industry standards develop from an ongoing statistical review of millions of loan applications across the nation and are incredibly predictive from a national perspective.

Portfolio lenders may be more familiar with the special circumstances in their region or in a particular applicant's situation. They often deviate from secondary mar-

| Exhibit 6-2 | Sample Qualification Worksheet |

FAIRFIELD SAVINGS ASSOCIATION
FIRST MORTGAGE LOAN INFORMATION

QUALIFICATION WORKSHEET

BORROWER(S)	SOC. SEC. #
Joseph F. Lynch	123-45-6789
Margaret J. Lynch	987-65-4321

INCOME EVALUATION: **PER MONTH**

BORROWER'S INCOME	$ 5000.00
COBORROWER'S INCOME	$ 4000.00
BONUS OR COMMISSION	$
INVESTMENT INCOME	$
OVERTIME	$
OTHER INCOME	$
TOTAL INCOME	$ 9250.00

CREDIT EVALUATION:

INTEREST RATE	6.000 %
TERM (YEARS)	30
POINTS	2.000%
AMOUNT	$ 189000.00
PRINCIPAL & INTEREST	$ 1133.16
REAL ESTATE TAXES	$ 250.00
INSURANCE	$ 75.00
OTHER	$ 39.38
TOTAL HOUSING EXP	$ 1497.54

INSTALLMENT DEBT	Incl	Mos	Balance
Peoples Bank	N	345	234255.00
Chase Auto Finance	Y	12	3000.00
Fleet Bank	Y	7	600.00
OTHER MONTHLY DEBT		$	$
TOTAL DEBT PAYMENTS			$ 365.91

CASH REQUIRED FOR CLOSING	$ 28310.76
CASH AVAILABLE FOR CLOSING	$ 22600.00
CASH RESERVE AFTER CLOSING	$ -5710.76

PROPERTY EVALUATION:

LOAN AMOUNT	$ 189000.00
SALES PRICE	$ 210000.00
APPRAISED PRICE	$ 210000.00
LOAN TO VALUE	90.00%

HOUSING STANDARDS:

HOUSING TO INCOME RATIO	16.19%
DEBT TO INCOME RATIO	20.15%

ket standards in their general policies or make exceptions in individual cases when, in their opinion, the industry standard is not the most appropriate guideline for their local lending area and prevents them from making an acceptable mortgage loan.

Historically, qualifying applicants for the secondary market meant following a single, specific formula into which the applicants needed to fit. As our society has evolved culturally, ethnically, and demographically, so has the approach to qualifying mortgage applicants. Although it may take a while, rest assured that our competitive, capitalist society will find creative solutions to opportunities in the marketplace! Secondary market guidelines are still structured (and with good reason), but qualifying, processing, and underwriting have evolved steadily and substantially since the mid-1980s with these changes. This chapter describes the conventional, traditional, or standard secondary market processing guidelines.

Today, lenders also have "alternative-," "streamlined-," "limited-," and even "no-documentation" programs from which to choose when selling loans on the secondary market. Separate sections in this chapter and in Chapter 7, "Underwriting the Residential Mortgage Loan," explain in further detail these and other programs. It is important to note that qualifying an applicant is a totally different issue from whether or not the lender will make a *profit* on the proposed loan. While this is a very important concern (especially for the lender), it is a separate consideration from how to qualify an applicant.

Loan Transaction and Program

Often, the first thing a loan officer discusses with the applicants is what their mortgage needs entail. A lender must obtain information about the real estate transaction and loan request. Once this information is developed, the loan officer must evaluate whether the lender's loan programs and policies can meet these needs. For example, an applicant might need a loan amount of $345,000 to complete a purchase, but the lender's loan limit is $322,700 (secondary market limit for single-family homes in continental 48 states for 2003). The applicants may qualify in all other aspects, but the lender does not offer a loan program for that amount.

Another example might be a refinance request in which the applicants need $110,000 to consolidate their consumer debt, but know this amount is 95 percent of the value of their property. In this case, the lender's loan policies might limit refinance transactions to a maximum of 90 percent of the value of the collateral (the secondary market limit for refinance transactions that take equity out of the collateral).

Mortgage bankers usually have less flexibility in this regard, so the loan officer must approve only those applications eligible for secondary market purchase. Lenders willing to hold loans in their portfolio may have more flexibility in accepting applications the secondary market deems nonconforming. Chapter 7, "Underwriting the Residential Mortgage Loan," contains more specific information on secondary market loan programs and transactions.

Debt/Income Ratios

After discussing the proposed loan transaction and program, the next qualifying area the loan officer must address is whether the applicant has the financial ability and willingness to repay the debt. A loan officer first conducts a comprehensive review of the applicant's income, debts, and credit history. This information is used to develop debt/income ratios for housing and total debt. These objective measures help evaluate the applicant's financial capacity.

Lenders calculate the housing ratio by dividing the total monthly housing expense by total monthly income. The secondary market guideline for this ratio is 28 percent, with some programs going to 33 percent or higher. The total debt ratio is total monthly debt payments divided by total monthly income. The secondary market guideline for this ratio is 36 percent, with some programs going to 38 percent or higher. Of course, if an applicant's FICO credit score is high, many lenders and investors (including Fannie Mae and Freddie Mac) place less importance on the total debt-to-income ratio.

Evaluating and verifying an applicant's qualifying income can be a complex process, depending on the circumstances. Since the loan officer may not have complete information at this time, these initial numbers are treated as estimates. Once the lender verifies all information, an underwriter determines the final figures.

Income of Applicant(s)

An applicant's income provides the means for the repayment of the mortgage debt, along with the applicant's other debts and everyday expenses. Lenders must evaluate the *amount* and the likely *continuation* of the income. Lenders must consider several sources of income in this analysis, but most income is received from the following sources:

- Wage or salary
- Self-employment
- Bonus or commissions
- Rental property
- Interest, dividends, investments, or trust
- Child support, alimony, or separate maintenance
- Retirement, pension, or disability
- Unemployment, welfare, or other sources

These sources of income have different characteristics. Lenders must consider the following questions: how regularly will it be received? Will the amount be consistent? How timely will it be paid? How reliable is the source? How long will it continue? As a result, how a lender will verify and use income to qualify an applicant varies dramatically according to its source. A precise evaluation can be difficult, because applicants receive income from many sources, and the factors affecting receipt of income are different with each application.

As is discussed later, certain regulations, particularly the Equal Credit Opportunity Act, limit the manner in which a lender can inquire about these sources of income, and privacy rules can affect what information a lender obtains and how an employer discloses it.

Lenders typically begin the income analysis by converting the applicant's disclosed income from all sources into a monthly amount, then comparing this figure with the most recent two years of income.

Wage or salary income is the most common form of income disclosed on mortgage applications. Lenders often qualify applicants using the current salary or wage level disclosed, since it is the most stable form of income. Wage or salary income is consistent

Exhibit 6-3   Sample Request for Verification of Employment

FannieMae

Request for Verification of Employment

Privacy Act Notice: This information is to be used by the agency collecting it or its assignees in determining whether you qualify as a prospective mortgagor under its program. It will not be disclosed outside the agency except as required and permitted by law. You do not have to provide this information, but if you do not your application for approval as a prospective mortgagor or borrower may be delayed or rejected. The information requested in this form is authorized by Title 38, USC, Chapter 37 (if VA); by 12 USC, Section 1701 et. seq. (if HUD/FHA); by 42 USC, Section 1452b (if HUD/CPD); and Title 42 USC, 1471 et. seq., or 7 USC, 1921 et. seq. (if USDA/FmHA).

Instructions: **Lender** - Complete items 1 through 7. Have applicant complete item 8. Forward directly to employer, named in item 1.
Employer - Please complete either Part II or Part III as applicable. Complete Part IV and return directly to lender named in item 2.
The form is to be transmitted directly to the lender and is not to be transmitted through the applicant or any other party.

Part I - Request

1. To (Name and address of employer)	2. From (Name and address of lender)
General Electric Corp. 2645 Stratfield Road Fairfield, CT 06825	Fairfield Savings Association 252 Main Street Fairfield, CT 06824

I certify that this verification has been sent directly to the employer and has not passed through the hands of the applicant or any other interested party.

3. Signature of Lender	4. Title	5. Date	6. Lender's Number (Optional)
Thomas Standa	Loan Origination	02/19/04	100101920

I have applied for a mortgage loan and stated that I am now or was formerly employed by you. My signature below authorizes verification of this information.

7. Name and Address of Applicant (include employee or badge number)	8. Signature of Applicant
Joseph F. Lynch (SS# 123-45-6789) 384 Katona Drive Fairfield, CT 06824	SEE ATTACHED AUTHORIZATION

Part II - Verification of Present Employment

9. Applicant's Date of Employment	10. Present Position	11. Probability of Continued Employment
07/17/00	Staff Accountant	Do not rate.

12A. Current **Gross** Base Pay (Enter Amount and Check Period)		13. For Military Personnel Only		14. If Overtime or Bonus is Applicable, Is Its Continuance Likely?

☒ Annual	☐ Hourly
☐ Monthly	☐ Other (Specify)
$ 60,000 — ☐ Weekly	

Pay Grade	
Type	Monthly Amount
Base Pay	$

Overtime	☐ Yes	☐ No
Bonus	☐ Yes	☐ No

12B. Gross Earnings

15. If paid hourly - average hours per week

Type	Year To Date	Past Year 16 2003	Past Year 16 2002			16. Date of applicant's next pay increase
Base Pay	Thru 2/15/19 $ 6,923.08	$ 59,743.20	$ 57,922.	Rations	$	
				Flight or Hazard	$	
Overtime	$	$	$	Clothing	$	17. Projected amount of next pay increase
				Quarters	$	
Commissions	$	$	$	Pro Pay	$	18. Date of applicant's last pay increase
				Overseas or Combat	$	
Bonus	$	$ 500.00	$			19. Amount of last pay increase
				Variable Housing Allowance	$	
Total	$	$ 60,243.20	$			

20. Remarks (If employee was off work for any length of time, please indicate time period and reason)

Part III - Verification of Previous Employment

21. Date Hired	23. Salary/Wage at Termination Per (Year) (Month) (Week)			
22. Date Terminated	Base	Overtime	Commissions	Bonus
24. Reason for Leaving		25. Position Held		

Part IV - Authorized Signature - Federal statutes provide severe penalties for any fraud, intentional misrepresentation, or criminal connivance or conspiracy purposed to influence the issuance of any guaranty or insurance by the VA Secretary, the U.S.D.A., FmHA/FHA Commissioner, or the HUD/ CPD Assistant Secretary.

26. Signature of Employer	27. Title (Please print or type)	28. Date
Harvey Beancounter	Senior Accountant	03/09/04
29. Print or type name signed in item 26 H BEANCOUNTER	30. Phone No.	

ITEM 7041L0 (9511)

GREATLAND ■ To Order Call: 1-800-530-9393

Fannie Mae
Form 1005 Mar. 90

and paid weekly, biweekly, semimonthly, or monthly. Total income from these payments are similar year to year (lenders expect to see variations of less than 15 percent).

The standard form developed by the secondary market to verify wage or salary income is the Request for Verification of Employment (Fannie Mae Form 1005, commonly called the VOE). If applicable, lenders also use this form to verify previous employment in the two-year history. Among other things, the VOE requests the following information from an employer:

- Date of employment
- Present position
- Type of income (base, overtime, commissions, bonus, military)
- Current and past two years' income
- Probability of continued employment, bonus, or overtime

To maintain the integrity of the information, the VOE must travel directly from the lender to the employer and back, not through a third party (such as the applicant or real estate broker). This can take anywhere from a few days to a few weeks, a relatively slow and cumbersome process.

Alternative Documentation

To expedite the process, the secondary market now accepts for wage or salary income verification alternative documentation ("alt doc"), consisting of paystub(s) covering the most recent month and IRS Form W-2s for the most recent two years. The applicant must bring originals to the loan officer, who copies them and certifies their authenticity. (This process of lender certification of alternative documentation is the same for verifying income, assets, debts, employment, or anything else.) For employment, alt doc requires a third step: the processor calls the employer to confirm employment and income.

The level of income on the VOE or alt docs must be consistent with the disclosed level of income used to qualify, or the underwriter may ask for additional information before final approval. Wage or salary earners rarely encounter this situation, unless substantial changes occurred during that time period.

When qualifying an applicant using other sources of income besides wage and salary, lenders frequently encounter substantial swings in total annual earnings. Overtime, bonus, part-time, interest/dividend, rental, self-employed, and even pension or retirement income levels frequently change with economic conditions, interest rates, and the employer and applicant's performance. Some income sources are discretionary, meaning the applicants have flexibility in the amount they choose to receive.

When using these sources of income to qualify an applicant, a lender will focus on the income trend over time instead of a particular income number for the current week or month. Lenders normally develop a two- or three-year average of these sources and do not rely on the current level of income. This method develops a clearer picture of the applicant's income and matches more closely the demands of repaying long-term mortgage debt.

Exhibit 6-4 Sample Tax Schedules Needed to Analyze Borrowers

Tax Schedules Needed to Analyze Borrowers

I. Sole Proprietorship
- Form 1040, signed
- Schedule C – Profit or Loss from Business or Schedule C-EZ – Net Profit from Business
- Form 4562 – Depreciation and Amortization

II. Partnership
- Form 1040, signed
- Schedule E – Supplemental Income and Loss
- K-1 (1065) – for the borrower to show percentage of ownership, whether the partnership is limited or general, and if partner is 25% or more owner
- Form 1065 – U.S. Partnership Return of Income, signed
- Form 4562 – Depreciation and Amortization
- Form 8582 – Passive Activity Loss Limitations

III. S Corporation
- Form 1040, signed
- Schedule E – Supplemental Income and Loss
- K-1 (1120S) – for the borrower to show percentage of ownership and if 25% or more owner
- Form 1120S – S Corporation Return, signed
- Form 4562 – Depreciation and Amortization
- Form 8582 – Passive Activity Loss Limitations

IV. Corporation
- Form 1040, signed
- Form 1120 – U.S. Corporate Income Return, signed
- Form 4562 – Depreciation and Amortization

V. Commission and Bonus Income
- Form 1040, signed
- Schedule A – Itemized Deductions
- Form 2106 – Employee Business Expenses
- Form 2106-EZ – Unreimbursed Employee Business Expenses

VI. Interest and Dividend Income
- Form 1040, signed
- Schedule B – Interest and Dividend Income

VII. Rental Income
- Form 1040, signed
- Schedule E – Supplemental Income and Loss
- Form 4562 – Depreciation and Amortization

VIII. Farm Income
- Form 1040, signed
- Schedule F – Farm Income
- Form 4562 – Depreciation and Amortization

Use of Tax Returns

The most common way to verify receipt of interest/dividend, rental, self-employed, pension/retirement income is by reviewing the applicants' signed, completed IRS returns (including all schedules) for the most recent two or three years. Overtime, bonus, and part-time income are commonly verified by IRS Form W-2s for the most recent two or three years (the secondary market requires this documentation if that income comprises 25 percent or more of the applicant's income). In special or unusual cases, a lender may find a more creative alt doc solution instead of IRS returns and W-2s.

At qualification a loan officer performs only an initial review with whatever documentation is available to help decide if the application should move forward. The processor will later obtain all the necessary documentation for these other sources of income and submit the loan file to underwriting. The underwriter performs a more detailed and final analysis of the IRS returns and other income documentation, along with all the other elements of the application. Chapter 7, "Underwriting the Residential Mortgage Loan," describes the steps and considerations for this review. The following sections discuss basic, additional information the loan officer seeks for qualifying an applicant with these particular sources of income.

Self-Employment

Self-employed borrowers represent the highest risk category for default. An applicant who owns 25 percent or more of a company is considered to be self-employed. In addition to the most recent two years of IRS returns, the loan officer should obtain a year-to-date, accountant-prepared, profit-and-loss statement and a balance sheet for the business. Self-employment income is considered stable income if the applicant has been self-employed for two or more years, during which time the net income is stable or increasing.

Qualifying income is calculated using the average of two years of net income from the business. Depending on the business, a lender may add back to net income the amount deducted for depreciation or other paper losses.

Interest, Dividends, Investments, and Trusts

Lenders calculate this income by averaging the past two year's income reported on the IRS returns. They may also accept as alt docs the brokers' statements, interest/dividend checks, or other account statements to verify this income. Trust income may require additional verification via the trust agreement or letter from the trust administrator.

The lender must consider whether the same assets generating this income will be available. For example, in purchase or home improvement transactions, the loan officer should determine whether the applicants will use any of these funds to complete the proposed purchase or home improvements. In these situations, those assets used for down payment, moving, or construction will not be available to generate future interest or dividend income and therefore cannot be included in qualifying income.

Rental Income

Applicants may rely upon rental income from either the subject property or other investment property. The lender must verify this income by obtaining copies of the lease agreement or IRS returns. Income from a current lease is typically discounted by 25 percent to allow for property maintenance, repairs, taxes, and a vacancy factor. This net amount is included in monthly income. Using IRS returns, net rental income is averaged over two years, with certain amounts added back to the net income figure if they are duplicated in the proposed housing expenses or elsewhere on the application.

Child Support, Alimony, or Separate Maintenance

Child support, alimony, or separate maintenance is a significant source of income for many loan applicants. Payment is mandated by a court order, divorce decree, separation, or other written agreement. Unfortunately, actual receipt of this income is typically dependent on another individual and may be inconsistent.

Lenders will use this income to qualify if verified by a review of the complete legal agreement or a letter from an attorney and payment is made in a regular manner. In some cases, lenders may verify actual receipt of the income by bank statements or copies of cancelled checks.

The loan officer must be mindful of the ECOA requirements when inquiring about this type of income. Basically, ECOA requires a lender to inform the applicant that the applicant can use this type of income but he or she can choose whether to divulge it or not.

Pension, Retirement, and Social Security

Pension, retirement, and social security income is usually a fixed amount or adjusted annually. The lender must verify this income by obtaining a letter from the company or organization providing the income or by obtaining a copy of the checks received. The lender must then compare this income to the level received in prior years for consistency and duration.

Unemployment and Welfare Payments

The ECOA states emphatically that all income must be treated equally when an applicant is trying to qualify for a mortgage loan. That includes income from unemployment, welfare payments, state assistance, or aid to dependent children. As with all other income, the lender must verify the amount received and establish its consistency and duration when determining whether it should be used to qualify applicants. If the income from these sources lasts long enough, the lender must make the loan if all other factors are in place.

Other Assets

In addition to verifying the income of an applicant, the lender will verify the assets of that applicant or coapplicant. A Request for Verification of Deposit (VOD) form should be used to verify depository accounts (savings/share, checking/draft, money market). Sometimes applicants will use these assets for the down payment, for any prepaid items such as credit report, appraisal, closing costs, moving expenses, and for those many other expenses associated with moving into a new house. If the applicants need these funds to complete the mortgage loan transaction, then the lender also must determine whether the applicants have enough verified assets to accomplish this.

If any of the funds used by an applicant come from relatives or others, a gift letter must appear in the file. The gift letter, signed by the donor, states that the funds are truly a gift and need not be repaid. The loan processor should verify that these funds exist and should be able to trace and document from where these funds came.

The applicants' ability to accumulate substantial financial assets can be an indication of how well they manage their fiscal responsibilities. An underwriter will view significant accumulated assets (such as liquid assets, retirement savings, equity real estate, or large investment portfolios) as a compensating factor to overcome a weakness in another area of the loan application.

Exhibit 6-5 Sample Request for Verification of Deposit

FannieMae
Request for Verification of Deposit

Privacy Act Notice: This information is to be used by the agency collecting it or its assignees in determining whether you qualify as a prospective mortgagor under its program. It will not be disclosed outside the agency except as required and permitted by law. You do not have to provide this information, but if you do not your application for approval as a prospective mortgagor or borrower may be delayed or rejected. The information requested in this form is authorized by Title 38, USC, Chapter 37 (If VA); by 12 USC, Section 1701 et.seq. (If HUD/FHA); by 42 USC, Section 1452b (If HUD/CPD); and Title 42 USC, 1471 et.seq. or 7 USC, 1921 et.seq. (If USDA/FmHA).

Instructions: Lender – Complete Items 1 through 8. Have applicant(s) complete Item 9. Forward directly to depository named in Item 1.
Depository – Please complete Items 10 through 18 and return DIRECTLY to lender named in Item 2.
The form is to be transmitted directly to the lender and is not to be transmitted through the applicant(s) or any other party.

Part I – Request

1. To (Name and address of depository)	2. From (Name and address of lender)
Bank of Fairfield **532 Main Street** **Fairfield, CT 06824**	**Fairfield Savings Association** **252 Main Street** **Fairfield, CT 06824**

I certify that this verification has been sent directly to the bank or depository and has not passed through the hands of the applicant or any other party.

3. Signature of lender	4. Title **Loan Origination**	5. Date 02/27/04	6. Lender's No. (Optional) 100101920

7. Information To Be Verified

Type of Account	Account in Name of	Account Number	Balance
CHECKING	**Joseph F. Lynch & Margaret J. Lynch**	**123-4059**	**$ 3000.00**
SAVINGS	**Joseph F. Lynch & Margaret J. Lynch**	**12-59690**	**$ 5000.00**
			$

To Depository: I/We have applied for a mortgage loan and stated in my financial statement that the balance on deposit with you is as shown above. You are authorized to verify this information and to supply the lender identified above with the information requested in Items 10 through 13. Your response is solely a matter of courtesy for which no responsibility is attached to your institution or any of your officers.

8. Name and Address of Applicant(s)	9. Signature of Applicant(s)
Joseph F. Lynch (SS# 123-45-6789) **Margaret J. Lynch (SS# 987-65-4321)** **384 Katona Drive** **Fairfield, CT 06824**	**SEE ATTACHED AUTHORIZATION**

To Be Completed by Depository

Part II – Verification of Depository

10. Deposit Accounts of Applicant(s)

Type of Account	Account Number	Current Balance	Average Balance For Previous Two Months	Date Opened
Sav	12.59690	$ 8733.82	$ Same	6/5/97
Checking	123.4059	$ 2321.07	$ Same	6/5/97
		$	$	

11. Loans Outstanding To Applicant(s)

Loan Number	Date of Loan	Original Amount	Current Balance	Installments (Monthly/Quarterly)	Secured By	Number of Late Payments
		$	$	$ per		
		$	$	$ per		
		$	$	$ per		

12. Please include any additional information which may be of assistance in determination of credit worthiness. (Please include information on loans paid-in-full in Item 11 above.)

13. If the name(s) on the account(s) differ from those listed in Item 7, please supply the name(s) on the account(s) as reflected by your records.

Part III – Authorized Signature - Federal statutes provide severe penalties for any fraud, intentional misrepresentation, or criminal connivance or conspiracy purposed to influence the issuance of any guaranty or insurance by the VA Secretary, the U.S.D.A., FmHA/FHA Commissioner, or the HUD/CPD Assistant Secretary.

14. Signature of Depository Representative Cindy Barlow	15. Title (Please print or type) Branch Manager	16. Date 3/5/04
17. Please print or type name signed in item 14 Cindy Barlow	18. Phone No.	

ITEM 7042L0 (0203) GREATLAND ■ To Order Call: 1-800-530-9393 □ Fax 616-791-1131

Fannie Mae
 Form 1006 July 96

Credit History

Of great concern to any mortgage lender is how the applicants handle their past credit responsibilities. Many lenders would argue that this is the most significant element of the mortgage application. A credit report provides objective information that helps lenders evaluate the applicants' current amount of outstanding debt and the payment history for active and prior debts. A basic credit report must be issued by an independent credit-reporting agency (or credit bureau) and lists the information it has for all of the applicants' debts that are disclosed on the application or found elsewhere. The credit-reporting agency relies on its own files, various national repositories of credit information, and public records. This may include the following information: loan type, account number, open or closed status and dates, highest and current balance, and monthly payment.

A lender should order a report for all applicants for every residential mortgage loan application. The lender needs the full name and Social Security number for each applicant. Married applicants are reported jointly, since many credit accounts are jointly held. If the applicants are not married to each other and wish to be co-borrowers, then the lender must order separate credit reports for each.

The credit report should verify all the information disclosed on the application, especially the number of creditors and amount of outstanding debt. Occasionally, there are discrepancies since many applicants cannot remember all details exactly. The lender should compare the credit report information to that disclosed on the application. If this comparison shows significant discrepancies, major omissions, or erroneous information of a serious nature for the most recent two years of credit history, then the applicant should provide a written explanation.

Additionally, some creditors do not report to a national credit repository or report infrequently, so the information is outdated. In these cases the lender will complete verification by mailing a Verification of Loan form to the creditor or by requesting the applicant provide a loan statement. In either case, the lender attempts to verify the same information that would be included in a credit report.

An applicant may not be aware of some of the information contained in a credit report, especially if the information is incorrect. If the applicant believes a mistake has been made, the lender should advise the applicant to discuss the information with the credit bureau directly. On occasion, credit bureaus receive wrong information that can be corrected by a discussion between the applicant and the credit bureau.

Credit-reporting agencies encounter many difficulties in trying to coordinate information into one format from the different computer systems of hundreds of thousands of creditors nationwide. In the past, these reports contained many errors, especially if the applicant changed names (such as through marriage), had a common name ("Davis," "Jones," "Smith," etc.), or was a Jr., II, III, and so forth. Although the system is not perfect, credit bureaus now produce more accurate credit information, partly as a result of better reporting by individual creditors.

On a monthly basis, credit-reporting agencies receive and store an enormous amount of confidential and sensitive information in the regular monthly reporting by creditors. As a result, the bureaus are held to strict standards by federal and state regulations (the Fair Credit Reporting Act, among others). Internet reporting raises

Exhibit 6-6   Explanation of a Credit Account

EXPLANATION OF A CREDIT ACCOUNT
The information on the report is set in columns as described below.

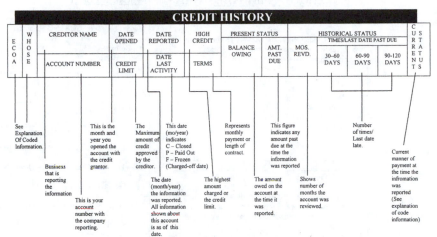

HOW TO READ A CREDIT ACCOUNT

ECOA	WHOSE	CREDITOR NAME / ACCOUNT NUMBER	DATE OPENED / CREDIT LIMIT	DATE REPORTED / DATE LAST ACTIVITY	HIGH CREDIT / TERMS	PRESENT STATUS BALANCE OWING	AMT PAST DUE	MOS. REVD.	30–60 DAYS	60-90 DAYS	90-120 DAYS	CURRENT STATUS
I	B	PEOPLES BANK 1234567891011	7/90 125k	11/98	125000 360 x 105	123620	1015	29	3 11/98	1 12/97	1 1/98	M02

2111111111143221111111111
*OPTIONAL – SEE BELOW

This is an individual account of the Borrower's with Peoples Bank. The account number is 1234567891011. The account was last reported on 11/98. The account was opened in 7/90, and the highest amount charged to the account was $125,000.00. The current balance owed on the account is $123,620.00, and the account is currently rated M02 (30 days past due). The amount past due is $1015.00. The terms of the loan are 360 months @ $105.00 per month. The account has been reviewed for 29 months and the prior paying history indicates that the account was 30 days past due 3 time(s), 60 days past due 1 time(s), and 90+ days past due 1 time(s). The most recent time the account was 30 days past due was November 1998. The most recent time the account was 60 days past due was December 1997, and the most recent time the account was 90 days or more past due was January 1998.

(*Optional) Up to 24-month payment pattern. The first entry corresponds to the date reported and proceeds back in time.

X – no history reported	03 – 60 days late
01 – payment on time	04 – 90 days late
02 – 30 days late	05 – 120 or more days late

Exhibit 6-6   Explanation of a Credit Account (continued)

EXPLANATION OF CODED INFORMATION

(ECOA)

The Equal Credit Opportunity Act designators explain who is responsible for the account and the type of participation you have with the account.

P - Participating
J - Joint
I - Individual
U - Undesignated
A - Authorized user
T - Terminated
M - Maker
S - Co-Maker

Type of Account

O - Open Account (30 days or 90 days)
R - Revolving or Option (open-end account)
I - Installment (fixed number of payments)
M - Mortgage
C - Line of Credit

WHOSE ACCOUNT

The Whose Account designators explain who is responsible for the individual accounts.

B – Borrower
C – Co-Borrower

COURT – CODES

MU – Municipal Court	M2 – 2nd Magisterial Court
SU – Superior Court	M3 – 3rd Magisterial Court
DO – Domestic Court	M4 – Quarterly Court
FE – Federal District Crt.	CC – County Clerk's Office
JU – Justice of the Peace	CH – Chancery Court
SC – Small Claims	GS – General Session
CI – Circuit Court	IC – Inferior Court
M1 – 1st Magisterial Crt.	PR – Probate Court

CURRENT MANNER OF PAYMENT

00 Too new to rate approved but not used
01 Pays (or paid) within 30 days of billing; pays account as agreed.
02 Pays (or paid) in more than 30 days, but not more than 60 days, or not more than one payment past due.
03 Pays (or paid) in more than 60 days, but not more than 90 days or two payments past due.
04 pays (or paid) in more than 90 days, but not more than 120 days, or three or more payments past due.
05 Pays (or paid) in more than 120 days
07 Making regular payments under wage earner plan or similar arrangements
08 Repossession
09 Charged to Profit & Loss.
09b Collection Account

Exhibit 6-6   Explanation of a Credit Account

Credit Information Bureau Mortgage Services
600 Saw Mill Rd., P.O. Box 26775
West Haven, CT 06516
203-931-2020

Page 1 of 6
ISSUED: 11/27/01
FNMA REF: A-111429832
Merged Report

Prepared for: B1234	Date: 11/27/01 $_.00
AMPSLink Test Customer	Loan Number: TESTER123
600 Saw Mill Rd	Requested By: ADB Analyst: VMV
West Haven, CT 06516	Repository Source: TU, EXP, EQX

—————————— Borrower ——————————   —————————— Co-Borrower ——————————

Name: VINCENT ATACOMMON	Name:
Address: 16 WALNUT DR	Address:
FANTASY ISLAND, IL 60750	
Since: Status:	Since: Status:
SSN: 111-42-9832 Age:	SSN: Age:
Marital Status:	Marital Status:
Employer:	Employer:
Position:	Position:
Hired:	Hired:
Verified: R On:	Verified: On:
Comment:	Comment:

—————————— Former ——————————   —————————— Former ——————————

Address:	Address:
From: To:	From: To:
Employer:	Employer:
Hired:	Hired:
Verified: R On:	Verified: On:
Comment:	Comment:

CREDIT HISTORY

E C O A	W h o s e	Creditor Name / Account Number	Date Opened / Credit Limit	Date Reported / Last Activity	High Credit / Terms	Balance Owing	Amount Past Due	Mos Rev	30-59 Days	60-89 Days	90-120 Days	Current Status
J	B	MELLON BK 2600493000000 DLA: 08/01 COMMENT: SECURED	06/96 $84750	08/01A 08/01	$84750 1020	$51731		61				I01 EQX
J	B	MELLON BK-N 4700000002600 CREDIT LINE SEC DLA: 10/01 COMMENT: 087 RD2 W MIDX 16159	08/98 $75000	10/01A	$12388 MIN137	$12398 111111111111111111111111	$0	39	0	0	0	C01 TU
J	B	CITIBK USA 549137100002 ESTIMATED MONTHLY PAYMENT: $64 DLA: 08/01 COMMENT: CREDIT CARD COMMENT: AMOUNT IN H/C COLUMN IS CREDIT LIMIT	02/96 $11600	08/01A 08/01	$11600	$1290		27				R01 EQX
J	B	MELLON BANK 54913710 CREDIT CARD DLA: 10/01	04/96 $11600	10/01A	$1828 MIN27	$1290 111111111111111111111111	$0	48	0	0	0	R01 TU

Exhibit 6-6 / Explanation of a Credit Account (continued)

Credit Information Bureau Mortgage Services		FNMA REF: A-111429832 Page 2 of 6

Borrower Name: VINCENT ATACOMMON   SSN:111-42-9832
Co-Borrower Name: SSN:

CREDIT HISTORY

E C O A	W h o s e	Creditor Name / Account Number	Date Opened / Credit Limit	Date Reported / Last Activity	High Credit / Terms	Present Status		Historical Status				Current Status
						Balance Owing	Amount Past Due	Mos Rev	30 - 59 Days	60 - 89 Days	90 - 120 Days	
J	B	KAUFMANNS 88790000 DLA: 07/01	07/91 $908	07/01A 07/01	$908 70	$503		99				R01 EQX
J	B	KAUFMANNS 8879 DLA: 10/01	09/91 $908	11/01A	$908 MIN60	$459 1111X11111111111111X11111	$0	48	0	0	0	R01 TU
I	B	GANTOS INC 102080000 DLA: 02/01 COMMENT: CHARGE	12/99 $168	07/01A 02/01	$168 15	$42		19				R01 EQX
I	B	JCP--MCCBG 77620120 DLA: 10/01	07/74 $654	10/01A	$654 MIN20	$42 11111111111111111111111	$0	12	0	0	0	R01 TU
I	B	JCP-MCCBG 6-077620120000 DLA: 08/01 COMMENT: CHARGE MAX DEL: 04/96 2	05/74 $654	08/01A 08/01	$654 20	$42		86	2	0	0	R01* EQX
I	B	GANTOS 10208 CHARGE ACCOUNT DLA: 10/01	02/00 $500	10/01A	$168 MIN15	$22 1111111111111111111XX1	$0	12	0	0	0	R01 TU
J	B	717 CR UN 251 LINE OF CREDIT DLA: 04/00	11/90 $6000	05/00A 04/00P	$6000	$0 1XXXXXXXXXXXXXXXXXXXXXXX	$0	48	0	0	0	C01 TU
S	B	717 CR UN 251 AUTOMOBILE	09/96 $10545	06/99A 05/99P	$10545 37M322	$0 X1111111111111111111111	$0	33	0	0	0	I01 TU
J	B	717 CR UN 2510000 DLA: 03/99 COMMENT: PAID ACCOUNT/ZERO BALANCE COMMENT: AUTO	07/96 $10545	04/99A 03/99	$10545 322	$0		33				I01 EQX
J	B	717 CR UN 2510000 DLA: 02/00 COMMENT: LINE OF CREDIT	09/90 $6000	03/00A 02/00	$6000	$0		44				R01 EQX

Exhibit 6-6 / Explanation of a Credit Account

Credit Information Bureau Mortgage Services   FNMA REF: A-111429832

Borrower Name: VINCENT ATACOMMON   SSN:111-42-9832
Co-Borrower Name: SSN:

CREDIT HISTORY

ECOA	Whose	Creditor Name / Account Number	Date Opened / Credit Limit	Date Reported / Last Activity	High Credit / Terms	Present Status — Balance Owing	Present Status — Amount Past Due	Historical Status — Mos Rev	30 - 59 Days	60 - 89 Days	90 - 120 Days	Current Status

```
------------------------------------------------------------------------------------
                                    SUMMARY
------------------------------------------------------------------------------------
                  *************** CURRENT STATUS ***************
ACCOUNT TYPE      #TRDS      CURRENT       CL/PD       UR       30      60      90+
------------------------------------------------------------------------------------
MORTGAGE            2           0            2          0        0       0       0
INSTALLMENT        11           1           10          1        0       0       0
REVOLVING          21          18            3          2        0       0       0
OPEN LINE OF CR     4           2            2          0        0       0       1
MISCELLANEOUS       0           0            0          0        0       0       0

TOTAL              38          21           17          3        0       0       1

------------------------------------------------------------------------------------
                                  ******* HISTORICAL STATUS ******
                                          #DEL
ACCOUNT TYPE      PAYMENT       BALANCE    TRDS         30              60          90+
------------------------------------------------------------------------------------
MORTGAGE            $0            $0         0           0               0           0
INSTALLMENT         $0        $51,731       0           0               0           0
REVOLVING         $215         $3,690       1           2               0           0
OPEN LINE OF CR   $137        $12,398       1           0               0           0
MISCELLANEOUS       $0            $0         0           0               0           0

TOTAL             $352        $67,819       2           2               0           0

AVAILABLE LINE OF CREDIT: $133,530

------------------------------------------------------------------------------------
        COLLECTIONS            INQUIRIES              PUBLIC RECORDS
       LAST 24MTHS            LAST 12MTHS              LAST 24MTHS
            0                      3                        0
------------------------------------------------------------------------------------
```

Exhibit 6-6   Explanation of a Credit Account (continued)

Credit Information Bureau Mortgage Services   FNMA REF: A-111429832

Borrower Name: VINCENT ATACOMMON   SSN:111-42-9832
Co-Borrower Name: SSN:

CREDIT HISTORY

ECOA	Whose	Creditor Name	Date Opened	Date Reported	High Credit	Present Status		Historical Status				Current Status
		Account Number	Credit Limit	Last Activity	Terms	Balance Owing	Amount Past Due	Mos Rev	30-59 Days	60-89 Days	90-120 Days	

```
-----------------------------------------------------------------------
                           SCORING SUMMARY
-----------------------------------------------------------------------
The point scoring shown is derived from the original infile data compiled from
each repository used, prior to the elimination of duplicate tradelines.

Trans Union
  01- NEW EMPIRICA: 690 [040, 010, 006, 014]
      (ATACOMMON, VINCENT M)
      REASON 1: DEROGATORY PUBLIC RECORD OR COLLECTION FILED
      REASON 2: PROPORTION OF BALANCES TO CREDIT LIMITS IS TOO HIGH ON BANK
                REVOLVING OR OTHER REVOLVING ACCOUNTS
      REASON 3: TOO MANY CONSUMER FINANCE COMPANY ACCOUNTS
      REASON 4: LENGTH OF TIME ACCOUNTS HAVE BEEN ESTABLISHED

Equifax
  01- BEACON: 761 [02, 10, 04, 05]
      (ATACOMMON, VINCENT S)
      REASON 1: LEVEL OF DELINQUENCY ON ACCOUNT
      REASON 2: PROPORTION OF BALANCES TO CREDIT LIMITS IS TOO HIGH ON BANK
                REVOLVING OR OTHER REVOLVING ACCOUNTS
      REASON 3: TOO MANY BANK OR NATIONAL REVOLVING ACCOUNTS
      REASON 4: TOO MANY ACCOUNTS WITH BALANCES
```

additional privacy concerns. As these privacy laws develop, lenders are responsible for ensuring that the credit bureau they use—acting as an agent for the lender—is currently and always will be in compliance with these increasingly complex regulations.

The secondary mortgage market requires a certain kind of credit report that includes more than just the computer-generated information that a simpler, standard factual credit report provides. The Residential Mortgage Credit Report (RMCR) provides the following additional information:

- Credit information from two national credit repositories
- Check of public records for divorce, liens, judgments, etc.
- Verification (if possible) of current employment and address of employer
- List of credit inquiries within previous 90 days
- Credit score or scores

RMCRs must be dated within 90 days of the mortgage closing date to be valid and must also contain a certification that they meet the standards of Fannie Mae, Freddie Mac, the VA, and HUD. At the time a lender orders a credit report, it should indicate to the credit agency or bureau the type of loan being considered for the applicant (i.e., conventional, FHA, or VA) and should be sure that any respective investors approve of that credit-reporting agency.

Credit Scores

Most credit reports today include a **credit score**—a numeric rating of the applicant's overall credit history. Several companies produce credit scores, each with its own proprietary formula for calculating the score. Many factors are considered in arriving at a score. Fair, Isaac and Company (the term *FICO* comes from its name) states that the factors used to score people are as follows:

- What is their payment history? Roughly 35 percent of score.
- Do they owe too much? 30 percent of score.
- How established is their credit? 15 percent of score.
- Do they have a "healthy" mix of credit? 10 percent of score.
- Are they taking on more debt? 10 percent of score.

A person's score also may be affected by repeated applications for credit, though the model treats multiple inquiries in a short period of time as a single inquiry, to avoid penalizing consumers for shopping for the best rate.

Secondary market programs have different guidelines for the use of credit scores, with many programs establishing a minimum value required for that loan program. Automated origination and underwriting systems may issue their own credit reports or may simply provide the lender with a summary evaluation of the credit history and account information.

Derogatory Items

When qualifying applicants, the loan officer should also explain how the lender defines an "acceptable credit history" in its loan policy or for that particular program. Most lenders consider only the most recent two years of credit history, with the following entries on a credit report categorized as "derogatory items," which adversely affect the credit decision:

- Late payments
- Past due and/or collection accounts
- Law suits
- Judgments
- Bankruptcy
- Concealed liabilities
- Numerous recent inquiries

Exhibit 6-7 / Determining Desktop Underwriter's Recommendation

FAIRFIELD SAVINGS ASSOCIATION
FIRST MORTGAGE LOAN INFORMATION

What factors does Desktop Underwriter consider?

If Desktop Underwriter is used to underwrite your loan, it will make a recommendation to your lender based upon the following risk factors:

Credit Report Factors	*Non-Credit Report Factors*
• Credit history	• Equity and loan-to-value ratio
• Delinquent accounts	• Liquid reserves
• Credit card accounts	• Debt-to-income ratio
• Public records, foreclosures, and collection accounts	• Loan purpose
	• Loan type
• Inquiries	• Loan term
	• Property type
	• Number of borrowers
	• Self-employed borrowers

None of these factors alone determines Desktop Underwriter's recommendation. Desktop Underwriter evaluates *all* of the risk factors to help the lender reach a decision about your loan application. When Desktop Underwriter determines that a loan application does not appear to meet its credit risk criteria, it refers the loan to the lender for further review and provides suggestions about where additional information could be helpful.

Desktop Underwriter's recommendation is taken into consideration by your lender, but it is not the definitive element in the final decision. The final decision to approve or deny your mortgage loan application is always made by your lender.

© 2000, Fannie Mae.

In some situations, a mortgage lender may not be able to justify a loan to an applicant regardless of current income or assets because of past credit problems. Unless the applicant supplies a written explanation with an acceptable reason for the credit problems, the lender may decline the application for an unacceptable credit history, delinquent credit obligations, or insufficient credit history. In all situations, applicants should be advised that if the loan is turned down because of adverse credit information, they may contact the credit bureau that furnished the derogatory information.

A mortgage lender must be aware of the Fair Credit Reporting Act and the limitations that are placed on credit information gathering. That law, as mentioned earlier, is designed to ensure the fair and accurate reporting of information regarding consumer credit. A mortgage lender seeking credit information from a consumer reporting agency must certify the purpose for which the information is sought and use it for no other purpose. This act prohibits investigative reports, which are based on interviews with noncreditors relating to character, general reputation, mode of living, and other subjective areas.

Collateral

At qualification the loan officer should also clarify the collateral and appraisal requirements for the mortgage loan. This means the loan officer should inquire about the house the applicants will be financing and explain how the lender will appraise it.

Housing standards vary tremendously from community to community across the country. Lenders develop fairly specific standards for property types they will finance based on local housing characteristics. These standards may specify property types (single- or multifamily, condominium, Planned Unit Development (PUD), vacation/seasonal, construction, land, etc.) and other features such as minimum square footage, heating and electrical, acreage, zoning restrictions, and flood insurance. Depending on the lender's charter, additional regulatory appraisal requirements may shape the appraisal policy and how it impacts mortgage applicants.

Lenders obtain an appraisal for the subject property to establish whether the condition and value of the property is sufficient for the loan amount and product requested. The standard appraisal form used is the Fannie Mae/Freddie Mac Form 1004/70. Most lenders use this form for all loan applications, but now the secondary market has developed less comprehensive forms. A lender can order this appraisal at application, but most wait until after the processor completes an initial review of the debt/income ratios and credit report. This saves the applicants the costly appraisal fee if other problems in the application jeopardize an approval.

Additionally, prior to application, the lender should make the applicants— especially first-time homebuyers—aware of the responsibilities and obligations a mortgage lien entails for both lender and borrower. The mortgage document the applicants sign at closing includes many covenants regarding lender's and borrower's rights and obligations regarding the property, including maintenance, access, defense of title, **hazard insurance**, taxes, and so forth.

Finally, at qualification, the loan officer should explain briefly the mortgage closing and lien process, along with other legal requirements. The loan officer should provide useful information, but should not attempt to explain the issues as a legal counsel. The loan officer should recommend the applicants engage an attorney for professional legal advice and counsel. Since a mortgage lien is a legal transaction recorded in public records, it involves a number of legal issues. In many states attorneys or other legal representatives such as title companies handle the mortgage transaction.

Again, the secondary market provides industry standards for both the appraisal process and for the mortgage (or deed of trust). It is highly recommended that lenders use the uniform documentation established by Fannie Mae and Freddie Mac for appraisals and legal forms—mortgages, riders, assignments, and so forth.

Other Compensating Factors

Loan officers, in their discussion with potential applicants at qualification, may discover an event that significantly impacted the applicants' financial situation. If this event was unique or unusual and nonrecurring, then the negative impact may be compensated for by another strength in the loan application. For example, the loan officer notices that last year's W-2 earnings are much lower than the current salary, but finds out that the applicant was injured in a car accident and out of work for several months. Other strengths, like high year-to-date earnings or large cash reserves may compensate for this negative feature, even with a high loan-to-value loan. An effective loan officer must develop a sense for discovering the reasons behind the events that negatively impact applicants' chances for loan approval.

Final Check

Before sending a residential mortgage loan file on to an underwriter, a loan processor should review the file to ascertain that all required documents are present and properly prepared. The file should include the following items:

- Application—both updated typed and preliminary applications
- Sufficient verification of employment, credit, and deposits via VOEs, VODs, VOLs, or alt docs
- Residential Mortgage Credit Report and credit explanations, if needed
- Appraisal report
- Compliance review to confirm that all federally mandated consumer protection requirements have been followed for

  1. ECOA
  2. RESPA
  3. Truth-in-Lending
  4. Flood insurance
  5. Fair housing
  6. Servicing
  7. Others (if applicable)

Exhibit 6-8   First Mortgage Loan Documentation

FIRST MORTGAGE LOAN DOCUMENTATION.

PRELIMINARY ANALYSIS.
> **Loan Products / Rate Sheet**
> **Pre-Qualification Worksheet**
> **Applicant Documentation List (what to bring to application)**

APPLICATION.
> **Processing Checklist / Borrower Contact Sheet**
> **Original Application**
> **Verifications of Employment, Deposit, Loan**
> **IRS Form 4506**
> **Application Fee Itemization**
> **Initial ARM Disclosure**
> **Truth-In-Lending Disclosure**
> **Good Faith Estimate**
> **Fair Lending Notice**
> **Servicing Transfer Notice**
> **Applicant Certification & Authorization**
> **Rate Lock-In Agreement**

PROCESSING.
> **Copy of Original Application**
> **Credit Report**
> **Sales Agreement**
> **Additional Documentation Request Form**

UNDERWRITING.
> **Underwriting Worksheet**
> **Underwriting Conditions/Summary Sheet**
> **Commitment Letter / Adverse Action Notice**
> **Underwriting Transmittal Summary**

PRE-CLOSING PACKAGE.
> **Closing Documentation Checklist**
> **Insured Closing Letter**
> **Instructions to Closing Agent**
> **Underwriter Conditions Needed**
> **Closing Disbursement Funds**
> **Initial Payment Letter**

FINAL CLOSING PACKAGE.
> **Executed Note**
> **Title Insurance Policy / Schedules / Endorsements**
> **Auto Insurance Binder / Policy**
> **Compliance Agreement**
> **W-9(s)**
> **Name Affidavit / Notarization**

REMOC ASSOCIATES, LTD.

• Proper fees collected for

1. Credit report
2. Appraisal
3. Points or discounts
4. Other third-party expenditures

The processor should forward to the underwriter a complete mortgage file as expeditiously as possible. It is not recommended that the person who processed a loan be the same person who underwrites the loan. The chances for error or fraud in this situation are too great. If a lending institution is too small for a full-time, qualified underwriter, it should use an independent underwriting service, one of the private mortgage insurance companies, or a secondary market automated underwriting service.

Discussion Points

1. In what three general ways have mortgage origination and processing changed in the last 20 years?

2. How has technology impacted mortgage origination and processing (discuss the benefits and drawbacks)?

3. What documentation should a consumer bring to a mortgage lender when applying for a loan?

4. What special challenges do Internet applications present?

5. What three issues must a lender identify when qualifying an applicant and why are they important?

6. Discuss the benefits and risks of using alternative documentation loan programs.

Underwriting the Residential Mortgage Loan

Introduction

Many segments in the American economy use the term *underwriting* to describe the process of analyzing information relating to risk and making a decision whether to accept that risk. Life and hazard insurance underwriting is an example of this risk analysis. In real estate, the purpose of an underwriting review is to analyze the features of the mortgage application, determine whether the cumulative risk is acceptable to the lender and falls within its lending guidelines, and establish the final conditions under which the lender will approve, deny, or make a counteroffer to the application.

Underwriting is an integral part of the mortgage-lending process, regardless of the type of transaction, loan product, borrower, or property involved. It follows a similar process for all different types of residential mortgage loans—conventional or government loans, or those loans intended to be sold or placed in portfolio. Any differences are more procedural and not of great significance.

Today, many lenders have turned to automated underwriting (AU) for an underwriting decision. An automated underwriting system, such as Fannie Mae's Desktop Underwriter, determines the creditworthiness of an applicant by assigning points to certain attributes and facts. These complex software programs use an enormous loan performance database for the basis of their calculations and analysis. AU is discussed later in this chapter.

This chapter first examines the underlying issues and risks, explains the practical steps involved in underwriting a residential mortgage loan, and reviews how underwriting has evolved and is practiced today.

Underwriting by a Mortgage Lender

No regulations require a residential mortgage lender to make a particular loan, nor do any provide specific underwriting guidelines. Regulations do make it clear, however, that mortgage lenders have a responsibility to attempt to satisfy any request for a mortgage loan, *as long as the risk is analyzed fully and deemed acceptable*. The desire to make loans must be balanced by a mortgage lender's fiduciary responsibility to protect whoever funds the loan: depositors, shareholders, or secondary market investors.

All lenders, of course, share the danger that even properly underwritten mortgages may become delinquent. The expense incurred in collecting these funds, or the losses suffered if uncollected, greatly exceed the income generated from originating and servicing the loan—that is how costly the collection process is. If several defaults occur, the costs of either curing the defaults or foreclosing could result in severe losses to the point where it jeopardizes the solvency of the lender.

Mortgage brokers and mortgage bankers have a unique problem. Unlike deposit-based mortgage lenders, mortgage brokers and mortgage bankers underwrite a loan knowing that the loan must be sold to a permanent investor. If a poorly processed or poorly underwritten loan is not secondary marketable at a reasonable price, it may result in considerable loss to a mortgage banker or broker. Since a deposit-based mortgage lender has the option of placing a mortgage into its own portfolio (instead of selling it to an investor), its loss potential for a poorly processed/underwritten mortgage is less than that of a mortgage banker.

In any event, the underwriting phase has significant, lasting financial effects. It is imperative that all mortgage lenders adopt prudent guidelines, maintain an objective reporting structure, develop professional underwriting expertise, and review underwriting performance through quality control.

Analyzing Risk

All mortgage loans involve the risk of possible financial loss to a mortgage lender, investor, or insurer. Depending on its circumstances, a single mortgage application may undergo four separate underwriting reviews at various stages by the following parties:

Stage 1.   Lender: The loan officer and/or processor review the application to determine whether it warrants full processing or an immediate credit decision. Automated underwriting may be used at this stage.

Stage 2.   Lender: After processing, the underwriter analyzes the application to determine whether to lend funds and under what conditions.

Stage 3.   Insurer/Guarantor: Before closing, a mortgage insurer or guarantor determines whether the submitted application is eligible for mortgage insurance or a guarantee.

Stage 4.   Investor: Before or after closing, a permanent investor determines whether the mortgage or mortgages as submitted will be purchased and at what price.

Each underwriter analyzes the loan package, estimates the risk to its organization, and determines whether the benefits are sufficient to balance the risk. The following kinds of risks are present in a typical residential mortgage loan:

- Credit
- Interest fate
- Collateral
- Default
- Compliance

- Price and market
- Liquidity
- Secondary market
- Portfolio

When reviewing an individual mortgage application, a lender's underwriter is mostly concerned with determining credit, collateral, compliance, and possibly secondary market risk, as they all relate to default risk. The other areas of risk are more toward management, operations, and finance—equally important, but typically not within the scope of the underwriter's file review.

The underwriting analysis quantifies the risk factors present and measures these against other strengths in the file to determine whether the strengths offset the weaknesses. The price of the mortgage—the interest rate and points paid by the borrower to the investor—rises *incrementally* with the number and extent of risk factors present in the loan. Although the price of the mortgage increases, the risk of default—and financial loss to the lender, insurer, guarantor, or investor—rises *exponentially* with each additional high-risk factor in the loan. Underwriters use the term *risk stacking* to describe this situation.

It is important to understand that these risks in mortgage lending are never eliminated completely—risks can only be managed. Mortgage lending is a risk business, and each party must assume some risk in order to earn a fee or make a profit. The questions are how much risk and for how much reward?

Underwriting Guidelines

The need for underwriting guidelines to address areas of risk in mortgage lending is evident. In addition, regulations—and sound business practice—require lenders to qualify applicants fairly and in a consistent manner from loan application to loan application. Clear loan policies and objective underwriting guidelines assist lenders in this challenging task. Such guidelines should explain how lenders must handle the most common scenarios and provide direction in more unusual circumstances.

Before the development and dominance of the secondary market, mortgage lending and underwriting was relatively fragmented. Each lender developed unique policies, programs, and procedures as a result of its charter, state/local laws, and financial situation. Each lender employed different underwriting rules and formulas.

Today, it is still the case that no single method of underwriting exists for all residential mortgage loans. In fact, no single uniform set of underwriting guidelines exists. And it is important to stress that only *guidelines* exist—not specific, precise formulas to apply to every applicant. This illustrates the scope of diversity and complexity involved in underwriting mortgage loans on a national basis.

However, most lenders follow the core underwriting guidelines of Fannie Mae and Freddie Mac as delineated in their separate *Seller/Servicer Guides*, or of government programs (such as FHA or VA). These industry standards develop from an ongoing statistical review of millions of loan applications submitted across the nation and are incredibly predictive from a national perspective. Today, similarities in underwriting guidelines for either conventional or government loans far outweigh their differences. Even lenders that don't intend to sell loans in the secondary mortgage market should follow these well-conceived underwriting guidelines. They provide the industry with much needed uniformity, ease of use, and have proved effective in avoiding delinquency.

Use of Technology for Underwriting

Although advances in technology have not resulted in one uniform set of underwriting guidelines, they have inspired an equally fundamental change. Improved data management and statistical analysis over the last decade now enable investors, secondary market players, and large lenders to analyze an unprecedented amount of loan data—millions of loans nationwide! They compare loan performance and identify more precisely what specific feature(s) affect repayment, default, and loan loss.

As a result, there is now a shift to base most (if not all) underwriting guidelines and reviews on empirical results derived from this data. Two positive results of this shift to technology are the number of loan programs now offered to the consumer and the measuring of various features statistically, which implies objectivity and fairness.

Negative results are complexity and confusion caused by these numerous loan programs. Different rates, points, and fees apply to each loan program, with adjustments for LTV, employment, **debt/income ratios**, cash reserves, property type, documentation, and credit score. Complicated underwriting matrices detail all these adjustments.

Conflicting Objectives?

The ability to perform these statistical analyses and their resulting program guidelines place underwriting at the focal point of two seemingly conflicting objectives:

- Regulator/consumer trend toward equal treatment of and uniformity for each application
- Investor/lender trend toward risk-based pricing of each application and, along with it, underwriting guidelines that reflect its unique risk profile

Although today's underwriter has access to sophisticated automated underwriting systems, credit scores, and mortgage scores, the time-honored industry saying still rings true: "underwriting is an art, not a science." A successful underwriter's greatest asset is not these powerful analytic tools, but applying common sense and creativity to the many situations that arise when qualifying mortgage applicants. More important than which underwriting guidelines a lender selects is how skillfully the underwriter follows them.

Underwriting Areas of Review

The areas of review set by a lender's underwriting guidelines should address the different risks inherent in mortgage lending (listed previously in this chapter). What does an underwriter review when making a loan decision? Which issues are significant and to what extent?

No discussion of mortgage underwriting would be complete without referencing the traditional areas of a loan application the underwriter must consider, the three Cs of lending: credit, capacity, and collateral.

- *Credit*—do the applicants have an acceptable credit history? Have they used credit responsibly?
- *Capacity*—do the applicants have the financial resources to repay the proposed and existing debts?
- *Collateral*—is the property sufficient collateral to secure the loan?

Lenders also look at a fourth "C"—that of character. Today, residential mortgage lenders consider this area in different ways—formally and informally—or fold it into other areas of review because it is subjective. *Character* is traditionally defined as the "willingness" to repay the debt—something very difficult to measure objectively. Lenders evaluate this from a review of the other "C's" listed above, considered within the context of the real estate transaction for which the applicants seek financing.

While this area is difficult to define, many lenders argue it may be the most influential factor in evaluating an application. Some borrowers with sufficient capacity elect not to repay their obligations. Others with "blemished" credit histories and low FICO scores are willing to make significant sacrifices and change their behavior to keep their mortgage current. The art of lending is developing the skill to distinguish which situation you have in front of you when making the credit decision. Local lenders tied more closely to their communities and their customers may argue they are better able to develop this history and skill than statistically-based automated underwriting systems or distant underwriters who have no experience and no other connection to their applicants.

Prequalifications of Applicants

The underwriting review in many ways mirrors the criteria loan officers consider when they prequalify applicants at application: loan transaction and program, debt/income ratios, credit history, collateral, and other compensating factors. The difference here is the underwriter now has verified information and can review the file to see whether "the whole picture" fits together. If it does not, the underwriter must consider under what terms a marginal application can be approved.

Historically, underwriters were perceived as those people who found ways to say, "No." Also, historically, secondary market underwriting meant following a single, specific formula into which the applicants needed to fit. As our society has evolved culturally, ethnically, and demographically, so has the approach to qualifying mortgage applicants. Secondary market guidelines still provide structure (and with good reason), but today's underwriting flexibilities allow an underwriter to view each situation creatively for its potential, instead of viewing it mechanically, as in the past. In this way, the underwriter works as a team with the loan officer, for many marginal loan applications require additional documentation and verifications or require changes in the loan offered (counteroffer).

Portfolio lenders often develop special loan programs that reflect their unique knowledge of special circumstances in their region. They create niche products that deviate from secondary market underwriting standards. When properly crafted, these programs provide the local lender a competitive advantage when competing with larger, national mortgage bankers who may offer better pricing but are limited to traditional underwriting guidelines.

Loan Transaction and Program

An underwriter first must determine whether the general terms of the application conform to the lender's loan policy (and secondary market standards or private investor's requirements, if so required). This involves reviewing the transaction type, loan product, loan amount, and loan-to-value ratios.

Some common eligibility issues that pop up at underwriting and often make a loan nonconforming are these:

- What was thought to be a purchase may now be a refinance
- A second mortgage appears when the applicants thought a particular loan they are obligated under was unsecured
- The property was "underappraised" from the original estimate
- Change in request from an ARM to fixed-rate loan
- Seller contributions now exceed 6 percent of sales price

Various mortgage-lending-industry studies rank different levels of default risk by loan transaction. Of highest risk are these:

- Investment property
- Construction loans
- Land loans

At the next tier are the following:

- Cash-out refinance transactions
- Purchase loans
- No cash-out refinances

Mortgage industry studies rank loan product in a similar fashion (risk highest to lowest):

- ARMs
- Interest-only mortgages
- **Balloon mortgages**
- Fixed-rate mortgages

The underwriter considers the performance and inherent risk in the loan transaction and product as a starting point in the file analysis. Within this context, the underwriter then reviews the individual application's specific features and associated risk.

Loan-to-Value Ratios

The loan-to-value ratio (LTV) measures the amount of collateral risk the lender takes and, conversely, the amount of equity the borrower risks losing. Industry studies find the LTV is the most significant risk factor affecting loan delinquency, default, and loss. It is arguably the most important underwriting ratio and has the greatest single impact on the other underwriting guidelines for an application.

The LTV may be calculated in the following manner (rounding up to the next whole number):

$$\frac{\text{Mortgage amount}}{\text{Lesser of Sales price or Appraised value}} = \text{LTV}$$

According to various studies, the following may be true:

- A 90 percent LTV loan is twice as likely to default as an 80 percent LTV loan
- A 95 percent LTV loan is nearly three times the default risk as an 80 percent LTV loan
- A 97 percent LTV loan is nearly six times the default risk as an 80 percent LTV loan

Ninety-five percent and higher LTV loans are especially vulnerable, as there is no equity in the property if the loan defaults shortly after closing. According to Mortgage Guaranty Insurance Corporation, "Once default occurs, there is a better than 50 percent chance of foreclosure, largely because of the borrower's inability to sell the property at a price high enough to cover the remaining loan balance plus selling costs and delinquent interest."

There are two reasons for this strong correlation between a high LTV ratio (over 80 percent) and default:

- Borrower has a low equity investment in the property and has less total dollars at risk for loss.
- Borrower quickly loses all equity in the property and then has less incentive to keep paying the mortgage.

This situation is worse if the property is located in a real estate market where property values decline and do not recover for several years, such as Texas in the early 1980s and California or New England during the early 1990s.

On the other hand, a low LTV (under 70 percent) may be an indication of the borrower's ability to handle his or her finances and accumulate wealth. This adds strength to the application and may offset a weakness, such as high income/debt ratios or low cash reserves.

A common industry practice and secondary market requirement is that any loan with an LTV over 80 percent be supported by mortgage insurance (discussed in detail in Chapter 8, "Government Insurance and Guaranty Programs," and Chapter 9, "Private Mortgage Insurance"). Additional underwriting guidelines change substantially as LTV rises. They usually become more stringent as LTV climbs above 80 percent and at each breakpoint above that important divide (i.e., 90, 95, 97, and even 100 or 103 percent). Expect to see more stringent income/debt ratios, credit scores, cash reserves, restrictions on gift or seller contributions, and property or loan types.

Combined LTV

As the mortgage marketplace became more complex in the 1980s, the secondary market players developed two additional LTV ratios acknowledging these changes: combined LTV (CLTV for Fannie Mae; TLTV for Freddie Mac) and home equity LTV (HCLTV for Fannie Mae; HTLTV for Freddie Mac).

CLTV equals LTV, unless the property has *subordinate financing*—any secured lien from borrowing that is junior to the proposed first mortgage. Subordinate financing can include a second mortgage or home equity line of credit, regardless of its source (lender, relative, employer, or builder). This ratio recognizes all mortgage debt on the property and the resulting amount of real equity the applicants have. CLTV may be calculated in the following manner:

$$\frac{\text{First mortgage amount} + \text{Second mortgage amount}}{\text{Lesser of Sales price or Appraised value}} = \text{CLTV}$$

Calculating the HCLTV or HTLTV has several conditions and they differ from each other, but thankfully both apply only to special situations. This ratio increases normal CLTV limits for applicants with good credit scores. It was developed as a convenience to those applicants who have demonstrated that their **Home Equity Line of Credit (HELOC)** is not active but who might have a CLTV issue because of their proposed loan amount.

Down Payment (Equity)

Down payment, or equity, is related to LTV, but represents the collateral risk the applicant takes in the transaction. Typically, purchase transactions refer to *down payment*; refinances refer to *equity*. The down payment in a purchase transaction may be calculated by simply subtracting the proposed mortgage amount and all other secondary financing from either the total acquisition cost or the **appraised value**, whichever is lower. The equity in a refinance transaction may be calculated by subtracting the proposed mortgage amount and all other secondary financing from the appraised value.

As with LTV, industry studies show the amount of down payment (or equity) the applicants put into the property is a very significant factor in default and loss. Increasing down payment/equity reduces lender default/loss risk. For this reason, underwriters examine the amount and source of down payment, as well the overall liquid and investment assets of the applicants.

A large down payment may not always be the result of applicant savings. Why is the source of down payment of concern? It gives underwriters a clearer picture of how the applicant acquired this equity—was it developed through savings or housing price appreciation, received as a gift, or obtained through other borrowing?

Down payment from accumulated savings, investments, retirement funds, or equity in another home sold is generally earned over time. It provides a good indication of the applicants' ability to handle debt and manage their income. As a general rule, the secondary mortgage market is interested in establishing that an applicant either saved or obtained through housing price appreciation at least 5 percent of the down payment for the mortgage loan. Secondary market players, other investors, and mortgage insurance (MI) companies place restrictions on gift funds, contributions from the builder or seller, and other down payment borrowing for applications with over 80 percent LTV.

Exceptions to this general rule do exist, such as under certain "affordable housing" programs that allow for a 3/2 split whereby the borrower has to produce only 3 percent of the purchase price from savings while the remaining 2 percent can come from another source, such as an employer. In all situations, the borrower is expected to be able to establish how the required money had been saved.

As mentioned, some or all of the down payment could come from a gift, but it is essential that a true gift has been made and that there is no expectation of that money being repaid. The grantor of gift funds must sign a legally binding gift letter and verify the source and transfer of the gifted funds to the applicants.

To establish the source of down payment/equity, the underwriter reviews a Verification of Deposits (VOD) or alt docs account statements. The underwriter looks for the following data:

- When was the account opened?
- How long have the funds been there?
- What is the current balance versus average balance?
- In whose name(s) are the funds held?

Recent substantial deposits in joint accounts, recently opened new accounts, and recent name changes on accounts often hide loans from family members, but not necessarily; a common practice when purchasing a home is to consolidate savings into one liquid account to complete the transaction, which confuses this analysis. Underwriters must use common sense in evaluating whether the applicants' activity and total amount of liquid or investment assets matches their income and debt levels, general spending and debt repayment habits, or any other significant features.

Income of Applicant(s)

As with the credit history, underwriters must evaluate the applicant's level and type of income. Of most concern are the applicant's income stability and the probability that income will continue. Industry studies confirm that over time the risk of default is not impacted by the applicant's specific position, industry, salary versus hourly, and similar factors. Of most importance is whether the borrower maintains the same level of income, regardless of its source.

Chapter 6, "Residential Mortgage Loan Origination and Processing," details much of the documentation and treatment of the different sources of income. Because applicants have most of this information at the loan interview, the loan officer has completed the basic analysis. The underwriter's main objective when verifying income is to confirm whether a complete two-year income/employment history is verified and to determine which information needs updating.

Economic events in the 1980s and 1990s changed the approach to reviewing income and employment history. "Job stability" now means consistent income level and employment in related lines of work, instead of having the exact same job. Moving from one job to another, especially if it is for more pay and is in the same field of endeavor, is a positive characteristic. On the other hand, extensive job changes without advancement or pay increases may be indicative of future financial instability. Gaps in employment may indicate possible future employment problems and should be adequately explained.

Since most applicants rely on employment income to repay the mortgage loan, the underwriter should review carefully the Verification of Employment (VOE) (or alt docs—paystubs and W-2s) for the following:

- Salary/wage corresponds with the application.
- Probability of continued employment is acceptable.
- Overtime/bonus income is likely to continue.
- Dates of employment correspond with the application.
- Name and signature of employer is on the form.

IRS and Sources of Income

A residential mortgage loan underwriter will review in detail IRS returns for applicants who rely on the sources of income listed in the following table. To qualify an applicant, an underwriter normally uses a two-year average of net income for the income source, as long as that source can be relied upon in the future. Certain deductions from the net income reported may be added back to reported income and included in qualifying income. These deductions typically include depreciation of over five years in duration; nonrecurring, discretionary expenses; housing expenses accounted for elsewhere in the application.

Financial statement analysis can be simple or very complex. Fannie Mae/Freddie Mac, private investors, and mortgage insurance companies provide specific guidelines and forms for completing this analysis, but in the end, the underwriter must rely on common sense to interpret the numbers, their relevancy, and the reliability of the documentation. Once the underwriter has established the income to be used for qualifying, the next step is debt/income ratio analysis.

Debt/Income Ratios

The most important test of whether applicants can afford a particular mortgage loan is by computing the various debt/income ratios. These ratios measure the level of housing and overall debt relative to the applicants' total income resources. The secondary

	IRS Forms Documenting Income		TABLE 7-1
Source	Personal IRS Form 1040	Other IRS Forms	
Commission/bonus/OT/pension		W-2/1099	
Interest/dividend	Schedule B	1098	
Self-employment	Schedule C/C-EZ	1099	
Investment	Schedule D		
Rental real estate/trust/royalty	Schedule E		
Partnership/ S corporation	Schedule E/K-1	1065/1120	
Farm	Schedule F		

mortgage market and insuring/guaranteeing entities have established acceptable levels through the years after reviewing millions of mortgage loans: 28 percent for the housing ratio and 36 percent for the total debt ratio.

Repayment and default risks rise as debt/income ratios exceed these standards. The presence of offsetting strengths may justify higher debt/income ratios. Underwriters should think of ratios in terms of ranges, not specific numbers. The difference in default risk for a loan with a 36.3 percent versus 36.4 percent total debt ratio is insignificant, but is substantially higher than loans with 21 to 24 percent total debt ratio. It is also important for underwriters to examine what kind of debt makes up the ratios—mortgage, installment, revolving, or other obligations.

Housing Ratio

The housing ratio (or front-end ratio, as it is sometimes called) measures the percentage of monthly income necessary to meet the monthly housing expense. Most lenders calculate the proposed monthly housing expense in a similar manner, but the maximum ratio allowed may differ for investor, loan product, and LTV. When computing the proposed monthly housing expense on a conventional loan, the following monthly charges or monthly share of annual expenses must be added:

- Principal
- Interest
- Hazard insurance premium
- Flood insurance premium (if required)
- Real estate tax
- Mortgage insurance premium (if required)
- Homeowners' association fee (if required)
- Ground rents (if required)
- Any payment on an existing or proposed second mortgage

Divide the proposed monthly housing expense by the verified gross monthly income. (*Gross monthly income* includes income before deductions of any type.) Generally, the ratio should not exceed 28 percent without compensating factors.

Total Debt Ratio

Individuals often have other monthly contractual debt obligations in addition to mortgage payments. Underwriters use the verified information from the credit report to determine other debt. The total debt ratio may be calculated using the following verified payments divided by the gross monthly income:

- Proposed monthly housing expenses (from housing ratio)
- Revolving charges
- Installment debts with more than 10 payments remaining
- Any alimony or child support payments
- Other legal obligations such as cosigned or endorsed loans, unless satisfactory repayment is documented for the other party

---

Figure 7-1   Calculation of the Total Debt Ratio

Example: Ed and Jane Smith want to borrow $120,000 in order to purchase a single-family detached house appraised at $150,000. He earns $35,000 a year as a bricklayer, and she earns $40,000 as an assistant professor of English. Their current debts include these monthly payments: car, $400; truck, $300 (both vehicles with 25 months remaining); credit cards, $100; child support, $400. Calculations are as follows:

Verified income:

Gross monthly income (borrower)	$2,917
Gross monthly income (co-borrower)	3,333
Total Monthly Income	$6,250

Projected monthly housing expense:

Principal and interest (7.5% for 30 years)	$838.80
Insurance escrow	35.00
Tax escrow	255.00
Total Projected Housing Expense	$1,128.80

Current long-term debts:

Car payments	$400.00
Truck payments	300.00
Child support	400.00
Credit cards	100.00
Total Long-Term Debts	$1,200.00

Total of All Monthly Payments	$2,328.80

Housing Expense Ratio: $1,128.80/$6,250 = 18 percent

Total Debt Ratio: $2,328.80/$6,250 = 37 percent

Higher ratios above 36 percent may be justified by mitigating factors, such as the following:

- Demonstrated ability of an applicant to allocate a higher percentage of gross income to housing expenses
- Larger down payment than normal
- Demonstrated ability of an applicant to accumulate savings and maintain a good credit rating
- Large net worth
- Potential for increased earnings because of education or profession

Equally important is for the underwriter to look beyond the total debt ratio number—to review the *type* of debt used and to identify the repayment risks involved. For example, an underwriter calculates other debt and comes up with a total of $300 per month, which represents a total debt ratio of 35 percent (just within the guideline maximum).

The underwriter should review this situation differently if the $300 payments were all charge accounts versus all installment debt. A $300 car loan payment is constant, so the underwriter knows the total debt ratio is constant. If the $300 is the total of four charge accounts in active use and with balances of over $1,000 each, then monthly payment is variable and more likely to change month to month. This means the total debt ratio would also change and, depending on the month chosen, may exceed the recommended guideline for that loan scenario.

Credit History

The total debt ratio measures only the current level of other debt—only a snapshot of the applicants' financial picture. By studying the credit report completely, the underwriter identifies the applicants' history of credit use—the type of credit used, highest balances, open accounts with no balances, as well as the current amounts outstanding, and repayment history. Additionally, only the past seven years of history are considered, with most emphasis placed on the most recent two years of history. It is important for the underwriter to not make a personal judgment on how consumers spend their money or use debt. The underwriter's concern is only how the applicants' use of debt and credit repayment history may impact the repayment of the proposed mortgage.

Use of Debt

Installment debt payments amortize the underlying principal amount over time, and the balance declines each month. Total repayment of this kind of debt "manages itself"—all the consumer has to do is make the same payment each month, and the loan gets paid off.

Revolving debt payments and balances can change dramatically from one month to the next. Additionally, the minimum payment generally is an amount that does not pay off the underlying principal. It is easy for inexperienced consumers to accumulate charge debt that will take several years to pay off with their current level of income. As a result, active users of revolving debt tend to stay active and carry the balance and payment. This debt is by its nature more difficult for consumers to budget and manage—it does not "manage itself" like installment debt. This variability presents a higher credit and repayment risk than does the structure of installment debt. If the applicants rely on income that is variable as well, this increases their risk of cash flow problems.

Repayment History

An additional key factor in underwriting an application for a mortgage loan is how an applicant has repaid credit in the past. If an underwriter verifies an applicant always pays debt obligations "as agreed" (according to contract terms), then that application should be considered in a positive manner. If, on the other hand, the credit history includes debt repayment problems ranging from delinquent or past due payments, to collection accounts, judgments, foreclosures, or bankruptcy, then an underwriter needs to analyze the credit history very carefully and may need to obtain additional documentation in order to make an informed loan decision. Credit reports measure delinquent or past due payments in terms of months (1×30, 2×60, etc.). It is important to review the frequency and extent of the problem. In the loan policy or underwriting guideline, lenders should establish specific credit standards so underwriters can complete this review consistently from application to application.

Minor Delinquency

One or two isolated 30-day delinquencies reported in the past two years, with several other "as agreed" accounts are considered to be minor. Example: a credit history with a single 30-day past due payment in the past five years is not a serious matter. Perhaps several other accounts were handled satisfactorily since then. The underwriter should not consider this application negatively or request an explanation.

Situational Delinquency

Delinquency that shows up on the credit report as a result of an event, not a pattern, is considered situational. Example: a credit history shows three consecutive 30-day and one 60-day delinquencies, but at all other times repayment on all accounts was excellent; this might then be a case of situational delinquency. If the delinquency was the result of non-recurring circumstances beyond the control of the applicant, then the information should not be viewed negatively. To verify this situation, the underwriter should request a satisfactory written explanation from the applicants with verification of the cause of the delinquency. Some common examples are unemployment, an accident or illness and time out of work, extensive medical bills, divorce, or other nonrecurring events.

Chronic Delinquency

These are unexplained delinquencies that are very serious in either frequency or severity (days past due). Example: a credit history that lists several accounts with 30-day delinquencies, three 60-day delinquencies, and a collection account spread out over different periods of the past five years is an indication of chronic delinquency. No one event or situation can explain the delinquent payment history. This kind of information may be a reason for denial.

Bankruptcy

The fact that a bankruptcy exists in an applicant's credit history does not in itself lead to a negative response to an application. As with the preceding example, the reasons for the bankruptcy and the type of filing are the most important factors for an underwriter to consider. If the circumstances are nonrecurring and beyond the applicants' control (such as a serious illness with no insurance), then the bankruptcy may not be the reason for a credit denial. As a general rule, if a bankruptcy exists in the credit history, additional credit may be extended if two years of excellent credit history have been maintained since the discharge.

A form of bankruptcy that has become common is a wage earner's petition. A *wage earner's petition* under Chapter 13 of the Bankruptcy Law provides for partial or full repayment of debts over a period of time, usually two to five years. When all payments have been satisfactorily made, underwriters should consider that accomplishment as reestablishing credit. Occasionally, applicants apply for a mortgage loan before full discharge of bankruptcy. In such a situation, the approval of the bankruptcy judge may be required. Certain other bankruptcies, such as those over seven years old, should not be given excessive consideration.

Past Foreclosures or Deed in Lieu

A past foreclosure or an agreement for a deed in lieu of foreclosure is evidence the applicant had a problem handling credit. The secondary mortgage market requires that these applicants have three years of excellent credit history since the foreclosure or deed in lieu. This type of credit problem is serious because it involves a mortgage loan—the same type of loan the applicants are requesting.

Credit Scores

A *credit score* is a numeric rating of applicants' use of debt and credit repayment history. Although the use of credit scores by consumer lenders was common in the 1980s, their use in mortgage lending was not widespread until the proliferation of automated underwriting systems in the mid-1990s. Scores range from the mid-800s (very good) to below 400 (extremely poor). Over 90 percent of the population has a score above 680.

Secondary market guidelines set minimum credit score levels for different loan programs and tailor the level of underwriting review to these "threshold" levels. Some recent examples are listed in the table, but exact numbers vary by lender, program, LTV, and constant refinement of the historical data from which they are derived.

Underwriters must be careful to not place too much emphasis on the credit score number alone—it is only as good as the information on which it is based. Incorrect reporting of delinquent and excessive credit or credit disputes eventually won by the consumer may negatively affect the credit score unfairly. Debts not reported to the credit bureaus would result in an artificially high credit score. Additionally, underwriters should also review carefully the credit scores reported on credit histories with recent, substantial changes in use of debt. These recent events may be very serious, and their impact on the credit score may be "diluted" by prior history.

Collateral

Although the lender relies primarily on the applicants' income and assets to fulfill the mortgage obligation, the mortgage lender must protect both its own position and that

Credit Score and Underwriting Review Levels	TABLE 7-2

Credit Score	Underwriting Review
720 and above	Streamlined or minimal review
660–719	Basic review
620–659	Full review
619 and below	Caution, full review

of any investor by having adequate security. The lender obtains an appraisal report to assist with this step (see Chapter 12, "Residential Real Estate Appraisal").

An *appraisal* is an opinion or estimate of market value made by a licensed or certified appraiser who is either an independent fee appraiser or employed by a mortgage lender. The appraiser has separate "underwriting" guidelines and standards to follow: the Uniform Standards of Professional Appraisal Practice (USPAP). The standard appraisal form that satisfies regulatory and secondary mortgage market requirements is the Uniform Residential Appraisal Report (URAR), Fannie Mae 1004/Freddie Mac 70. Underwriters review this report to determine whether the subject property is sufficient collateral for the mortgage loan. The property must conform to the lender's property standards, provide sufficient value, and be in marketable condition.

Property and Appraisal Standards

Regulatory agencies have similar requirements for lenders regarding appraisals and their use. The lenders should include the particular requirements for both appraisals and property standards. Underwriters should be familiar with these requirements, since they review appraisals daily. It is recommended that either the underwriter or another qualified person review appraisals regularly for violations in policy or unacceptable appraisal practices, such as redlining. *Redlining* is the withdrawal of mortgage funds from an area due to perceived risks in that area based on racial, social, religious, or ethnic factors. It is similar to property discrimination. The lender must not designate any area or neighborhood as being unacceptable—nor allow any appraiser to do so—for illegally discriminatory reasons.

When reviewing the appraisal, an underwriter is concerned with the risks the property represents to the lender in the event of foreclosure and subsequent sale by the lender. The collateral-related characteristics listed in the table may affect loan repayment, property value, and marketing time (listed from highest risk to lowest).

Descriptive information from the front page of the appraisal describes the overall market conditions, neighborhood, site, improvements, and condition of the subject property. Information on this page details the condition of the subject property and identifies any legal or flood zone issues.

Collateral-Related Characteristics of Property		TABLE 7-3
Property Type	Location	Property Value
Investment	Rural	Decreasing
Construction/land	Urban	Stable
Vacation/second home	Suburban	Increasing
Cooperative		
Condominium		
PUD		
Single family		

The descriptive information on the first page must support the market conditions, comparable selections, and adjustments to value found on the second page of the appraisal. This page details the analysis the appraiser performs to establish market value.

Throughout the appraisal form are comment sections that should contain explanations for any unusual or significant conditions, characteristics, or adjustments. The processor and underwriter should establish an effective relationship with the appraiser to resolve quickly any issues, questions, or requests for additional documentation or an addendum.

Underwriter's Review of Appraisal

The underwriter's review should include the previously mentioned items and the following additional property considerations for their impact on value, marketability, and property eligibility:

1. *Location/Site*. This is always the most critical of all evaluating factors.
   a. Property must be residential in nature, not agricultural or commercial.
   b. Adequate sewage and water facilities and other utilities are present.
   c. Property is readily accessible by an all-weather road.
   d. No danger is posed to health and safety from immediate surroundings (including environmental hazards).

2. *Physical security*. The age, equipment, architectural design, quality of construction, floor plan, and site features are considered in establishing the adequacy and future value of the physical security.
   a. Evidence of compliance with local codes should be in file for underwriter's review.
   b. Topography, shape, size, and drainage of a lot are equally important.
   c. View, amenities, easements, and other encroachments may have either a positive or negative influence on market value.

3. *Local government*.
   a. The amount of property tax can have a great effect on future marketability.
   b. Building codes, deed restrictions, and zoning ordinances help to maintain housing standards and promote a high degree of homogeneity.

4. *Comparable sales*. This is a critical section for residential real estate loans.
   a. The comparables are truly similar to the subject in regards to location, type of real estate, and time of sale.
   b. The adjustments exceed 10 percent for any line item.
   c. The total of all adjustments, disregarding plus and minus signs, exceeds 25 percent.
   d. Adjusted sales prices "bracket" the market value of the subject property.

In the overwhelming majority of appraisals, the sales comparison approach to value is the greatest determination of the property's market value. Comparable selection is the most subjective step in the appraisal process and has the greatest impact on market value. Analyzing comparable selection is one of the most difficult and important skills for an underwriter to develop.

The underwriter must use common sense to evaluate whether all the technical data, market assumptions, and sales comparable selections realistically support the market value.

Underwriting Worksheet and Summary

It is of vital importance for the lender to document the analysis and conclusions of the underwriting review. Normally, the underwriter completes a worksheet showing the calculations supporting the analysis and a summary form itemizing the conditions under which the loan will be approved and can close. There are several benefits to adhering to this practice:

- Highlights the key issues in the credit decision
- Ensures a consistent underwriting review process
- Explains the methodology used for income and other calculations
- Enables secondary market investors to understand the decision
- Allows faster review during processing
- Summarizes commitment or denial conditions in one place

Conditions on the underwriting worksheet and/or summary should be included on the commitment letter to the applicants (and later forwarded to the closing agent). This consistency in communication minimizes confusion between the many parties involved: lender, applicant, underwriter, processor, closing agent, loan committee, loan review/quality control, and private investor.

Automated Underwriting Systems

As discussed earlier, two systems exist for evaluating the creditworthiness of an applicant: judgmental (manual) and empirical (automated). Historically, mortgage lenders used the judgmental system, which relies on trained underwriters to evaluate each application on a case-by-case basis. The same standards are applied to each application in the same manner. Exceptions are allowed, but the reason must be clearly demonstrable. For example, if a larger-than-normal down payment is made, then an increased total debt ratio of 40 percent of gross monthly income may be acceptable. This system attempts to be objective, but people (who are subjective by nature) perform the analysis.

The second system—automated underwriting system (**AUS**)—determines the creditworthiness of an applicant by having a computer software program assign values to certain attributes and facts for each application. To analyze and calculate these values, the AUSs use as their database enormous loan portfolios, which track the performance of millions of loans over several years. AUSs evaluate and score each application, much like the credit-scoring systems discussed earlier. "Earning" a minimum number of points in certain areas provides the basis for approval. ECOA regulations state that these systems must be "demonstrably and statistically sound and empirically derived."

When these systems were first introduced, lenders were wary of using them because of the complexities of lending and potential for unintended discrimination. Information on how these AU systems work is proprietary (as with credit-scoring

Exhibit 7-1 / Sample Underwriting Worksheet

REMOC ASSOCIATES, LTD.
UNDERWRITING WORKSHEET

FSA Loan Applic. #: 100101920

Processor/ Underwriter: T Pinkowish
Originator: W Lodovico

Lynch, Joseph F.
Applicant

Subject Property Address: 89 Harvester Road
Fairfield, CT

Lynch, Margaret J.
Co-Applicant

Loan Terms

Loan Amount: **$ 189,000.**   Loan Type: **Fixed Rate**   Interest Rate: **6.000 %**   Term: **360**

Amortization Type: **Monthly P&I**   Lien Position: _X_1st ___2nd   2nd Financing (Y / N)   **$ 0.**

Transaction Type	Occupancy	Property Type	Loan To Value	
[X] Purchase	[X] Owner-Occupied	[X] Single Family (SF)	LTV (%)	90 % (e)
[ ] Limited Cash-out Refinance	[ ] Second Home	[ ] PUD (P)	CLTV (%)	90 % (e)
[ ] Cash-out Refinance	[ ] Investment	[ ] Condo (C)		
		[ ] 2-4 Family (2F)		

Assets and Monthly Obligations

REFER TO PRINTED APPLICATION FOR SPECIFIC ACCOUNTS

Current Monthly Housing Expense	$ 929.	**HOUSING EXPENSE RATIO (%):**	30 %
Proposed Monthly Housing Payment	**$ 1,498.**	**TOTAL DEBT RATIO (%):**	37 %

Total Revolving Debt	$ 100.	**Cash Verified**	
Total Installment Debt	$ 265.	Purchase Deposit	(2,100.)
Other Debt(s):	$ 0.	Deposits_____	$ 11,054.
Other Debt(s):	$ 0.	**Other: Equity in present home** $	12,195.
Total Other Debt	**365.**	**Other: GE Stock**	$ (10,000.)
Total Monthly Obligations	**$ 1,863.**	**Total:**	$ 33,249.

Credit History		**Cash Needed To Close**
IFCU Credit Score(s): B 690 Empirica CB 761 Beacon	*	Down Payment / Payoffs $ 21,000.
		Prepaid Costs $ 3,280.
Significant Credit Delinquencies/Comments:		Closing Costs $ 4,032.
None.		PITI Reserves $ 2,996.
		Total: $ 31,308.
		LOAN PROCEEDS: $ 0.

* **Paid off at Closing: None.**

Exhibit 7-1 / Sample Underwriting Worksheet (continued)

Job / Tenure & Income & Source

B1	Base	$	5,000.
B2		$	0.
B1		$	0.
B2		$	0.
	Total Verified Income	**$**	**5,000.**

Other Income Comments: Applicant discloses 4 years with current employer; co-applicant discloses 1 year, but income not used to qualify as applicant has sufficient income. Used base earnings to qualify applicant; can verify co-applicant income if needed. Income verified by VOE and YTD paystub.

Property

Appraiser Name: **TBD**   Appraised Value: **$,000.**

Land Value / %: **$ 0,000. /   %**   Sales Price/ Acquisition Cost: **$ 0.**

Appraisal Made: "As Is" / Subject to Repairs, Alterations, Inspections, or Conditions / Subject To Completion

Existing / New Construction / Proposed   Flood Hazard: N   Flood Zone: X   Water / Sewer: Public / Sewer

Sales Price Range: from $,000   to $,000   **Predominant Value: $,000**

Property Values : Increasing / **Stable** / Declining   Marketing Time: **3-6 Mos.**   Urban / **Suburban** / Rural

Sales Comparables/Adjustments OK: Sales comps. rated _____ average.

Other Appraisal/Property Comments:

Comprehensive Risk Assessment Summary

Comprehensive Risk Assessment: **Low/Moderate - Contributory risk factors decrease overall CRA.**

Primary Risk Factors: **Moderate**
(Equity Investment / Credit History)

Contributory Risk Factors: **Decreases Risk**

	Signif. Increases	Increases	Satisfies	Decreases	Signif. Decreases
Financial Liquid Reserves				X	
Employment Classification			X		
Transaction Type			X		
Mortgage Term			X		
Product Type			X		
Type of Property			X		
Presence of Co-Borrowers				X	
Total Debt-to-Income Ratio			X		
Previous Mortgage Delinquency				X	
Prior Bankruptcy or Foreclosure			X		

Underwriting Comments & Conditions

Purchase of primary residence. LTV 90 % CLTV 90 % (e).

Fixed Rate product requested with 30-yr. Term.

Overall very good credit history; excellent income stability, liquid assets. Need verification of GE stock, appraisal, and PMI approval/certificate prior to closing. HUD-1 on present home at closing.

Thomas Pinkowish   03/11/04
Underwriter   **Date**

Exhibit 7-2 / Sample Underwriting Summary

REMOC ASSOCIATES, LTD.
LOAN UNDERWRITING SUMMARY

Review Date: 03/11/04

Thomas Stavola
Mortgage Loan Officer
Fairfield Savings Association
252 Main Street
Fairfield, CT 06824

Application #: 100101920
Name: Lynch, Joseph F.
Property Address: 89 Harvester Road
                  Fairfield, CT
Loan Amount: $ 189,000.
Loan Program: Fixed Rate

REMOC ASSOCIATES, LTD. has reviewed the application for the following mortgage loan and recommends approval, subject to the following conditions listed below:

UNDERWRITING CONDITIONS:

Underwriter Review Recommended [*]

[X] This loan must close by 06/14/04 for the current documents to be valid. **Rate lock EXPIRES 04/14/04.**

[X] The maximum allowed interest rate for this loan is: 7.000%

[X] Final corrected, typed Loan Application and all other revised documents to be signed at loan closing.

[X] Verification of GE stock in the amount of at least $ 10,000 prior to closing.

[X] PMI approval and certificate prior to closing; PMI escrow at closing.

[X] HUD-1 Settlement statement for the sale of Katona Drive, verifying proceeds of at least $12,000 at closing.

[*] Satisfactory appraisal on subject property and all conditions resulting from its review prior to closing.

NOTE: The following condition(s) are recommended to meet secondary market guidelines:
[X] FSA to certify all title, flood insurance, deposit, loan, and credit documentation to secondary market standards.

Please review the conditions to this recommendation detailed above. If you have any questions regarding this recommendation, please do not hesitate to contact me.

Sincerely,

Thomas Pinkowish
REMOC ASSOCIATES, LTD.

systems), but since the late 1990s most lenders either own or have access to AU systems. Fannie Mae/Freddie Mac, MI companies, and large private lenders rely on AUSs for much of their originations.

Fannie Mae and Freddie Mac developed the most widely used systems. Over 50 percent of all loans purchased by Fannie Mae in 2001 were submitted using Desktop Underwriter, its AUS. Freddie Mac experienced the same level of use with its AUS, Loan Prospector. Government loans (FHA, VA) can also be submitted through these systems, as well as subprime loans (A– credit) that Fannie Mae/Freddie Mac avoided until recently.

All AUSs operate in a similar manner. The lender logs on to the system, inputs and submits the completed loan application information, then receives within a few minutes what is formally called an underwriting recommendation from the AUS. The basic recommendations are to approve, refer, or "caution" (which realistically means there is no way the loan as submitted will be purchased by the investor).

It is important to recognize that the accuracy and soundness of AUS recommendations depend totally on the knowledge, skill, and ability of the person inputting the information. Lenders retain liability for the accuracy of what is submitted. If the secondary market player later determines (in a "postclosing review" performed by a human underwriter) the information upon which its recommendation was based is inaccurate, then the lender is subject to repurchase of the loan.

AUSs provide the potential for enormous cost savings and faster approval and closings. As they develop, the capacities and services of these AUSs go way beyond providing a credit decision. Now lenders can manage their mortgage pipelines; sell loans to investors; and order credit reports, appraisals, flood and tax determinations, and so forth with AUSs.

AUSs provide important benefits in the processing area as well. An "accept" recommendation includes a list of exactly which processing documentation is needed for closing. This minimizes the time and extent of processing.

Streamlined Underwriting Guidelines

Through these AUSs, Fannie Mae/Freddie Mac and large lenders now offer several additional loan programs that reduce even further the amount and extent of processing. This allows even more flexible underwriting guidelines or eliminates the verification process altogether. The secondary market players and other investors who developed these programs could not have done so without the analytical horsepower that advanced technology now offers. Their AUSs recognize and rate an application that qualifies for these special programs. Although traditional underwriters believe some guidelines are too lax, the guidelines are based on national statistical data for loan repayment, default, and loss.

Fannie Mae and Freddie Mac use such terms as *streamlined* or *accept plus* to signify applications that qualify for limited documentation programs. Limited documentation expedites the processing and closing of applications identified as "low risk" (remember—risk is never eliminated, just managed). AUSs recognize the low-risk profiles for these applications, such as LTV below 50 percent, credit scores over 720, or cash reserves in excess of 10 months of total debt obligations.

Fannie Mae/Freddie Mac and large lenders use the same statistical analysis to develop the other extreme of the risk scale, "subprime" mortgage loan programs. These applications have higher risk profiles than "prime" or standard secondary market guidelines permit. Rather than denying the application under standard programs, the

AUS identifies them as eligible for these "Alt-A" or "A–," or "Expanded Approval" guidelines. Higher risk profiles might include high debt/income ratios over 50 percent, credit scores below 620, or no income verification.

Applicants in these programs pay higher interest rates and origination fees than a standard program in order to compensate for the higher risk. Each high-risk factor adds approximately 0.25 to 0.5 percent to the rate and/or origination fees. Lenders expect higher delinquency in these loans and price them accordingly.

Comprehensive Risk Assessment

Clearly, the development and implementation of AUSs provide the mortgage-lending industry with many benefits as described. In recent years, secondary market players invested heavily in developing AUSs and placed a heavy emphasis on cultivating the market of lenders who use them, since this is the most efficient way for Fannie Mae and Freddie Mac to receive and sell mortgages on a flow basis.

There is a drawback to secondary market players relying exclusively on AUSs for the delivery of loans. A significant number of lenders choose not to use these systems. Some feel the guidelines are not appropriate for their market; others find it either economically or operationally impractical. To avoid alienating this significant mortgage origination market, in 2002, Fannie Mae updated its *Selling Guide* to include underwriting guidelines for lenders who do not submit loans through Desktop Underwriter (DU). Fannie Mae calls this a *Comprehensive Risk Assessment*. It is similar to the risk analysis format described at the beginning of this chapter, but it focuses only on default risk. The assessment guidelines are based on the analysis of millions of Fannie Mae mortgage loans. Fannie Mae recommends that a lender complete the following steps in this assessment:

- Evaluate primary risk factors
- Evaluate each contributory risk factor
- Use information from both evaluations to make a Comprehensive Risk Assessment of the application

The assessment differentiates between "primary" and "contributory" risk factors. Fannie Mae identifies two primary risk factors that most significantly impact default risk: equity investment (LTV and CLTV) and credit history. The two factors may not impact equally the default risk of a particular loan, but the overall dynamic is similar. Loans with the same LTV have different repayment histories, depending on the credit history. Loans with the same credit scores have different repayment histories, depending on the LTV.

The lender must consider the *combined impact* of these factors on mortgage default and identify it as low, moderate, or high primary risk. Fannie Mae lists three representative combinations of primary risk factors that it considers moderate risk:

- Generally, LTV/CLTV ratio of 91 to 100 percent and a representative credit score of mid-600 to low 700
- Generally, LTV/CLTV ratio of 81 to 90 percent and a representative credit score of low 600 to mid-600
- Generally, LTV/CLTV ratio of 80 percent or less and a representative credit score in the low 600 range

Once the lender completes its primary risk assessment, it next assesses contributory risk factors. These factors individually are insufficient to form an underwriting decision, but when combined may significantly affect mortgage default risk (and therefore, a lender's underwriting decision). Fannie Mae identifies the following contributory risk factors (the categories are added in parentheses to help organize them):

1. **(Financial)**
   - Liquid financial reserves
   - Total debt/income ratio
   - Employment classification

2. **(Transactional)**
   - Mortgage term
   - Mortgage product type
   - Transaction type
   - Property type

3. **(Credit)**
   - Previous mortgage delinquency
   - Prior bankruptcy and/or foreclosure

To complete risk assessment in this step, the lender categorizes in the following manner the impact each contributory risk factor has on default risk:

- Significantly decreases risk
- Decreases risk
- Satisfies basic risk tolerances (neutral effect on risk)
- Increases risk
- Significantly increases risk

In its *Selling Guide*, Fannie Mae provides more detail on how to assess and document each contributory risk factor using the preceding categories. (For example: two months of principal, interest, taxes, and insurance (**PITI**) reserves would satisfy the basic risk tolerance for liquid financial reserves, over 12 months of reserves would decrease risk, and no reserves would significantly increase risk; a debt-to-income ratio in the mid-30 percent range would satisfy the basis risk tolerance, a ratio of 45 percent or greater significantly increases risk, a ratio of 10 percent or less significantly decreases risk.)

Once the lender completes this step for each contributory risk factor, it then considers the cumulative effect of its primary and contributory assessments to form a Comprehensive Risk Assessment. This final assessment should document the application's strengths, weaknesses, layering of risk factors, and offsetting factors. This assessment determines whether the application is eligible for sale to Fannie Mae:

- *Low Comprehensive Risk*—Low probability of default.
- *Moderate Comprehensive Risk*—Moderate probability of default.
- *High Comprehensive Risk*—High probability of default. The lender should not deliver this loan to Fannie Mae (unless it has access to DU and Expanded Approval programs).

It is important to note the evolution in terms and language used here. This recent format focuses on the assessment and evaluation of the loan application's risk factors, not on cultural or subjective issues. Additionally, Fannie Mae stresses that assessments are on a gradient. Each factor may have a different weight in the overall loan decision and again may differ from one application to the next. The Comprehensive Risk Assessment attempts to quantify in objective terms the underwriting review process, but still allows for individual circumstances (not so easily quantifiable) to have an impact on the loan decision.

Like AUSs, the Comprehensive Risk Assessment mainly (if not exclusively) relies on past history and does not incorporate recent economic events or other factors specific to a local geographic area. The basis for AUSs and Comprehensive Risk Assessment is a blend or national data over a long period of time, a method that may distort the real impact of a factor in a particular area of lending.

As is stated in advertisements for financial investments, "Past performance is no guarantee of future results." It is dangerous for a local or regional lender, or one that portfolios loans regularly, to rely exclusively on the findings of AUSs or Comprehensive Risk Assessments without taking into account current or local conditions that may impact mortgage repayment. Additionally, it is important for lenders to realize that underwriting guidelines developed by Fannie Mae/Freddie Mac, large lenders, or other private investors are tailored to their unique risk tolerance level. For a variety of reasons, this level is not necessarily the same for a local or regional lender or one who portfolios most of its mortgage loans. All lenders must take into account the validity and applicability of any externally developed underwriting guidelines to their lending operation and business objectives.

The Underwriting Decision

When the lender has a fully processed mortgage loan application, the lender provides the applicants a credit decision that either accepts, rejects, or modifies the mortgage loan application. The lender must notify the applicant of this decision within 30 days of the date of a "completed" loan application. In this context, *completed* means fully processed—when the lender has obtained all the documentation normally needed to make a decision.

If the application is accepted, a mortgage lender sends a commitment letter to the approved applicants and explains the procedures for loan closing. If the application is modified by any action, such as offering less credit or credit at different terms, and the applicants accept the counteroffer terms, the loan application proceeds as with a normal loan acceptance. If the lender denies an application or the applicants reject the counteroffer terms, the lender must notify the applicant of that decision in writing, include the reason for denial, and provide the ECOA notice of nondiscrimination. A Statement of Credit Denial usually accomplishes this requirement.

Underwriting Guidelines and Loan Application Register

The lender's underwriting standards should be clearly written, nondiscriminatory, and available for review by the general public. These standards should be reviewed periodically to assure continuing compliance with evolving legislation and good business practices. All mortgage lenders (excluding credit unions) also need to be concerned with the Community Reinvestment Act (CRA). This regulation establishes guidelines for taking care of the credit needs of the community.

Discrimination and the Federal Government

Unfortunately, discrimination in residential mortgage lending is not a new issue. Chapter 16, "Compliance," describes in detail several regulations involving civil rights issues that shape the federal government's policy and role regarding discrimination in lending. Several regulations were drafted in the 1970s in part because of actual and perceived inequities in the way mortgage applicants were handled. Their objectives are to ensure that each individual receives equal treatment when applying for a mortgage loan and to eliminate all discriminatory lending practices.

Through these regulations, the federal government actively monitors the fairness of underwriting guidelines. This shift in the underwriting concept makes a mortgage lender liable for civil and/or criminal penalties for violating the letter and spirit of the various antidiscrimination laws. In essence, the burden shifted from the applicant, who had to demonstrate he or she was qualified for a mortgage loan, to the lender, who must establish that the applicant is not so qualified.

Regrettably, this issue still challenges mortgage lenders. Early 1990 data collected from lenders (required by the Home Mortgage Disclosure Act) reveals that denial rates for minorities are still much higher than denial rates for whites. (The *denial rate* for a particular category—white, black, Hispanic, male, female, and so forth—is the number of denied applications divided by the total number of applications.) The data indicates that, although a bit different than in the past, inequities in mortgage lending still exist.

As a result of this data, the federal government renewed its emphasis on determining why the same pattern of declinations continues even after the enactment of many consumer and discrimination safeguards. The 1992 Housing and Community Development Act requires government-sponsored enterprises (Fannie Mae/Freddie Mac) to promote nondiscriminatory lending practices in their underwriting. It also requires these secondary market players to discourage discrimination by loan originators, and it authorized HUD to call upon these two players to help monitor originators for signs of discrimination.

In response, secondary market players developed affordable housing and community outreach programs targeting minority applicants and low- to moderate-income census tracts. These programs offer different underwriting guidelines that recognize cultural and economic differences between minority and nonminority applicants and low/moderate-income and higher-income census tracts. The secondary market players actively market and encourage lenders to participate in these programs, but with limited success. Often these transactions require substantial time and effort and present unique underwriting challenges that are difficult to resolve.

Another part of the federal government's strategy to encourage lending to minorities was the enactment—and recent reassessment—of the Community Reinvestment Act (CRA), which required lenders to serve their local communities. Mortgage lenders found not serving the local community's borrowing needs receive "poor" or "needs to improve" Community Reinvestment Act (CRA) ratings. In some of these situations, federal regulators denied their requests for charter revisions. In other situations, federal regulators denied lenders with poor CRA results the opportunity to purchase other lending institutions or change branch structure.

All mortgage lenders have an obligation to review their mortgage-lending underwriting standards and the effects of their lending policies to avoid overt discrimination and disparate impact on minority applicants.

Discussion Points

1. Identify the types of risks present in residential mortgage lending. Which of these does an underwriter evaluate?

2. How do underwriting guidelines mitigate the risks in mortgage lending?

3. What are the pros and cons of automated underwriting systems?

4. How does the loan-to-value ratio (LTV) and combined LTV (CLTV) affect the way the underwriter reviews a mortgage application? Why are these ratios so important?

5. What compensating factors might offset a total debt ratio that exceeds a lender's guideline?

6. What are credit scores? How does the secondary market use credit scores, and how are they different from mortgage scores?

7. In what ways does a Comprehensive Risk Assessment differ from other underwriting reviews?

Government Insurance and Guaranty Programs

Introduction

Insurance of any type is designed to spread the economic risk or loss from a particular hazard over a large group—that is, the insured group. Mortgage insurance is a financial guarantee provided to a mortgage lender in return for a premium paid, usually by a mortgage borrower (however, there are some exceptions), which insures a lender against all or most of the losses that would be suffered if a borrower defaults on a mortgage obligation. All types of mortgage insurance or guarantees perform this function, whether they are government sponsored or private.

The various classifications of mortgage insurance or guarantees are as follows:

- Federal Housing Administration (FHA) insurance
- Veterans Administration (VA) guarantee
- USDA Rural Housing Services (RHS) guarantee
- Private mortgage insurance (PMI)—covered in Chapter 9, "Private Mortgage Insurance"

The social benefit derived from mortgage insurance is that it allows for more people to purchase homes. The reason is that lenders are willing to accept smaller downpayments than the normal 20 percent if a type of mortgage insurance is present. Since lower downpayments are allowed, more people are capable of saving the reduced downpayment amount and thus purchasing a home of their own. In addition, the use of mortgage insurance disperses the risk and makes mortgage investments more attractive to mortgage investors.

Before examining current government and private mortgage programs, a brief review of the historical development of mortgage insurance will be helpful in order to gain an understanding of present practices.

The Beginning

Early title insurance companies began mortgage insurance in the 1890s by insuring the repayment of mortgages in addition to the validity of title. The first statutory law providing for this type of insurance was enacted in New York State in 1904.

The social and demographic changes in the United States that emerged after 1900 (particularly following World War I) led mortgage lending into a more important position in the U.S. economy. As mortgage lending became more prevalent and important, mortgage insurance became more accepted and desired. Because of this increased interest, title insurance companies became involved in providing this financial service as a no-cost add-on to title insurance.

The residential mortgage-lending and title insurance business was practiced differently then from the way it is practiced today. It was customary during this period for a mortgage company to exchange a new mortgage for a defaulted one or to buy back a troubled loan sold to an investor. As the real estate boom of the 1920s continued, this custom gave way to the actual guaranteeing of principal and interest by a new entity— the mortgage guaranty company.

During their peak years (1925–1932), as many as 50 of these companies were in operation, located primarily in the state of New York. These companies prospered by originating and selling mortgages with a guarantee to institutional investors or to individual investors as mortgage participation bonds. The units sold to individual investors were usually in $500 or $1,000 denominations. Yield and apparent safety made the units very attractive. A trustee would hold the mortgages and be responsible for foreclosure if any default in payment occurred. The prevailing viewpoint during this period was that real estate values would continue to appreciate, and, if any lax underwriting or appraising occurred, the resulting questionable mortgage would be saved by inflation. This optimism affected the investing public. Large portions of accumulated savings were invested in mortgage bonds issued by apparently successful mortgage guaranty companies.

Due to the general optimism about the economy and the laissez-faire attitude of the government, these mortgage guaranty companies were virtually unregulated. Lack of regulation often led to poor underwriting, self-dealing, fraud, and ultimately to a lack of adequate reserves to meet any meaningful emergency.

Even before the stock market crash of 1929, the real estate industry was in serious trouble. Real estate values started to drop and foreclosures resulted, which further depressed values. It was inevitable that these companies would not survive the bank holiday declared by President Roosevelt in March 1933. Institutional investors lost many billions of dollars with similarly tragic results for private investors because of the failure of these companies.

The collapse left such an ugly mark on the real estate finance industry that private mortgage insurance did not reappear for almost 25 years.

Government Insurance

Federal Housing Authority (FHA) Insurance

The years immediately following the stock market crash witnessed much debate on the proper roles of the government in the nation's economy. Many in Congress urged action; others were against it. Most, however, agreed that government action would benefit real estate by helping put a floor under real estate prices. Those in favor of stimulation reasoned that expanding waves from a healthy real estate industry would have a multiplier effect on the remainder of a depressed economy. The National Housing Act (1934) contains provisions to help stimulate the construction industry. The act created the Federal Housing Administration (FHA) to encourage lenders to make real estate mortgages again by providing government-backed mortgage insurance as protection. Title I of this law provides insurance, initially free, to lenders who would loan money for home improvements and repairs.

Title II provides for the establishment of a Mutual Mortgage Insurance Fund to be funded by premiums paid by mortgagors out of which any claims by the protected lenders could be satisfied. Initially, the mortgagor paid an annual insurance premium of one-half of 1 percent based on the original amount.

This insurance premium has changed through the years and most recently has been affected by federal legislation regarding mortgage insurance. The current practice for single-family and 2–4-family homes is of paying an upfront premium of 1.50 percent of the original mortgage amount for the first year and, on loans with a term greater than 15 years, 0.50 percent annual premium, paid monthly. The annual premium on mortgage loans with a term of 15 years or less and with a downpayment of 10 percent or less is 0.25 of 1 percent, paid monthly. Mortgage loans with a term of 15 years or less and an LTV less than 90 percent do not have a monthly premium after the initial upfront premium is paid. Condominiums are not subject to the upfront premium and require only a monthly premium based on the same terms and LTV limits as 1–4-unit houses.

Regardless of the computed loan to value, all but 15-year mortgages have annual premiums for the greater of five years or until the amortized loan to value reaches 78 percent. The annual mortgage insurance premiums (MIPs) automatically are cancelled once the unpaid principal balance reaches 78 percent of the lower of the appraised value or the initial sales price.

Now a part of the Department of Housing and Urban Development (HUD), FHA has other insurance programs, each designed to meet a specific need. But the Mutual Mortgage Insurance Fund remains the largest and most important.

Early Opposition

Initially, the legislation to establish FHA was faced with opposition from some thrift institutions that believed the federal government should not get involved in housing. Even after enactment, FHA did not meet with great acceptance among financial centers, since many felt that mortgage insurance as a concept was discredited or felt strongly that government should not get involved in what was basically a private enterprise.

History, however, has proved this to be a shortsighted belief, especially in view of the many changes for which FHA has paved the way in real estate finance. As an example, FHA insurance has allowed for the development of a national mortgage market by providing for the transferability, and thus the liquidity, of mortgage instruments. The FHA-insured mortgage was attractive to many investors because it established property and borrower standards with a corresponding reduction in risk.

The FHA mortgage insurance program allowed life insurance companies to justify a successful request, to state insurance commissioners, for the purchase of loans with higher loan-to-value ratios and with lower downpayments. The program also gave

Mortgage Delinquencies and Foreclosures Started: 1986–2000*											TABLE 8-1
	Delinquency Rates								Foreclosures Started		
	Total Past Due			90 Days Past Due							
Period	All	Conv.	FHA	VA	All	Conv.	FHA	VA	All	Conv.	FHA	VA
	Annual Averages										
1986	5.56	3.80	7.16	6.58	1.01	0.67	1.29	1.24	0.26	0.19	0.32	0.30
1987	4.97	3.15	6.56	6.21	0.93	0.61	1.19	1.17	0.26	0.18	0.34	0.32
1988	4.79	2.94	6.56	6.22	0.85	0.54	1.14	1.14	0.27	0.17	0.37	0.32
1989	4.81	3.03	6.74	6.45	0.79	0.50	1.09	1.09	0.29	0.18	0.41	0.37
1990	4.66	2.99	6.68	6.35	0.71	0.39	1.10	1.04	0.31	0.21	0.43	0.40
1991	5.03	3.26	7.31	6.77	0.80	0.46	1.25	1.11	0.34	0.27	0.43	0.42
1992	4.57	2.95	7.57	6.46	0.81	0.47	1.35	1.15	0.33	0.26	0.45	0.40
1993	4.22	2.66	7.14	6.30	0.77	0.45	1.40	1.16	0.32	0.24	0.48	0.42
1994	4.10	2.60	7.26	6.26	0.76	0.45	1.44	1.19	0.33	0.23	0.56	0.48
1995	4.24	2.77	7.55	6.44	0.74	0.43	1.46	1.17	0.33	0.23	0.53	0.50
1996	4.33	2.78	8.05	6.75	0.63	0.32	1.40	1.10	0.34	0.25	0.58	0.46
1997	4.31	2.82	8.13	6.94	0.58	0.32	1.22	1.15	0.36	0.26	0.62	0.51
1998	3.97	2.53	8.57	7.55	0.58	0.27	1.50	1.23	0.30	0.17	0.45	0.33
1999	3.97	2.53	8.57	7.55	0.58	0.27	1.50	1.23	0.30	0.22	0.59	0.44
2000	4.02	2.54	9.07	6.84	0.56	0.25	1.61	1.22	0.29	0.22	0.56	0.38

Source: National Delinquency Survey, Mortgage Bankers Association.

them the opportunity to lend across the nation. With this new authorization, life insurance companies could lend in those areas of the country that desperately needed capital. Subsequently, they could receive a higher yield than what was previously available in the capital-surplus area of New England, where most of the major life insurance companies were located. Mortgage companies were the principal intermediaries for moving this capital from capital-surplus areas to capital-deficit areas by originating mortgages with FHA insurance and then selling them to life insurance companies.

Mortgage-Lending Benefits Derived from FHA

One of the primary reasons for the increase in homeownership (from about 40 percent of all homes occupied in 1930 to about 68 percent today (in 2003) is the leadership provided by FHA that led to the following:

- More liberal underwriting criteria
- Established property and borrower lending standards
- Reintroduced mortgage insurance
- Self-amortizing mortgage loans
- Higher loan-to-value ratios
- Longer mortgage terms

These factors contributed not only to the higher percentage of homeownership but also to a financial environment conducive to a rebirth of private mortgage insurance.

Mortgage loans to be insured by FHA can be originated by any of the various mortgage intermediaries, although as a practical matter, about 75 percent of all FHA mortgages are originated by mortgage bankers. Initially, this high percentage of origination was due to the local lending philosophy of the other mortgage lenders and the correspondent system that developed between mortgage bankers and life insurance companies. Most FHA-insured mortgages are still originated by mortgage bankers.

FHA Insurance Today

FHA and its various insurance programs have been in existence for nearly 70 years and have assisted approximately 30 million families that might not otherwise have been able to purchase a home. In 2001, FHA production reached a record $131 billion (in a year with total residential production of $2 trillion). In that year, over 79 percent of FHA-insured mortgages were for first-time homebuyers and nearly 35 percent were for minority borrowers. Originations for minority borrowers have increased for the past three years.

During the past 70-plus years, FHA has often been a leader in innovation and has helped shape the way residential mortgage lending is done today. These years have not all been smooth, as witnessed by the dramatic falloff in loans insured during the 1970s and early 1980s. Some of the reasons for this decline in insured loans are these:

- Internal reorganization and change of FHA's status within HUD
- Fraud, abuse, and influence peddling by some lenders and loan originators
- Excessive government red tape and paperwork delay

These issues were addressed, and the amount of FHA insurance began to increase again, reaching record levels in the second half of the 1980s. But then another problem developed. By the end of the 1980s, Congress realized that radical changes had to occur to remedy persistent high default and foreclosure rates. These changes included the following:

- Higher insurance premiums
- Underwriting changes (use of gross income)
- Elimination of investor loans

Section 203(b)

Today, as in prior years, the most important FHA program is Section 203(b). The maximum loan amount permitted and other requirements periodically change, but the most recent limit for high-cost areas is $261,609 and is set according to the state and county in which the property is located.

The low downpayment requirement for an FHA mortgage is what makes this program so popular. The downpayment amount varies according to property value and occupancy, but once the maximum loan to value is established, the following tests are applied to calculate the actual downpayment:

1. Multiply the lesser of the sales price or appraised value (plus or minus any adjustments for repairs, seller or financing concessions) by the LTV factor to calculate the maximum mortgage amount.

2. Add the sales price to the allowable closing costs that the borrower is paying to calculate the acquisition cost.
3. Subtract the maximum mortgage amount from the acquisition cost to calculate the actual investment amount.
4. The actual investment amount *cannot be less than 3 percent of the sales price.*

Acquisition cost includes the contract price of the property or appraised value (whichever is lower) plus allowable closing costs for the purchase. FHA allows a borrower to finance the origination fee, survey, appraisal, title insurance, and up to $200 of the home inspection cost. However, the loan maximum is 97.75 percent of the home price if the home price is greater than $50,000 (98.75 percent if the home price is less than $50,000). The maximum term is 30 years, and the loan is assumable (with some limitations) with no prepayment penalty to a qualified borrower.

Processing

While processing procedures and requirements have become more uniform between the conventional and government sectors during the past decade, FHA-insured loans still have issues particular to themselves that must be mentioned.

Until recently, HUD required a face-to-face interview with potential borrowers. This rule has been abandoned, but the borrower must still be given the option for a face-to-face interview in every case.

Documentation

There are several additional documents required in the origination and underwriting of an FHA-insured loan:

- *Addendum to the URLA (HUD 92900-a)*: This is the borrower's application for FHA insurance.
- *Mortgage Credit Analysis Worksheet (92900-WS)*: The underwriter presents facts and the numbers (maximum mortgage calculation, income, debt, assets, funds to close, and ratios) in this document. This is HUD's version of the FNMA 1008.
- *Social Security number*: All borrowers on a HUD-insured mortgage must provide evidence (except when specifically excluded) of a Social Security number.

EXAMPLE

If Mr. and Mrs. O. K. Byrne want to purchase a home that has a sales price of $135,000, the borrower's minimum investment would be $4,050 ($135,000 × 3 percent).

The maximum mortgage is $131,962.50 ($135,000 × 97.75 percent) and the acquisition cost is $137,763 (sales price + allowable closing costs).

The borrower's actual investment would be $5,801 for downpayment and allowable closing costs, but only $4,050 of that would be required for the downpayment.

Acceptable documentation is a copy of a Social Security card, paystub, driver's license, or IRS form W2.

- *Real Estate Certification*: This must be signed by the buyers, sellers, and all real estate agents or builders involved in the transaction. It certifies that the terms and conditions of the sales contract are true to the best of each party's knowledge.
- *Conditional Commitment/Direct Endorsed Underwriter Statement of Appraised Value (HUD 92800-B)*: Although a full URAR and additional certifications by an approved appraiser are required, HUD requires that all properties have this form completed by a direct endorsed underwriter, who states the property value and any conditions or repairs that are required to be met prior to closing to substantiate that value.
- *Important Notice to Homebuyers*: This is a multifaceted disclosure advising borrowers regarding the setting of their interest rate and points, fraudulent practices, and the possible refund of mortgage insurance premiums.
- *"For Your Protection Get a Home Inspection"*: This brochure emphasizes the importance of a home inspection and requires the borrowers to decide *prior* to signing a sales contract whether they desire a home inspection.
- *Amendatory clause to the real estate contract*: When the appraised value has not been disclosed to the borrower prior to signing the contract, this amendment is required to be signed by both the buyers and the sellers. It states that they understand that if the appraised value comes in under the contracted sales price, the borrowers would no longer be bound by the contract and would also be entitled to a full refund of any deposit monies.

Income and Employment

Although sources of income are treated much the same as conventional lending for the calculation of income used in underwriting, much more emphasis is placed on the stability of the borrower's income than on job stability. FHA allows a much more liberal look at borrowers with gaps in employment, frequent job changes, and so forth if the continuity of stable income can be established.

Source of Funds

One major difference between conventional lending and HUD-insured loans is that on an FHA-insured loan, the borrower is not required to provide a minimum investment from his or her own savings. All downpayment and closing costs can be gifted as long as the donor is an acceptable source such as a relative, close friend whose relationship can be clearly explained, employer, labor union, charitable or nonprofit organization, government agency, or other public entity. The lender must be certain that there is no relationship to or interest in the real estate transaction and the gift donor. Downpayment assistance programs can also be utilized in some instances, but, again, the lender must be sure there is no relationship between the source of the downpayment and/or closing cost funds and the loan transaction.

Seller contributions toward the mortgage insurance premium, closing costs, prepaid items, and escrows are allowed as long as the contribution does not exceed 6 percent of the property's selling price.

HUD has recently established a Homeownership Bridal Registry Account to encourage young couples to save for homeownership. The account, which is not limited to newlyweds, allows cash gifts from friends and relatives to be deposited, and then when the borrower purchases a new home, the funds from the lender-supervised account would be available and documented as gift funds.

Credit/Liabilities

Historically, HUD's view of credit, credit reestablishment, or credit history has been and continues to be more liberal than conventional lending. HUD does require acceptable explanations that clearly establish whether derogatory credit was due to extenuating circumstances or poor financial management; however, the time and amount of reestablished credit tends to be shorter than that required by Fannie Mae or Freddie Mac.

There is an area in which HUD tends to be somewhat more conservative than conventional underwriting, however, and that is in dealing with liabilities with less than 10 months remaining. Although HUD does not require they be used in underwriting, it strongly advises that the amount of the monthly obligation and its remaining term be carefully weighed against the strengths and weaknesses of the rest of the loan because the borrower will be expected to meet that obligation along with the new mortgage payment in the first few months of the new mortgage loan. HUD views placing borrowers in a hardship position wherein they are unable to meet all obligations as negligence on the part of the lender and the exercise of poor underwriting judgment.

FHA Ratios

The HUD ratios of 29/41 are not strictly adhered to if a lender can establish the presence of compensating factors justifying the loan approval with higher ratios. Some, but not all, acceptable compensating factors include the following:

- Borrower has made a large downpayment (10 percent or more) toward the purchase of the property.
- Minimal increase (less than 120 percent) in housing expense from current rent to the newly proposed housing expense.
- Substantial cash reserves.
- Conservative use of credit, ability to save, and a history of devoting a larger portion of monthly income to rent and or housing debts.

Borrower Eligibility

In addition to normal underwriting requirements and those listed previously, HUD requires that borrowers not be listed on HUD's Limited Denial of Participation (LDP) or the General Services Administration (GSA) List of Parties Excluded from Federal Procurement or Nonprocurement Programs.

Borrowers who are currently delinquent on any federal debt (VA-guaranteed loan, federal student loan, Title I loan, SMA loan, or federal taxes) are not eligible for an FHA-insured loan until such delinquency is brought current, paid off, or has had a satisfactory repayment plan approved in writing from the federal agency involved.

Lenders must also check HUD's Credit Alert Interactive Voice Response System (CAIVRS) to screen borrowers who currently have a HUD-insured loan in default or prior claim paid (within the past three years) by HUD. Borrowers whose names and Social Security numbers show up during this screening are ineligible for a HUD-insured loan. Exceptions may be made by contacting HUD in some cases, such as divorce, assumption, or bankruptcy situations.

Automated Underwriting

Surprisingly in the forefront of technology, HUD joined forces with Freddie Mac in 1996 in piloting an automated underwriting system. Since then, HUD has approved a configuration for Fannie Mae's Desktop Underwriter that can be used to underwrite FHA loans. Like conventional lending, HUD's automated underwriting system has stretched income, ratio, and credit guidelines beyond traditionally excepted standards, resulting in homeownership opportunities for many millions of American families.

Veterans Administration

VA-Guaranteed Loans

As a gesture to returning World War II veterans, Congress enacted the Servicemen's Readjustment Act (1944), which authorized the Veterans Administration (VA) to guarantee loans (among other benefits) made to eligible veterans. This guaranteed loan program, now administered by the Department of Veterans Affairs, no longer represents a large segment of originations each year, but still serves the needs of many active and retired military personnel.

The original guarantee was for the first 50 percent of the loan amount or $2,000, whichever was less. This has been increased through the years to the current loan entitlement of $60,000 for purchase, new construction, and Interest Rate Reduction Refinancing Loans (IRRRL). A veteran who has full entitlement and no downpayment can borrow four times this amount or $240,000. Additionally, Ginnie Mae will purchase VA-guaranteed loans up to $300,700, including the financed VA funding fee, but the cash downpayment plus the guarantee must equal at least 25 percent of the sales price or Certificate of Reasonable Value, whichever is less. Regular refinance transactions are limited to an entitlement of $36,000 or $144,000 loan amount.

VA Program Today

The percentage of total residential originations that are VA guaranteed has continued to drop in recent years. In 2001, only $35.5 billion was originated (in a year with total originations of $2 trillion). During the last major refinancing period (1999), originations were nearly $50 billion.

Many differences exist between VA-guaranteed lending and conventional lending, but most of the differences are of minimal importance, such as the way the VA establishes value of real estate. The VA requires an appraisal to establish the "reasonable value" of the real estate and, based upon that appraisal (or the sales price, if lower), issues a Certificate of Reasonable Value (CRV). The maximum guarantee is based on

History of Increases in VA Maximum Guarantees	TABLE 8-2

Change Date	Increased to (dollars)
September 16, 1940	$4,000.00
April 20, 1950	7,500.00
May 7, 1968	12,500.00
January 1, 1975	17,500.00
January 1, 1978	25,000.00
October 7, 1980	27,500.00
February 1, 1988	36,000.00
January 1, 1990	46,000.00*
October 13, 1994	50,750.00*
December 28, 2001	60,000.00*

*Only available on purchases when the loan amount is in excess of $144,000. Otherwise, the maximum guarantee is $36,000.

the loan amount, not the appraised value. The loan amount is based on the lesser of the sales price or appraised value. Another difference is the underwriting debt-to-income ratio, which is slightly higher for a VA-guaranteed loan (41 percent) than for a conventional loan. This underwriting difference and others are discussed in greater detail in Chapter 7, "Underwriting the Residential Mortgage Loan."

VA Downpayment

Originally, this program was designed to allow veterans to buy homes with no money down. It still operates on that concept, although a veteran now must pay a *funding fee*, which is the guarantee or MI premium. A downpayment might be required if the loan amount exceeds a certain limit. A veteran with a service-related disability acknowledged by the Veterans Administration is exempt from the funding fee. The funding fee schedule is based on the amount of downpayment.

Currently, a veteran (or any other eligible person) can buy a home costing up to $240,000 with no downpayment with a mortgage guaranteed by the VA, assuming

VA Funding Fee Schedule (funding fee is based on the amount of downpayment)						TABLE 8-3

Down-payment (%)	First-Time User (%)	Multiple User (%)	Nat'l Guard Purchase (%)	Nat'l Guard Multiple (%)	Stmline Refi (%)	Cashout Refi (%)
0–<5%	2.00%	3.00%	2.75%	3.00%	0.50%	2.75%
5%–<10	1.50	1.50	2.25	2.25	0.50	2.75
10% or more	1.25	1.25	2.00	2.00	0.50	2.75

income is sufficient to support the mortgage payment. The current maximum guarantee ($60,000) is the reason lenders will accept no downpayment. Although a lender makes a $240,000 mortgage, only $180,000 ($240,000 − $60,000 = $180,000), or 75 percent of its value, is made with any risk. If foreclosure is necessary, the real estate should bring at least the $180,000 the lender had at risk. This amount, combined with the $60,000 guarantee, should make the lender whole.

If a veteran wants to buy a home appraised at more than $240,000, a lender would probably require a downpayment equal to 25 percent of the amount in excess of $240,000 to keep the loan within the 75 percent loan-to-value ratio.

Eligibility

VA-guaranteed loans are only available to qualified current or former armed service personnel, un-re-married surviving spouses of veterans whose deaths were caused by a service-related injury or ailment, or spouses of members of the armed services who have either been missing in action or a prisoner of war for more than 90 days, active duty personnel, and National Guard reservists.

A veteran is eligible for a VA-guaranteed mortgage if the service record indicates active service:

- World War II: 90 days between September 16, 1940, and July 25, 1947
- Pre-Korean: 181 days between July 26, 1946, and June 26, 1950
- Korean Conflict: 90 days between June 27, 1950, and January 31, 1955
- Post-Korean: 181 days between February 1, 1955, and August 4, 1964
- Vietnam Era: 90 days between August 5, 1964, and May 7, 1975
- Post-Vietnam: 181 days between May 8, 1975, and September 7, 1980
- Pre–Desert Storm: 24 months between September 8, 1980, and August 22, 1990
- Desert Storm: 90 days between August 22, 1990, and present
- Post–Desert Storm: 24 months continuous service
- National Guard reservists

Veterans who believe they are eligible for a VA-guaranteed loan must apply to the VA for a Certificate of Eligibility that establishes eligibility and the amount of the guarantee available. The 1974 law, which increased the guarantee, also provided for restoration of veterans' entitlement.

Restoration of Veteran's Entitlement

Before the 1974 law change, once a veteran's entitlement was used, it could not be restored. The 1974 law provided for partial and, in some situations, full restoration of benefits. This change was partially motivated by Congress's desire to stimulate housing during that economic downturn. A veteran's entitlement can be restored if the following conditions can be met:

- Real estate was sold for reasons of health or condemnation
- Real estate was destroyed by fire or a natural hazard
- Loan was paid in full

EXAMPLE

A veteran purchased a home in January 1993 for $150,000. The maximum entitlement at that time was $46,000. This veteran wants to purchase another home today for $200,000 using the remaining entitlement.

$150,000   loan amount on first home
× 0.60
─────────
$ 90,000   amount of entitlement used

The amount of guarantee used exceeds the amount available, but the amount is 50 percent of the purchase price, which exceeds the 25 percent required by a lender.

Maximum loan available now is established by subtracting the entitlement used from the current entitlement: $60,000 current entitlement minus $46,000 entitlement used multiplied by 4 equals $140,000 remaining entitlement; thus, $56,000 maximum loan with no downpayment. In this case, the veteran will have to put $36,000 down ($200,000 price − $56,000 maximum loan = $144,000 divided by 25 percent downpayment = $36,000).

The veteran obtaining a release of liability also restores eligibility. A veteran's entitlement is restored to the extent it was not used.

Assumptions

Unlike most conventional loans, a VA-guaranteed loan can be assumed without an increase in the mortgage interest rate. This feature makes homes with a VA guarantee more attractive to purchasers, especially during periods of rising interest rates. The purchaser does not have to be a veteran, although the purchaser must be judged to be a creditworthy borrower. As mentioned, the interest rate is not increased, but the VA charges the assumptor a modest funding fee equal to 0.05 percent of the outstanding loan balance.

VA No-Bids

The VA's normal way of handling foreclosures changed in the late 1980s, to the detriment of mortgage lenders. Before this change, the VA would acquire the title to foreclosed property after the foreclosure sale for an amount up to the guarantee. The VA would then market the foreclosed property, hoping to recoup as much of the guarantee amount as possible. The VA learned that in many cases it actually lost more money by taking title to the property and attempting to sell it. As a result, the VA now requires an appraisal before the foreclosure sale. If that appraisal indicates a value that will produce a loss to the VA greater than its guarantee, the VA issues "nonspecific" bidding instructions. The effect of this "no-bid" is that the servicer acquires the property at foreclosure and must market the property themselves. The VA will provide no more than the maximum amount of its guarantee.

Processing

The Veterans Administration, as might be surmised, is not unlike other military offices and has an abundance of paperwork and procedures that are unlike other loan programs, whether conventional or other government-backed programs.

Documentation

The Veterans Administration is like all government agencies in that it has an abundance of paperwork and procedures that are unlike any other residential mortgage loan program. In addition to the standard origination forms used for conventional lending, the VA has the following requirements:

- *Interest Rate and Discount Disclosure Statement*: This form basically educates the veteran/borrower about interest rates and points, **rate locks**, and the consequences rate changes could have on an already-approved loan.
- *VA Addendum to the URAR (VA form 26-1802a)*: This form is the veteran's application for the VA guarantee.
- *VA Amendatory Clause*: This is a clause in the sales contract that is required to be signed by both the veteran and the sellers. It states that they understand that if the Statement of Reasonable Value is less than the agreed upon sales price, the veteran is not bound by the contract and may be entitled to a full refund of any deposit monies.
- *Name and address of the veteran's closest living relative*: This information is required to be on file for collection purposes, should the VA loan ever go into default.
- *Original VA Certificate of Eligibility*: This is light green for full-time armed forces and goldenrod for reservists and National Guard. It shows the veteran's entitlement for VA programs and any use of the entitlement.
- *Request for a Certificate of Eligibility for VA Home Loan Benefits (VA 26-1880)*: This form is completed by the veteran, outlining his or her military service data and any previous VA loan data, and then it is sent to the nearest VA office as a request for a copy of the veteran's most recent Certificate of Eligibility when the certificate is not available from the veteran.
- *Child Care affidavit or statement*: This form is required when the veteran has minor children under the age of five years. The form states who is responsible for the child's daily care and what the monthly or weekly expense of that care is. This amount would be used as a monthly debt in underwriting.
- *Military Discharge Papers (VA DD214)*: These forms are required when the veteran has been out of the military for less than two years. The discharge papers help document a full two-year employment history as well as provide evidence that the veteran is working in a line of work similar to his or her military experience and/or training.
- *Verification of VA Benefit-Related Indebtedness (VA 26-8937)*: This document is now required only if the veteran is receiving VA disability benefits or if the veteran would be entitled to VA disability benefits except for the receipt of retirement pay, has received VA disability benefits in the past, or the borrower is a surviving spouse of a veteran who died during active duty or as a result of a service-related disability. The form is submitted to the VA during the processing of the loan file to verify how much, if any, indebtedness the veteran has to the VA.
- *Leave and Earnings Statement (LES)*: If the borrower is on active duty, is a reservist, or is in the National Guard, this form is used to show earnings, dates in service, and position.
- *Counseling Checklist for Military Homebuyers (26-0592)*: This document is required for active-duty military. This form notifies the borrower of the responsibilities and

Exhibit 8-1   Sample Request for Certificate of Eligibility

OMB Approved No. 2900-0086   Respondent Burden: 15 minutes

Department of Veterans Affairs	**TO**	Department of Veterans Affairs Attn: Loan Guaranty Division
REQUEST FOR A CERTIFICATE OF ELIGIBILITY		

NOTE: Please read information on page 2 before completing this form. If additional space is required, attach a separate sheet.

1. FIRST-MIDDLE-LAST NAME OF VETERAN	2. DATE OF BIRTH	3. VETERAN'S DAYTIME TELEPHONE NO.
SCOTT E VETERAN		703-555-5555

4. ADDRESS OF VETERAN (No., street or rural route, city or P.O., State and ZIP Code)	5. MAIL CERTIFICATE OF ELIGIBILITY TO: (Complete ONLY if the Certificate is to be mailed to an address different from the one listed in Item 4)
8709 KENNILEWORTH DRIVE SPRINGFIELD, VA 22151	

6. MILITARY SERVICE DATA (ATTACH PROOF OF SERVICE - SEE PARAGRAPH "D" ON PAGE 2)

A. ITEM	B. PERIODS OF ACTIVE SERVICE DATE FROM	DATE TO	C. NAME (Show your name exactly as it appears on your separation papers or Statement of Service)	D. SOCIAL SECURITY NUMBER	E. SERVICE NUMBER (If different from Social Security No.)	F. BRANCH OF SERVICE
1.	1-1-1950	1-5-1975	SCOTT E. VETERAN	123-45-6781		NAVY
2.						
3.						
4.						

7A. WERE YOU DISCHARGED, RETIRED OR SEPARATED FROM SERVICE BECAUSE OF DISABILITY OR DO YOU NOW HAVE ANY SERVICE-CONNECTED DISABILITIES? ☐ YES ☒ NO (If "Yes," complete Item 7B)	7B. VA CLAIM FILE NUMBER C-

8. PREVIOUS VA LOANS (Must answer N/A if no previous VA home loan. DO NOT LEAVE BLANK)

A. ITEM	B. TYPE (Home, Refinance, Manufactured Home, or Direct)	C. ADDRESS OF PROPERTY	D. DATE OF LOAN	E. DO YOU STILL OWN THE PROPERTY? (YES/NO)	F. DATE PROPERTY WAS SOLD (Submit a copy of HUD-1, Settlement Statement, if available)	G. VA LOAN NUMBER (If known)
1.	N/A					
2.						
3.						
4.						
5.						
6.						

I CERTIFY THAT the statements herein are true to the best of my knowledge and belief.

9. SIGNATURE OF VETERAN (Do NOT print) *Scott E. Veteran*	10. DATE SIGNED Jan. 10, 2004

FEDERAL STATUTES PROVIDE SEVERE PENALTIES FOR FRAUD, INTENTIONAL MISREPRESENTATION, CRIMINAL CONNIVANCE OR CONSPIRACY PURPOSED TO INFLUENCE THE ISSUANCE OF ANY GUARANTY OR INSURANCE BY THE SECRETARY OF VETERANS AFFAIRS.

FOR VA USE ONLY

11A. DATE CERTIFICATE ISSUED Feb. 1, 2004	11B. SIGNATURE OF VA AGENT

VA FORM **26-1880** SUPERSEDES VA FORM 26-1880, MAR 1999,
FEB 2000 UM50 0004.03 WHICH WILL NOT BE USED.

VMP **-416** (0004).01   VMP MORTGAGE FORMS - (800)521-7291

Page 1 of 2   DOC #:81401   APPL #:8009781272   LOAN #:8009781272

Exhibit 8-2 / Sample Counseling Checklist for Military Homebuyers

 Department of Veterans Affairs

COUNSELING CHECKLIST FOR MILITARY HOMEBUYERS

1. Failure on the part of a borrower on active duty to disclose that he/she expects to leave the area within 12 months due to transfer orders or completion of his/her enlistment period may constitute "bad faith." If your loan is foreclosed under circumstances which include such bad faith, you may be required to repay VA for any loss suffered by the Government under the guaranty. (In ANY case in which VA suffers a loss under the guaranty, the loss must be repaid before your loan benefits can be restored to use in obtaining another VA loan.)

2. Although real estate values have historically risen in most areas, there is no assurance that the property for which you are seeking financing will increase in value or even retain its present value.

3. It is possible that you may encounter difficulty in selling your house, recovering your investment or making any profit, particularly if there is an active new home market in the area.

4. Receiving military orders for a permanent change of duty station or an unexpected early discharge due to a reduction in force will not relieve you of your obligation to make your mortgage payments on the first of each month.

5. "Letting the house go back" is NOT an acceptable option. A decision to do so may be considered "bad faith." A foreclosure will result in a bad credit record, a possible debt you will owe to the government and difficulty in getting more credit in the future.

6. If unexpected circumstances lead to difficulty in making your payments, contact your mortgage company promptly. It will be easier to resolve any problems if you act quickly and be open and honest with the mortgage company.

7. YOUR VA LOAN MAY NOT BE ASSUMED WITHOUT THE PRIOR APPROVAL OF VA OR YOUR LENDER.

8. DO NOT BE MISLED! VA does not guarantee the CONDITION of the house which you are buying, whether it is new or previously occupied. VA guarantees only the LOAN. You may talk to many people when you are in the process of buying a house. Particularly with a previously occupied house, you may pick up the impression along the way that you need not be overly concerned about any needed repairs or hidden defects since VA will be sure to find them and require them to be repaired. This is NOT TRUE! In every case, ultimately, it is your responsibility to be an informed buyer and to assure yourself that what you are buying is satisfactory to you in all respects. Remember, VA guarantees only the loan - NOT the condition.

9. If you have any doubts about the condition of the house which you are buying, it is in your best interest to seek expert advice before you legally commit yourself in a purchase agreement. Particularly with a previously occupied house, most sellers and their real estate agents are willing to permit you, at your expense, to arrange for an inspection by a qualified residential inspection service. Also, most sellers and agents are willing to negotiate with you concerning what repairs are to be included in the purchase agreement. Steps of this kind can prevent many later problems, disagreements, and major disappointments.

10. Proper maintenance is the best way to protect your home and improve the chance that its value will increase.

11. If you are buying a previously owned house, you should look into making energy efficient improvements. You can add up to $6,000.00 to your VA loan to have energy efficient improvements installed. Consult your lender or the local VA office.

I HEREBY CERTIFY THAT the lender has counseled me and I fully understand the counseling items set forth above.

Jan. 10, 2004	*Scott E Veteran*
Date	SCOTT E VETERAN -Borrower
	Christina B. Veteran
	CHRISTINA B VETERAN -Borrower
	-Borrower
	-Borrower

I HEREBY CERTIFY THAT the borrower has been counseled regarding the counseling items set forth above.

1-10-04	*Ben Johnson*
Date	Navy Federal Credit Union -Lender

VA FORM **26-0592**   EXISTING STOCK OF VA FORM 26-0592, JUL 1990,
JUN 1995   WILL BE USED

VMP **-438** (9509).01 UM50 9509.01
VMP MORTGAGE FORMS - (800)521-7291
DOC #:048301LOAN #:8009781272

Exhibit 8-3 Sample Department of Veteran Affairs Loan Analysis Form

OMB Control No. 2900-0523
Respondent Burden: 30 minutes

Department of Veterans Affairs **LOAN ANALYSIS** | LOAN NUMBER 8009781272
72-727260799012

PRIVACY ACT INFORMATION: The information requested on this form is authorized by 38 U.S.C. 3710. The information will be used to determine whether a veteran-borrower qualifies for a VA-guaranteed loan and the lenders adherence to VA credit standards. Responses may be disclosed outside VA only if the disclosure is authorized under the Privacy Act, including the routine uses identified in the VA system of records, 55VA26, Loan Guaranty Home, Condominium and Manufactured Home Loan Applicant Records, Specially adapted Housing Applicant Records, and Vendee Loan Applicant Records - VA, published in the Federal Register.

RESPONDENT BURDEN: VA may not conduct or sponsor, and respondent is not required to respond to this collection of information unless it displays a valid OMB Control Number. Public reporting for this collection of information is estimated to average 30 minutes per response, including the time for reviewing instructions, searching existing data sources, gathering and maintaining the data needed, and completing and reviewing the collection of information. If you have comments regarding this burden estimate or any other aspect of this collection of information, call 1-800-827-1000 for mailing information on where to send your comments.

SECTION A - LOAN DATA

1. NAME OF BORROWER	2. AMOUNT OF LOAN	3. CASH DOWN PAYMENT ON PURCHASE PRICE
SCOTT E VETERAN	$ 137,100.00	$

SECTION B - BORROWER'S PERSONAL AND FINANCIAL STATUS

4. APPLICANT'S AGE	5. OCCUPATION OF APPLICANT	6. NO. OF YEARS AT PRESENT EMPLOYMENT	7. LIQUID ASSETS (Cash, savings, bonds, etc.)	8. CURRENT MONTHLY HOUSING EXPENSE
38	Analyst	2yrs	$ 8,997.87	$ 1,258.00

9. UTILITIES INCLUDED	10. SPOUSE'S AGE	11. OCCUPATION OF SPOUSE	12. NUMBER OF YEARS AT PRESENT EMPLOYMENT	13. AGE OF DEPENDENTS
☐ YES ☒ NO	46	Nurse	21yrs	16,14

NOTE: ROUND ALL DOLLAR AMOUNTS BELOW TO NEAREST WHOLE DOLLAR

SECTION C - ESTIMATED MONTHLY SHELTER EXPENSES (This Property)

	ITEMS	AMOUNT
14.	TERM OF LOAN: 15 YRS.	
15.	MORTGAGE PAYMENT (Principal and Interest) @ 5.500 %	$ 1,120.22
16.	REALTY TAXES	161.78
17.	HAZARD INSURANCE	39.75
18.	SPECIAL ASSESSMENTS	
19.	MAINTENANCE	79.50
20.	UTILITIES (Including heat)	159.00
21.	OTHER (HOA, Condo fees, etc.)	58.00
22.	TOTAL	$ 1,618.25

SECTION D - DEBTS AND OBLIGATIONS
(Itemize and indicate by (✓) which debts considered in Section E, Line 41)
(If additional space is needed please use reverse or attach a separate sheet)

	ITEMS	(✓)	MO. PAYMENT	UNPAID BAL.
23.			$	$
24.	See Attached "Liabilities" Page			
25.				
26.				
27.				
28.				
29.				
30.	JOB RELATED EXPENSE (e.g., child care)			
31.	TOTAL		$ 4,843.83	$ 453,591.00

SECTION E - MONTHLY INCOME AND DEDUCTIONS

	ITEMS	SPOUSE	BORROWER	TOTAL
32.	GROSS SALARY OR EARNINGS FROM EMPLOYMENT	$ 5,882.93	$ 5,416.67	$ 11,299.60
33.	FEDERAL INCOME TAX	874.77	804.23	
34.	STATE INCOME TAX	301.00	307.06	
35.	DEDUCTIONS — RETIREMENT OR SOCIAL SECURITY	450.04	414.37	
36.	OTHER (Specify)			
37.	TOTAL DEDUCTIONS	$ 1,625.81	$ 1,525.66	$ 3,151.47
38.	NET TAKE-HOME PAY	4,257.12	3,891.01	8,148.13
39.	PENSION, COMPENSATION OR OTHER NET INCOME (Specify)		705.00	705.00
40.	TOTAL (Sum of lines 38 and 39)	$ 4,257.12	$ 4,596.01	$ 8,853.13
41.	LESS THOSE OBLIGATIONS LISTED IN SECTION D WHICH SHOULD BE DEDUCTED FROM INCOME			3,010.70
42.	TOTAL NET EFFECTIVE INCOME			$ 5,842.43
43.	LESS ESTIMATED MONTHLY SHELTER EXPENSE (Line 22)			1,618.25
44.	BALANCE AVAILABLE FOR FAMILY SUPPORT		GUIDELINE $ 1,003.00	$ 4,224.18
45.	RATIO (Sum of items 15, 16, 17, 18, 21 and 41 ÷ sum of items 32 and 39)			36.573 %

46. PAST CREDIT RECORD	47. DOES LOAN MEET VA CREDIT STANDARDS? (Give reasons for decision under "Remarks," if necessary, e.g., borderline case)
☒ SATISFACTORY ☐ UNSATISFACTORY	☒ YES ☐ NO CAIVR #1 - A101002051 CAIVR #2 - A101002056

48. REMARKS (Use reverse or attach a separate sheet, if necessary) EXCELLENT RESIDUAL
GOOD ASSETS
STABLE INCOME

CRV DATA (VA USE)

49a. VALUE	49b. EXPIRATION DATE	49c. ECONOMIC LIFE
$180,000.00		40 YRS.

SECTION F - DISPOSITION OF APPLICATION AND UNDERWRITER CERTIFICATION

☒ Recommend that the application be approved since it meets all requirements of Chapter 37, Title 38, U.S. Code and applicable VA Regulations and directives.

☐ Recommend that the application be disapproved for the reasons stated under "Remarks" above.

The undersigned underwriter certifies that he/she personally reviewed and approved this loan. (Loan was closed on the automatic basis.)

50. DATE	51. SIGNATURE OF EXAMINER/UNDERWRITER
Feb. 1, 2004	Tony Turlow

52. FINAL ACTION	53. DATE	54. SIGNATURE AND TITLE OF APPROVING OFFICIAL
☒ APPROVE APPLICATION ☐ REJECT APPLICATION	Feb. 1, 2004	Cory Notchman

VA FORM 26-6393
DEC 2001
EXISTING STOCK OF VA FORM 26-6393, JUL 1992, WILL BE USED.

DOC #: 963071

LOAN #: 8009781272

VMP -406 (0112)
VMP MORTGAGE FORMS - (800)521-7291

potential difficulties of homeownership in the face of serving in the military and must be signed by the borrowers and lender.

- *VA Request for Determination of Reasonable Value (real estate) (VA 26-1805)*: This is the order form for an appraisal and the VA's review of said appraisal and determination of value. This form *must* be typed, not handwritten.
- *Loan Analysis (VA 26-6393)*: This form is the Veterans Administration's version of a Loan Summary (FNMA 1008) and summarizes the veteran's income, debt, ratio calculation, loan terms, and so forth.

Income and Employment

The Veterans Administration's considerations of information when determining a veteran's qualifications for a mortgage loan are quite conservative. The basis of the strictness in its guidelines is understandable, as these historically are loans with no downpayment and, therefore, very high risk. The VA closely follows conventional underwriting guidelines when considering a veteran's employment history and the income used to qualify. There are a few additional regulations required, starting with the veteran's pay stubs. While certified copies are accepted, the VA prefers that at least one original pay stub for each borrower be included in the loan package. In addition, active-duty military personnel whose tour ends within one year of a home purchase using a VA Guaranty must state their intention and plans to reenlist and must obtain their commanding officer's written statement verifying whether they are eligible to reenlist *or* they must provide written evidence of a commitment or contract for a new job in a similar or the same field. If rental income is used to qualify when purchasing a 2–4 family house, the veteran must show evidence of six month's reserves and a two-year history of property management, including the collection of rents. Income from a nonsubject rental property may be used to offset the mortgage debt of that same property. The VA does allow verifiable nontaxable and tax-free income to be grossed, however.

Source of Funds

Because the Veterans Administration does not require a downpayment, the emphasis on source of funds is toned down on a VA loan; however, any funds used for downpayment and/or closing costs must be verified. The seller is allowed to pay any closing costs, the VA funding fee, prepaid, or escrows. Seller concessions are limited to 4 percent of the reasonable value as stated by the VA. If a downpayment is made, the VA allows all gifts, grants, and normal sources of savings.

Credit/Liabilities

Lenders participating in making loans with VA Guaranty are also required to check HUD's Credit Alert Interactive Voice Response System (CAIVRS) to screen borrowers who currently have a HUD-insured loan in default or prior claim paid (within the past three years) by HUD. Borrowers whose names and Social Security numbers show up during this screening may be ineligible for a VA Guaranty.

Again, because of the nature of risk associated with a no-downpayment loan, the VA's credit standards are also quite strict, and the reestablishment of credit must show

12 month's clean credit from the date the last derogatory was resolved. All explanations must make perfect sense and be documented. Personal or installment loans with less than 10 months remaining may only be excluded from liabilities if the monthly payment is less than or equal to $100. Child care expenses for children under five years of age must be documented and included as a monthly debt.

Underwriting

The VA is critically different from conventional or FHA lending in the calculation of underwriting ratios. The VA uses one ratio of 41 percent that includes the monthly PITI of the subject property and all of the veteran's debts. There is no separate housing ratio. The 41 percent ratio can be exceeded if the veteran's monthly housing debt is not increasing more than 20 percent, but the increase must stay within reason based on the other strengths and merits of the loan. If the housing is increasing beyond 20 percent and the ratio is over 41 percent, the loan must have a minimum of two compensating factors justifying the underwriting decision.

In addition to the underwriting ratio, VA Guaranty loans must also pass the residual income test. The veteran's income is reduced by federal, state, and local taxes that apply, further reduced by the monthly housing (PITI), a fee for heat, utilities, and maintenance, and all debt. The remaining income (residual income) must be equal to or more than a published minimum balance based on family size, loan amount, and geographical region.

Delegated underwriting authority is given only to lenders who are approved for automatic processing or who are being supervised by a lender who is approved. All other lenders must submit their loan files directly to the VA for prior approval. Various other circumstances also require prior approval, such as a loan for two veterans who are not married to each other and who are using both of their entitlements, loans to a veteran and a nonspouse, veterans receiving VA non-service-related pension income, loans to veterans rated incompetent by the VA, and interest rate reduction loans for which the monthly payments are three or more months in arrears.

Automated Underwriting

In 1998, the Veterans Administration approved the use of automated underwriting in conjunction with VA-guaranteed loans. Originally, this approval was for Freddie Mac's Loan Prospector system, but it has now been expanded to include Fannie Mae's Desktop Underwriter. The VA warns lenders to be cautious because although an automated underwriting system can evaluate the risk associated with a loan and recommend levels of documentation based on that risk, it does not supply a loan approval or rejection; that decision still lies with the lender. The lender is also fully responsible for ensuring that the VA's lending and eligibility criteria are met.

U.S. Department of Agriculture

Rural Housing Services (RHS) Guarantee

An agency of the U.S. Department of Agriculture (USDA), the Rural Housing Service (RHS) offers a wide range of programs under the USDA's Rural Development Mission.

The RHS assistance comes in the following forms:

• Direct loans made and serviced by the USDA
• Loan guarantees of loans made by banks and other lenders
• Grants to individuals or organizations

These programs provide the following:

• Assistance to tenants and developers of multifamily housing
• Community facilities
• Farm labor housing
• Funding for housing rehabilitation and preservation
• Financing for individual homeownership

Programs are offered to applicants who fit specific eligibility criteria and who are dealing with real estate in rural areas (open country or rural towns) usually with a population of no more than 20,000. An annual publication in the *Federal Register* entitled "The Notice of Funding Availability" (NOFA) describes types of funding available and provides a contact in each state for application submission. The RHS programs are available for home purchase, renovations, or rental assistance.

Single Family—Direct Loan Program (Section 502)

Since most RHS applicants are not eligible for conventional lending programs, the Direct Loan Program enables many more families to enjoy the benefits of homeownership. The Direct Loan Program provides financial assistance to individuals or families in the form of a home mortgage loan at affordable rates. Typically, the individual or family income is 80 percent or below median income for the community in which the borrowers choose to live. Funds can be used to purchase an existing home or to build a new home.

Single Family—Loan Guarantee Program

When an individual or family applies for financing to purchase or to repair a home through a private lender or bank, the mortgage loan is then guaranteed through RHS so that in the event of default, RHS pays the lender. The program is designed to assist low-income families, who may have a household income of up to 115 percent of median income in an area. Income limits are set for each area. The family must have a reasonable credit history and must be capable of paying the principal, interest, taxes, and insurance themselves.

RHS Single-Family Housing Loan Guarantees are offered for a 30-year term only and the individual lender sets the interest rate. No downpayment is required, but underwriting ratios of 29/41 are strictly adhered to. The property, located in a rural area, must meet the Voluntary National Model Building Code adopted by the state within which it is located as well as RHS thermal and site standards.

Manufactured housing must be permanently installed and must meet HUD's Manufactured Housing Construction and Safety Standards and RHS thermal and site standards. Houses must be modest in design, cost, and size. Existing manufactured housing is not eligible for the Single-Family Loan Guarantee Program unless it is an REO (real estate owned) of or is currently financed by an RHS direct or guarantee loan.

Discussion Points

1. Discuss the positive and negative ways in which government-sponsored mortgage programs impact housing.

2. How is mortgage insurance (FHA or PMI) different from a mortgage guarantee (VA or USDA)?

3. Why has FHA mortgage lending increased so dramatically in recent years?

4. How do FHA mortgage programs differ from conventional mortgage programs?

5. How do VA-guarantee programs work?

6. What eligibility issues and restrictions does the VA impose?

Private Mortgage Insurance

Why Is Private Mortgage Insurance so Important in Today's Market?

As a general rule, regulatory agencies prohibit lenders from making mortgage loans with a loan-to-value exceeding 80 percent without some form of mortgage insurance. In addition, Fannie Mae and Freddie Mac are prohibited from buying residential mortgage loans with a loan-to-value over 80 percent unless the loan is insured or guaranteed or has some other type of credit enhancement. Private mortgage insurance provides an answer to both of these issues.

Introduction

Following the failures of mortgage insurance during the Great Depression, private mortgage insurance companies (PMIs, or simply, MIs) returned in 1957 after a lapse of a quarter of a century. In the early years of rebirth, MI programs were not as dominant as the government insurance programs, which were generally the first choice of consumers who qualified for them. MI companies offered an alternative to the successful VA and FHA mortgage insurance programs for which many consumers and some properties were ineligible.

The return of private mortgage insurance was important for potential homebuyers who had difficulty saving the 20 percent downpayment and who did not qualify for either FHA or VA loans. Further, mortgage lenders not offering FHA or VA programs were then able to approve a mortgage with small downpayments—if the mortgage was covered by private mortgage insurance.

Since the return of PMI, private mortgage insurance companies have evolved into the dominant player in mortgage insurance today. Information from the Mortgage Insurance Companies of America (MICA, **www.micanews.com**) shows that since 1994 MI is in place on more loans than FHA or VA.

Since 1997, MI insures more than *twice* the dollar amount of mortgage debt in the United States as these federal government insurance programs combined. In 2001, nearly 64 percent of the dollar volume of *insured* mortgage originations was provided by private mortgage insurance (30 percent FHA, and 6 percent VA). This is quite an accomplishment for a segment of the industry that disappeared from the 1930s until 1957. This chapter explains how PMI works and which factors helped it gain so much ground in the mortgage insurance business.

Number of Insured Mortgage Originations				TABLE 9-1
Year	FHA	VA	Private	Private as Percentage of Insured
1997	839,712	254,671	974,298	47.1%
1998	1,110,530	384,601	1,473,344	49.6
1999	1,138,086	441,642	1,455,354	48.0
2000	783,990	186,695	1,236,214	56.0
2001	1,062,867	281,510	2,035,546	60.2

Sources: MICA, FHA, VA.

Private Mortgage Insurance
Recent History and Evolution

A successful strong regulatory structure ensured that MI companies were stable and committed to the industry. The first of the reborn mortgage insurance companies was the Mortgage Guaranty Insurance Corporation (MGIC), organized in 1957 under a Wisconsin state law passed in 1956. Several additional companies followed.

Of great importance to the rapid growth of MI was the Emergency Home Finance Act (1970). This act first authorized Fannie Mae and Freddie Mac to purchase loans with less than 20 percent downpayment, as long as the loans had MI, which was required on these loans to reduce the lender's exposure down to 75 percent of value (lesser of sales price or appraisal).

High-ratio conventional mortgages became increasingly popular in the 1970s, as home prices appreciated steadily and the 20 percent downpayment eluded more and more potential borrowers. Once these mortgages could trade in the secondary market, more mortgage lenders (in particular, savings associations) offered them. Today, Fannie Mae and Freddie Mac purchase high-LTV loans regularly with MI and with many different insurance programs and levels of coverage (see Chapter 11, "Secondary Mortgage Market," for a discussion of credit enhancements).

Loan Quality and Portfolio Risk

Any discussion of MI necessarily involves a discussion of risk in mortgage lending. Mortgage lenders, investors, and regulators are very interested in the quality of mortgage loans, but for mortgage insurers quality of loans is a critical issue. While the other parties manage portfolios with a mix of loan to values, the *entire* portfolio of loans insured by MI companies has high loan to values: 80 percent and higher. As a result, the first party to lose money in a default and foreclosure situation is the mortgage insurance company with exposure. It is the function of an MI company to analyze the different risks in a loan (or portfolio) and to charge a premium based on that risk. The mortgage insurance company then spreads its portfolio risk over a large geographic area (unlike a local lender, with a much higher geographic concentration). This helps

| Figure 9-1 | Geographic Distribution of New Insurance Written, 2000 |

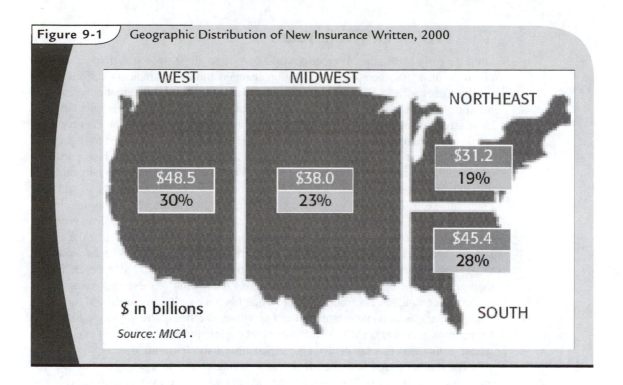

manage risk, as the national economy is a combination of numerous local economies and real estate markets.

Geographic distribution of high-LTV loans does not eliminate all MI portfolio risk. Mortgage insurance volume is tied to the home purchase market and generally rises and falls with it. Understanding this market provides an understanding of the mortgage insurance industry. More specifically, the *first-time* home purchase market has a closer impact on MI activity, as these borrowers typically have not accumulated 20 percent equity from prior homeownership. The typical first-time homeowner is at the beginning of his or her income-earning years, does not have substantial accumulated wealth and retirement funds, and has other consumer debt. This makes him or her more sensitive to affordability and interest rate levels, as compared to a middle-age borrower who is relocating for business or needs additional room for a family.

The Federal Financial Institutions Examination Council (FFIEC), other regulators, and community groups are interested in affordable housing and lending to low/moderate-income areas. The FFIEC compiles PMI activity by census tracts via information reported for the Home Mortgage Disclosure Act. PMI, FHA, and VA use this information to monitor their effectiveness in this area of mortgage lending. This information can be obtained online at **www.ffiec.gov/hmda/mica.htm**.

Because it manages a portfolio with high collateral risk, a central foundation for the MI business strategy is maintaining quality loan originations and servicing. Adding to the difficulty is the distance of the MI company from the parties directly involved in the transaction. As a result, since the 1980s, MI companies have been very active providing education to lenders in identifying fraud and other loan-quality issues.

The 1980s: Difficult Years

Until the early 1980s, the MI process worked well and all parties to the transaction benefited. In the l980s, the economic situation changed and the MI industry suffered spectacular losses with $5 billion paid out in claims to policyholders. Dramatic increases in inflation and interest rates resulted in a general slowing of property appreciation in most areas and significant property depreciation in entire regions of the country. As a result, many homeowners could not sell their property and pay off their mortgages to avoid foreclosure. Lenders who foreclosed faced the same situation. This poor real estate market, combined with the recent popularity and expansion of 95 percent loan-to-value lending in the years immediately preceding this economic recession and coupled with exotic ARM loan programs, significantly raised delinquency and foreclosure rates nationwide. Soon to follow were sharp increases in the claims incidence for MI.

Many MI companies discovered, to their financial disappointment, that the claims level on loans written in the early 1980s were five or six times that of loans written in the 1970s. (Delinquency and claims on loans originated in the early 1990s were higher than preceding years as well, but not as severe.) As a result of these staggering losses to the MI companies, confrontations developed between MI companies and mortgage lenders over questionable origination and servicing practices. The Mortgage Insurance Companies of America (MICA) estimates that during this period, 5 out of every 1,000 lender policyholders were denied claims because of some irregularities.

The decade ended with the MI industry paying claims to mortgage lenders in the amount of billions of dollars. Such large payouts are strong evidence of the value of mortgage insurance during periods of economic downturn and deflation in housing values. If MI companies had not absorbed these losses, then lenders would have had to suffer the losses, with the resulting economic chaos. As it turned out, the losses were too much for some MI companies, and they either stopped writing new business or merged with larger, better-capitalized MI companies.

The 1990s: Golden Years?

The MI companies benefited tremendously as a result of the economic expansion throughout the 1990s, a welcome period after the painful 1980s. Although current business and financial performance for MI companies was stellar, the MI companies had learned a painful lesson in the 1980s and in the 1990s developed programs that would hedge the potentially negative effects of a poor home purchase market.

A comparison of FHA/VA/private insurance certificate volume for 1991 through 2000 reveals some of the dynamics of "today's" mortgage insurance. It is important to note that volume for all three insurance sources reacted to economic changes in generally the same way, but with some differences and some exceptions.

From 1990 to 2000, home purchase activity remained consistent and grew steadily as strong economic conditions sustained the consumer confidence level needed to commit to such a large purchase. Although overall purchase activity did not decline, mortgage insurance activity declined sharply in 1994 and 1999 as increases in interest rates impacted the first-time home purchase market disproportionately to overall housing activity.

| Figure 9-2 | Certificate Comparison for FHA/Private/VA |

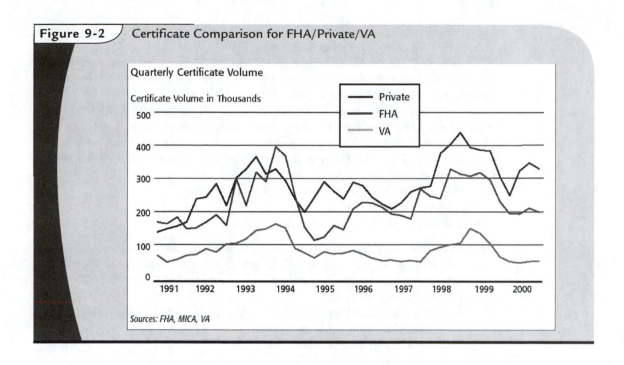

Quarterly Certificate Volume

Certificate Volume in Thousands

Legend: Private, FHA, VA

Sources: FHA, MICA, VA

Although the three sources of mortgage insurance increased and decreased in unison (mostly) during these economic turning points, the severity and duration of increase/decrease differed. This illustrates the differences in these types of insurance. From 1990 to 2000, both FHA and private mortgage insurance volume were more volatile compared to the more consistent (although lower) VA volume. This is largely a result of the eligibility requirement for VA versus more of the general public being eligible for FHA and PMI. Since the market for VA loans is severely restricted by eligibility, changes in interest rates have less impact on VA mortgage volume compared to the general public.

FHA is more restrictive than PMI as well because of its loan limits. FHA determines a maximum loan amount in each county of the country for one-, two-, three-, and four-unit properties. The highest single-family amount is approximately $260,000, but in many areas of the country, the limit is around $150,000. This amount is approximately one-half of the 2003 Fannie Mae/Freddie Mac loan limit, which excludes many

2000 Average Insured Loan Amount	TABLE 9-2

PMI	$131,964
VA	$118,953
FHA	$100,344

Source: MICA.

loan transactions that are eligible for PMI. This also explains why the average-size loan insured by PMI and VA is higher than that by FHA.

Since 1996, FHA volume is less volatile than PMI volume. Private mortgage insurance increased dramatically and now accounts for 62 percent of the mortgage insurance market. The loan limits do not explain this change. Instead, while the FHA program remained relatively constant, during this period, PMI companies implemented new insurance programs that work in conjunction with less stringent automated underwriting guidelines from Fannie Mae and Freddie Mac. Additional programs evolved, which increased insured LTV to 97 percent, then insured 100 percent, and now 103 percent LTV. Many of these new programs have not seen a strong recession, so the performance of these loans is questionable (remember the 1980s?).

Additional reasons for the rebirth of the MI companies and their impressive growth since the 1950s include the following:

- Extensive use of the secondary market by mortgage bankers
- Eligibility of MI loans for secondary mortgage market sale
- Government-sponsored enterprise (**GSE**) requirement that loans over 80 percent LTV must have MI
- Relatively slow loan processing with state/federal government programs
- Lower loan limits for FHA mortgages
- Increase in high-LTV conventional lending

MI Coverage Amount

For many years, secondary market mortgage insurance requirements fell into one standard MI program. With the addition of their automated underwriting and "expanded" (subprime) programs, Fannie Mae and Freddie Mac now list several MI coverage levels in addition to the standard MI program. The following table lists typical coverage levels required by Fannie Mae and Freddie Mac for 30-year fixed-rate primary residence mortgage loans (subject to change).

Reduced and custom MI programs are available only on loans that pass through the proprietary automated underwriting systems of Fannie Mae and Freddie Mac (GSE). While on the surface, it appears that consumers benefit from this reduced coverage, Fannie Mae and Freddie Mac adjust their pricing to reflect this increased risk. Generally, for loans with custom or reduced coverage, Fannie Mae and Freddie Mac charge an additional 0.375 percent on the price for a loan with standard coverage. In

| Required MI Coverage Levels | | | TABLE 9-3 |
LTV	Standard Coverage (%)	Custom Coverage (%)	Reduced Coverage (%)
80.01–85 LTV	12%	12%	12%
85.01–90 LTV	25	12	17
90.01–95 LTV	30	18	25

Figure 9-3 Mortgage Insurance Claims Settlement Example

Assume a home appraised at $100,000 is purchased with a 10 percent down-payment at a fixed rate of 8 percent interest for 30 years. Default has occurred and a claim against the mortgage insurance company is filed. The lender obtained 25 percent coverage.

Principal balance	$88,500
Accumulated interest from default at 8 percent	3,300
	$91,800
Attorney fees—3 percent	$2,754
Property taxes	700
Hazard insurance	250
Preservation of property	250
Statutory disbursements	+ 100
	$95,854
Escrow funds	(350)
Claim Total	$95,504
Percentage with coverage	× 0.25
Payoff to lender	$23,876

As an alternative approach, the mortgage insurance company could pay the claim off ($95,504), take title to the property, and sell it. Assuming property sold for $85,000:

Sales price	$85,000
Less 6 percent sale commission	– 5,100
Less expenses	– 1,000
Less carrying cost of money	– 2,000
	$76,900
Payoff to lender	95,504
Proceeds of sale	76,900
Net loss to MI company	$18,604

---

this way the GSE (and investors who receive some of this premium) in effect "self-insure" a percentage of these high-LTV loans and charge the lender (and therefore the consumer).

In certain situations, lenders may require more extensive coverage to below the normal 75 percent coverage for certain loan products and in certain geographical areas. Many state-sponsored mortgage programs require MI (or FHA) coverage on high-LTV loans and, in some cases, on all loans regardless of LTV.

Claims

Because mortgage lending is a business that has risk, defaults by mortgage borrowers occur even in the best of times. When a default is not cured (usually through the sale

Figure 9-4   Sample Private Mortgage Insurance Disclosure

Private Mortgage Insurance Disclosure
Northland Mortgage Company

Borrower Name: **Lisa Dennis-Valvo**
Address: **1190 North Benson Drive**
Hollywood, Illinois 60062

Account Number: 1234567

You are required to maintain private mortgage insurance in connection with the above referenced mortgage loan. Private mortgage insurance protects lenders and others against financial loss in the event borrowers default on their loans. Mortgage insurance enables you to purchase a home with a downpayment of less than 20 percent, which might otherwise not be possible.

Under certain circumstances, the federal Homeowners Protection Act of 1998 gives you the right to cancel private mortgage insurance or requires that such insurance automatically terminate. This disclosure describes those circumstances. Also enclosed is an amortization schedule that shows the principal and interest due on your mortgage loan and the remaining balance after each scheduled payment.

Requesting Cancellation of Private Mortgage Insurance
You have the right to request that private mortgage insurance be canceled on or after:

(a)   (See attached amortization schedule) 04/04/10, which is the date the principal balance of your mortgage loan is first *scheduled* to reach 80 percent of the original value of the property securing the loan; or

(b)   The date 04/04/10 when the principal balance of your loan *actually* reaches 80 percent of the original value of the property.

"Original value" means the lesser of the contract sales price of the property or the appraised value of the property at the time the loan is closed.

Private mortgage insurance on your loan will be canceled only if all of the following conditions are met:

(a)   You submit a written request for cancellation;

(b)   You have a good payment history (meaning, no payments 60 or more days past due within two years and no payment 30 or more days past due within one year of the cancellation date); and

(c)   We receive, if requested and at your expense, evidence satisfactory to the holder of your loan that the value of the property has not declined below its original value, and certification that there are no subordinate liens on the property.

Automatic Termination
When you are current on your loan payments, the mortgage insurance on your loan will automatically terminate on the date the principal balance of your loan is first *scheduled* to reach 78 percent of the original value of the property. That date is 06/01/11 (see attached amortization schedule). If you are not current on your loan payments as of that date, the private mortgage insurance will automatically terminate only when you become current.

High-Risk Loans
The rights to cancellation and automatic termination described above do not apply to certain loans that may present a higher risk of default. As your loan is not designated a "high-risk" loan, the cancellation and automatic termination provisions described above do apply to your loan.

I/we acknowledge having received, read, and understood this Initial Disclosure for fixed-rate mortgage; or it has been thoroughly explained to me/us.

_____   _____
Lisa Dennis-Valvo   Date

You should consult your attorney with respect to this act.

of the home and the subsequent payoff of the mortgage), a claim on a mortgage insurance company could result. Claims are settled in three ways:

1. The mortgage insurance company reimburses the lender the percentage of loss specified in the policy.
2. At its option, the mortgage insurance company pays the lender the entire loan amount and takes title to the property, later selling it to mitigate the loss to the MI company.
3. The sale of the home in default is preapproved by the MI company.

Strengths of MI Today

Strong regulatory control coupled with sound actuarial reserves, two elements missing in the old mortgage insurance business, are now present with the new MI. The laws of the state in which MI companies are organized as well as the states in which they do business carefully regulate all mortgage insurance companies. The regulating entity is normally the state insurance commission or department. The specific regulations vary by state but generally provide that a MI company can insure first liens on 1–4 family residences that do not exceed 95 percent of fair market value.

Authority has been expanded to include the various alternative mortgage instruments. Before a mortgage insurance company can begin insuring loans, it must meet minimum limits for paid-in capital and surplus. Then its insurance exposure is limited to 25 times the value of its capital, surplus, and contingency reserves. In other words, MI companies set aside $1 of capital for every $25 of risk they insure. *Insured risk* is defined as the percentage share of each loan that is actually covered by the individual insurance policy.

Rating agencies, such as Moody's, Fitch, and Standard & Poor's, also rate mortgage insurance companies on their financial strength and performance.

Net Industry Risk/Capital (dollars in thousands)				TABLE 9-4
	1997	1998	1999	2000
Net primary risk in force	$122,036,185	$127,824,601	$138,818,689	$139,481,548
Net pool risk in force	$5,502,172	$5,913,885	$7,235,327	$8,298,755
Total Net Risk in Force	$127,538,357	$133,738,486	$146,054,016	$147,780,302
Policyholders surplus	$2,378,366	$2,853,914	$2,857,239	$3,689,362
Contingency reserve	$5,151,672	$6,510,450	$7,949,831	$9,501,271
Total Capital	$7,530,038	$9,364,364	$10,807,070	$13,190,633
Risk-to-Capital Ratio	16.94	14.28	13.51	11.20

Source: MICA.

Types of Reserves

Mortgage insurance companies must maintain three types of reserves:

1. *Unearned premium reserve*: Premiums received but unearned for the term of a policy are placed in this reserve.
2. *Loss reserve*: This reserve is established for losses or potential losses on a case-by-case basis as the company learns of defaults and foreclosures.
3. *Contingency reserve*: This is a special reserve required by law to protect mortgage lenders against the type of catastrophic loss that can occur in severe economic periods. Half of each premium dollar received goes into this reserve and cannot be used by a mortgage insurance company for 10 years, unless losses in a calendar year exceed 35 percent of earned premiums and the insurance commissioner of the state in which the insurer is domiciled concurs in the withdrawal.

Evolving MI Business

After nearly a half century of progress and service, mortgage insurance companies have recently evolved into one of the more innovative members of the real estate finance business. In addition to insuring mortgage loans of all types, these companies also offer the following products and services:

- Serve as intermediaries between mortgage loan originators and investors
- Maintain extensive involvement in private mortgage-backed securities
- Operate conduits to pool and sell privately insured mortgage-backed securities
- Provide contract underwriting during periods of peak origination
- Assist in the portfolio restructuring of lenders
- Offer cutting-edge technology products and services
- Develop innovative affordable housing programs

These added functions are logical extensions of the mortgage insurance business and have assisted in the tremendous growth of MI companies recently. For example, MI companies deliver their insurance product through satellite underwriting offices across the country and employ a significant sales force that regularly calls on lenders. From

Industry Assets and Reserves (dollars in thousands)				TABLE 9-5
	1997	1998	1999	2000
Admitted assets	$10,528,316	$12,083,431	$13,800,478	$16,149,811
Unearned reserve premium	$572,598	$492,025	$479,979	$503,098
Loss reserve	$3,478,716	$3,884,484	$1,985,822	$1,923,089
Contingency reserve	$5,151,672	$6,510,450	$7,949,831	$9,501,271

Source: MICA.

this delivery structure, MI companies can easily bring together originators and investors to facilitate secondary market transactions. Often this secondary market assistance is provided free or at a reduced fee with the hope that this service and others will be repaid with additional insurance business for the MI company.

Contracting with a Mortgage Insurance Company

In order to do business with a mortgage insurance company, the lender first must be approved and must receive a master policy. MI companies screen mortgage lenders that apply for master policies and look for experience in originating and servicing first-mortgage loans. This screening process may include conducting interviews with the lender's mortgage-processing, underwriting, and servicing staff, as well as management. The MI companies want to ensure the loans they will be insuring have been originated in a thorough and professional manner. They also wish to establish that the servicing lender has the experience to manage the ongoing insurance policy requirements. Once the MI company issues a master policy to an approved lender, it then issues individual insurance commitments within a day or two of reviewing the individual loan application package submitted by the lender. According to MICA numbers, in the last five years the approval percentage of applications submitted to MI companies ranged from 74 to 83 percent.

Pool Insurance

With the explosion of subprime lending on the secondary market through private investors and through Fannie Mae and Freddie Mac, a recent trend for MI companies has been to insure pools of mortgages. These mortgages are not necessarily over 80 percent LTV, but instead may present some other greater risk than traditional "investment quality" secondary market loans (for example, lower credit scores, no income verification). The MI company insures the entire pool of loans to improve them to investment grade. Usually, the **pool insurance** reduces both investor and MI company exposure to a certain percentage of the original pool loan amount negotiated, usually 5 to 25 percent.

Three Companies Comprise 94 Percent of the $19 Billion of Pool Insurance (2000)	TABLE 9-6

Name	Market Share (%)
PMI	37%
Radian	31
MGIC	26

Source: Inside Mortgage Finance.

This source of MI business has grown appreciably in recent years, but not all seven MI companies actively participate. MI companies began reporting this volume separately in the third quarter of 2001. According to *Inside Mortgage Finance*, pool insurance accounted for 12 percent of the total insurance originated in that period.

Private Mortgage Insurance Companies

Private mortgage insurance companies' activity is tracked by the Federal Financial Institutions Examination Council (FFIEC) and can be obtained online at **www.ffiec.gov/hmda/mica.htm**.

Noninsured Residential Loans

As mentioned earlier in this chapter, most financial institutions' regulatory bodies require some type of mortgage insurance or guarantee if the loan to value of a residential loan is over 80 percent. Both Fannie Mae and Freddie Mac require mortgage insurance, guarantee, or other credit enhancements for residential mortgage loans with a loan to value over 80 percent.

Private Mortgage Insurance Company Activity (2001)			TABLE 9-7
Private MI Company	Market Share Percentage	Primary Insurance (billions)	Primary in Force (billions)
Mortgage Guaranty Insurance Corporation Milwaukee, WI	25%	$71	$173
PMI Mortgage Insurance Co. San Francisco, CA	18	$52	$118
Radian Mortgage Assurance Company Philadelphia, PA	16	$45	$108
GE Capital Mortgage Insurance Companies Raleigh, NC	15	$44	$119
United Guaranty Corporation Greensboro, NC	13	$36	$95
Republic Mortgage Insurance Company Winston-Salem, NC	9	$25	$66
Triad Guaranty Insurance Corporation Winston-Salem, NC	4	$10	$20
Industry Totals		$283	$699

Source: Inside Mortgage Financing (**www.imfpubs.com**).

Yet, in today's market it is common practice for mortgage lenders to offer so-called **piggyback loans**. These structured transactions feature multiple loans (a first mortgage and a second mortgage combined or "piggybacked") that are closed at the same time and limit the exposure of each mortgage to under 80 percent of the value of the security. For example, a mortgage lender would be willing to make a person a 75 percent first mortgage loan, and at the same time, make a 15 percent second (equity) mortgage. The combined loan to value is 90 percent, but the borrower is not required to purchase mortgage insurance. The reason no mortgage insurance is needed in this situation is because the first mortgage loan itself has a loan to value of 80 percent or below and, assuming other requirements are satisfied, is eligible for sale to either Fannie Mae or Freddie Mac or a private investor.

Therefore, the combined loan to value of 90 percent in this transaction is not the deciding factor in whether mortgage insurance is required—individual loan exposure is what determines whether mortgage insurance is required. The logic behind this approach is that a lender could make a 75 or 80 percent LTV today (with no mortgage insurance) and the borrower could come back a month later and obtain a 10 or 15 percent (in some cases, borrowers may obtain loans with a combined LTV of 100 percent!) with no requirement for mortgage insurance. Thus, what difference does a month make? The exposure for both the borrower and lender is the same.

Mortgage lenders adopting this approach have become quite numerous in today's market. They may sell the first mortgage into the secondary market while retaining the second mortgage within their own portfolio (or sell it to some investor other than Fannie Mae or Freddie Mac). By utilizing the piggyback loan structure, mortgage lenders limit their risk and consumers can save money by avoiding mortgage insurance premiums.

Discussion Points

1. How is private mortgage insurance (PMI) different from government insurance and guaranty programs?

2. Explain the recent growth of PMI compared to government-sponsored programs.

3. What is pool insurance and how is it used?

4. How have PMI companies performed in the 1980s and 1990s? Why the difference?

5. Discuss how PMI impacts the housing market and the secondary mortgage market.

6. How do you calculate a PMI premium?

Selling Residential Mortgage Loans

Introduction

In the current residential mortgage loan market, most mortgage originators sell some or all of their current loan production to others. The ability to quickly obtain commitments and sell mortgage loans is crucial to profitability, interest rate risk management, and market share for most originators. The entire function or process of obtaining investor commitments, managing interest rate risk, and preparing and shipping loan packages is traditionally referred to as *the marketing of residential mortgage loans*. In this chapter, in order to better describe this activity, the entire function is called *selling residential mortgage loans*. Frequent reference is made in this chapter to Chapter 11, "Secondary Mortgage Market," because they are closely interrelated.

Selling Mortgage Loans as a Business Strategy

Selling residential mortgage loans has become increasingly important today for all classifications of mortgage originators. The growth of the secondary mortgage market bears witness to that importance with yearly secondary market transactions often exceeding $1 trillion a year. The critical importance of selling residential loans to a successful mortgage-lending strategy has been evident since the 1960s. Before 1961, the only originating lender concerned with selling loans was the mortgage banker, and that was the result of necessity. Practically all other mortgage originators at that time were portfolio lenders and thus were not concerned with selling loans.

In 1961, savings and loan institutions were authorized by their regulators to buy and sell whole loans originated outside their normal lending area, and with that change selling residential loans became more common. The Depository Institutions Deregulation and Monetary Control Act (1980) completed the evolution, as it revised federal lending regulations to the extent that any federally chartered thrift institution could buy and sell whole loans or participations under the exact terms as if originating such a loan. Other lenders, including commercial banks and credit unions, became sellers in the 1980s and 1990s as originations exceeded their ability to portfolio loans.

Most Originations Should Be Saleable

Today, the vast majority of mortgage loans produced by mortgage originators is "standard" (sometimes referred to as *conforming loans*), which means they conform to the standards of the secondary mortgage market. (The term *conforming mortgage* is also used to describe the maximum original principal balance that Fannie Mae or Freddie

Mac can purchase.) Today, the majority of mortgage originators realizes that most residential mortgage loans should be saleable (i.e., capable of being sold) in the secondary mortgage market even though the intent at origination is for those loans to be placed in a lender's portfolio.

Nonstandard Mortgages

Mortgage lenders, especially portfolio lenders, understand that originating some nonstandard mortgages could assist them in meeting the housing finance needs of their community. Nonstandard mortgage loans include unusual ARM types, low- and no-documentation loans, and so-called subprime or Grade B loans. These loans are important for lenders that want to be perceived as local lenders or ones that must meet their community reinvestment goals. These loans are also ones that are important to some borrowers, especially for low-income borrowers or first-time homebuyers; lenders should definitely make some of these loans. But these lenders should limit their portfolio exposure to these mortgages to a level supported by their capital or have an investor who is interested in purchasing these mortgages. As should be obvious, mortgage lenders that originate mortgages not suitable for sale in the secondary mortgage market at a reasonable price face the possibility of disaster when interest rates move up or liquidity is needed for whatever reason.

Some lenders believe that since all loans can ultimately be sold (especially after seasoning), why should they worry if their mortgage loans don't meet the requirements or standards of the secondary market? That belief is partially justifiable—all mortgage loans can be sold to someone—but the discounted price these loans command may be so low that a sale isn't really a viable option.

In all situations, a mortgage originator should require that the legal foundation (correct security agreement, note, title insurance, etc.) is present. Many underwriting deficiencies can be overcome by the loan remaining on the books for a year or two with no delinquencies, but legal foundation deficiencies prevent a loan from being sold to many investors.

Generic Mortgage Banking

Sound modern asset management dictates that all mortgage lenders involved in residential lending also be engaged in what is generically called *mortgage banking*. This prudent approach should be followed even if current economic conditions and investment philosophy dictate retaining some or all residential mortgage loan production in portfolio. The term *mortgage banking* in this sense refers to the process of originating mortgages that are saleable (even if not actually sold) in the secondary mortgage market. (See Chapter 3, "The Mortgage Lenders.")

Growth of Residential Lending and the Secondary Mortgage Markets

One of the most important reasons for the sharp increase in real estate lending activity since the end of World War II has been the demand for and the supply of mortgage money at reasonable rates. The demand for housing credit resulted from the pent-up housing needs, population growth, and the migration of many people to the Sun Belt states. The ready supply of mortgage money from the secondary mortgage market (see discussion in Chapter 11, "Secondary Mortgage Market") provided the funds for these housing demands. For example, the movement of many people to the Sun Belt would have been very difficult without the secondary mortgage markets, the reason being that that geographical area did not have sufficient capital to meet credit demands. Therefore, easy availability of capital from the secondary market was essential for continued economic growth. During periods of tight money or credit restraints, such as existed in the 1970s and 1980s, the activity of the secondary market provides the funds needed for a large portion of the residential lending that occurs.

Today, the activity of the secondary market is greater than ever and provides the foundation for all residential mortgage lending in this country. As the need for more and cheaper credit for housing grows in the first decade of the new century, it is estimated that the secondary market will fund 80 percent of this credit. In particular, the use of mortgage-backed securities will allow for a direct path of needed funds from the capital markets to the mortgage markets.

Marketing Alternatives

In today's sophisticated mortgage market, all classifications of mortgage lenders have the same strategic alternatives for placement of their loan production. These alternatives include the following:

1. Retaining some or all loan production in the lender's own portfolio
2. Selling whole loans or participations to government-sponsored enterprises—Fannie Mae/Freddie Mac or Federal Home Loan Banks
3. Selling whole loans or participations to private secondary market entities
4. Directly issuing mortgage-backed securities (MBSs)
5. Selling loans to conduits for packaging into MBSs

These selling alternatives are available, conceptually, to all mortgage lenders, but some of these lenders will not use one or more for various reasons. Mortgage bankers, for example, can never retain production in portfolio since a traditional mortgage banker does not have a portfolio like a depository institution and therefore must sell all loans originated. Some smaller thrifts and credit unions, on the other hand, may opt for the portfolio alternative most of the time. Except in those situations in which a lender will not or cannot consider one or more alternatives (e.g., a mortgage banker and portfolio lending), a mortgage lender should constantly consider all alternatives before selecting the most advantageous for that period of time. Part of this strategic decision should be deciding how to handle the servicing issues inherent in selling loans. The various servicing alternatives are discussed in Chapter 14, "Mortgage Loan Servicing and Administration."

Retaining Production in Portfolio

For many years, the only option available to thrifts, credit unions, and commercial banks was to retain residential mortgage production in their portfolios. This strategy served them well for many decades. In the early 1960s, a few thrifts began selling some of their loan production, but until the late 1970s most thrifts were primarily portfolio lenders. In fact, one type of thrift, mutual savings banks, which are located primarily in the capital-surplus Northeast, could not generate sufficient loan production and as a result had to balance savings deposits with mortgages purchased from mortgage bankers. Savings banks, as a result, had their mortgage portfolios made up of their own production supplemented by that of mortgage bankers.

High Interest Rates of Early 1980s

In the highly volatile interest rate environment that existed in the United States in the early 1980s, portfolio lending became a very dangerous strategy. The number of thrifts that were forced to close or merge in the 1980s illustrates vividly these dangers. As a general rule, these institutions failed because their portfolio yield could not keep pace with their cost of funds and because many of these loans could not be sold. The spread between a depository institution's cost of funds and portfolio yield normally needs to be between 200 and 300 basis points for profitable lending. For the period of 1981 to 1983, the spread for most thrifts was actually negative, resulting in financial failure of the weakest and shrinking net worth for the remainder. If these thrifts had had residential mortgage loans that were saleable and had sold some of these loans, they could have decreased the interest rate risk of loans held in portfolio.

Some Exclusive Portfolio Lenders Remain

Even though the most common residential mortgage-lending strategy today involves selling some or all of current production, it is expected that some mortgage lenders in the new century will continue to portfolio loans. Some of them, such as credit unions, have valid reasons for keeping some or all of the mortgages in their portfolio. Credit unions often have trouble putting all of the share deposits to work, so they keep many of their mortgages in portfolio to put that excess liquidity to work. Other lenders have similar problems or see similar investment opportunities in their own mortgages. (Of course, these mortgages should still be saleable so that if a need ever develops, the loans can be sold.)

Asset/Liability Management

In the more sophisticated mortgage market of today, those mortgage lenders that elect to be portfolio lenders have ways to protect themselves against the risks inherent in portfolioing loans. As mentioned earlier, the principal dangers to a portfolio lender are increasing interest rates (which increases the cost of funds) and a portfolio of fixed-rate mortgages (which does not respond to changed market conditions). Better asset/liability management can minimize these dangers but not eliminate them completely. *Asset/liability management*, as it relates to residential mortgage lending, generally refers to a lengthening of the maturity of liabilities (deposits and certificates) and a shortening of the maturity of assets (e.g., when the mortgages will reprice) and/or indexing the interest rates on those assets. The desired change on the liability side can be achieved by obtaining more core deposits (low- or no-interest checking), longer terms for certificates of deposit, and possibly by borrowing from a Federal Home Loan Bank. In regards to assets, a portfolio lender wants to originate as many variable-rate loans (both first and equity loans) as possible. These suggested changes will help all lenders but especially those mortgage lenders that opt for portfolio lending.

Risk in the Primary Mortgage Market

Through the years, mortgage originators have learned that an investment in a residential mortgage loan can be risky. The risk can be as simple as credit risk (i.e., a borrower cannot or will not repay the loan) or as complex as interest rate risk (i.e., the cost of funding a loan exceeds the yield on the loan). In addition to the economic functions performed by the secondary mortgage market, the market helps mortgage originators manage the following risks:

- Credit risk
- Interest rate risk
- Prepayment risk
- Liquidity risk

Credit risk is discussed in detail in Chapter 7, "Underwriting the Residential Mortgage Loan."

Interest Rate Risk

The interest rate risk from investing in mortgage loans that could last up to 30 years has forced many originators into the secondary mortgage market. The risk is the result of the fact that mortgage investors do not have a source of funding for an investment that could last up to 30 years (potentially). Most mortgage investors, other than the secondary market players, are depository institutions. These institutions fund their investments in mortgage loans from short- and long-term funds with the maximum term for any deposit generally being five years. Thus, if a depository institution retained 30-year fixed-rate mortgages in its portfolio and funded them with five-year deposits, it runs the risk that the cost of the deposits could eventually exceed the yield on the mortgages. This was exactly what happened to savings and loans in the early 1980s when, for a couple of years, the cost of funds was higher than the yield on the mortgage portfolio. Selling some or all mortgage loans to investors transfers the interest rate risk to them or to the investors in mortgage-backed securities. Of course, most 30-year mortgages do not last 30 years. Over the past 50 years, the average life of a 30-year mortgage has never been higher than 12 years (during periods of high interest rates) and often no more than five years (during periods of lower interest rates).

Prepayment Risk

Prepayment risk is derived from mortgage borrowers paying more principal and interest than is necessary to amortize their loans over the full term of their loans. This activity is beneficial for a borrower since it pays off a loan quicker. But prepayments force a mortgage lender to take the funds from the prepayment and put them to work elsewhere. Prepayments often occur when interest rates are falling and are usually made by the borrower who is refinancing the existing loan. The purpose of the refinancing is, of course, to lock in the lower interest rate for the life of the loan. During periods of low rates, such as occurred in 2001–2002, over half of the 1–4 family mortgage loans originated during those record years were refinancings. Mortgage lenders who held mortgage loans in their portfolio were forced to reinvest the proceeds from the refinancings into mortgages at lower rates. Selling mortgage loans to investors transfers this risk to the investor.

Liquidity Risk

When a mortgage loan cannot be sold because it does not meet the requirements of the secondary market or private investors, it is referred to as illiquid in the sense that the mortgage loan cannot be converted into cash. The reason the loan cannot be sold may be because of the underwriting standards used, the type of property serving as collateral, or other similar reasons. (It is important to reiterate that all loans can be sold to some investor, but it is simply a matter of price.) Having mortgage loans that cannot be readily converted into cash presents a mortgage investor with a major problem that can lead to serious consequences, as witnessed by some savings and loan associations in the 1980s.

When discussing mortgage loans, liquidity risk also refers to the different cash flows from long-term mortgage loans. For example, the cash flow from a five-year automobile loan is quite different from the cash flow from a 30-year mortgage loan. Financial institutions that retain both loans in their portfolio must manage their liquidity needs in consideration of the slower cash flow of principal from a long-term investment.

Selling Loan Production to Investors

All mortgage originators are now authorized (by regulation) to sell residential mortgage loans to either Fannie Mae or Freddie Mac (both are referred to as government-sponsored entities, or GSEs) or to private investors. Both GSE investors and most private players buy whole loans or participations, conventional or FHA/VA, and fixed-rate or adjustable-rate mortgages. An extensive review of the programs, fees, and commitment requirements of Fannie Mae and Freddie Mac is made in Chapter 11, "Secondary Mortgage Market."

For a residential mortgage originator, the advantage gained from selling loans to these major secondary market players or other participants is based on the following factors:

- No portfolio risk from changing interest rates
- Increased ability to meet local housing demand
- Instant liquidity
- Increased servicing volume and income
- Potential for marketing profit
- Participation leverage

As previously discussed, mortgage bankers must sell their loan production to some investor. Although they can choose from many investors, they usually sell the production that does not go into Ginnie Mae mortgage-backed securities to Fannie Mae or Freddie Mac. Other residential originators, on the other hand, can sell to either of these agencies, other investors, or can retain loan production in their portfolio. The deciding factors include type of loan, price, servicing fees, underwriting requirements, and commitments outstanding.

Becoming an Approved Seller/Servicer

Before any mortgage lender can sell mortgage loans to any investor, it must become an approved lender with that investor. Fannie Mae and Freddie Mac refer to approved lenders as *Approved Seller/Servicers*. As a general rule, a mortgage lender must be approved to be both a seller of loans and servicer of loans. In some circumstances, a lender can sell loans to either of these investors and have the servicing transferred to another approved servicer.

The process of becoming an Approved Seller/Servicer requires a mortgage lender to apply for approval from the investor. The first step is stipulating the type(s) of loans to be sold, for example:

1. 1–4 family first mortgages
2. 1–4 family second mortgages
3. Reverse mortgages
4. Rural housing mortgages
5. Cooperative mortgages
6. Rehabilitation loans
7. Multifamily mortgages

The approval process includes the following steps:

1. Applicant submitting application for approval
2. Applicant paying nonrefundable fee
3. Examination of applicant's financial condition
   a. Fannie Mae requires a minimum net worth of $250,000
   b. Freddie Mac requires $1 million
4. Reviewing mortgage-lending experience of lender in
   a. Origination
   b. Secondary market operations
   c. Servicing
5. Establishing whether applicant is properly licensed in jurisdiction
6. Establishing whether staff has sufficient experience in
   a. Originating investment quality mortgage loans
   b. Servicing loans for investors
7. Reviewing fidelity bond and errors and omissions coverage
8. Reviewing acceptability of
   a. Quality control plan
   b. Loan-servicing systems in place

Once an originator of residential loans is approved to sell loans to an investor, the next step is obtaining secondary market commitments.

Direct Sales to Private Secondary Mortgage Market Entities

The direct sale by mortgage bankers to private investors of mortgage loans originated in one part of the country and sold in another was the only alternative to portfolio lending until the start of Fannie Mae in 1938. Mortgage companies in the late 1890s were originating farm mortgages in the Ohio Valley and selling those loans to wealthy individuals or life insurance companies located in the northeastern states. This activity started the loan correspondent system and produced the first use of commitments in mortgage lending. The various types and the use of commitments is discussed in a later section.

Oftentimes, when the term *secondary mortgage market* is used, mortgage lenders automatically think of Fannie Mae or Freddie Mac (and recently the Federal Home Loan Banks), but there also exists a thriving private secondary mortgage market. Although Fannie Mae and Freddie Mac account for between 50 and 60 percent of secondary mortgage market activity, the remaining 40 to 50 percent involves the following players:

- Commercial banks
- Savings banks
- Savings and loan institutions
- Life insurance companies
- Pension funds
- Private conduits

Mortgage bankers, at times, also purchase mortgages originated by other lenders, but never for their own portfolios. This purchase activity is always to fill an outstanding commitment or to issue a Ginnie Mae or private mortgage-backed security (MBS). All mortgage lenders, including mortgage bankers, periodically purchase mortgages from other lenders **servicing released** (see discussion in Chapter 14, "Mortgage Loan Servicing and Administration"). These mortgage lenders in turn sell the loans to the government-related agencies with the servicing rights retained. In this way, mortgage lenders are able to grow their servicing portfolio without the expense of origination. Some mortgage lenders purchase mortgage loans from other lenders because of a permanent or temporary imbalance of deposits and loan production.

Details of Sale

The direct sale to private secondary mortgage market players can be either on a continuous basis supported by outstanding commitments or on a case-by-case negotiated basis. The details of the sale of residential mortgage loans includes the following items:

1. Type of mortgage loans to be delivered:
   a. FHA/VA or conventional
   b. Whole loan or participation
   c. Fixed-rate or variable-rate
2. Total dollar amount of this sale (plus or minus any amount?)
3. Type of pricing (discount/par/premium)

4. Yield (net) to the investor
5. Servicing requirements and fees:
    a. Amount of servicing fee
    b. Whether released or retained
6. **Commitment fees** (if any) charged to seller:
    a. How much
    b. Refundable or not
7. Delivery requirements to purchaser:
    a. Immediate delivery
    b. Future delivery and date
8. Underwriting standards to be used:
    a. Fannie Mae/Freddie Mac standards
    b. Other standards (whose?)
9. Type of loan documentation to be used
10. Recourse to seller:
    a. Whether for mortgage default
    b. Whether for breach of warranties
11. Method of monthly reporting and remittance to investor
12. Loan characteristics of mortgages to be delivered:
    a. Type of properties, for example:
        (1) Single-family detached
        (2) Condominiums
        (3) Second homes
    b. Location (geographic)
    c. Maximum loan amount per mortgage loan
    d. Coupon rates of loans
    e. Loan-to-value maximums
    f. Whether mortgage insurance required
13. Other requirements to be negotiated

As a general rule, these private secondary market purchasers use the same underwriting and documentation requirements as Fannie Mae and Freddie Mac. At times, though, these private market purchasers may vary these requirements slightly, such as increasing certain ratios, or decreasing some documentation to make them more competitive with Fannie Mae/Freddie Mac.

To a mortgage lender, the principal advantage of these direct transactions with private investors is that the nonconforming mortgage loans that cannot be sold to Fannie Mae or Freddie Mac (because they are above the statutory loan limit or have other unique features) are saleable. In addition, the marketing profit to an originating lender may be greater in a direct sale on a negotiated basis than in the more competitive environment of dealing with Fannie Mae or Freddie Mac.

Mortgage Electronic Registration System (MERS)

MERS, modeled after the electronic system for tracking ownership of securities, allows mortgage lenders to register new mortgage loans and to record ownership transfers of mortgage loans and servicing in a similar fashion. At the end of 2001, about 1 out of 3

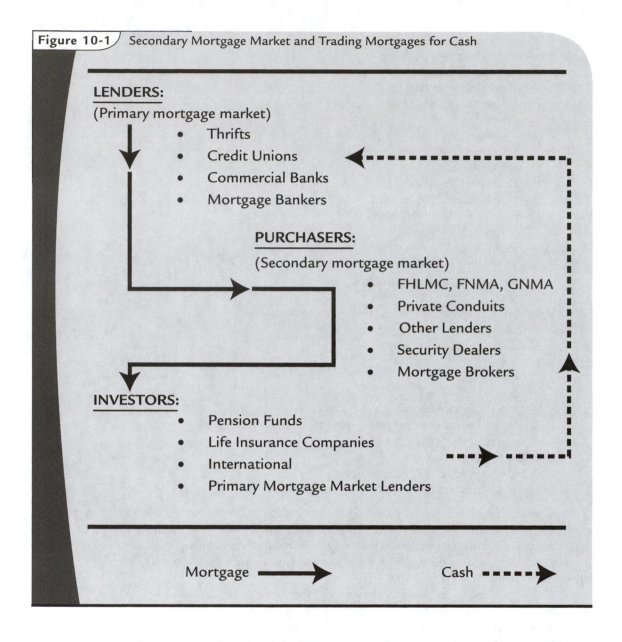

Figure 10-1 Secondary Mortgage Market and Trading Mortgages for Cash

LENDERS:
(Primary mortgage market)

- Thrifts
- Credit Unions
- Commercial Banks
- Mortgage Bankers

PURCHASERS:

(Secondary mortgage market)

- FHLMC, FNMA, GNMA
- Private Conduits
- Other Lenders
- Security Dealers
- Mortgage Brokers

INVESTORS:

- Pension Funds
- Life Insurance Companies
- International
- Primary Mortgage Market Lenders

Mortgage ⟶   Cash ▪▪▪▪▶

newly originated mortgage loans were being registered on this electronic registry. Projections are that 1 out of 2 newly originated mortgage loans will be registered in the future. The reason MERS has become so successful is that lenders do not have to go to the local courthouse or recorder to register ownership changes. These ownership changes normally cost at least $25 per loan. The cost of registering on MERS is currently less than $4. The MERS system was tested and proved its worth during the massive refinancing boom in 2001. Lenders saved considerable time and money by not having to record every assignment or new mortgage loan at the courthouse. A new web-enabled, turnkey system was recently added that allows smaller lenders to obtain mortgage identification numbers and register loans on the system.

Directly Issuing Mortgage-Backed Securities

Until 1977, the mortgage-backed securities (MBSs) field was the exclusive turf of government and government-related agencies. This changed in 1977 when the Bank of America issued the first private MBS. Since then, many other private concerns, including many different types of mortgage lenders, have issued MBSs. This entire subject is covered extensively in Chapter 11, "Secondary Mortgage Market."

Even though mortgage bankers do not have the problem of securing existing portfolios, they have been very active in direct-issue MBSs. Practically all of the Ginnie Mae MBSs that have been issued to date are backed by FHA/VA loans originated or purchased from other lenders by mortgage bankers. Today, all types of mortgage lenders have directly issued mortgage-backed securities.

Selling Loan Production to Conduits for Packaging into MBSs

The number of **conduits** in the marketplace that will buy loans from mortgage lenders and then package those mortgages with other mortgages from other lenders is growing every year. One example, CUNA Mortgage Corporation, buys mortgages only from credit unions and in turn sells those mortgages to Fannie Mae or Freddie Mac, who then issues MBSs. Wall Street companies and mortgage insurance companies have also been active in purchasing mortgages from many lenders and then directly issuing MBSs themselves.

Secondary Mortgage Market Commitments

Commitments are critical to successful mortgage lending for those lenders that sell mortgages. A commitment is an undertaking by either a mortgage lender to make a loan or an investor to buy a loan. A commitment is legally binding as a contract if it agrees completely with the loan application or the offer to sell. If a commitment varies the terms of an application or offer, then it becomes a counteroffer and must be accepted by the borrower or seller before a binding contract can result.

Commitments from investors to buy mortgage production are essential for successful marketing. During the early 1970s, a few mortgage lenders originated mortgages for later sale without a commitment from a permanent investor to purchase those loans. Because interest rates moved so slowly during that period, the interest rate exposure of an originator was limited. But practices changed later in that decade as interest rates became more volatile. After a few mortgage bankers were forced out of business because of severe losses occasioned by not having their production covered, the business changed to mortgage bankers protecting the majority of loan production from interest rate swings by obtaining commitments for future delivery.

For all practical purposes, that was the end of the practice of not covering loan originations by either a firm (mandatory) or standby commitment. Of course, those mortgage lenders who do not originate loans for sale (but for their own portfolios instead) still continue to originate loans without the need of protection from commitments to sell.

Master Commitments

Most mortgage lenders who sell to Fannie Mae and/or Freddie Mac negotiate a master commitment with one or both of these major secondary market players. A master commitment locks in the program, product availability, volume agreement, and specific credit and documentation terms. In addition, a master commitment can establish price arrangements.

Mandatory Delivery Commitments

The most common secondary market commitment is a mandatory delivery under which a lender agrees to sell a specified dollar amount of loans to an investor at agreed-upon prices within a specific period of time. If the lender fails to meet all of the terms of the contract, it may have to pay a penalty or, as it is called, a pair-off fee. (Making a good delivery to Fannie Mae, for example, means that a lender must deliver at least 95 percent up to a maximum of 105 percent of the original commitment amount—or come within $10,000 of the original commitment, whichever is greater.) In some situations, a lender may request a 30-day extension on delivery of loans under the commitment. This type of commitment is used to sell loans for cash or to swap loans for securities.

Pair-Off

Before a commitment expires, a lender may request a full or partial **pair-off** (repurchase) of the outstanding amount of the commitment. The fee will always be at least one-eighth of 1 percent of the commitment and could be more based on the amount of the commitment, type of loan, and the direction of interest rates. If a lender did not request a pair-off and still does not fulfill the commitment, an investor will automatically pair off the remaining unfulfilled commitment.

Best Efforts

In the typical best-effort transaction, a mortgage lender agrees to sell a specific whole loan to a buyer (usually a mortgage wholesaler) at a specific price. In this transaction, both the loan and the servicing rights are often included. These transactions are referred to as **best efforts** because only those mortgage loans that actually close are obligated to be delivered. The benefit of this transaction is that there is no penalty if a loan does not close as there would be in a mandatory delivery commitment. The disadvantage of this transaction is that a lender often must transfer the servicing of the loan to the purchaser, thus placing another institution in contact with the borrower. Recently, Fannie Mae added a best-efforts commitment that allows lenders to retain servicing rights on their loans while not facing a pair-off fee if loans do not close.

Standby Commitments

A **standby commitment** obligates the issuer to purchase mortgages at a certain yield for a certain period of time, but it does not obligate the originator to whom it is issued to deliver any loans. Both parties recognize the likelihood that the mortgage loans may not be delivered and that the standby is a type of insurance for the mortgage originator. This process is valuable to an issuer because it is a fee generator. The fees required for both types of commitments are, as a general rule, established by the marketplace. **Standby fees** are usually twice as much as those required for mandatory delivery. This is because an investor must be compensated for holding funds at the ready to purchase loans, which may or may not be delivered.

Establishing Custodial Accounts

In order to do business with an investor in the secondary mortgage market, a mortgage lender must set up a **custodial account** that allows for collecting payments from the borrower and passing those funds through to the investor. For example, if a lender is selling loans to Fannie Mae, the lender must deposit borrowers' monthly payments into two specific accounts: one for principal and interest, and another for any tax and insurance escrow funds that must be collected. Further, a "drafting" arrangement must be established that authorizes Fannie Mae to draft commitment and other fees.

Uniform Documentation

In order for mortgages to be readily saleable in the secondary market, a degree of uniformity must exist. Before Freddie Mac joined Fannie Mae in the secondary market, the required uniformity existed because all mortgages sold in the secondary market were either FHA insured or VA guaranteed. After 1970, conventional mortgages could also be bought and sold in the secondary market and a need developed for uniform documentation.

Both Fannie Mae and Freddie Mac have worked diligently to produce the state-by-state uniform documents that all mortgage lenders should use for all originations. Ginnie Mae has also adopted these forms, which include the following, among others:

- Mortgage note
- Deed of trust
- Mortgage
- Loan application
- Appraisal form
- Verification documents

These forms can also be used for VA-guaranteed mortgages if a VA-guaranteed loan rider is added to the mortgage or deed of trust to make the mortgage instrument conform to special VA requirements. These forms regrettably cannot be used for FHA-insured loans; FHA-approved forms must be used, but this may change in the future. These uniform forms may contain some minor variations to comply with different state laws.

Pricing in the Secondary Mortgage Market

The price an investor will pay for a mortgage loan (i.e., the yield on the mortgage) determines the value of that loan in the secondary market. Put another way, the secondary mortgage market players (meaning, in this context, Fannie Mae and Freddie

Mac) through posted yields, establish the price they will pay for a net yield (or pass-through rate) on a residential mortgage. Investors will buy mortgage loans at one of the following:

- **Par** (which means the mortgage loan is worth 100 percent of face value)
  Example: A $100,000 mortgage with a 9 percent interest rate would produce $100,000 in cash to the seller and at that price would produce a yield of 9 percent to the investor.

- Discount (which means the mortgage is worth less than 100 percent of face value)
  Example: A $100,000 mortgage with a 9 percent interest rate sold at 98 (98 percent of face value) would produce $98,000 in cash to the seller and deliver a yield of 9.184 percent to the investor.

- Premium (which means the mortgage loan is worth more than 100 percent of face value)
  Example: A $100,000 mortgage with a 9 percent interest rate sold at a price of 102 (102 percent of face value) would produce $102,000 in cash to the seller and deliver a yield of 8.823 percent to the investor.

Pricing information is available from a number of sources, including Fannie Mae's **MORNET** and Freddie Mac's MIDANET. The various financial news outlets (e.g., Bloomberg) can also provide this information.

Remittance Options

In addition to the net yield on a mortgage, the price paid by investors for a residential mortgage loan is also affected by the remittance option selected by the servicer. Once a loan has been sold to an investor, the principal and interest payments (minus any servicing fee) belong to the investor. How and when the principal and interest (P & I) collected by the servicer is remitted to the investor obviously impacts the price the investor will pay for the loan. The options a servicer has for remittance include remitting P & I to the investor

- As collected
- When a certain dollar level is reached
- At some date in the future (e.g., 15th of month after collected)

The longer it takes for an investor to receive the principal and interest, the lower the price the investor is willing to pay for a loan. Some mortgage lenders are willing to take a slightly lower price for their mortgages when they sell (e.g., they have selected a longer period to remit the payments) because they believe they can make more money on the use of the P & I before it is remitted.

Another option a seller has to be concerned with is which remittance option to select for principal and interest. This decision concerns whether to select one of the following:

- **Actual/Actual (A/A):** A type of remittance requiring the lender to remit to the investor only the principal and interest payments actually collected from borrowers.

- **Scheduled/Actual (S/A)**: A type of remittance requiring the lender to remit to the investor the scheduled interest due (whether or not it is collected from borrowers) and the actual principal payments collected.
- **Scheduled/Scheduled (S/S)**: A type of remittance used with mortgage-backed securities that requires the servicer to remit to the issuer the scheduled interest due and the scheduled principal due (whether or not payments are collected from borrowers).

Pipeline Management

If a mortgage originator is planning to sell some or all of the mortgage loans it originates, that lender must be concerned about the interest rate risk inherent in originating mortgage loans. This interest rate risk occurs between the time a lender commits to an interest rate to the borrower and the time that lender receives a commitment from an investor to sell that loan at a certain yield to that investor. The length of time of the interest rate risk could be zero (if the lender immediately gets a commitment to sell the mortgage loan) or could be months (if the lender holds the loan[s] in the warehouse for a period before obtaining a commitment to sell it). Managing this interest rate risk is often referred to as *pipeline management*. The term **pipeline** is used to portray and explain the flow of a mortgage from application to sale. The management part is derived from controlling or limiting the risk while the loans are in the pipeline.

Locking Rates at Application

In a perfect world, a mortgage lender would only commit on interest rates to a loan applicant at or very near closing the mortgage loan so as to not have the potential mismatch between rates committed first to the applicant and then to investors. But, if one lender is willing to commit to borrowers at application, other lenders will normally be forced by market pressures to do the same thing even though they would prefer not to do so. A problem many lenders face is what to do if rates drop after the lender has committed to a rate to the applicant. Should it require the loan applicant to close at the agreed-upon rate? What happens if the applicant refuses and goes to another lender with lower rates? If the transaction is a purchase money mortgage, an applicant may not have the time to shop for another mortgage and wait for the loan to be processed, but if the mortgage is to refinance an existing mortgage, the applicant is not under any time constraints and may look for another lender with lower rates.

Many lenders have decided that the better business practice is to close the loan at the lower rate. If they don't and the applicant goes to another lender, the first lender may find it can only replace the lost loan with a new loan at the lower rate anyway. Some lenders attempt to manage the situation when rates drop before closing by charging a fee for locking rates at application. This strategy can work if other lenders are charging a fee to lock rates, but if only one lender charges a fee, applicants may take their business to those lenders who don't charge a fee for the lock.

Interest Rate Volatility

Even during periods of relative interest rate stability as existed in the United States during the 1990s and into the first decade of the new century, mortgage interest rates rise

| Figure 10-2 | Interest Rate Risk |

Assume $1 million package of 30-year, fixed-rate mortgages originated at 7.00 percent. Yields required in the secondary market have increased to the following figures:

Yields Required (%)	Discount Factor	Dollar Value of Package
7.00%	100.00	$1,000,000
7.50	96.31	$963,100
8.00	92.80	$928,000

and fall over short periods of time and these changes can be significant enough to painfully hurt a lender without a commitment for future delivery to an investor. For example, between January 15 and February 15, 1992 (volatility result of Desert Storm), mortgage rates increased 110 basis points. To illustrate this risk, assume a lender committed to an applicant at a certain interest rate on January 15 and closed that loan four weeks later without having protected itself from interest rate movements. If that lender had to sell the mortgage loan, the price the lender would receive from an investor would have to be discounted to make up for the difference in yield. This risk can be better understood by examining the above figure.

Mortgage Pipeline Segments

The residential mortgage-lending pipeline is defined as that period of time between when an applicant applies for a mortgage loan and the loan is sold. This pipeline should be viewed as consisting of two segments:

- *Production segment*: Period of time between the acceptance of the loan application and the closing of the loan
- *Inventory segment*: Period of time between closing and sale of the loan

The distinction between the two segments is important since a lender has different risk in a loan that has not and may not close and one that has closed.

At first glance, it would appear the best strategy is to simply provide an interest rate commitment to the mortgage applicant and obtain a commitment to deliver a net yield to an investor at the same time. The problem with this strategy is that the loan may not close, either because the applicant doesn't qualify or interest rates drop and the applicant doesn't want to close at the rate quoted at application. This risk of a loan not closing is called **fallout risk**, which means a lender has a commitment to deliver loans at a certain net yield but doesn't as yet have the loans.

Some lenders manage their pipeline risk by establishing what percentage of their applications will always close, no matter what happens to interest rates, and obtaining commitments to sell those loans at the same time they commit to the applicants. If the lender's history is that 50 percent of applicants will always close, while 10 percent never close, that lender has an easier problem in having to manage only 40 percent of the pipeline and not 100 percent. As the loans flow through the pipeline and get closer to closing without falling out, the lender can increase the amount of coverage on those loans by obtaining investor commitments so that by the time the loans close, the lender has nearly 100 percent coverage.

Another pipeline risk a lender has is product risk. *Product risk* is created by a lender obtaining commitments to deliver one type of loan (e.g., 15-year, fixed-rate mortgage) but not being able to close that type of loan. This risk is created because investors don't always value different loan products the same way as interest rates change directions. (For example, if rates are declining, an ARM loan is less attractive to investors than is a fixed-rate mortgage. If rates are rising, just the opposite is true.)

Pipeline Reports

Before a lender can manage the pipeline risk successfully, management must have the necessary tools, and the most important tool is information. The loan-processing system should contain a module that allows for the preparation of reports that management can use to track the following information:

- Dollar amount of loans in the pipeline
- Types of loans
- Interest rates committed to applicants
- When loans are expected to close
- Outstanding commitments to investors

Once management has the appropriate pipeline reports, it will be able to manage the risks inherent with the mortgage loans in the pipeline. There are two basic methods for managing the price and product risk inherent in mortgages in the pipeline. The most obvious is to obtain from investors commitments to buy the loans at a certain yield sometime in the future—a **forward sale**. Most lenders use this method to protect themselves. A few of the large originators use substitute sales to protect themselves. Substitute sales are accomplished with debt market instruments, such as futures contracts, which are sold at an agreed-upon price for delivery on a specified future date. Before the contract expires, the lender purchases an equivalent security to offset the existing position. The normal result is a loss in one market offset by a gain in the other market, thus protecting the original transaction. These transactions can be expensive and don't always work. For that reason, few lenders use substitute sales. The vast majority is served well by obtaining commitments for forward sales.

Yield Calculations

Yield is defined as the return on an investment over a specified period of time, usually expressed as a percentage of the original investment amount. Mortgage loans are generally sold based on the yield (often net) of the mortgage or loan package to the investor. The establishment of some yields (e.g., yield to maturity) is neither an easy nor exact task. Yield to maturity, for example, is impacted by defaults, foreclosures, and principal prepayments. When investors have a large enough package, they can establish to a degree the impact of these events. Mortgage-backed securities are marketed to investors based on certain assumptions regarding yield to maturity.

Our concern in this chapter is determining current yield. Yield is determined by dividing the annualized income by the money invested; for example:

$$\frac{\$90,000 \text{ annualized income}}{\$1,000,000 \text{ invested}} = 9 \text{ percent yield}$$

Put another way, what would an investor pay to receive $90,000 annually when the investor is looking for a 9 percent yield?

$$\frac{\$90,000}{9 \text{ percent}} = \$1,000,000$$

If the investor, with the same amount of annual income, wanted a 10 percent yield, the calculation would be as follows:

$$\frac{\$90,000}{10 \text{ percent}} = \$900,000$$

Thus, if an investor paid $900,000 for a $90,000 annualized income, the yield to the investor would be 10 percent.

Net Yield

As a general rule, when yield to an investor is being negotiated, it refers to a net yield to that investor. Therefore, if a mortgage lender originates a package of mortgages at 9.00 percent and wants to retain 25 basis points servicing, the net yield to an investor would be 8.75 percent. Put another way, if the net yield requirement for an investor with delivery in 60 days is currently 8.75 percent, the originating lender will want to originate mortgages with an average coupon rate of 9.00 percent. If the investor is charging a commitment fee, the fee must also be subtracted in order to correctly establish the yield for the lender. Yield conversion tables are required to arrive at an exact yield, but as a general rule, a 1 percent commitment fee equals 14 basis points.

Weighted-Average Yield

Seldom does the mortgage market rate remain constant long enough for a lender to originate a package of loans with the same coupon (interest) rate. If a lender has mortgages with varying interest rates, the yield to an investor will be calculated on a weighted-average basis. For example, assume a lender has an outstanding commitment requiring delivery of $10 million in mortgages with a net yield to the investor of 9.00 percent. The following calculations will occur:

1. Lender determines which loans in the pipeline will be used to fulfill commitment. Assume:

$5 million at 9.50 percent
$3 million at 9.25 percent
+ $2 million at 9.00 percent
_____
$10 million

2. Yields are then converted into annualized income:

$5 million × 9.50 percent = $475,000
$3 million × 9.25 percent = $277,500
$2 million × 9.00 percent = $180,000

$932,500 annual income

3. Divide annualized income by loan package to establish weighted-average yield:

$$\frac{\$932,500}{\$10,000,000} = 0.09325 \text{ percent}$$

In this example, minus the 25-basis-point servicing fee, the weighted-average yield of 0.09075 is more than the commitment of 0.09 net yield to the lender. When an originator is faced with this situation, it can do one of the following:

- Keep the difference as excess servicing
- Sell the loans at a slight premium
- Substitute a few more 9 percent mortgages to bring the yield down

Price for a Package

Once a package of loans has been put together, the yield can be adjusted by the price paid by the investor for the package. Assume an originator has put together a $10 million package of fixed-rate mortgages for sale to an investor with a weighted-average yield of 8.75 percent. Further, assume that the originating lender predicts rates will remain steady so does not obtain a **forward delivery** commitment. As a result, now that the package is ready for delivery, the market requires an 8.75 net yield. The package of mortgages must be discounted to produce the required net yield to the investor. (With an 8.75 percent weighted-average yield on the underlying mortgages, minus the 25-basis-point servicing fee, the mortgages deliver a net yield to the investor of 8.50.) In this case, minus the servicing fee, the annualized income would be $850,000; thus, the calculation would be as follows:

$$\frac{850,000}{0.0875} = 0.9714$$

Thus, the package will be sold at a discounted price of 0.9714, or

$$\frac{850,000}{0.9714} = 8.75 \text{ yield}$$

Occasionally, a mortgage originator will sell mortgages (probably from portfolio) with coupon rates higher than those required in the secondary market. In those situations, the loans could be sold at a premium. Assume the investor's required net yield is 8.50, and the lender wants to sell $10 million in mortgages with a weighted-average yield of 9.00 percent. After subtracting the 25-basis-point servicing fee, the net yield would be 8.75 percent, or $875,000:

$$\frac{\$875,000}{0.0850} = \$10,294.177, \text{ or a price of } \$102.94$$

Discussion Points

1. Describe the business strategy of selling mortgage loans. Why is it the most popular residential mortgage loan strategy today?

2. What alternatives does a mortgage originator have for the residential mortgage loans that have been originated? What are the pros and cons of each?

3. Identify and discuss the inherent risk of residential mortgage origination.

4. What are the major benefits that a mortgage lender derives from selling loans into the secondary mortgage market?

5. What steps must a mortgage lender go through before it can sell loans into the secondary market?

6. What are loan commitments and why are they so important in secondary mortgage market transactions?

7. Explain the pricing options that a lender has when selling loans into the secondary mortgage market.

Secondary Mortgage Market

Introduction

This chapter examines the role the secondary mortgage market plays in residential mortgage lending and reviews the major players in that market. The major players include the two government-sponsored enterprises, Fannie Mae (Federal National Mortgage Association) and Freddie Mac (Federal Home Loan Mortgage Corporation), who together purchase, on average, approximately 50 to 60 percent of the 1–4 family mortgage loans originated each year. These government-sponsored enterprises (GSEs) are so identified because the federal government was involved in the creation of both of these now private corporations. The importance of the GSE classification is that the debts of the GSEs are often treated in the marketplace as "United States agency" securities even though neither is now a part of the federal government. Since the marketplace equates GSE debt securities as agency debt backed by the U.S. government, this debt is sold at lower rates than similar corporate debt.

On the other hand, Ginnie Mae (Government National Mortgage Association) is an actual federal agency (under the Department of Housing and Urban Development) and thus carries the "full faith and credit of the federal government." All three of these organizations are sometimes referred to as the "government-sponsored" secondary mortgage market to distinguish them from the private secondary mortgage market.

Marketing of residential mortgages and the activity of the secondary mortgage market have taken on new importance since the near disaster faced by thrifts in the early 1980s. The size of the secondary mortgage market is now nearly as large as the primary market was just a few years ago. In the first half of the 1990s, for example, for every four mortgage loans originated in the primary market, approximately three were sold into the various secondary mortgage market outlets. Total secondary mortgage market transactions for 2001 were approximately $1.3 trillion, a figure higher than originations in the primary market for any year before 1998.

Primary Markets and Secondary Markets

The distinction between the primary and secondary mortgage markets is not always clear, especially today with so many originations being funded from sources other than deposits at financial intermediaries. However, most authorities agree that a primary mortgage market exists when a lender extends mortgage funds directly to a borrower. This process includes origination, processing, underwriting, and closing the mortgage loan. This same process occurs, of course, whether a lender is originating the mortgage for its own portfolio, for direct sale to an investor, or for sale into the secondary mortgage market.

The secondary mortgage market, on the other hand, is that market wherein existing mortgages are bought and sold. The most common transaction in this market occurs when a mortgage originator sells existing mortgages to one of the government-sponsored enterprises. This activity could occur as part of the normal course of business for a mortgage lender, or should be utilized only during periods of credit restraints. Thus, the primary market involves an extension of credit to borrower, and the secondary market, a sale of that credit instrument.

Economic Functions of the Secondary Mortgage Market

In order to provide the needed economic assistance to residential mortgage lenders and the primary market, the secondary mortgage market performs these four important economic functions:

1. *Provides liquidity.* Assuming the mortgages are of sufficient investment quality, any originator, portfolio lender, or investor can buy or sell mortgage loans in the market at any time. This ability allows a seller to meet any immediate needs for capital (e.g., to meet deposit withdrawals, fund other loans, or satisfy other demands). Many investors who have not traditionally invested in residential mortgage loans (such as pension funds and trust accounts) are now beginning to invest because the required liquidity for mortgages is present. These investors, attracted by the higher yields available with mortgages, realize that a ready market exists if they are forced to liquidate their holdings.

2. *Moderates the cyclical flow of mortgage capital.* During periods of general capital shortage, the funds available for residential mortgages are usually very scarce, and real estate activity slows down. Institutions operating in the secondary market during these periods purchase existing mortgages from primary mortgage lenders and, in this way, provide funds for additional mortgages to be originated. This availability of capital for mortgages helps to lessen the countercyclical nature of real estate. Today, the secondary mortgage market also serves as a link between the mortgage market and the capital market by the sale of mortgage-backed securities.

3. *Assists the flow of capital from surplus areas to deficit areas.* The operations of the secondary market allow an investor in a capital-surplus area, such as New England, to invest in mortgages originated in a capital-deficit area, such as the South or West, thus providing capital for needed mortgage activity. Capital-surplus areas are the older, slower-growing areas of the country that have excess capital exceeding the demand of homebuyers. Capital-deficit areas are those where the demand for housing credit exceeds the supply of capital created by the savings of individuals.

4. *Decreases the geographical spread in interest rates and allows for portfolio diversification.* The mobility of capital allows for a moderation of the geo-

graphical differences in mortgage interest rates since capital flows to areas of high interest, thus pressuring rates downward. In addition, regional risk (e.g., a large industry closing) is spread to more investors, thus lessening its effect.

Finally, selling mortgage loans in the secondary market usually allows an originator to increase mortgage originations, which normally leads to an increase in profits. The reason is that as a lender sells mortgage loans, it can originate more mortgages with the proceeds of the sale and repeat the cycle again, eventually generating economies of scale in both the origination and service sides of the business.

Participants in the Secondary Mortgage Market

The major players in the secondary mortgage market are the so-called government-sponsored enterprises (GSEs). As mentioned earlier the GSEs include the following entities:

- Federal National Mortgage Corporation (better known as Fannie Mae)
- Federal Home Loan Mortgage Corporation (better known as Freddie Mac)

In addition to these two GSEs, two other players are actually federal agencies:

- Federal Home Loan Banks (offering the Mortgage Partnership Finance program, or MPF)
- Government National Mortgage Association (better known as Ginnie Mae)

Fannie Mae and Freddie Mac are the players most often associated with the secondary market as they fulfill their fundamental role in the U.S. housing finance system by linking the domestic mortgage market and the global capital market. They are often referred to as mortgage investors because they purchase such a large percentage of total originations each year. For example, in both 2001 and 2002, they purchased a combined $1.3 trillion of the $2.0 trillion originated in the primary market in each of those years. Not only do Fannie Mae and Freddie Mac purchase mortgage loans, they are also meaningful holders of mortgage debt. Their combined holdings of outstanding U.S. residential debt is an astonishing 20 percent! These two GSEs are also described as conduits since they purchase loans from many originators and then pool these loans into mortgage-backed securities. Other private investors also purchase loans for their own portfolios or package them into mortgage-backed securities that are insured privately.

The significant advantage Fannie Mae and Freddie Mac enjoy in secondary mortgage market transactions is the result of the magnitude of their secondary activities and their GSE status. An example of the magnitude of these two players is that their combined holding of residential debt (whole loans and mortgage-backed securities) has increased from 36 percent in 1980 to over 70 percent currently.

To a great degree, these two GSEs have established the various standards (documentation, underwriting, loan to value, etc.) for first-mortgage loans. Their advantages have served thus far to prevent any significant penetration by other entities into the secondary market for conforming mortgages. Ginnie Mae, on the other hand, currently does not purchase mortgage loans the way Fannie Mae and Freddie Mac do. Instead,

Ginnie Mae provides a mechanism for lenders to sell FHA/VA mortgages into the secondary mortgage market by wrapping the "full faith and credit of the U.S. government" around mortgage-backed securities backed by FHA/VA mortgages. In recent years, it has been suggested by various housing industry groups that Ginnie Mae could expand its involvement in the secondary market by buying some types of mortgage loans. This addition of another player in the secondary mortgage market could provide additional funds for housing.

Federal Home Loan Banks

The new entrants into the action of buying mortgage loans are the various Federal Home Loan Banks (FHLBs). At year-end 2002, nearly 300 financial institutions were approved to sell loans under the FHLB's Mortgage Partnership Finance (MPF) program. In 1997, the Federal Home Loan Bank of Chicago became the newest entrant into the secondary mortgage market when it purchased from LaSalle Bank a loan used to fund the purchase of a home in Chicago, thus initiating the MPF program. Most other Federal Home Loan Banks soon joined the FHLB of Chicago. FHLB member institutions—including local commercial banks, thrifts, credit unions, and insurance companies—have sold nearly $40 billion conventional and FHA/VA mortgage loans under the Mortgage Partnership Finance program.

The MPF program was created to give local mortgage lenders new options when selling first-mortgage loans. Before 1997 and the introduction of the MPF program, local lenders could either retain first mortgages in their portfolios or sell them to the GSEs. The MPF program provided a new concept whereby the credit expertise of a local lender is combined with the funding and hedging advantages that an FHLB has as a governmental agency. This concept works by allowing lenders to retain the credit risk and customer relationship of their loans while transferring the interest rate and prepayment risks to the FHLB. A major financial advantage of this new program is that a lender is paid a credit enhancement fee for its credit expertise rather than being charged a guarantee fee when loans are securitized with Fannie Mae and Freddie Mac. Because each lender shares in the credit risk with the FHLB, the local lender has ultimate control over the underwriting of loans it originates.

Competition between the Major Players

Just as competition in the primary mortgage market is intense, so is competition in the secondary market. The two GSEs compete intensely and directly with each other year in and year out, although certain requirements (such as the conforming loan limit) are the same for both. Fannie Mae and Freddie Mac are now structured similarly and have basically the same business plan. Mortgage lenders should be approved to do business with both of these corporations since, at any given time, the product mix, price, or services rendered may be better at one than the other. Lenders may take advantage of pricing differences on a daily basis for improved loan sale executions.

At the present time, Fannie Mae and Freddie Mac appear to have the secondary market, for all practical purposes, to themselves. But it is important to understand that these two players purchase on average about 50 to 60 percent of the 1–4 family mortgage debt originated each year. That amount may equal about 65 to 70 percent of the loans actually sold into the secondary market. Therefore, other private entities are buying mortgage loans either for their portfolios or so they can issue mortgage-backed securities.

Are These Two GSEs Regulated?

The Federal Housing Enterprises Financial Safety and Soundness Act of 1992 created a regulatory oversight structure for both GSEs. The U.S. Department of Housing and Urban Development (HUD) has oversight responsibilities for the housing mission of the GSEs. Safety and soundness regulation is vested in the Office of Federal Housing Enterprise Oversight (OFHEO). The OFHEO is within HUD but operates independently of the secretary of HUD. It has the responsibility of monitoring and enforcing safety and soundness standards for both Fannie Mae and Freddie Mac.

The new risk-based capital standards require the GSEs to be able to withstand 10 years of extreme and sustained credit and interest rate fluctuation without exhausting their capital bases.

Federal National Mortgage Association (Fannie Mae)

Any discussion of the secondary mortgage markets must start with the Federal National Mortgage Association, generally referred to as "Fannie Mae." Fannie Mae is the most active participant in the secondary markets historically and currently is the largest holder of residential mortgage debt (over $705 billion) in the world. It is also the largest purchaser of mortgages each year. In 2001, Fannie Mae purchased nearly $800 billion, or about 40 percent of all loans produced that year. This massive amount of money allowed over 5 million Americans to purchase or refinance a home during that year.

Fannie Mae is a congressionally chartered, shareholder-owned, privately managed corporation that is the fifth largest corporation in the United States. Currently, Fannie Mae purchases residential mortgages from nearly 3,000 originators across the United States, including mortgage bankers, commercial banks, thrifts, housing finance agencies, and credit unions.

The importance of an effective secondary market has been recognized since 1924, when a bill was introduced in Congress to establish a system of national home loan banks that could purchase first mortgages. The legislation failed to become law. The first federal attempt to establish and assist a national mortgage market was the Reconstruction Finance Corporation (RFC), created in 1935 and followed in 1938 by a wholly-owned subsidiary, the National Mortgage Association of Washington, soon renamed the Federal National Mortgage Association.

Separation of Ginnie Mae

In 1950, Fannie Mae was transferred to the Department of Housing and Urban Development (HUD) and was later partitioned into two separate corporations by an amendment to the Housing and Urban Development Act of 1968. This was done to permit the "new" Fannie Mae to more actively support the mortgage market outside the federal budget. The new entity, named the Government National Mortgage Association (GNMA, or "Ginnie Mae") remained in HUD and retained the special assistance and loan liquidation functions of the old Fannie Mae. Ginnie Mae is discussed in greater detail in a later section.

The new Fannie Mae corporation was to be basically private, though some regulatory control remained with HUD. In addition, Fannie Mae retained a $2.25 billion line of credit with the U.S. Treasury (which has not been used to date). It also retained the Federal National Mortgage Association's name as well as the assets and responsibilities for secondary market operations. Today, the corporation is run by an 18-member board of directors, consisting of 13 selected by stockholders and 5 appointed by the president of the United States.

From its beginning until 1970, Fannie Mae purchased only FHA/VA mortgages that were originated predominantly by mortgage bankers. In 1970, Congress (in the same bill that created the Federal Home Loan Mortgage Corporation) authorized Fannie Mae to purchase conventional mortgages. The first conventional mortgages were purchased in 1971, and today, Fannie Mae purchases more conventional mortgages than any other type of mortgage loan.

How Fannie Mae Finances Its Operations

Fannie Mae finances its secondary market operations by tapping the private capital markets using short-, medium-, and long-term obligations. Currently, the largest portion of the debt is short term. During recent years, callable debentures have become the most important funding vehicle for the corporation, thus providing some interest rate protection. Purchasers of Fannie Mae debentures include international concerns (largest purchasers), pension funds, local governments, and individuals.

Fannie Mae's Earnings

Although Fannie Mae produces revenue from three sources, the first two are by far the most important:

- *Net interest income.* The spread between its borrowing costs and the yield on its mortgage investment
- **Guaranty fees**. The fee charged for providing a guaranty that the principal and interest will be paid to investors holding their MBSs on a timely basis ($1.48 billion in guaranty fees were earned in 2001)
- *Fee income.* From financial and information services such as the issuance of Real Estate Mortgage Investment Conduits (**REMIC**)

Secondary Market Operations

Fannie Mae, like other institutions in the secondary mortgage market, has made extensive changes in its programs and in the way it operates in an attempt to adapt to changing economic conditions. These changes occur often, even monthly; therefore, any discussion of Fannie Mae's current programs runs the risk of becoming dated quickly. Recognizing that risk, a text without at least an overview of current practices and programs of Fannie Mae would appear to diminish the importance of this major player in the secondary mortgage market.

Fannie Mae purchases mortgages only from Approved Seller/Servicers that have obtained delivery commitments. To become a Fannie Mae Approved Seller/Servicer, a lender must have a minimum net worth of $250,000. Fannie Mae requires an appropriate level of experience on a lender's part and will periodically review the volume of loan originations and amount of serviced loans. Fannie Mae wants assurance that a lender's quality control system contains written procedures, identifies discrepancies, and takes corrective action.

Obtaining Commitments

In order to actually sell mortgage loans to Fannie Mae (Freddie Mac acts in a similar way), a mortgage originator must obtain a contract from the investor that spells out the details of the transaction—the product to be sold, the price, and the delivery terms. This contract is called a commitment. Commitments are obtained by agreeing to sell loans at a specific net yield with **delivery** within a commitment period. (Fannie Mae offers 5-, 10-, 30-, 60-, and 90-day commitments.) The net yield (which does not include the required servicing by a servicer) for specific loan products is quoted over the telephone or is available through various financial information systems (such as MORNET or Bloomberg). Commitments are discussed extensively in Chapter 10, "Selling Residential Mortgage Loans."

The servicing fee, which Fannie Mae requires a lender to collect, ranges from 25 to 50 basis points, depending on the type of mortgage and the volume and experience of the mortgage lender.

Mortgage Loans Fannie Mae Buys

Fannie Mae offers standard purchase and negotiated purchase programs for many different types of first- and second-mortgage loans, including both fixed-rate and adjustable-rate loans. Multifamily and cooperative loans are also eligible to be purchased. The mortgages that Fannie Mae buys for cash or swaps for MBSs include current production and seasoned loans:

- First and second mortgages
- Biweeklies
- Conventional, HUD/FHA, and VA mortgages
- Fixed-, adjustable-, balloon-, and graduated-rate mortgages
- Multifamily and cooperative mortgages

Fannie Mae Activity (in millions of dollars)			TABLE 11-1
Year	Purchases	Year-End Portfolio	
1960	$980	$2,903	
1970	5,078	15,502	
1980	8,099	57,327	
1990	23,959	113,875	
2000	154,231	610,122	
2001	270,584	707,476	

Source: Fannie Mae Annual Report.

Figure 11-1	Fannie Mae Year-End 2001 Residential Mortgage Portfolio	
	Conventional, long-term, fixed-rate	78 percent
	Conventional, intermediate-term, fixed-rate	10 percent
	Adjustable-rate	3 percent
	FHA/VA	6 percent
	Multifamily	3 percent
		100 percent

Source: 2001 Fannie Mae Annual Report.

If a lender does not find the program it wants, it may also negotiate a special transaction with Fannie Mae.

Fannie Mae may only purchase single-family mortgage loans with a maximum original principal balance up to the conforming loan limit—which, in 2001, was $300,700 (this maximum loan amount changes January 1 of each year). This is the same limit for Freddie Mac (Alaska, Hawaii, and the Virgin Islands are 50 percent higher). Higher limits apply to loans secured by dwelling units for two, three, or four families. Conforming loan limits are adjusted annually to reflect changes in the average purchase price of single-family conventionally financed homes, as reported by the Federal Housing Finance Board.

Whole Loans or Participations

Both GSEs purchase whole loans and participation interests in a pool of mortgages. A whole loan sale is the sale of a 100 percent interest in a loan or group of loans. Whole loan sales originally required that all loan documentation be transferred to the purchas-

Conforming Single-Family Loan Limits for Fannie Mae and Freddie Mac (Continental United States; Hawaii and Alaska 50 percent higher)		TABLE 11-2
	1975	$ 55,000*
	1980	$ 93,750*
	1985	$115,300
	1990	$187,450
	1995	$203,150
	2000	$275,400
	2003	$322,700

*Determined by Congress.

Source: Fannie Mae and Freddie Mac.

EXAMPLE

A lender originates $1 million package of 10 percent loans and sells a 90 percent interest at 9.75 percent. Its yield on the retained 10 percent will be 12.25 percent. (Investor receives 9.75 × $900,000 = $87,750; seller receives difference, $100,000 − $87,750 = $12,250 or a yield of 12.25 percent on the $100,000 retained.

ing investor. The secondary market changed this by requiring only the transfer of the promissory note, the security interest, and any mortgage insurance or guaranty forms.

A participation sale is the sale of a partial interest in a loan or group of loans. The sale of interests increases in 5 percent increments between 50 and 95 percent. The most common transaction is the sale of a 90 percent interest in a pool of mortgages with the originator retaining a 10 percent interest. Many lenders favor participation sales because the actual sale requires only two documents: the participation agreement and the participation certificate. **Participations** are also favored by originators because of the possibility of leverage on the remaining 10 percent interest.

Maximum Loan-to-Value Ratios for Standard Purchases

The following maximum loan-to-value ratios currently apply to Fannie Mae's standard purchases:

- 95 percent for fixed-rate mortgages if owner-occupied principal residence
- 90 percent for adjustable-rate if owner-occupied principal residence
- 90 percent for fixed- and adjustable-rate on owner-occupied refinances
- 80 percent for investment properties and second homes

Mortgage Insurance Requirements and Credit Enhancement

Both secondary mortgage market investors are required by their charter from the federal government to obtain mortgage insurance on all mortgage loans if the loan-to-value (LTV) ratio at the time of purchase is greater than 80 percent. In the past, this meant mortgage insurance or guaranty was required for all loans if the LTV was over 80 percent. Today, both GSEs allow loans with over 80 percent LTV to be purchased without mortgage insurance or guaranty if another form of "credit enhancement" is available. This could take the form of pool insurance on a large group of mortgage loans or recourse arrangements whereby the seller agrees to repurchase loans that become delinquent. Credit enhancements are becoming a large part of the business for both GSEs. For instance, 33 percent of Fannie Mae's total mortgage purchases in 2001 were credit enhanced.

Delivery Requirements

During much of Fannie Mae's history, most of its programs were optional delivery. These contracts resulted in Fannie Mae being on the receiving end of a put contract and were not always beneficial to Fannie Mae's financial position. Practically all of Fannie Mae's programs now require mandatory delivery of at least 95 percent of the commitment amount. On occasion, a mortgage lender may be unable to fulfill a commitment; in that situation, the lender can "buy back" the commitment by paying a fee that compensates Fannie Mae for the lost yield. The buyback is called a pair-off. On the other hand, if an outstanding commitment has at least one additional dollar outstanding, another loan can be delivered under that commitment.

As mentioned earlier, most of the standard products no longer require the lender to pay a commitment fee. For a standby commitment, Fannie Mae charges a modest fee.

Federal Home Loan Mortgage Corporation (Freddie Mac)

The second major player in the so-called organized secondary mortgage market is the Federal Home Loan Mortgage Corporation, also known as Freddie Mac. The Emergency Home Finance Act of 1970, in addition to giving Fannie Mae the power to purchase conventional mortgages, authorized the establishment of a new secondary market player. Because it was originally a government-sponsored enterprise, it carries the GSE designation. This player was originally intended to provide secondary market facilities for members of the Federal Home Loan Bank System, which meant savings and loan associations. The corporation's initial capital was from the sale of $100 million of nonvoting common shares to the 12 district Federal Home Loan Banks (FHLBs). The charter of Freddie Mac has been modified to include all mortgage lenders; therefore, any originator of mortgage loans that meets the financial and experience qualifications of Freddie Mac may sell to this GSE.

Today, Freddie Mac is a publicly owned corporation similar to Fannie Mae and listed on the New York Stock Exchange with 60 million shares outstanding. Freddie Mac is managed by a board of directors consisting of 18 members, 13 of whom are elected by the shareholders and 5 are appointed by the president of the United States.

A part of the enabling legislation authorized Freddie Mac to request that the FHLB guarantee Freddie Mac debts or help it raise funds. This authorization has not been used to date. Although Freddie Mac is not formally a part of the federal government, its ties to the FHLB have led investors to classify it as a quasi-governmental agency. As a result, its debt offerings, like Fannie Mae, sell at governmental or near-governmental rates.

Largest Purchaser of Conventional Loans

Freddie Mac's stated mission is to improve the quality of life by making the dream of decent, accessible housing a reality to U.S. citizens. Over the years, Freddie Mac has been the largest purchaser of conventional loans, with financing provided for more than 30 million homes. In 2001, Freddie Mac purchased approximately $475 billion worth of mortgages from various lenders. These loans were purchased from the over 5,000 lenders approved to do business with Freddie Mac. Fulfilling its secondary mortgage market function in addition to its purchases, Freddie Mac issued nearly $390 billion in original issue mortgage securities in 2001.

In 1992, Freddie Mac made a major strategic decision to begin adding loans to its own portfolio. This action allows Freddie Mac to have the same strategic alternatives available as Fannie Mae during periods of volatility in interest rates. At the end of 2001, Freddie Mac had a residential mortgage portfolio of approximately $508 billion.

Business Overview

Freddie Mac finances most of its mortgage purchases with the sale of guaranteed mortgage securities called mortgage participation certificates (PCs), for which Freddie Mac ultimately assumes the risk of borrower default. Mortgages financed in this way are referred to as the *sold portfolio*.

Freddie Mac's Earnings

Freddie Mac's revenue base consists of three components:

- Management and guarantee fees, which consist of the fee income or effective spread earned on the corporation's sold portfolio. The effective spread is the difference between the effective interest rate received on sold mortgages and the effective rate paid to the holders of mortgage securities.
- Net return on Freddie Mac's retained mortgage and investment portfolios.
- Net float benefit or loss, which is the difference between interest earned and interest paid on cash flows generated by the sold portfolio held by Freddie Mac pending remittance to investors. **Float** arises because of inherent timing differences between the remittance of principal and interest payments to Freddie Mac by mortgage servicers and the pass-through of such payments to security holders.

Secondary Market Operations

Similar to Fannie Mae, before a lender sells loans to Freddie Mac, it must become an Approved Seller/Servicer. The major difference between the two GSEs is that Freddie Mac requires a higher net worth ($1 million) before granting approval to a lender. Lenders telephone special numbers or go online to receive current quotes on yield requirements. If a lender decides to obtain a commitment, it gives its identification number and tells the operator the type and amount of loan(s) the lender wants to sell and the delivery period desired. The operator confirms the commitment over the phone and mails two copies of the written contract to the lender. When received, the lender must sign and return the contract within 24 hours. The yield to Freddie Mac is a net yield; that is, it does not include the lender's servicing fee.

Freddie Mac also offers *master commitments*, which allow a mortgage seller the opportunity to sell mortgages over a specified period of time that typically covers 6 to 12 months. Once a seller decides to deliver a specified amount of mortgages to Freddie Mac in accordance with the master commitment, a separate purchase contract is executed for the specific delivery and sale.

Mortgage Characteristics

Freddie Mac, under either the Cash Program or the Guarantor Program, offers to purchase from Approved Sellers the following residential mortgage loans:

- 15-, 20-, and 30-year fixed-rate mortgages
- 5- and 7-year balloon/reset mortgages
- 1-, 3-, and 5-year adjustable-rate mortgages

Financing Mortgage Purchases

Freddie Mac finances its secondary mortgage market operations somewhat differently than Fannie Mae. Freddie Mac previously financed its purchases of mortgage loans by issuing mortgage-backed securities. Today, it has also added the use of debt securities sold in the capital market to fund the loans retained in its portfolio, similar to Fannie Mae. One of the early successes was the Guarantor Program, under which a mortgage lender sold mortgages to Freddie Mac and, in turn, Freddie Mac sold back to the lender an MBS secured by those same mortgages. For this action, Freddie Mac earned a guarantee fee.

In effect, Freddie Mac finances its mortgage purchases with capital generated from the sale of either whole mortgages (rarely) or participations (generally) in groups of mortgages. It effectively buys and sells mortgages on a constant basis. Some capital is generated by the sale of debt securities.

The practical result of this activity is the sale of so-called **participation certificates (PCs)**, which are sold to thrift institutions, pension funds, and others. PCs are mortgage-backed securities that have the timely payment of principal and interest guaranteed by Freddie Mac. These PCs give the investor an undivided interest in the pooled mortgages.

The most important recent mortgage securitization program development by Freddie Mac has been the Gold Mortgage Participation Certificate (Gold). Under this program, introduced in 1990, investors receive borrowers' mortgage payments more quickly than under previous PC programs.

Delivery Requirements

Freddie Mac, similar to Fannie Mae, expects a mortgage lender to deliver the dollar amount of mortgages it contracted to deliver when it obtained a commitment. Though their requirements are slightly different, both secondary mortgage market investors allow a slight variance up or down from the commitment amount.

Documents Delivered to Secondary Market Investors

After agreeing to purchase a mortgage, neither Freddie Mac nor Fannie Mae wants to keep all the documents a mortgage lender finds necessary to have when processing a mortgage loan. As a general rule, they only want the original mortgage, note, assignment of the mortgage, and a loan schedule whereby the characteristics of the mortgage(s) sold are listed. The mortgage lender, on the other hand, must keep these documents either in their original form or recorded on microfilm. These documents must be available at all times if an investor wants to perform its own quality control audit or if the loan becomes delinquent.

Recourse

Mortgage lenders that sell mortgage loans to Fannie Mae or Freddie Mac (or, for that matter, to other investors) face the possibility of recourse. **Recourse** can be defined as the contingent liability a seller of a mortgage loan has to repurchase the loan if the sale of the loan breaches one of the warranties or representations the seller made when the loan was sold. For instance, a seller of a mortgage loan warrants to Fannie Mae that a loan sold was originated according to Fannie Mae's Seller/Servicer Guide. If the loan was not originated according to the requirements, then the seller faces the risk of having to repurchase the loan. Sometimes an investor's quality control efforts identify a deficient loan and the seller is ordered to immediately repurchase the loan. If it is not identified in this manner and the loan never becomes delinquent, then no one is harmed and nothing will happen. But, if the loan was not originated according to the requirements of the investor and the loan does become delinquent and a causal connection can be drawn between the delinquency and breach of warranty, then the seller will be required to repurchase the loan.

With or Without Recourse?

A seller has the option of whether to sell a mortgage loan with or without recourse. If the seller finds an investor who will purchase mortgages with no recourse, the net yield to that investor will be higher than normal. Therefore, the seller's decision is whether to give up yield to acquire no contingent liability to repurchase mortgages. On the other hand, a seller could also contract that loans are sold with full recourse, which means if the loan ever becomes delinquent, the seller will repurchase the loan even if the seller did nothing wrong. This type of arrangement is strongly recommended against (except for the most sophisticated lenders) because a seller could be forced to repurchase many mortgages that defaulted (possibly because of economic events, such as a factory closing), which could put that seller out of business.

In conclusion, three levels of recourse exist:

- *Full recourse*. Seller must repurchase the loan if loan becomes delinquent for any reason.
- *Normal recourse*. Seller must repurchase after delinquency, but only if seller did not process or underwrite the loan according to the investor's requirements and that was the reason for the default.
- *No recourse*. Seller is not obligated to repurchase any loans (with the exception of fraud), even if delinquent, but gives up yield to the investor (net yield is 10 to 15 basis points higher).

Most loans sold into the secondary mortgage market are with normal recourse. Although investors don't want to disclose how many loans are forced back on sellers, it has been suggested that the percentage of delinquent loans repurchased by sellers is approximately 8 to 10 percent. This definitely varies by lender; some lenders produce higher-quality loans than other lenders and thus have fewer delinquencies.

Secondary Market Fraud Issues

Although both Fannie Mae and Freddie Mac (and other investors) attempt to address the risk of fraud when purchasing mortgages in their underwriting and servicing guidelines and requirements, certain types of fraud are difficult to address. Mortgage fraud takes many forms in both the origination and secondary market sales environment. From the secondary market sales side, some of the more common types of fraud include the following:

- *Double selling*. Selling loans to one investor that have already been sold to another investor

- *Sale of nonexistent mortgages*. Sale of illusory loans evidenced by falsified documents and not secured by any interest in real estate
- *Deceptive underwriting practices*. For example, overstating a borrower's income
- *Conversion of funds*. Funds held for an investor's benefit in custodial accounts

Although fraud in secondary market transactions is not common, it does happen. The result of the few bad apples is often increased work for the vast majority of ethical lenders. Those that are convicted of fraud are not allowed to work in the industry again.

Private Secondary Mortgage Market

In addition to the government and government-related agencies, private companies have recently become quite active and thus important in the secondary mortgage market. Reasons for the emergence of the private secondary mortgage market include the following:

- Deregulation and a shift in political sentiment to less government
- Government-related agencies borrowing in the capital markets at the same time excessive federal deficits drive up interest rates and thus crowd some other borrowers out
- Perception of unfair competition, since government-related agencies borrow more cheaply than private companies
- Growth of primary and secondary mortgage markets providing profit opportunities for private entities

Much of the activity of these private entities is with those mortgage loans classified as nonconforming. These loans are so classified because they exceed the set statutory loan limit above which Fannie Mae and Freddie Mac cannot purchase mortgages. The private companies, as a general rule, cannot compete with Fannie Mae and Freddie Mac on loans below that loan limit because government-related agencies have a substantial advantage with their lower cost of funds.

Mortgage-Backed Securities (MBSs)

Mortgage economists' project 1–4 family residential mortgage originations to average over a trillion dollars annually for the first decade of the new century. Some economists have predicted that outstanding single-family mortgage debt will double during the first decade. Even in an economic environment without excessive federal deficits and their resulting demands on credit, this projected growth cannot be met by traditional sources of capital. Mortgage-backed securities (MBSs) provide one of the few ways to meet this demand.

Importance of MBS Today

For the past 20 years, the use of MBSs has become an important tool for mortgage lenders and secondary mortgage market players because of the increased amount of housing that could be financed with MBSs. Further, MBSs have been important to financial institutions because of capital requirements placed on them by their regulators. Because MBSs are considered safer than most other investments an institution can have in its portfolio, the capital requirements for MBSs are lower than for most other investments. In fact, because Ginnie Mae MBSs carry the "full faith and credit of the U.S. government," the capital requirement for them is the same as for Treasury securities— zero. Fannie Mae's and Freddie Mac's MBSs carry a very low capital requirement, much less than for whole loans. As a result of these lower capital requirements, many financial institutions have securitized some of their residential mortgage portfolio.

Concept of MBSs

The basic concept behind MBSs is simple: to provide a way for more capital to flow into housing. Disintermediation among the traditional mortgage lenders in the late 1960s and early 1970s resulted in a shortage of capital for housing and focused attention on the need to develop additional sources of finance. These additional sources were the so-called nontraditional mortgage lenders (i.e., those institutions that traditionally had not invested in mortgages) such as pension funds, retirement systems, life insurance companies, and trusts, among others. The challenge was to provide a way for these nontraditional mortgage lenders to get involved in residential mortgage financing. The answer was mortgage-backed securities.

How Successful Have MBSs Been?

In 1970, the traditional mortgage lenders (not including mortgage companies that sold all their originations) held 78 percent of the outstanding residential mortgage debt. In contrast, at the end of 2002, these same investors held only 30 percent of the outstanding debt, while MBSs held 54 percent of outstanding residential mortgage debt. The other 16 percent was divided between Fannie Mae and Freddie Mac and all other holders. MBSs now constitute the largest classification of holders of residential debt, with over $3 trillion outstanding at the end of 2002!

Why Were Nontraditional Investors Afraid of Mortgages?

Nontraditional mortgage investors were not interested in residential mortgage debt before MBSs because of the cumbersome nature of mortgage investments and the high cost for each transaction. In addition, these investors were concerned about the following more basic drawbacks:

- Diverse state real estate and mortgage laws (e.g., foreclosure, redemption)
- Lack of liquidity (ability to sell quickly) of mortgages
- Lack of day-to-day evaluation of mortgages
- Monthly cash flow of principal and interest that required monthly reinvestment decisions

Considering that the alternative to mortgages were government and corporate bonds with little default risk, substantially lower administrative expenses, and fewer state-related differences to worry about, it is not surprising that these investors had little interest in mortgages before MBSs.

MBSs: A Capital Market Security

What was needed was a way to make mortgage debt a more attractive investment for more investors. The tool used to make mortgage debt attractive was an instrument investors were already familiar with—a **capital market security**. That's the whole key to the success of MBSs: a capital market instrument that is standardized and understood by investors and readily traded in capital markets.

MBSs: An Old Idea

This critical need for more capital was addressed by reviving an old idea—the use of a capital market instrument backed by a pool of mortgages. Some large mortgage insurance companies that sold participation bonds to the general public had used this concept in the 1920s. Neither these mortgage insurance companies nor the bonds they guaranteed survived the Great Depression. Because of the severity of the losses caused by these bonds, mortgage-backed securities were dormant for nearly 50 years.

Types of MBSs

If all of the various types of mortgage-backed securities are considered, all represent either an equity or a creditor position for an investor. That is to say, MBSs either provide an investor with an undivided ownership interest in a pool of mortgages or the pool of mortgages secures a debt.

Pass-Through Certificates

In the first type, an equity position, the investor has a fractional undivided ownership in a pool of mortgages represented by an investment trust. (The trust does not actually manage the mortgages; therefore, no federal income taxes are due from the trust.) The pool of mortgages is created when a mortgage lender assembles a group of mortgages that are alike in type of mortgage instrument, term, and interest rate. The security issuer or pool sponsor is usually one of the traditional originators of residential mortgages. Mortgage bankers have issued more MBSs than any other, but recently savings and loans, commercial banks, sponsors of conduits (e.g., GE), and Wall Street have increased their activity.

When a mortgage lender structures a mortgage pool, the individual loans are actually sold; thus, pass-through certificates involve a sale of assets and are not a debt instrument that would be carried on the books of the issuer. The MBS is then sold to investors who now are the owners of an undivided interest in the pool of mortgages. The monthly principal, interest, and any prepayments from the mortgagors are collected by a servicer (usually the issuer) and are then passed through to the investors.

The pass-through payments can be made in one of three ways, depending on the type of security. The simplest type is the straight pass-through, which is used primarily in private placements. With this instrument, principal and interest are paid to an investor when collected, but if a default by a mortgagor occurs, the investor's cash flow is reduced by that amount.

Some of the early Ginnie Mae MBSs were of the second type, the partially modified pass-through. With this type, the monthly principal and interest due an investor are paid as collected, but if a default occurs, an issuer is only obligated to pass through a predetermined percentage of what is owed.

Neither of these first two was very attractive to investors since investors require greater certainty of cash flow in order for mortgages to be considered as investments. The third form, the modified pass-through, became the instrument accepted in the marketplace and is the one used almost exclusively today.

Modified Pass-Through MBSs

The modified pass-through is the MBS that best meets the needs of investors since it offers near certainty of monthly cash flow. This certainty is an absolute guarantee in some situations; witness the full faith and credit of the federal government backing the monthly payment of principal and interest for Ginnie Mae. With this instrument, the issuer of a certificate is required to pass through to investors principal and interest even if not collected. If the investor is unable to pass through this amount, then Ginnie Mae (or Fannie Mae or Freddie Mac, if they provided the guarantee) will make the payment. This makes the instrument very attractive to investors since monthly cash flow is ensured. Many mortgage investors, including pension funds (the most sought after), invested heavily in Ginnie Mae because of the full faith and credit of the federal government, making modified pass-throughs the most popular pass-through for nontraditional mortgage investors.

Government National Mortgage Association (Ginnie Mae)

To understand MBSs more fully, one must start with the Government National Mortgage Association (GNMA), or as it is called, Ginnie Mae. As mentioned, Ginnie Mae was not the first to use mortgage-backed securities. The first MBS was issued in the 1920s. Because many financial institutions and individual investors lost considerable money with these instruments, the return of MBSs might not have been so successful if the federal government were not involved as a guarantor.

The way a Ginnie Mae MBS works is as follows: First, an issuer, most often a mortgage banker, will seek a commitment from Ginnie Mae to guarantee a pool of acceptable FHA, Farmers Home Administration (FmHA), or VA mortgages. (Originally, only fixed-rate mortgages were used in MBSs, but now adjustable-rate mortgages can make up the pool.)

After receiving the guarantee, a security is issued, backed by a pool of FHA, FmHA, or VA mortgages that have been originated for this purpose, taken out of portfolio, or purchased on the secondary market. These mortgages are then placed in a custodian account as collateral for a Ginnie Mae–guaranteed security.

This MBS is sold through a securities dealer to investors based on the guarantee that the issuer will pay all principal and interest due even if not collected. This guarantee of timely payment of principal and interest by the issuer is backed by Ginnie Mae, which, in return, is backed by the full faith and credit of the federal government. By the end of 2002, nearly $650 billion Ginnie Mae MBSs of all types were outstanding.

Rate of MBS Is Lower than Coupon Rate of Underlying Mortgages

The face rate of a Ginnie Mae MBS is 50 basis points less than the coupon rate of the mortgages underlying the security. Originally, all Ginnie Mae MBSs issued required that all of the mortgages in the pool have the same interest rate. (The Ginnie Mae II MBS allows a 1 percent spread.) If all of the mortgages in a pool carry a coupon rate of 9 percent, then the face rate of the MBS will be 50 basis points less, or 8.5 percent.

The 50 basis points are split, with 44 basis points going to the servicer and 6 basis points going to Ginnie Mae. These fees are to compensate the following:

- The servicer, for its risk of making monthly payments to investors even if principal and interest was not collected from the borrower
- Ginnie Mae, for its guarantee, backing up the servicer

Conventional MBSs

Since the late 1970s, housing finance has been evolving rapidly because of the changes brought about by deregulation of financial institutions, a bout of inflation, and changes in capital requirements, among others. Portfolio lending is no longer the advisable strategy it once was for many lenders. Most residential mortgage originators follow the mortgage-banking strategy that emphasizes originating mortgage loans for sale into the secondary mortgage market and the securitizing of mortgage portfolios. To accomplish these tasks, many lenders have turned to conventional MBSs. Conventional MBSs have allowed mortgage originators to tap the capital markets as a source of funds for housing. A conventional MBS is one that contains only conventional mortgages (either fixed-rate or adjustable-rate, but not mixed together). The underlying conventional mortgages may or may not have private mortgage insurance.

A conventional MBS issuer may remit principal, interest, and any principal prepayments to investors on a specific date of the month when collected or, possibly, the next month. Since mortgagors typically pay their mortgages on or about the first of the month, this delay in payment results in a slight decrease in yield to an investor. This float can be very profitable to issuers based on the amount of MBSs they have issued. Offsetting this slight decrease in yield to an investor is the monthly cash flow, which increases the bond equivalent yield, since a bond typically has interest paid semiannually.

Credit Rating

The rating a private conventional MBS receives from a rating agency is very important since that rating helps establish the yield requirements of investors. Ratings depend on three major items:

- Type of mortgages in the pool
- Experience of the servicer
- Pool mortgage insurance

The so-called prime pool, which gets the highest rating, consists of mortgages that fit within the parameters established by a rating agency in the following table. Other types of properties can be in a pool, but the required amount of pool insurance will be higher since the perceived risk is higher.

Since a conventional MBS is a pass-through, an investor is ensured monthly cash flow from the servicer. If the servicer does not collect it from the mortgagors, the servicer pays it out of its own funds. Thus, the financial strength of the servicer is also of concern to the rating agency.

Mortgage Bonds

In contrast with the equity position an investor has with a pass-through, a mortgage bond puts an investor in a creditor position, with a pool of mortgages serving as collateral. Since the issuer is in a debtor position, mortgage bonds are carried on the balance sheet as liabilities. Two types of bonds have been used: the pay-through or cash flow bond and the straight or traditional bond. The collateralized mortgage obligation is a type of bond, but is unique enough that it is discussed separately.

Pay-Through Bonds

The primary difference between the two mortgage bonds is how the mortgages are valued. With the pay-through bond, the mortgages serve as the source of cash flow to pay off the bond. The monthly principal and interest collected from the mortgagor—the cash flow—is used to make the bond interest payment. That payment can be monthly, quarterly, or semiannually.

Characteristics of Prime Mortgage Collateral Pool	TABLE 11-3
Mortgage security	First lien on single-family (one-unit) detached properties
Mortgage payment	Fixed-rate, level payment, fully amortizing loans
Mortgagor status	Mortgagor's primary residences
Location of properties	Well dispersed throughout an area having a strong diversified economic base
Mortgage size	Less than Fannie Mae/Freddie Mac maximums
Loan to value	80 percent or less
Mortgage documentation	Fannie Mae/Freddie Mac uniform documents

Pay-through bonds have the ability to stand on their own since the cash flow necessary to make the bond interest payment comes from the mortgages that are serving as the security. The cash flow generated by the underlying mortgages is put in the hands of a fiduciary—a trustee. This action removes the possibility that creditors of the issuer could seize the funds if the issuer experiences financial difficulty. Therefore, with the cash flow going to a trustee, the money is able to flow through to investors.

Issuers of Conventional MBSs

Freddie Mac was the first issuer of conventional MBSs in 1971 when it sold participation certificates (PCs) backed by conventional loans purchased from savings and loan associations. Today, Freddie Mac continues to issue PCs, but they can be backed by conventional mortgages (fixed-rate or adjustable-rate) purchased under the cash program from any mortgage lender. The guarantee on the timely payment of principal and interest on PCs issued by Freddie Mac is in its own name and not that of the federal government; thus, there has always been a slight decrease in the yield to investors when compared to Ginnie Mae securities. At the end of 2002, nearly $1 trillion of Freddie Mac PCs was outstanding.

Fannie Mae was a decade behind Freddie Mac in issuing its first MBS in October 1981 but now has surpassed its primary competitor. Fannie Mae backs MBSs consisting of either fixed-rate or adjustable-rate-type mortgages, which can be either conventional or FHA/VA mortgages. By the end of 2002, Fannie Mae had over $1 trillion in MBSs outstanding.

In 1987, Fannie Mae introduced a new concept with its Fannie Majors program, under which mortgage originators could combine their mortgage loans into a multiple-lender MBS. The lender received back a portion of the larger MBS equal to the principal amount of mortgages it had contributed to the pool. This process provided the benefits of geographical diversification to small lenders and lower-volume pooling requirements. Lenders can do one loan at a time in Majors, as contrasted with needing a least $1 million to do a single-issue MBS.

Both Fannie Mae and Freddie Mac can issue only MBSs backed by mortgages (fixed-rate or adjustable-rate) with a principal balance below their conforming loan limit.

Mortgage-Backed Securities Outstanding by Type (dollars in billions)					TABLE 11-4
Year	GNMA	FHLMC	FNMA	Private	Total
1980	$ 94	$ 17	$ 0	N.A.	$111
1985	212	100	55	N.A.	367
1990	401	316	300	53	1,070
1995	472	515	583	236	1,806
2000	612	822	1,058	549	3,041

Sources: Ginnie Mae, Freddie Mac, and Fannie Mae.

Private Issuers of MBSs

Many private MBSs are sponsored by or affiliated with private mortgage insurance companies that use the conduit concept. Other private issuers are Wall Street companies and large financial institutions. A conduit works by channeling the originations of a number of traditional mortgage originators into a single security. This is attractive to investors because it provides them with greater economic and geographical diversity in the mortgage pools. Mortgage insurance companies are interested in sponsoring these conduits because both primary mortgage insurance and pool insurance are normally required. The mortgage insurance companies hope this insurance is purchased from them. Privately issued MBSs have grown rapidly and had nearly $550 billion outstanding in securities at year-end 2000.

Prepayment Considerations

Normally, when evaluating capital market securities, the yield to maturity is the most important consideration. But with MBSs, a prepayment factor seriously impacts all yield calculations. Prepayments occur because people move and sell their homes, refinance, or have other reasons for not letting a mortgage run the full 30 years. For many years, investors used the prepayment assumptions derived from FHA experience. The FHA experience is explained by the conclusions drawn from actual FHA studies on the average life of 30-year fixed-rate mortgages. For example, if all FHA mortgages originated in 1960 are examined, the propensity for prepayment can be established, since all have now been paid off. Some of these mortgages were paid off only months after being originated; others paid off after 1, 10, or 20 years; and some were not paid off until the full 30 years had expired. From these studies, it was concluded that 30-year FHA mortgages show a propensity to be repaid in 12 years. Therefore, a pool of mortgages backed by FHA and VA mortgages is going to show the same propensity for repayment as the individual mortgages in the pool. Based on such studies, it was assumed that a Ginnie Mae MBS will prepay in 12 years, and the yield is calculated on that assumption.

This assumption has been challenged and shown to be very inaccurate during certain interest rate cycles. Further, conventional mortgages have demonstrated a different propensity to prepay than FHA/VA mortgages. For example, when an MBS is said to have a 200 percent experience, it means the pool will prepay twice as fast as a pool of FHA/VA mortgages. The assumption will also vary based on when the mortgage was originated. For example, the propensity to prepay a fixed-rate mortgage originated in 1982 at a rate of 17 percent is probably one or two years. On the other hand, fixed-rate mortgages originated in 2001, when rates were as low as 6.50, may have an average life closer to the old FHA assumption of 12 years.

PSA Model

In 1985, the Public Securities Association developed a new model for measuring prepayments—the PSA Model. This model is used more often today because it better represents the differences between seasoned securities and new securities. For example, seasoned mortgages have been shown to have a more stable prepayment rate, while new mortgages display very low but increasing prepayment rates over the early months and years of their lives. Securities representing these mortgages should show the same propensity. The PSA model has provided interesting conclusions about average life of 30-year mortgages. Recently, the model has shown that the average life of a 30-year fixed-rate mortgage originated after 1998 has been less than 5 years. That very short average life is the direct result of the major downward movement of interest rates over that period of time. As rates begin to head upward again, the average life is expected to also increase.

Conceptual Problems with MBSs

Mortgage-backed securities have accomplished what they were designed to do. They have allowed more dollars to flow into housing. But they are not a perfect solution. There are still some very basic conceptual problems with MBSs. Probably the most important is the irregular cash flow. This refers not to the monthly cash flow but to pre-payments. The biggest problem with prepayments is that they usually come at the wrong time. Mortgagors tend to start prepaying when interest rates are falling just when an investor wants to be able to lock in a yield. On the other hand, when interest rates are going up and an investor would like to get some of the money back so it can be reinvested at a higher yield, prepayments fall off.

Call protection is another problem casting a shadow on MBSs. The issue of call protection is also tied into monthly cash flow of principal and interest for some investors. Many investors would like to have an issuer reinvest the cash flow rather than have it flow through. In other words, if an investor puts money out at 10 percent and then interest rates drop, the investor will get the monthly payment of principal and interest, but it probably cannot reinvest it at 10 percent. In this situation, an investor would like some protection on its yield. The problem is that providing active management of an investment trust for mortgages in order to protect yield would incur some tax liabilities.

There are five items to keep in mind when discussing conceptual problems of MBSs. Already discussed are the reinvestment and prepayment risks. There are three others:

- The market price could change, although that's a risk with any type of commodity subject to market price.
- Credit risk can also impact liquidity and price of MBSs. Although this risk is not as strong now, in 1981–1982, questions surfaced about some of the security issuers. The credit risk concerns the ability of a servicer to make required payments if mortgagors default.
- A liquidity risk exists, which concerns the ability to resell a security. There is no liquidity risk with Ginnie Mae, Freddie Mac, or Fannie Mae because of their real or perceived link with the federal government. But as more financial and nonfinancial institutions issue MBSs, there may be some initial liquidity risk until the marketplace has fully accepted the integrity of the issuer.

Collateralized Mortgage Obligations (CMOs)

As mentioned, the lack of any call protection was a major impediment preventing non-traditional mortgage investors and others from becoming extensive purchasers of MBSs. This problem has been addressed for a time by collateralized mortgage obligations (CMOs), which were introduced by FHLMC in 1983.

These debt instruments have been described as serial pay-through bonds that allow for any nonscheduled payments (prepayments) to be distributed first to one of the various classes of holders. As an example, the first FHLMC CMO has three classes of holders with different maturities:

- Class I—3.2 years maturity
- Class II—8.6 years maturity
- Class III—20.4 years maturity

Through semiannual sinking fund payments, Class I bonds will be fully retired before any principal reduction occurs in Class II or Class III. In other words, all principal payments go to one class until it is fully retired, and then to the next. The maturity of each class is derived from the scheduled mortgage cash flow and the prepayment assumptions based on the characteristics of the mortgages in the pool. The PSA Model is used to predict prepayments rather than the older, less accurate FHA experience. By investing in CMOs, investors have some degree of assurance that their investment will earn the stated yield and not be called before maturity.

Real Estate Mortgage Investment Trusts (REMIC)

The 1986 Tax Reform Act provides that any issuer that meets the requirements of the law may be treated as a trust for taxation purposes. The primary purpose of the REMIC legislation was to provide more efficient and flexible financing arrangements than those that existed for CMOs under the prior tax law. The provisions of this law became effective January 1, 1987, and provided that CMOs may continue to be used until January 1, 1992, after which only REMIC would be used. The requirements, which issuers had to meet, related to the type of mortgages that qualified for REMIC and the trust status and how the cash not yet distributed to security holders could be invested. Issuers of REMIC are allowed to treat these securities as the sale of assets and not as a debt obligation that might create capital inadequacy issues. The law did provide, however, for REMIC transactions to be treated as debt for accounting purposes while reporting it as a sale of assets for tax purposes. These new provisions result in taxation on only the security holders.

Discussion Points

1. What economic functions are performed by the secondary mortgage market?

2. Identify the major players in the secondary market and their specific roles.

3. What types of mortgage loans will Fannie Mae and Freddie Mac buy?

4. What is the difference between whole loan sales and participation sales?

5. What are credit enhancements? Why are they important in today's market?

6. What does *recourse* mean? How can a lender avoid this risk?

7. What are mortgage-backed securities? Why are they so important?

Residential Real Estate Appraisal

Introduction

Throughout the economic activity of humankind, no meaningful business decision is made, nor does any significant investment of any type occur, without first obtaining an appraisal. An appraisal establishes an estimate of value. There are different types of appraisals designed for different types of investment problems.

This chapter provides an overview of residential real estate appraisals, defines the standard terminology used, and explains the common methodology of estimating value. It then explains briefly how lenders use and underwrite appraisals in mortgage lending. Because of its overall complexity and because of important recent developments in this field, the subject of appraising residential real estate requires more extensive reading and additional course work for a complete understanding of the technical processes and requirements.

Hiring the Appraiser

All mortgage lenders should clearly understand that it is their responsibility to order the residential mortgage loan appraisal. In no situation should a mortgage lender allow applicants to order an appraisal from an appraiser of their choosing or bring an appraisal report in with them when they apply for a mortgage loan. The reason for this is obvious: the applicant will simply shop for an appraiser who will produce the highest appraised value. When a mortgage lender is determining who the appraiser should be for a particular assignment, the lender should consider the best appraiser available from a list of approved (by the lender) appraisers. If a mortgage lender hires the best appraiser available, that lender will get the best results from the appraisal. One of the premier attributes a lender should be looking for is the ability of the appraiser to accurately communicate information about the property that will secure the mortgage loan. The narrative on an appraisal report is equally as important as the value listed on the back of the appraisal report.

Purpose of the Appraisal

The primary purpose in obtaining an appraisal report is to help the lender determine whether the collateral is sufficient security for the loan. The secondary purpose of obtaining an appraisal report is to meet the requirements of state and federal laws and regulations and to sell the loan in the secondary mortgage market.

Prudent mortgage underwriting requires that the lender somehow consider the collateral pledged as security for the loan requested. This involves two considerations, and the most commonly used appraisal forms can be divided into two sections to address them:

- What is the condition of the property?
- What is the value of the property?

Describing the condition of the property involves assembling factual data about the land, buildings, and immediate area around it. It is more than simply inspecting the property. The condition of some properties can be relatively straightforward to assess, but many others require years of experience to evaluate the condition accurately. After ascertaining the condition of the property, estimating its value is an even more complex skill for the appraiser to master.

Value

A residential appraisal report should describe clearly its estimate of value and the method(s) used to arrive at that value. *Value* is generally defined as the relationship between an object desired and the person desiring it. Translating the value of this object into a more universal commodity, usually money, results in a clearer estimate of value. Value, stated as a price, is that point at which supply and demand coincide or intersect. Value is also quite subjective. Two individuals might not pay the same price for the same object; thus, its value is different to each of them.

Lenders must always remember this underlying subjectivity of value when reviewing an appraisal report and relying on its value for a loan decision. Although an appraiser uses objective methods, details factual information, and performs empirical calculations in producing an appraisal report, the appraiser makes certain (subjective) judgments based on years of experience and training to select the most appropriate information and methods. The lender relies on the skill of the appraiser to complete the report as objectively as possible and to minimize subjectivity. Although completed in a totally professional manner, at its essence, the appraisal report's estimate of value contains a certain amount of subjectivity.

Uniform Residential Appraisal Report

Appraisers and the appraisal process were under intense scrutiny in the mid- to late 1980s because of the extremely high residential delinquency rates, wide swings in market value of real estate, and the resulting losses to the mortgage industry. Lenders, investors, and mortgage insurance companies all experienced terrible losses because of higher than anticipated real estate delinquency and foreclosures. Many consumers lost all the equity in their homes when they either sold or lost their homes. Some important players in the real estate lending business blamed the high losses on inflated and poorly prepared appraisals. Fannie Mae and several private mortgage insurance companies were among the more vocal in their criticism of the current level of appraisal practices. As a result of this criticism and a desire to improve their profession, the various appraisal organizations worked with the five government agencies involved in residential real estate to develop a single form acceptable to all agencies.

Exhibit 12-1 / Sample Uniform Residential Appraisal Report

Integrated Loan Services, Inc.

Page #4

UNIFORM RESIDENTIAL APPRAISAL REPORT   File No.

Property Description

Property Address **123 Any Street**	City **Melrose** — State **Mass** — Zip Code **02176**
Legal Description **Book , Page**	County **Middlesex**
Assessor's Parcel No. **Map # Lot #**	Tax Year **1996** — R.E. Taxes $ **3,518.81** — Special Assessments $ **0.00**
Borrower **Mr & Mrs Anyone** — Current Owner **Mr & Mrs Anyone**	Occupant: ☒ Owner ☐ Tenant ☐ Vacant
Property rights appraised ☒ Fee Simple ☐ Leasehold — Project Type ☐ PUD ☐ Condominium (HUD/VA only)	HOA $ /Mo.
Neighborhood or Project Name	Map Reference **4-F** — Census Tract **3363**
Sale Price $ **Refinance** — Date of Sale **N/A**	Description and $ amount of loan charges/concessions to be paid by seller **N/A**
Lender/Client **Any Bank USA** — Address **123 Main Street**	
Appraiser **Integrated Loan Services, Inc.** — Address **1017 Turnpike Street, Canton, MA 02021**	

NEIGHBORHOOD

Location	☐ Urban ☒ Suburban ☐ Rural	Predominant occupancy	Single family housing	Present land use %	Land use change
Built up	☒ Over 75% ☐ 25-75% ☐ Under 25%		PRICE $(000) / AGE (yrs)	One family **90**	☒ Not likely ☐ Likely
Growth rate	☐ Rapid ☒ Stable ☐ Slow	☒ Owner	Low **120** / Low **10**	2-4 family **5**	☐ In process
Property values	☐ Increasing ☒ Stable ☐ Declining	☐ Tenant	High **270** / High **100+**	Multi-family	To:
Demand/supply	☐ Shortage ☒ In balance ☐ Over supply	☒ Vacant (0-5%)	Predominant	Commercial **5**	
Marketing time	☐ Under 3 mos. ☒ 3-6 mos. ☐ Over 6 mos.	☐ Vac.(over 5%)	**190** / **60**		

Note: Race and the racial composition of the neighborhood are not appraisal factors.

Neighborhood boundaries and characteristics: The subject is bounded to the north by Upham Street, to the south by Malden City line, to the east by Saugus line, and to the west by Lebanon Street.

Factors that affect the marketability of the properties in the neighborhood (proximity to employment and amenities, employment stability, appeal to market, etc.): There were no adverse factors noted upon inspection that would have a negative effect on the marketability or overall value of the subject property. The subject property is located in a residential neighborhood in its equilibrium stage of its life cycle. Employment stability is average. Proximity to employment and support services is average and typical. The overall appeal of the neighborhood is average and typical of the community.

Market conditions in the subject neighborhood (including support for the above conclusions related to the trend of property values, demand/supply, and marketing time -- such as data on competitive properties for sale in the neighborhood, description of the prevalence of sales and financing concessions, etc.): Market conditions in the subject neighborhood reflect a level of stability. Supply and demand appear to be in balance. Conventional financing with no concessions are prevalent in competitive transactions. The average marketing time for properties in the subject's neighborhood is between 60 & 120 days. The subject is expected to sell at the appraised value given a reasonable marketing time of 120 days based on data obtained from comparable closed sales in the community in the past year.

PUD

Project Information for PUDs (if applicable) - - Is the developer/builder in control of the Home Owners' Association (HOA)? ☐ Yes ☐ No **N/A**
Approximate total number of units in the subject project **N/A** — Approximate total number of units for sale in the subject project **N/A**
Describe common elements and recreational facilities: **N/A**

SITE

Dimensions **60.05' + 28.94' frontage**		Topography	**Level**
Site area **7,712 SF**	Corner Lot ☒ Yes ☐ No	Size	**Typical**
Specific zoning classification and description **SRB (10000 sf/80'min frnt)**		Shape	**Mostly Rectangular**
Zoning compliance ☐ Legal ☒ Legal nonconforming (Grandfathered use) ☐ Illegal ☐ No zoning		Drainage	**Appears Adequate**
Highest & best use as improved: ☒ Present use ☐ Other use (explain)		View	**Neighborhood**

Utilities	Public	Other	Off-site Improvements	Type	Public	Private		
Electricity	☒		Street	**Asphalt**	☒		Landscaping	**Typical**
Gas	☒		Curb/gutter	**Granite**	☒		Driveway Surface	**Asphalt**
Water	☒		Sidewalk	**None**			Apparent easements	**None apparent**
Sanitary sewer	☒		Street lights	**Electric**	☒		FEMA Special Flood Hazard Area	☐ Yes ☒ No
Storm sewer	☒		Alley	**None**			FEMA Zone **C** — Map Date **8/5/86**
							FEMA Map No. **250206-0003B**	

Comments (apparent adverse easements, encroachments, special assessments, slide areas, illegal or legal nonconforming zoning use, etc.): There were no known easements, encroachments, or special assessments noted as of the date of inspection as indicated through a search of available records.

DESCRIPTION OF IMPROVEMENTS

GENERAL DESCRIPTION		EXTERIOR DESCRIPTION		FOUNDATION		BASEMENT		INSULATION	
No. of Units	**1**	Foundation	**Concrete**	Slab	**Full**	Area Sq. Ft.		Roof	☐
No. of Stories	**2**	Exterior Walls	**Clapboard**	Crawl Space	**N/A**	% Finished	**N/A**	Ceiling	☐
Type (Det./Att.)	**Detached**	Roof Surface	**Asphalt**	Basement	**N/A**	Ceiling	**N/A**	Walls	☐
Design (Style)	**Split**	Gutters & Dwnspts.	**Aluminum**	Sump Pump	**None noted**	Walls	**N/A**	Floor	☐
Existing/Proposed	**Existing**	Window Type	**Double Hung**	Dampness	**None noted**	Floor	**N/A**	None	☐
Age (Yrs.)	**31**	Storm/Screens	**Yes**	Settlement	**None noted**	Outside Entry	**N/A**	Unknown	☒
Effective Age (Yrs.)	**8**	Manufactured House	**No**	Infestation	**None noted**				

ROOMS	Foyer	Living	Dining	Kitchen	Den	Family Rm.	Rec. Rm.	Bedrooms	# Baths	Laundry	Other	Area Sq. Ft.
Basement												
Level 1	X					1		1	1	X	Utility	840
Level 2	X	1	1	1				3	1			1,236

Finished area above grade contains: **8** Rooms; **4** Bedroom(s); **2** Bath(s); **2,076** Square Feet of Gross Living Area

INTERIOR	Materials/Condition	HEATING		KITCHEN EQUIP.		ATTIC		AMENITIES		CAR STORAGE	
Floors	**WW/Good**	Type	**FHW**	Refrigerator	☐	None	☐	Fireplace(s) # **2**	☒	None	☐
Walls	**Drywall/Good**	Fuel	**Gas**	Range/Oven	☒	Stairs	☐	Patio	☒	Garage	# of cars
Trim/Finish	**Wood/Good**	Condition	**Avg**	Disposal	☒	Drop Stair	☒	Deck	☒	Attached	
Bath Floor	**Ceramic/Gd**	COOLING		Dishwasher	☒	Scuttle	☐	Porch	☐	Detached	
Bath Wainscot	**Ceramic/Gd**	Central	**CAC**	Fan/Hood	☒	Floor	☒	Fence	☐	Built-In	**1 Car**
Doors	**Wood/Good**	Other	**No**	Microwave	☒	Heated	☐	Pool **Inground**	☒	Carport	
		Condition	**Avg**	Washer/Dryer	☐	Finished	☐			Driveway	**2+ Cars**

Additional features (special energy efficient items, etc.): Additional features include 2 fireplaces, inground pool, Patio.

COMMENTS

Condition of the improvements, depreciation (physical, functional, and external), repairs needed, quality of construction, remodeling/additions, etc.: The subject is in good overall condition. No items of deferred maintenance were noted as of the date of inspection. Physical depreciation appears due to normal wear and tear. There were also no items of functional or external obsolescence noted at the time of inspection.

Adverse environmental conditions (such as, but not limited to, hazardous wastes, toxic substances, etc.) present in the improvements, on the site, or in the immediate vicinity of the subject property.: There were no adverse environmental conditions observed or known by this appraiser as of the date of inspection. See addendum.

Freddie Mac Form 70 6/93 — PAGE 1 OF 2 — Fannie Mae Form 1004 6/93

Form UA2 — "TOTAL for Windows" appraisal software by a la mode, inc. — 1-800-ALAMODE

Exhibit 12-1 / Sample Uniform Residential Appraisal Report (continued)

Page #5

UNIFORM RESIDENTIAL APPRAISAL REPORT File No.

Valuation Section

COST APPROACH			
ESTIMATED SITE VALUE	= $	90,000	Comments on Cost Approach (such as, source of cost estimate, site value, square foot calculation and for HUD, VA and FmHA, the estimated remaining economic life of the property): Square foot cost amounts were derived through a correlation of data from the Marshall & Swift Valuation Journals and conversations with local builders and developers in the community.
ESTIMATED REPRODUCTION COST-NEW-OF IMPROVEMENTS:			
Dwelling 2,076 Sq. Ft. @$ 75.00 = $	155,700		
Sq. Ft. @$ =			
2FPs/Pool/Patio	=	25,000	
Garage/Carport 216 Sq. Ft. @$ 8.00 =	1,728		
Total Estimated Cost New = $	182,428		The estimated effective age of the subject is 8 years; the economic life is based on a 60 year period; and the estimated remaining economic life is 52 years.
Less Physical Functional External			
Depreciation 24,318 =$	24,318		
Depreciated Value of Improvements =$	158,110		
"As-is" Value of Site Improvements =$	8,000		
INDICATED VALUE BY COST APPROACH =$	256,110		

ITEM	SUBJECT	COMPARABLE NO. 1		COMPARABLE NO. 2		COMPARABLE NO. 3	
Address	123 Any Street Melrose	39 Ridgewood Lane Melrose		107 Ellis Farm Lane Melrose		121 Boston Rock Road Melrose	
Proximity to Subject		.25 Mile - 22 DOM		.6 Mile - 92DOM		1 Mile - 142 DOM	
Sales Price	$ Refinance	$	210,000	$	232,000	$	249,000
Price/Gross Living Area	$	$ 134.62		$ 130.04		$ 135.03	
Data and/or	Inspection	Ext.Insp /MLS #30101608		Ext.Insp /MLS #30072224		Ext.Insp /MLS#30072467	
Verification Source	Pub. Records	Public Records		Public Records		Public Records	
VALUE ADJUSTMENTS	DESCRIPTION	DESCRIPTION	+(-)$ Adjust.	DESCRIPTION	+(-)$ Adjust.	DESCRIPTION	+(-)$ Adjust.
Sales or Financing		Conventional		Conventional		Conventional	
Concessions		None noted		None noted		None noted	
Date of Sale/Time		6/28/96Clsd		1/16/96Clsd		4/15/96Clsd	
Location	Good	Similar		Similar		Similar	
Leasehold/Fee Simple	Fee Simple	Fee Simple		Fee Simple		Fee Simple	
Site	7,712 SF	8,098 SF		7,500 SF		11521 SF	
View	Neighborhood	Neighborhood		Neighborhood		Neighborhood	
Design and Appeal	Split/Avg	Split/Avg		Split/Avg		MultiLvl/Avg	
Quality of Construction	Average	Average		Average		Average	
Age	31	38		41		33	
Condition	Good	Inferior	+15,000	Similar		Similar	
Above Grade	Total Bdrms Baths	Total Bdrms Baths		Total Bdrms Baths		Total Bdrms Baths	
Room Count	8 4 2	7 3 2.5	-2,000	6 3 2		8 5 2	
Gross Living Area	2,076 Sq. Ft.	1,560 Sq. Ft.	+10,320	1,784 Sq. Ft.	+5,840	1,844 Sq. Ft.	+4,640
Basement & Finished	Slab	Slab		Full	-5,000	Full	-5,000
Rooms Below Grade	N/A	N/A		2 Rooms/Bath	-10,000	2 Rooms/Lav	-8,000
Functional Utility	Average	Average		Average		Average	
Heating/Cooling	FHW/CAC	FHW/Wall	+2,500	FHW/None	+3,000	FHW/Wall	+2,500
Energy Efficient Items	Standard	Standard		Standard		Standard	
Garage/Carport	1 Car Garage	2 Car Garage	-1,000	2 Car Garage	-1,000	1 Car Garage	
Porch, Patio, Deck,	Patio	Enc Porch	-3,000	Patio		Scr Porch	-2,000
Fireplace(s), etc.	2 Fireplaces	1 Fireplace	+2,000	2 Fireplaces		2 Fireplaces	
Fence, Pool, etc.	IG Pool	None	+5,000	None	+5,000	IG Pool	
Net Adj. (total)		☒ + ☐ - $	28,820	☐ + ☒ - $	2,160	☐ + ☒ - $	7,860
Adjusted Sales Price		Net 13.7 %		Net 0.9 %		Net 3.2 %	
of Comparable		Gross 19.4 % $	238,820	Gross 12.9 % $	229,840	Gross 8.9 % $	241,140

Comments on Sales Comparison (including the subject property's compatibility to the neighborhood, etc.): The subject neighborhood compatibility is average and typical. Lavs adjusted at $2000, GLA adjusted at $20 per sf for any differences in excess of 100 sf. All other adjustments as noted. All comparables weighed equally.

ITEM	SUBJECT	COMPARABLE NO. 1	COMPARABLE NO. 2	COMPARABLE NO. 3
Date, Price and Data Source, for prior sales within year of appraisal	No recorded sale in past year.B&T/MLS	There has been no recorded sale in the past year. B&T/MLS	There has been no recorded sale in the past year. B&T/MLS	There has been no recorded sale in the past year. B&T/MLS

Analysis of any current agreement of sale, option, or listing of subject property and analysis of any prior sales of subject and comparables within one year of the date of appraisal: There has been no prior sale, option, or listing of the subject in the last year. Other than noted above, there has been no reported sales of the comps within the past year as per public records.

INDICATED VALUE BY SALES COMPARISON APPROACH .... $ 238,500

INDICATED VALUE BY INCOME APPROACH (if Applicable) Estimated Market Rent $ N/A /Mo. x Gross Rent Multiplier N/A = $

This appraisal is made ☒ "as is" ☐ subject to the repairs, alterations, inspections or conditions listed below ☐ subject to completion per plans & specifications.

Conditions of Appraisal: There are no repairs required as a condition of this appraisal.

Final Reconciliation: Single family properties are purchased based on comparable property sales rather than reproduction cost or income generating potential. The Sales Comparison Approach is most reliable in estimating current market value as it directly reflects the actions of typical buyers & sellers.

The purpose of this appraisal is to estimate the market value of the real property that is the subject of this report, based on the above conditions and the certification, contingent and limiting conditions, and market value definition that are stated in the attached Freddie Mac Form 439/FNMA form 1004B (Revised 6/93).

I (WE) ESTIMATE THE MARKET VALUE, AS DEFINED, OF THE REAL PROPERTY THAT IS THE SUBJECT OF THIS REPORT, AS OF September 12, 1996 (WHICH IS THE DATE OF INSPECTION AND THE EFFECTIVE DATE OF THIS REPORT) TO BE $ 238,500

APPRAISER:	SUPERVISORY APPRAISER (ONLY IF REQUIRED):	
Signature *Kathleen Murphy*	Signature *Supervisory signature*	☐ Did ☒ Did Not
Name Kathleen Murphy	Name	Inspect Property
Date Report Signed September 13, 1996	Date Report Signed September 13, 1996	
State Certification # Cert Res #4005 State Mass	State Certification # Cert Gen #98	State MA
Or State License # State	Or State License #	State

Freddie Mac Form 70 6/93 PAGE 2 OF 2 Fannie Mae Form 1004 6-93

Form UA2 — "TOTAL for Windows" appraisal software by a la mode, inc. — 1-800-ALAMODE

The result was the Uniform Residential Appraisal Report (URAR) in 1986. Use of this form allows appraisers to produce professional reports that are self-contained and that logically support the final value estimate given. The January 1993 revision of this form was required by Fannie Mae, Freddie Mac, the Federal Housing Administration, the Veterans Administration, and the Farmers Home Administration for all mortgage loans until the development of newer forms that accompanied automated underwriting systems in the late 1990s.

The first page of the URAR contains extensive descriptive information about the property, its condition, the neighborhood in which it is located, and the market conditions at the time of the appraisal. The form provides descriptive information in the following major areas:

- *Subject*. Address, ownership rights, legal description, occupancy
- *Neighborhood*. Market conditions, price ranges, land use, boundaries
- *Site*. Dimensions, zoning, off-site improvements, utilities, flood zone
- *Description of improvements*. Exterior, foundation, room count, interior, heating, venting, and air conditioning (HVAC), kitchen, amenities

The second page of the URAR develops the three approaches to value (described later) and overall estimate of market value for the property:

- *Cost approach*. Site value, reproduction cost, depreciation
- *Sales comparison analysis and value*. Three or more comparable sales, detailed value adjustments, sources
- *Income approach*. Estimated market rent, gross rent multiplier
- *Reconciliation*. Final reconciliation, estimate of market value, appraiser signature(s)

Completion of the URAR is part of the appraisal process (described later). The appraiser delivers this report directly to the client—the lender, not the applicants—however, regulations now require that the lender offer a copy to the applicants. The guidelines by which the appraiser completes this or any other appraisal form and makes an estimate of market value are set by the Uniform Standards of Processional Appraisal Practice.

Uniform Standards of Professional Appraisal Practice

In 1986, the various appraisal organizations also developed a set of professional practice standards that govern appraisers in preparing the URAR (and subsequent forms). These standards are called the Uniform Standards for Professional Appraisal Practice, or USPAP. These standards were an important step forward for the profession, since they are the first uniform standards ever adopted by the appraisal industry as a whole. Although the specific forms have changed since 1986, these standards remain as the basis for the objective practice of appraising real estate.

In 1993, the Financial Institution Reform, Recovery and Enforcement Act (FIRREA) legislation addressed the issue of appraisals as a part of the real estate lending process and formally adopted the USPAP. This process was facilitated by the appraisal industry through the nonprofit body known as the Appraisal Foundation.

The FIRREA legislation also required that beginning on January 1, 1993, all real estate transactions needing an appraisal must include one performed by either a state-licensed or certified appraiser. A licensed appraiser is one who possesses a basic level of skills and education in real estate appraising sufficient to prepare a "noncomplex" residential assignment. A certified residential appraiser is one whose experience and education level is such that that appraiser is qualified to handle all residential properties, in particular those deemed complex or above a certain transaction level, currently $1 million.

Principles of Real Estate Value

Lenders may need an estimate of value at almost any stage of a real estate transaction or activity. For example, at any given moment, an appraisal of real estate may be needed to estimate any of the following:

- Market value for mortgage-lending purposes
- Assessed value for taxation purposes
- Insurance value
- Market value for sale or exchange purposes
- Compensation for condemnation/municipal acquisition
- Investment value for rental income purposes

The value determined for the same piece of real estate can vary according to the ultimate purpose of the appraisal assignment. For example, the estimated value for insurance purposes could be much different than the value estimated for condemnation purposes. Most mortgage lenders are regulated by law to lend according to a certain percentage of market value, the focus of this discussion.

Market Value

Market value is defined by the Appraisal Foundation and the Uniform Standards of Professional Appraisal Practice as "the most probable price which a property should bring in a competitive and open market under all conditions requisite to a fair sale, the buyer and seller, each acting prudently and knowledgeably, and assuming the price is not affected by undue stimulus." Implicit in this definition is the consummation of sale as of a specific date and the passing of title from seller to buyer under conditions whereby

- Buyer and seller are typically motivated.
- Both parties are well informed and well advised and acting in what they consider their best interests.
- A reasonable time is allowed for exposure in the open market.
- Payment is in terms of cash in U.S. dollars or in terms of financial arrangements comparable thereto.
- The price represents the normal consideration for the property sold unaffected by special or creative financing or sales concessions granted by anyone associated with the sale.

Market Price

The *market price* is that price for which the real estate actually sells. In theory, market value and price should be the same, but they rarely are. For example, a seller may decide to accept less (market price) than asked (presumed market value) in order to facilitate the sale if the seller believes time is more valuable than the difference in money.

Factors Affecting Market Value

For almost 30 years, from 1950 to 1980, residential real estate appreciated steadily across the country, increasing at an average rate of 3 to 6 percent per year. This stability reinforced the mind-set developed in consumers and industry professionals that investment in residential real estate was a no-risk investment.

But the value of a particular piece of real estate does not remain constant. It changes over time, because of economics, governmental intervention, and the changing tastes of consumers. Value does not constantly go up, as mortgage lenders and consumers in the Southwest learned during the early 1980s and in New England during the late 1980s. For example, in 1986–1987, it was not uncommon in some areas of Texas, notably Houston, for real estate values to drop 30 to 40 percent a year. Here is a general list of factors that affect the value of real estate:

- Population growth or decline
- Economic developments
  - Micro or local changes
  - Macro or national changes
- Financial factors
  - The rate of inflation
  - Cost of financing
  - Type of financing available
- Shifts in consumer preference
- Governmental regulations
  - Zoning
  - Building codes
  - Taxation
- Shifts in traffic patterns or public transportation
- Physical forces
  - Water supply
  - Soil contamination
  - Location on an earthquake fault

Even if these factors remain constant, market value may still change as a result of even more basic value determinants. The most basic is supply and demand. Like all other marketable commodities, real estate value increases or decreases based on its supply and the demand. Supply conditions result from the number of housing units available in the market at any given time—the number of new units being constructed, the number of building permits issued, as well as the number of units lost or destroyed. Demand conditions depend on the level of employment, the level of income, inflation rates, family size, and saving rates, along with other economic factors of this type.

In addition to the preceding factors, other economic principles of value influence the appraisal of real estate:

- Highest and best use
- Diminishing returns
- Substitution

Market value of real estate is influenced to a great extent by whether or not the real estate is put to its "highest and best use." This use is defined as the use that creates the highest present value. The Uniform Standards state, "Two separate highest and best uses exist for each property site: one for the site as though it were vacant, and one for the site as though it were improved. The first looks through the existing building as though it did not exist and estimates the best use of the site as if it were vacant. The second estimates the best use of the site and building(s) with all improvements together."

Four important considerations determine highest and best use for a property:

- Physical possibility
- Legal permissibility
- Appropriate support
- Financial feasibility

If all of these conditions are present, the result will be a property's highest and best value.

The principle of diminishing returns recognizes that, after a certain point, additional improvements to the property will not continue to increase its total value by the amount of new improvements. For example, if we add a second bathroom to a house, the property might increase in value by an amount equal to the cost of the new bathroom. But if we add a third, fourth, or fifth bathroom, the value will increase by an amount greatly less than the cost of the additional bathrooms.

Finally, the principle of substitution demonstrates that the upper range of value for a property tends to be established by the cost of acquiring an equally desirable substitute property, or the cost of building a similar structure.

As with mortgage underwriting, no single formula applies to all properties and situations. An experienced appraiser must consider and blend these various principles and factors to produce a professional estimate of market value for the proposed collateral.

The Appraisal Process

The first step in the appraisal process is to plan the appraisal. Since the appraisal is intended to solve a problem—to estimate value of a particular property—it must be clearly stated as to what type of value is being sought. The process required to produce this estimate of value necessitates identification of the following:

- Real estate to be appraised
- Type of value sought
- Effective date of the appraisal
- Character of the property
- Property rights
- Character of the market in which the property is located

The next step in the appraisal process is to identify the data that the appraiser needs. The data required by the appraiser can be found in the public records and obtained from mortgage lenders, other appraisers, or real estate agents. Other sources include the local chamber of commerce, planning and zoning authorities, and even

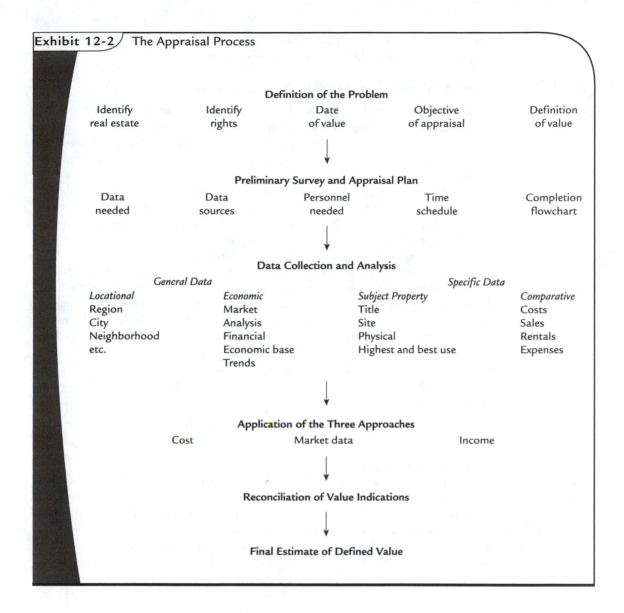

Exhibit 12-2 The Appraisal Process

Definition of the Problem

| Identify real estate | Identify rights | Date of value | Objective of appraisal | Definition of value |

Preliminary Survey and Appraisal Plan

| Data needed | Data sources | Personnel needed | Time schedule | Completion flowchart |

Data Collection and Analysis

General Data   *Specific Data*

Locational	*Economic*	*Subject Property*	*Comparative*
Region	Market	Title	Costs
City	Analysis	Site	Sales
Neighborhood	Financial	Physical	Rentals
etc.	Economic base	Highest and best use	Expenses
	Trends		

Application of the Three Approaches

| Cost | Market data | Income |

Reconciliation of Value Indications

Final Estimate of Defined Value

local homebuilders. Finally, the appraiser has the professional dual responsibilities of keeping this data current and relying only on accurate data.

Alternative Approaches to Value

Appraisers use three very specific appraisal techniques when developing a real estate appraisal: the direct sales comparison approach, the cost approach, and the income approach. Although one of these "approaches," or techniques, may be more appropriate under certain circumstances, the combination of the three is intended to provide the most complete solution to the appraisal problem.

Direct Sales Comparison Approach

The direct sales comparison approach is considered to be the most reliable determinant of market value for most residential properties. This approach assumes that an informed and rational purchaser will pay no more for a property than the price or cost of a substitute property with the same characteristics and utility. As a result, this approach relies on the ability of the appraiser to locate similar, or "comparable," properties that have recently sold in that neighborhood. Although no two properties are identical, nevertheless the two homes can be compared and a reasonable value established using an appropriate adjustment process. The principle of substitution is evident with this approach since the value of a property similar to the subject property should closely approximate the value of the subject property.

An appraiser will use as many recent sales of similar or comparable properties as possible; the more used, the more accurate the estimate. The URAR requires the use of at least three comparable sales, or "sales comps." The market prices of the comparables are adjusted for the physical differences between the comparable and the subject property. Appraisers adjust the features of the sales comp to the subject property. If the sales comp has a feature missing in the subject property, the appraiser calculates a negative adjustment to that sales comp equal to the market value of that feature. If the sales comparable lacks a feature present in the subject property, the appraiser makes a positive adjustment to that sales comp. The basic formula is as follows:

Sales Price of the Comparable ± Adjustment = Value of the Subject

Financing Concessions

Seller-paid financing concessions complicate the effectiveness of the direct sales comparable approach. The seller, for example, may pay all of the buyer's closing costs, pay something to buy down the interest rate, or pay some other concession to facilitate the sale. This increases the speed of selling the property and increases the number of buyers capable of buying the property. The net result of these actions is an increase in the sales price to cover the cost of providing these concessions.

EXAMPLE

Sales comp 1 (SC1), which has a finished basement worth $15,000, recently sold for $115,000. Except for the finished basement, this property is otherwise comparable to the subject property (SP), so the estimate of value for the SP would be $100,000.

SC1 value – Value of Basement = SP Value
$115,000 – $15,000 = $100,000

The appraiser recognizes the impact of sales concessions when preparing an appraisal that relies on comparables with these characteristics. This is important to a mortgage lender because the mortgage should be secured by the value of the real estate alone, not by real estate plus some concession. To assist the appraiser in these situations, the Uniform Standards require that the appraiser request a copy of the sales contract during the information-gathering phase of the appraisal. A mortgage lender is required to provide the appraiser with a copy of the sales contract and as much information on the sale as possible.

Cost Approach

The cost approach is the second most important method used for estimating the market value for residential real estate. It relies on the appraiser's ability to calculate an estimate of the current cost of production, which is defined as the reproduction cost, or the cost to build an exact replica of the improvements. More specifically, the cost approach can be explained using the following formula:

Cost of Reproduction – Depreciation + Land Value = Value of Subject Property

When figuring costs, the appraiser includes both direct costs and indirect costs. Direct costs include building materials and supplies, labor, and profits. Indirect costs include various fees, taxes, and financing costs.

Next, the appraiser recognizes that a newly reproduced structure will not be *exactly* the same value or condition as the subject property because of its effective economic age. Every physical thing of economic use eventually wears out or its condition deteriorates with age. Think of the value of a new car versus last year's model with less than 100 miles on it, or the value of a new computer versus one that is a year old but never been used. All comparables have effectively the same usefulness and may have the same features, but the new car and computer appeal to more buyers and are easier to sell, so they are more expensive. In real estate, the older subject property has depreciated in value from when it was new—some features of the subject experience wear out or are not as valuable as new ones with improved features. Although the subject may appear to be in the same condition with no noticeable deterioration, it has, by virtue of time, a shorter economic life. The appraiser adjusts the reproduction cost to reflect depreciation in value from three possible forms:

- *Physical deterioration.* A loss in value from the cost of a new structure is equal to the loss of economic life in the subject property caused by wear and tear. Physical deterioration may be "curable" or "incurable," meaning it may or may never be brought to current standards (such as a roof that is 15 years old that can be replaced, or a termite-infested wood frame that is rotted and cannot be fixed so that the entire structure must be razed).
- *Functional obsolescence.* A loss in value resulting from structural components that are outmoded or inefficient, as judged by current standards (such as bathrooms or the overall design or layout of the structure).
- *Economic obsolescence.* A loss in value resulting from changes external to the property (such as changes in zoning classifications, traffic patterns, or environmental hazards).

EXAMPLE

Assume the appraisal assignment is to estimate the value of a 10-year-old Cape Cod that has depreciated 15 percent. The cost of building a comparable structure is $185,000. The estimate of value is made in this way:

Cost of Reproduction − Depreciation = Adjusted Value + Land Value
= Value of Subject Property
$185,000 − $27,750 = $157,250 + Land Value = Value of the Subject Property

Finally, the appraiser includes the value of the land upon which the structure stands, plus any improvements to it such as landscaping, stone walls, public sewer and water connections.

The idea of the cost approach starts to break down the older the improvements become. Generally, properties older than 25 years cannot be reliably appraised with the cost approach because there is too much depreciation to estimate and the changing skills and techniques in home construction make it too speculative. Generally, the cost approach sets the upper limit to value, because a house will not be worth more than a house built new. Again, this breaks down the older the property gets. At some point, a house's value has dropped so low because of disrepair and the lack of maintenance that the land is worth more than the improved property. This is because it costs more to demolish the house than the improvements are worth.

Income Approach

The income approach to estimating market value uses the net operating income of the property, but is similar to the cost and direct market approaches. The income approach assumes there is a strong relationship between the rental income a property earns and the price someone would prudently pay for that property. This method also reflects the choice that the buyer has in the marketplace between renting and buying a similar unit or property (from the buyer's standpoint, "Why should I pay more for a property when I can rent a similar property for less?"). The appraiser developing the income approach selects sales comparables with rental unit(s) similar to those in the subject property, then reviews both the rents for similar units and the sales prices for similar properties.

Obviously, this approach makes the most sense for those properties that have or can produce rental income. Generally, the sales comparison approach and the cost approach apply more to residential real estate, and the income approach is more suitable to income-producing properties, such as offices or apartment buildings. But a special technique called the gross rent multiplier (GRM) can be used to either estimate value for a single-family residence or to serve as a check against the other approaches. The theory behind the GRM is that the same economic influences affect both sales prices and rents. This relationship can be expressed as a ratio:

$$\frac{\text{Sales Price}}{\text{Gross Monthly Rental Income}} = \text{GRM}$$

EXAMPLE

If a house recently sold for $125,000 and was rented for $750 per month, the GRM would be the following:

$$\frac{\$115,000}{\$750} = 153.33, \text{ rounded to } 153$$

Thus, if the appraisal assignment is to estimate the value of another similar property that is being rented for $675 per month, the result would be $675 \times 153 = \$103,275$, rounded to $103,000 (value of the subject house using the income approach).

Reconciliation and Final Value Estimate

Although most appraisal problems call for a single final estimate of market value, the Uniform Standards require that appraisers consider all three approaches on their way to the final estimate of value. While each method can serve as a check against the other approaches, it is true that certain types of properties lend themselves more to one method than the others. For example, the cost approach lends itself to a property currently under construction, and the income approach applies best to a duplex rental property.

In most situations, the estimates of value using all three approaches should be fairly similar. If the estimates are widely divergent, the data-gathering method and analysis for each approach should be carefully reviewed. If the estimates remain far apart, the appraiser must consider the purpose of the appraisal. If the appraisal is to estimate market value for mortgage-lending purposes, the sales comparison approach is most important. For insurance claim purposes, the cost approach may be most important. If, on the other hand, the subject property is a residential rental property, then the income approach will be the most applicable.

It is in the correlation of value that an appraiser's skill and experience comes to the forefront and the problem of estimating market value is resolved. This reconciliation process and final value estimate is not simply a mathematical exercise. It is, however, a process of judgment, analysis, and reason that results in a professional, logical, and supportable estimate of market value.

Required Forms

The secondary market has developed several standardized appraisal forms for residential mortgage lending. Their use depends on the type of property appraised. They include the following:

- *For single-family property.* URAR (Fannie Mae Form 1004/Freddie Mac Form 70)
- *For 2–4 family property.* Small Residential Income Property Form (Fannie Mae Form 1025/Freddie Mac Form 72)

• *For condominium or cooperatives.* Individual Condominium Form (Fannie Mae Form 1073/Freddie Mac Form 465)

• *PUD properties.* URAR Form or Individual Condominium Form

The following attachments must be a part of each appraisal report:

• Original photos of the subject property (front, rear, and street)
• Original photos of the comparable sales (front)
• Location map showing the subject and the comparable sales
• Exterior sketch of the subject dwelling, with measurements
• Certification and Statement of Limiting Conditions (Fannie Mae Form 1004B)
• Addendum warranting compliance with all pertinent FIRREA requirements

Streamlined Appraisals and Automated Valuation Models

In the mid-1990s, Fannie Mae and Freddie Mac adopted new appraisal requirements and developed new appraisal forms as part of their automated underwriting systems (AUSs)—Desktop Underwriter (DU) for Fannie Mae and Loan Prospector (LP) for Freddie Mac. Driven by the desire of large lenders and investors for faster decision making and delivery in secondary market transactions, in 1996, Fannie Mae and Freddie Mac developed shorter "abbreviated" appraisal forms to expedite the underwriting process in their proprietary AUSs.

Lenders who submit loans to either DU or LP have several options for appraisals in addition to what is now considered the "full" appraisal using the URAR Fannie Mae Form 1004/Freddie Mac Form 70. The new appraisal standards and options include streamlined appraisals and automated valuations (AVs). These abbreviated forms provide less descriptive and market information and require less time to complete than the industry standard URAR Fannie Mae Form 1004/Freddie Mac Form 70. In some cases, Fannie Mae and Freddie Mac require only a "drive-by" inspection of the property. The following sections describe the forms most commonly used.

Streamlined Appraisals

1. *DU or LP Quantitative Analysis Appraisal Report (Fannie Mae Form 2055)— Exterior Inspection and/or Interior Inspection.* This form differs from the standard URAR Fannie Mae Form 1004/Freddie Mac Form 70 in several areas:
   • Fewer areas for comments
   • Less descriptive neighborhood, site, improvement, and sales comparison sections
   • Elimination of income and cost approaches
   • Only an exterior, drive-by inspection required, depending on the recommendation from the AUS

2. *DU Qualitative Analysis Appraisal Report (Fannie Mae Form 2065)—Interior Inspection Only.* This form differs from the standard URAR Fannie Mae 1004/Freddie Mac 70 Form in all the same areas as detailed for the Fannie Mae Form 2055, in addition to the following areas:

- Sales comparison adjustments do not contain dollar values, only a +, –, or = value when compared to the subject property.
- Only an exterior drive-by inspection is required—no internal inspection.

Automated Valuation Models (AVMs)

The appraisal process for AVMs differs substantially from the normal appraisal process. AVMs use high-powered econometric models designed to emulate the marketplace and predict the value of a property based on the surrounding actions within the property's marketplace. The statistical model, not the appraiser, develops the estimate of market value. Sources of information that are compared to the subject property or methods used to produce an estimate of value include the following:

- Repeat sales in the subject property's area
- "Hedonic models," which focus on property characteristics
- Property tax and assessments
- Prior lending information
- Economic, cost-of-living, and home price appreciation statistics

In these situations, GSEs (and the lender and investor) rely on the AUS valuation methodology to estimate market value, not on the appraiser or inspection form. Other companies involved in real estate lending have developed AVMs. Lenders can now select from private companies, credit bureaus, title companies, and other large lenders or investors.

Use of Streamlined Appraisals and AVMs

Although Fannie Mae and Freddie Mac would like the streamlined appraisals and AVM valuation process to replace the industry standard URAR form, not all loans submitted through AUS can use them. Lenders and appraisers, always ultimately responsible for all information submitted to the GSE, must pay particular attention to the condition of the property, its conformity to the neighborhood characteristics, and its overall marketability. If adverse or uncertain factors exist, then the appraiser must recommend a more complete analysis.

Only loans with other strong factors to offset this increased collateral risk may be approved by the GSE for this limited documentation. An ideal loan application for AVM would include features such as a no-cashout refinance with an LTV of under 50 percent, a home located in a clearly defined and uniform neighborhood with a high level of maintenance, and applicants who have lived in the house for over five years and have excellent credit and cash reserves. Properties in declining markets or neighborhoods with deferred maintenance, where real estate price stability and property condition are variable, may require a more comprehensive valuation method such as the URAR.

Initially, these changes met with mixed reception in the lending and appraising communities. Both appraisers and lenders were concerned with the less stringent standards and quality that would result from these appraisals, but most realized how these changes were a part of the evolution in technology in mortgage lending.

These changes, without question, provide lenders and secondary market investors with benefits: faster processing and turnaround time, less work and time needed for appraisers, fewer documents and steps for many loans. The changes may also bring some drawbacks: less accurate reporting of property condition and value, more fraudulent information used in completing appraisal reports, and an increase in delinquency and/or foreclosure as a result of inaccurate appraisal valuation. MI company studies indicate fraudulent appraisals are on the increase, but no clear information has emerged to confirm an increase in delinquency as a result of these new appraisal requirements and forms.

Since streamlined appraisals and AVMs require less work and time to complete and do not apply to complex properties or real estate markets, they cost less than the standard URAR. Depending on the type of property appraised and the general cost of living in the area of the country in which the appraisal is performed, typical appraisal price ranges are as follows:

- *Standard URAR*—$200.00 to $500.00
- *Streamlined appraisals*—$125.00 to $250.00
- *AVMs, drive-bys, and other limited appraisals*—$35.00 to $175.00

In many cases, lenders do not always pass on to consumers the savings from the reduced cost of streamlined appraisals and AVMs, as promised by Fannie Mae and Freddie Mac in their public relations statements. The savings on appraisal costs are now replaced with AUS fees or other items lenders now charge in addition to the application fee.

Proponents of the changes explain that these changes apply to only those loan applications with low overall risk factors or to applications where collateral risk is low—*not* to high-risk applications or to applications where collateral risk is high.

Development and adoption of streamlined and automated valuation guidelines come after research on millions of loan applications with years of repayment history, and these AUSs have a predictive ability for delinquency over 10 times better than conventional underwriting. Applying these less-stringent appraisal requirements to loan applications selected by AUSs does not affect their investment quality or likelihood of delinquency or loss in any significant way.

Finally, the streamlined and AVM guidelines state that the appraiser should recommend and follow a more comprehensive analysis (such as the URAR) if, in the appraiser's opinion, these reports cannot establish satisfactorily the condition and marketability of the property. In this way, streamlined and AVM appraisal and property inspection forms represent additional tools for the appraiser to use when appropriate.

Critics of these changes liken the new appraisal process to valuing a car by riding by it on a bicycle and taking a snapshot of it—never seeing the other side of the vehicle or finding out whether it starts or runs. An external, drive-by inspection or assimilation of property tax and home sale information does not reveal reliable information about the condition of the property structure or interior and its effect on marketability. In other words, the appraiser doesn't know what he or she is missing, so accuracy suffers.

Age of Appraisal Report

The appraisal report must be signed and dated within 120 days of the date the mortgage loan is closed. If an appraisal is older than that, it can be "recertified"—updated by the original appraiser certifying that the value has not declined since the original appraisal was prepared. (Fannie Mae and Freddie Mac allow the appraisal to be up to 180 days old from the date the loan closes if the property is considered new construction.) If the appraisal report is older than one year, a new appraisal is required.

Discussion Points

1. What two main areas of consideration does an appraisal report help a lender evaluate? How does the appraisal report do this?

2. Explain the appraisal process an appraiser would follow developing a traditional appraisal report.

3. What three approaches to value are used in developing an appraisal? When is each approach most appropriate?

4. What factors can affect the market value of the subject property?

5. Why are sales comparable adjustments necessary to estimate the value of the subject property?

6. How do other appraisal forms differ from the Uniform Residential Appraisal Report (URAR)? Why are these differences significant?

7. Discuss the benefits and drawbacks to a lender using streamlined appraisals and automated valuation models (compared to traditional appraisals).

Closing the Residential Loan

Introduction

After the decision is made to approve a residential mortgage loan application (either by an authorized individual, a loan committee, or automated underwriting), the mortgage-lending process proceeds to the closing of that mortgage loan. The closing of a mortgage loan should not be interpreted to mean that the end of the mortgage-lending process has been reached, but only that the production phase has ended. The mortgage loan may exist for as long as 30 years and during that time will require servicing.

A residential mortgage transaction is closed by the delivery of the mortgage (or deed of trust) and note to the mortgage lender and the disbursement of the mortgage funds to the mortgagor or pursuant to the mortgagor's direction. The term *loan closing* as used in residential mortgage lending refers to the process with the following characteristics:

- Formulating, executing, and delivering all documents required to create an obligation to repay a debt and to create a valid security instrument
- Disbursing the mortgage funds
- Protecting the security interest of the lender or investor (e.g., **recording**)
- Establishing the rights and responsibilities of the mortgagor

A clear distinction should be drawn between this type of closing and a real estate sales closing in which a different set of documents is required, such as a purchase agreement, deed, sales contract, and a closing statement, among others. Of course, as is typical, when the sale of real estate also involves financing, both sets of documents or a combination of the two are usually required.

State law governs most of the steps necessary to close a mortgage loan and create a valid security interest in the real estate. As a result, this text cannot establish the exact requirements for closing any residential mortgage loan. Mortgage lenders must be careful to understand the requirements of their state, and the best way to understand these requirements is to have a competent closing agent.

Federally Related Mortgage Loans

As previously mentioned, RESPA must be followed when closing federally related mortgage loans. Practically all residential mortgage loans today are federally related. Thus, the act requires the following:

- Good faith estimate of likely settlement service charges (provided within three business days of application)
- Notice of Servicing Disclosure (signed at application)
- The HUD booklet, *Settlement Cost and You*, provided by lender
- Use of a HUD settlement sheet
- Limits on escrow (or impounds) accounts

Process of Loan Closing

The process of loan closing actually begins with the taking of the mortgage application and the issuance of a commitment letter to the borrower and concludes in the exchange of documents and funds and the recording of all pertinent instruments. As mentioned, it is important to realize that a loan closing is not the end of the mortgage-lending cycle, which continues through servicing until the loan is finally repaid or refinanced.

The Handling of Loan Closing

Loan closing, depending on the law or custom in the jurisdiction, can be handled by any of the following professionals:

- Outside attorney for either the seller or buyer
- Escrow agent
- Title insurance company
- Staff of the mortgage lender

Insured Closings

For first-mortgage loan closings, an insured closing is recommended. Today, most investors require these insured closings. An insured closing agent can be anyone, such as an attorney, who has been approved and accepted by a title company. The title company is, in effect, insuring that the loan is closed according to the lender's directions as well as the title company's requirements and that it is insuring against any fraud or dishonesty on the part of the loan closer.

At one time, an outside attorney handled most closings, and many still do, but more and more mortgage lenders have staff members who are qualified loan closers. These professionals have the competency to prepare and analyze all necessary closing documents and, as a general rule, can do it more inexpensively than an outside attorney. Care must be taken, though, to ascertain whether state law requires a licensed attorney to close a loan.

Whichever method is used, the purpose of loan closing is to ensure that the loan is closed according to all laws of that state. The expected result, of course, is to provide the mortgage lender with a first lien on the property.

There are many types of loan closings, including the closing of construction loans, loans to be warehoused, and loans with permanent investors. This chapter is concerned primarily with the closing of a permanent residential mortgage loan.

Steps in Closing a Residential Mortgage Loan

When the underwriter indicates that the loan application is acceptable, certain steps are taken to close the loan. These steps include the following:

1. Advise applicant of loan acceptance by a commitment letter (and, if applicable, set rate, terms, etc.)
2. Order final title report (and survey, if separate) and any other documents or verifications still outstanding
3. Schedule closing and prepare closing documents
4. Conduct closing, obtain all required signatures, and disburse funds
5. Return all closing documents to mortgage lender for inclusion in loan file
6. Record mortgage

Commitment Letter

Although most residential mortgage lenders use a commitment letter to inform applicants that their applications have been approved and the conditions of the loan, some lenders do not. Lenders that don't use a commitment letter should review that policy with a view toward using one. The commitment letter serves as the lender's acceptance of the mortgagor's application as submitted. If the lender makes a counteroffer, the applicant must accept that offer. The commitment letter is what creates the contractual right of the borrower to receive a mortgage loan. It also helps to clearly establish in the borrower's mind what is expected in regard to what has to be done, such as addressing conditions, for the loan to close.

Besides the legal implications of a commitment letter, lenders must acknowledge the marketing or public relations benefits of using a commitment letter. The letter can start off by congratulating the applicants on their approval for a mortgage loan. The letter can then spell out the specifics of the loan for which they have been approved by listing the amount of the loan, term of the loan, interest rate, and so forth. This letter can also tell applicants that they must have a hazard insurance policy or binder at closing and how the mortgagee payable clause should read. In addition, in the commitment letter a lender can inform the applicant of a need for flood insurance, what the closing fees will be, the date of closing, and other items. The issuance of a commitment letter should be the policy for all residential mortgage lenders.

Contents of a Commitment Letter

Most loan-processing systems contain a commitment letter. If a lender does not have one on its system, it can easily develop one. The contents of a commitment letter should cover the following subjects:

- For whom the loan is approved
- The real estate that will secure loan
- The way the title will be held
- Type of loan (fixed rate or variable rate)
- Loan amount
- Interest rate

Exhibit 13-1 Sample Commitment Letter

First County Bank
P.O. Box 1415
Stamford
Connecticut 06904-1415

203/462/4200
FAX 203/462/4443

June 13, 2002

James Smith
Susan Smith
10 Hill Avenue
Madison Boro, NJ 07940

Re: 300 Saw Mill Lane
Westport, CT 06880
Application #100107745

Dear Mr. And Mrs. Smith:

We are pleased to inform you that your application for a Fixed Rate Mortgage in the amount of **$650,000.00** for a term of **30** years and an interest rate of **7.125%** has been approved.

This loan must be secured by a mortgage on property located at:

300 SAW MILL LANE
WESTPORT, CT 06880

The monthly payment of principal and interest will be **$4,379.18**.

The monthly payment must also include 1/12 of the annual property taxes. The estimated amount is **$509.92**.

A non-refundable loan commitment fee of **$6,500.00** is payable upon acceptance of this commitment.

A non-refundable loan discount fee of **$6,500.00** is payable at closing.

Closing funds must be in the form of a certified check or cashiers check.

TITLE: The title to the real estate must be in the following name(s):

JAMES SMITH AND SUSAN SMITH

MORTGAGE PROMISSORY NOTE to be signed by the following:

JAMES SMITH
SUSAN SMITH

CONDITIONS OF COMMITMENT: Approval of your mortgage loan is subject to certain conditions. You are responsible for fulfilling these conditions *prior* to your loan closing. Conditions marked with an asterisk (*) may be satisfied at the time of closing.*

Exhibit 13-1	Sample Commitment Letter

1)   Provide a $325.00 check or money order payable to First County Bank for application fee.

2)   Borrower to provide one additional pay stub - dated within 30 days of closing.

3)   Provide signed copies of 2000 and 2001 personal, federal income tax returns with all schedules and attachments.

4)   Provide a copy of the fully executed sales contract for the sale of 10 HILL AVENUE, MADISON BORO, NJ.

5)   At closing, provide a copy of the fully executed HUD-1 Settlement Statement from the sale of 10 HILL AVENUE, MADISON BORO, NJ.

6)   Provide a copy of the fully executed Purchase Contract of Sale for 300 SAW MILL LANE, WESTPORT, CT which evidences a purchase price of $950000.00, with no sales concessions, rebates or secondary financing.

7)   Sign, initial and/or complete the following disclosures/documents:
a) Truth In Lending disclosure
b) Good Faith Estimate of Settlement and Closing Costs
c) Form 4506
d) W-9 Statement
e) Signed pages from 2000 and 2001 income tax returns

CANCELLATION OF COMMITMENT: First County Bank, at its option, may cancel this commitment if we discover any materially adverse fact regarding the property or your finances which you have not previously revealed to us.

EXPIRATION OF COMMITMENT: The financing terms of this commitment will expire on 02/08/01 unless the loan is closed and funded by that date. If you are currently floating the financing terms of this loan request, the Bank will issue a new commitment expiration date when you lock-in the interest rate. If applicable, this new commitment expiration date will be sixty (60) days from the date of the interest rate lock-in.

RE-PROCESSING FEE: This loan will be subject to a $250.00 re-processing fee if it does not close on or before 08/02/02. You will also be required to submit updated verification documentation (pay stubs, bank statements, etc.) if this loan does not close on or before 08/02/02.

ACCEPTANCE OF COMMITMENT: This commitment is not valid unless it has been signed and returned to the Bank within ten days of the commitment date.

By signing below I am acknowledging that I have read and accept the terms as outlined above:

James Smith
JAMES SMITH   Date _6/13/02_

Susan Smith
SUSAN SMITH   Date _6/13/02_

Very truly yours,

Robert Halpin
Robert Halpin
Executive Vice President

- Term of the loan
- Any escrow provisions
- Payment amount (initial payment if an ARM loan)
- Requirements for insurance
  - Hazard
  - Flood
  - Mortgage insurance
- When the loan must close
- Other provisions
  - Pest inspections
  - Certificate of occupancy

Most lenders require the borrowers to sign the commitment letter indicating they accept the terms of the loan.

Reviewing Title and Title Insurance

A mortgage lender must establish with certainty that the mortgagor has good title to the real estate that will secure the mortgage debt. The obvious reason is if another person has a superior interest in the real estate securing the mortgage loan and exercises that interest, the mortgage lender will have an unsecured personal loan. A mortgage lender therefore demands that all questions pertaining to ownership rights be resolved before the loan is closed. Questions of ownership can be raised by misfiled legal documents, undisclosed heirs, mistaken interpretations of wills or intestate statutes, confusions about marital status, or other legal problems.

The most common method of reviewing legal title and providing protection to mortgage lenders is through the purchase of **title insurance**. In some states, title insurance is not available or is available only in certain areas. In those states, an attorney's opinion based on an abstract of title is used. In other states, such as New York, a registration system of land title is used (referred to as the Torrens system of land registration).

When Should Title Insurance Be Ordered?

Today, with the emphasis placed on getting a loan approved as fast as possible, some lenders use the strategy of ordering title insurance as soon as the applicant(s) has been determined to have acceptable credit. This could be done by automated underwriting or by a loan officer reviewing a credit report. Obviously, some of the loans for which title insurance has been ordered do not close for other reasons (for example, the appraisal is not sufficient). In these situations, many title insurance companies will not charge for the work they have put into reviewing the title. This courtesy is provided in recognition that lenders are attempting to be timely in loan closing for competitive reasons. A lender should ask a title insurance company if it follows this policy.

Content of the Title Commitment

It is very important that the title commitment from the title insurance company be reviewed very carefully. The items that should be reviewed include the following:

- Name(s) of the seller (if a sale) or the name(s) of the applicants (if a refinance) in the title commitment are the same as on the loan application

Exhibit 13-2 / Sample Title Insurance Policy

FIDELITY NATIONAL TITLE INSURANCE COMPANY OF NEW YORK
COMMITMENT FOR TITLE INSURANCE
SCHEDULE A

1. Effective Date: **June 6, 2002**   File No.: **C1234567**

2. Policy or Policies to be issued:

   a) [ ] ALTA Owner's Policy - 1990 (Rev. 10-17-92)   Amount: **$**
      [ ] ALTA Leasehold Owner's Policy - 1990 (Rev. 10-17-92)
      [ ] TitlePLUS Owner's Policy One-to-Four Family Residence (6-1-87) - Enhanced Version

      PROPOSED INSURED:

   b) [X] ALTA Loan Policy - 1990 (Rev. 10-17-92)   Amount: **$16,700.00**
      [ ] ALTA Leasehold Loan Policy - 1990 (Rev. 10-17-92)
      [ ] TitlePLUS Loan Policy One-to-Four Family Residence (6-1-87) - Enhanced Version

      PROPOSED INSURED:
      ABC Lending Company, its successors and/or assigns as their interest may appear

3. The estate or interest in the land described or referred to in this Commitment and covered herein is **Fee Simple**.

4. Title to the estate or interest in said land described or referred to in this commitment is at the effective date hereof vested in:

   John M. Doe and Jane P. Doe

5. The land referred to in this Commitment is described as follows:

   444 Anywhere Lane, Middletown, Connecticut

   SEE ATTACHED DESCRIPTION

Countersigned:

Donald B. Official
Donald B. Official/Authorized Signatory

Form 5836 - A(6/93)   This Commitment is invalid unless the Insuring Provisions and Schedules A and B are attached.

Exhibit 13-2   Sample Title Insurance Policy (continued)

FIDELITY NATIONAL TITLE INSURANCE COMPANY OF NEW YORK
COMMITMENT FOR TITLE INSURANCE
SCHEDULE B

File No.: C1234567

I. **The following are the requirements to be complied with:**

A. Payment to or for the account of the grantors or mortgagors of the full consideration for the estate or interest to be insured.

B. Proper instrument(s) creating the estate or interest to be insured must be executed and duly filed for record to-wit:

   1. Mortgage deed from **John M. Doe and Jane P. Doe** in favor of **ABC Lending Company** securing the insured loan.
   3. The Borrower must execute the Company's Owner's Affidavit.

C. Payment and release of the following:

   1. Second half Real Estate Taxes due July 1, 2002 to the Town of Middletown in the amount of $1,265.37 should be paid at closing.

NOTE: The Company may make other requirements or exceptions upon its review of the proposed documents creating the estate or interest to be issued or otherwise ascertaining details of the transaction.

- Legal description in the title commitment is the same as the real estate being offered as security for the loan
- Whether any liens or encumbrances on the property will not be removed with this loan
- Whether any mechanics liens, lis pendens, tax liens, or any other condition on the title must be resolved

Depending on state law, the title insurance policy may contain a clause covering survey matters and, thus, a separate survey is generally not required. In other states, a survey is needed either for all mortgage loans or only if the loan is a purchase money mortgage.

Mortgagor's Policy

It is important that mortgagors understand that they are not protected under the lender's policy against any defects in their title to the real estate. The policy that borrowers are required to provide to lenders and pay for protects only the interest of the lender. If borrowers want title insurance that protects their interest, they can purchase it from the same insurer as issued the lender's policy. This is a decision made solely by the mortgagor, since mortgage lenders do not require that mortgagors purchase this insurance.

The policy should be an American Land Title Association's standard policy. The amount of title insurance should be equal to the original loan amount.

Documents Required for a Properly Closed First-Mortgage Loan

Essential documents that should be contained in a complete residential first-mortgage file vary by state as well as by the type of loan—conventional or FHA/VA. A lender's peculiar requirements can also add to the list. As in any discussion involving legal documents, a review of the requirements of each state's law is required. When establishing a loan-closing process, competent counsel should be consulted on state law concerning any of the documents discussed. Mortgage lenders should realize that the required documentation for an equity loan, especially a home equity line of credit, is different than the documentation needed for a first-mortgage loan.

The following documents are discussed relative to the closing of a residential first-mortgage loan. The process of gathering, producing, and preparing the necessary documents and the careful checking of all forms is often referred to as a preclosing procedure. The documents normally required in a closed residential mortgage loan file are listed subsequently. Mortgage lenders should realize that in some states, state law or custom might require additional documents to those listed here. Mortgage loan documents need not appear in any particular order in a loan file. However, some secondary mortgage market transactions may require the documents to be arranged in a specified order.

Lenders may find it helpful to have printed on the inside cover of their loan files the documents that should be in such files. In that way, lenders can double-check that all required documents are included.

First-Mortgage Checklist

This checklist is an important tool that should be used in mortgage lending for each of the following types of loans:

- First-mortgage loan
  - Fixed-rate mortgage
  - Adjustable-rate mortgage
- Equity loan
  - Closed-end second
  - Line of credit

The checklist reminds the loan processor, closing personnel, servicers, and loan quality review personnel what should be in a properly closed loan file.

The following documents are listed in alphabetical order and include a discussion of the reason for their requirement in the loan file.

Adjustable rate rider. If the mortgage is an adjustable-rate mortgage, a statement signed by the borrower acknowledging that he or she understands that the interest rate could increase should be in the loan file.

Figure 13-1	First-Mortgage Checklist

APPLICANT(S): _____

APPLICATION #_____ DATE_____

PURCHASE____ REFINANCE____ LOAN AMT: _____ TERM_____

RATE_____ PAYMENT_____

SECONDARY FINANCING AMT: _____ TERM_____ RATE_____

PAYMENT_____

PROPERTY ADDRESS:

_____

SINGLE-FAMILY ____ PUD ____ CONDO ____ OTHER_____

PROJECT NAME_____

APPRAISED AMT: _____ NEW CONSTRUCTION? _____

LTV _____ CLTV _____ HOUSING RATIO _____ TOTAL DEBT RATIO _____

APPLICATION

_____ Application

_____ HUD Booklet

_____ Good Faith Estimate/Good Faith Addendum/Truth in Lending

_____ RESPA Servicing Disclosure

_____ ECOA/Occupancy/Appraisal/Employment Certification

_____ IRS 4506

_____ IRS W9

_____ Fair Credit Reporting

_____ Application Fee Itemization

_____ Borrowers Certification & Authorization

_____ Verification of Employment (W2s or tax returns—2 years tax returns if self-employed)

_____ ARM Disclosure

_____ PMI Disclosure

PROCESSING/ORDERING

_____ Credit Report

_____ Flood Certification

_____ Appraisal Type: ____ Automated Valuation ____ Streamlined ____ Full Appraisal

_____ Appraisal Received and Reviewed

_____ Title Insurance Ordered   Date Ordered:_____

_____ Title Insurance Received and Reviewed

_____ Income Verification: ____ VOE ____ Paystubs ____ W2s ____ IRS Returns ____ Other: _____

_____ Asset Verification: ____ VOD ____ Statements ____ Other: _____

_____ Loan Verification: ____ VOL ____ Statements

_____ Other: ____ Sales Contract ____ Divorce Decree ____ Gift Letter

_____ Other: _____

| Figure 13-1 | First-Mortgage Checklist |

UNDERWRITING

_____ Underwriting Worksheet

_____ Underwriting Conditions/Summary Sheet

_____ Commitment Letter/Adverse Action Notice

_____ Underwriting Transmittal Summary

_____ Preliminary Title Search/Policy

_____ Other: _____

_____ Approving Officer Conditions Received

_____ Denying Officer Reasons: _____

    Date Notice Sent: _____

CLOSING

_____ Closing Instruction Sheet

_____ Note

_____ Mortgage/Riders: _____ 1–4 Family _____ ARM _____ PUD _____ Condo _____ Construction

_____ Hazard Certificate/Insurance With Paid Receipt

_____ Hazard Insurance Binder / Policy

_____ Flood Insurance Binder (if applicable)

_____ HUD-1/1A Settlement statement

_____ Final Typed Application

_____ Final Truth-in-Lending

_____ Escrow Waiver Agreement   _____ Initial Escrow Disclosure

_____ Closing Disbursement Funds

_____ Occupancy Affidavit

_____ CPI Notice

_____ Error and Omissions

_____ Payoff information

_____ Others:

_____

POST CLOSING

_____ COPY: Mortgage or Trust Deed Executed for Note and Wire Transfer Dollar Amount

_____ RECORDED ORIGINAL MORTGAGE: If Applicable: Riders Recorded: _____

_____ Title Policy: $ Amount_____ (MUST MATCH MORTGAGE)

_____ Notice of Right to Cancel (Refinance Only)

_____ HMDA REPORTING: Enter information on P.C. Data Sheet for HMDA reporting

_____ Letter To Borrower

_____ Other:

_____

I verify that this mortgage loan file is complete:

_____ Posted

_____ All pertinent documents accounted Date: _____

Loan officer:_____

ARM disclosure. A separate disclosure explaining each ARM plus the booklet *Consumer Handbook on Adjustable-Rate Mortgages (CHARM)* must be given to ARM applicants.

Application. Both the original and the typed final application are required for a closed loan. Be sure all lines are completed and all required signatures appear.

Appraisal. A recent appraisal (or valuation) is strongly recommended for all real estate loans (but is not required by many regulators if the loan amount is for less than $250,000). If the loan is a single-family detached conventional mortgage and is to be sold to the secondary mortgage market, the Uniform Residential Appraisal Report should be used. If the loan is for another type of residential real estate, care should be exercised that the correct appraisal form is used for that type of loan (e.g., condominium loan).

Assignment of mortgage. If the mortgage is being purchased from a mortgage lender who originated it for later sale, an instrument assigning the mortgage to a permanent investor and an estoppel certificate should be included in the loan file.

Building restrictions. Any local building restrictions that affect the mortgaged premises should be contained in the loan file with a statement as to whether this property meets local building restrictions. This may be contained in a lawyer's opinion.

Cancelled mortgage. If the loan being closed is for the purpose of refinancing a previous loan, a copy of the refinanced mortgage and note (the original is returned to the consumer, unless the existing loan is a modification) should appear in the file and be cancelled with the satisfaction of that mortgage recorded.

Certificate of occupancy. In all new construction and refurbishing projects that require it, a certificate issued by the local authorities should appear declaring that the building is habitable.

Chattel lien. If personal property is serving as a security in addition to the real estate, a financing statement or other document creating the lien is required.

Closing instructions. These instructions to the closing agent informing him or her of what to do and how should be retained to help establish whether the closing was executed correctly.

Closing statement. The closing statement for a mortgage closing (like a closing statement for a real estate sale) determines how the proceeds are to be apportioned to the parties. The purchase price; adjustments to the purchase price; prorations of rents, taxes, and other revenue and expense items related to the property; and the allocation of the costs of the transaction between the buyer and the seller should be itemized. A receipt signed by the mortgagor is required, indicating that loan proceeds have been disbursed according to instructions.

Commitment letter. A commitment letter should be examined closely since it establishes the contractual rights and obligations between the lender and the borrower. Comparison should be made between this commitment letter and the application for the loan to determine whether the applicant is receiving everything required. If the mortgage is to be insured, guaranteed, or sold to a third party, those commitment letters should also appear.

Contract of sale. If a loan is requested for the purchase of an existing property, the contract of sale should be in the loan file to verify an actual sale and to assist later in verifying the appraisal of the property.

Credit report. A credit report on the borrower is required on all mortgage loans. The correct credit report for a mortgage loan is typically a Residential Mortgage Credit Report provided by a local credit bureau with a tie-in to a national repository of credit information. Today, many lenders require only a consumer credit report.

Deed. If a loan is to purchase real estate or refinance an existing mortgage, a copy of the deed should be included in the loan file along with instructions to record.

Disclosures, federally mandated. In addition to federally mandated disclosures already listed, others necessary include notice of right to a copy of the appraisal, disclosure of whether servicing will be transferred and what percentage had been transferred within the past three years, disclosure of business relationship if a particular provider of services is required.

Disbursement papers. Instructions are required on how funds are to be delivered to the mortgagor or other involved parties.

Escrow. If the transaction involved has been closed in escrow, a copy of the escrow agreement should be in the loan file. When the term *escrow* or *impounded* is used to describe the way monthly payments of taxes and insurance are made, this agreement should also be in the loan file.

FHA/VA. All documents required by an FHA-insured or VA-guaranteed loan (e.g., credit report, verification of employment, building certificate, certificate of occupancy, flood insurance) should be in the loan file.

Flood certification. A statement that the property is or is not in a flood area is required and, if in a flood area, a statement of whether flood insurance is available and provided. Life of loan coverage is strongly suggested whereby a third party will monitor the status of the property securing the mortgage loan.

Good Faith Estimate of Closing Costs. Lender must provide a loan applicant with a written estimate of charges payable at settlement within three business days of application. A signed, dated receipt of this Good Faith Estimate should be in the file. This estimate may also be combined with the Truth-In-Lending loan cost and APR disclosure. In addition, the HUD booklet *Settlement Costs and You* must be given out within the three business days.

Home Owners Association agreement. If the property is a condominium, the association agreement binding all homeowners is required in the file.

Insurance (hazard) policies. In a residential file the required insurance policy (probably a homeowners policy) covering losses for fire, liability, and any other hazard should exist with a mortgagee loss payable clause. The hazard insurance policy provider is selected

Exhibit 13-3   Sample Open-End Mortgage Deed

After Recording Return To: **FIRST COUNTY BANK**
117 PROSPECT STREET
STAMFORD, CT 06901

——————————————— [Space Above This Line For Recording Data] ———————————————

OPEN-END MORTGAGE DEED

DEFINITIONS

Words used in multiple sections of this document are defined below and other words are defined in Sections 3, 11, 13, 18, 20 and 21. Certain rules regarding the usage of words used in this document are also provided in Section 16.

(A) **"Security Instrument"** means this document, which is dated   **December 15, 2000**   , together with all Riders to this document.
(B) **"Borrower"** is **James Smith And Susan Smith**

Borrower is the mortgagor under this Security Instrument.
(C) **"Lender"** is **First County Bank**
Lender is a   organized and existing under
the laws of **The State Of Connecticut**   . Lender's address is
                        117 Prospect Street, Stamford, Connecticut, 06901

                                                        . Lender is the mortgagee under this Security Instrument.
(D) **"Note"** means the promissory note signed by Borrower and dated   **December 15, 2000**   The Note
states that Borrower owes Lender **Six Hundred Fifty Thousand Dollars And No Cents**
                        Dollars (U.S. **$650,000.00**   ) plus interest. Borrower has promised
to pay this debt in regular Periodic Payments and to pay the debt in full not later than   **January 1, 2031**
(E) **"Property"** means the property that is described below under the heading "Transfer of Rights in the Property."
(F) **"Loan"** means the debt evidenced by the Note, plus interest, any prepayment charges and late charges due under the Note, and all sums due under this Security Instrument, plus interest.
(G) **"Riders"** means all Riders to this Security Instrument that are executed by Borrower. The following Riders are to be executed by Borrower [check box as applicable]:

☐ Adjustable Rate Rider   ☐ Condominium Rider   ☐ Second Home Rider

☐ Balloon Rider   ☐ Planned Unit Development Rider   ☐ Other(s) [specify]

☒ 1-4 Family Rider   ☐ Biweekly Payment Rider   **"Schedule A"**

CONNECTICUT—Single Family—Fannie Mae/Freddie Mac UNIFORM INSTRUMENT   Form 3007 1/01
                                                                        GREATLAND ■
ITEM 1855L1 (0011)   *(Page 1 of 11 pages)*   To Order Call: 1-800-530-9393☐ Fax 616-791-1131

FIRST PAGE ONLY! TEN OTHER PAGES OF UNIFORM CONVENANTS.
----

by the borrower from an approved insurer. The amount of insurance should be equal to the *lesser* of 100 percent of the insurance value of the improvements or the unpaid principal balance of the mortgage as long as it equals the minimum amount (80 percent) required to compensate for damages on a replacement cost basis.

Internal Revenue Service reporting form. IRS form 1009-B reports the gross proceeds of the sale.

Mortgage or deed of trust. A mortgage or deed of trust creating the security interest must appear in the loan file. Any chattel liens on personal property or any financing statements should also appear. Recording instructions are required to protect all parties. See the sample Open-End Mortgage Deed in Exhibit 13-3.

Mortgagor's affidavit. A mortgagor should be required to sign certain affidavits attesting to any current position regarding divorce proceedings, judgments or liens, or any recent improvement on the real estate or other pertinent facts that would affect the mortgage loan.

Note. It is essential to include a properly executed promissory note. This note creates the obligation to repay the debt that is secured by the mortgage; it should state the amount of the loan, the term, the interest rate, and any other pertinent conditions.

Payoff statement. This form states the encumbrances to be paid off and released at the closing.

Perc test. If the property has or will need a septic tank, the result of a percolation test must be in the loan file.

Pest control report. When normally performed for termites and other destructive insects, this report must be in the loan file.

Photographs. Photographs of good, clear quality are required of the front, rear, and street scene for the appraisal to adequately show the mortgaged real estate.

Private mortgage insurance documents. All documents required by mortgage insurance company to issue its insurance, as well as a copy of its commitment, should appear in the loan file.

Real estate taxes. In some states a form showing that all past due taxes have been paid is required. In most states, unpaid real estate taxes and other liens appear in the title report.

Right to Cancel notice. Whenever a mortgagor puts up a primary residence as security, the notice of a three-day right of rescission is required. Not required for a purchase money mortgage.

Survey. Since the real estate is the loan security, it is in the mortgagee's interest that a survey is made to identify the property correctly and determine whether any encroachments exist. In some states a separate survey is not required since the title insurance covers this area also. There are several survey standards, the most exacting and universally accepted are those adopted by the American Land Title Association (ALTA)

Exhibit 13-4   Sample Promissory Note

NOTE

December 15, 2000	Stamford,	Connecticut
[Date]	[City]	[State]

300 Saw Mill Lane, Westport, Connecticut, 06880

[Property Address]

1. BORROWER'S PROMISE TO PAY

In return for a loan that I have received, I promise to pay U.S. **$ 650,000.00**   (this amount is called "Principal"), plus interest, to the order of the Lender. The Lender is

First County Bank

I will make all payments under this Note in the form of cash, check or money order.

I understand that the Lender may transfer this Note. The Lender or anyone who takes this Note by transfer and who is entitled to receive payments under this Note is called the "Note Holder."

2. INTEREST

Interest will be charged on unpaid principal until the full amount of Principal has been paid. I will pay interest at a yearly rate of   **7.125**   %.

The interest rate required by this Section 2 is the rate I will pay both before and after any default described in Section 6(B) of this Note.

3. PAYMENTS

(A) Time and Place of Payments

I will pay principal and interest by making a payment every month.

I will make my monthly payment on the   **1st**   day of each month beginning on **February 1, 2001**
I will make these payments every month until I have paid all of the principal and interest and any other charges described below that I may owe under this Note. Each monthly payment will be applied as of its scheduled due date and will be applied to interest before Principal. If, on   **January 1, 2031**   , I still owe amounts under this Note, I will pay those amounts in full on that date, which is called the "Maturity Date."

I will make my monthly payments at **117 Prospect Street**

Stamford, Ct, 06901

or at a different place if required by the Note Holder.

(B) Amount of Monthly Payments

My monthly payment will be in the amount of U.S. $ **4,379.18**

4. BORROWER'S RIGHT TO PREPAY

I have the right to make payments of Principal at any time before they are due. A payment of Principal only is known as a "Prepayment." When I make a Prepayment, I will tell the Note Holder in writing that I am doing so. I may not designate a payment as a Prepayment if I have not made all the monthly payments due under the Note.

I may make a full Prepayment or partial Prepayments without paying a Prepayment charge. The Note Holder will use my Prepayments to reduce the amount of Principal that I owe under this Note. However, the Note Holder may apply my Prepayment to the accrued and unpaid interest on the Prepayment amount, before applying my Prepayment to reduce the Principal amount of the Note. If I make a partial Prepayment, there will be no changes in the due date or in the amount of my monthly payment unless the Note Holder agrees in writing to those changes.

Exhibit 13-4 / Sample Promissory Note

5. LOAN CHARGES

If a law, which applies to this loan and which sets maximum loan charges, is finally interpreted so that the interest or other loan charges collected or to be collected in connection with this loan exceed the permitted limits, then: (a) any such loan charge shall be reduced by the amount necessary to reduce the charge to the permitted limit; and (b) any sums already collected from me which exceeded permitted limits will be refunded to me. The Note Holder may choose to make this refund by reducing the Principal I owe under this Note or by making a direct payment to me. If a refund reduces Principal, the reduction will be treated as a partial Prepayment.

6. BORROWER'S FAILURE TO PAY AS REQUIRED

(A) Late Charge for Overdue Payments

If the Note Holder has not received the full amount of any monthly payment by the end of 15 calendar days after the date it is due, I will pay a late charge to the Note Holder. The amount of the charge will be 5.000 % of my overdue payment of principal and interest. I will pay this late charge promptly but only once on each late payment.

(B) Default

If I do not pay the full amount of each monthly payment on the date it is due, I will be in default.

(C) Notice of Default

If I am in default, the Note Holder may send me a written notice telling me that if I do not pay the overdue amount by a certain date, the Note Holder may require me to pay immediately the full amount of Principal which has not been paid and all the interest that I owe on that amount. That date must be at least 30 days after the date on which the notice is mailed to me or delivered by other means.

(D) No Waiver By Note Holder

Even if, at a time when I am in default, the Note Holder does not require me to pay immediately in full as described above, the Note Holder will still have the right to do so if I am in default at a later time.

(E) Payment of Note Holder's Costs and Expenses

If the Note Holder has required me to pay immediately in full as described above, the Note Holder will have the right to be paid back by me for all of its costs and expenses in enforcing this Note to the extent not prohibited by applicable law. Those expenses include, for example, reasonable attorneys' fees.

7. GIVING OF NOTICES

Unless applicable law requires a different method, any notice that must be given to me under this Note will be given by delivering it or by mailing it by first class mail to me at the Property Address above or at a different address if I give the Note Holder a notice of my different address.

Any notice that must be given to the Note Holder under this Note will be given by delivering it or by mailing it by first class mail to the Note Holder at the address stated in Section 3(A) above or at a different address if I am given a notice of that different address.

8. OBLIGATIONS OF PERSONS UNDER THIS NOTE

If more than one person signs this Note, each person is fully and personally obligated to keep all of the promises made in this Note, including the promise to pay the full amount owed. Any person who is a guarantor, surety or endorser of this Note is also obligated to do these things. Any person who takes over these obligations, including the obligations of a guarantor, surety or endorser of this Note, is also obligated to keep all of the promises made in this Note. The Note Holder may enforce its rights under this Note against each person individually or against all of us together. This means that any one of us may be required to pay all of the amounts owed under this Note.

9. WAIVERS

I and any other person who has obligations under this Note waive the rights of Presentment and Notice of Dishonor. "Presentment" means the right to require the Note Holder to demand payment of amounts due. "Notice of Dishonor" means the right to require the Note Holder to give notice to other persons that amounts due have not been paid.

10. UNIFORM SECURED NOTE

This Note is a uniform instrument with limited variations in some jurisdictions. In addition to the protections given to the Note Holder under this Note, a Mortgage, Deed of Trust, or Security Deed (the "Security Instrument"), dated the same date as this Note, protects the Note Holder from possible losses which might result if I do not keep the promises which I make in

---

MULTISTATE FIXED RATE NOTE—Single Family—Fannie Mae/Freddie Mac UNIFORM INSTRUMENT   **Form 3200 1/01**
GREATLAND ■
ITEM 1646L2 (0011)   *(Page 2 of 3 pages)*   To Order Call: 1-800-530-9393 □ Fax 616-791-1131

Exhibit 13-4 Sample Promissory Note (continued)

this Note. That Security Instrument describes how and under what conditions I may be required to make immediate payment in full of all amounts I owe under this Note. Some of those conditions are described as follows:

If all or any part of the Property or any Interest in the Property is sold or transferred (or if Borrower is not a natural person and a beneficial interest in Borrower is sold or transferred) without Lender's prior written consent, Lender may require immediate payment in full of all sums secured by this Security Instrument. However, this option shall not be exercised by Lender if such exercise is prohibited by Applicable Law.

If Lender exercises this option, Lender shall give Borrower notice of acceleration. The notice shall provide a period of not less than 30 days from the date the notice is given in accordance with Section 15 within which Borrower must pay all sums secured by this Security Instrument. If Borrower fails to pay these sums prior to the expiration of this period, Lender may invoke any remedies permitted by this Security Instrument without further notice or demand on Borrower.

Borrower has executed and acknowledges receipt of pages 1 through 3 of this Note.

WITNESS THE HAND(S) AND SEAL(S) OF THE UNDERSIGNED

_____ (Seal)　　_____ (Seal)
James Smith　　　　　　　　　　　 -Borrower　　Susan Smith　　　　　　　　　　　　 -Borrower

_____ (Seal)　　_____ (Seal)
　　　　　　　　　　　　　　　　　 -Borrower　　　　　　　　　　　　　　　　　　 -Borrower

_____ (Seal)　　_____ (Seal)
　　　　　　　　　　　　　　　　　 -Borrower　　　　　　　　　　　　　　　　　　 -Borrower

[Sign Original Only]

MULTISTATE FIXED RATE NOTE—Single Family—Fannie Mae/Freddie Mac UNIFORM INSTRUMENT　　　　Form 3200 1/01
ITEM 1646L3 (0011)　　　　　　　　　　*(Page 3 of 3 pages)*　　　　　　GREATLAND ■
　　　　　　　　　　　　　　　　　　　　　　　　　　　　　　To Order Call: 1-800-530-9393 □ Fax 616-791-1131

and the American Congress of Surveying and Mapping (ACSM). The most recent revisions of these standards were made in 1992.

Title insurance or examination. In all cases, it is essential that title be examined or that an approved American Land Title Association (ALTA) title insurance policy or binder be included. This requirement establishes who has right to the real estate and, therefore, who must execute the mortgage to encumber it. The title examination should also disclose any prior encumbrances, tax liens, or other interests. (In some states, a Torrens certificate will be used.)

Truth-in-Lending. The loan file must contain a Loan Cost Disclosure statement that discloses both the Annual Percentage Rate (APR) and the total finance charge. This may be combined with the Good Faith Estimate of Closing Costs.

Uniform Settlement Statement (HUD-1 or HUD-1A). This statement is required at loan closings by the Real Estate Settlement Procedures Act of 1974 (RESPA). The statement offers the borrower and seller a full disclosure of known or estimated settlement costs. The HUD-1A is used when only one party is involved, such as in a refinance.

Verification reports. The mortgage lender should verify all relevant statements made on the loan application by obtaining verifying documentation. The most commonly used verification forms are those for employment and deposits.

Final Requirements

Because most residential mortgage lenders understand the necessity of creating conforming mortgage loans, they must be aware of general requirements of the secondary mortgage market in regard to closing documentation. As mentioned previously, the secondary mortgage market players have these requirements because of their desire to combat fraud when loans are sold to them.

The note and mortgage are the most important documents in the first-mortgage package. As such, they require special attention and care in completion. Some of these requirements include the following:

- All blanks on uniform instruments must be completed.
- All corrections on forms must be initialed by the borrowers.
- No correction fluid or tape can be used on the documents.
- Documents should contain original signatures.
- Names of signers must be consistent through all documents and signatures should be the same as name.
- Legal description and property address should be consistent throughout and agree with title policy.
- Note and security instrument should be signed on same date.
- Signatures should be notarized according to state requirements.

Exhibit 13-5 / Sample Uniform Settlement Statement (HUD1)

A.	U.S. DEPARTMENT OF HOUSING AND URBAN DEVELOPMENT **SETTLEMENT STATEMENT**	B. TYPE OF LOAN	OMB No. 2502-0265

		B. TYPE OF LOAN	
		1. ☐ FHA 2. ☐ FMHA 3. ☐ CONV. UNINS.	
		4. ☐ VA 5. ☒ CONV. INS.	
		6. FILE NUMBER: 100101920	7. LOAN NUMBER: 127-9500
		8. MORTGAGE INS. CASE NO.:	

C. NOTE: This form is furnished to give you a statement of actual settlement costs. Amounts paid to and by the settlement agent are shown. Items marked "(p.o.c.)" were paid outside the closing; they are shown here for informational purposes and are not included in the totals.

D.	NAME OF BORROWER:	Joseph F. Lynch, Margaret J. Lynch
	ADDRESS OF BORROWER:	384 Katona Drive
		Fairfield, CT 06824
E.	NAME OF SELLER:	James Williams, Sally Jefferson Williams
	ADDRESS OF SELLER:	89 Harvester Road
		Fairfield, CT 06825
F.	NAME OF LENDER:	Fairfield Savings Association
	ADDRESS OF LENDER:	252 Main Street
		Fairfield, CT 06824
G.	PROPERTY	89 Harvester Road
	LOCATION:	Fairfield, CT 06825
H.	SETTLEMENT AGENT:	SEDENSKY & MYERS
	PLACE OF SETTLEMENT:	100 CAPITAL AVENUE
		Bridgeport, CT 06601
I.	SETTLEMENT DATE:	02/13/04

J.	SUMMARY OF BORROWER'S TRANSACTION		K.	SUMMARY OF SELLER'S TRANSACTION	
100. GROSS AMOUNT DUE FROM BORROWER:			**400. GROSS AMOUNT DUE TO SELLER:**		
101. Contract sales price		210,000.00	401. Contract sales price		210,000.00
102. Personal property			402. Personal property		
103. Settlement charges to borrower (from line 1400)		8,935.76	403.		
104.			404.		
105.			405.		
ADJUSTMENTS FOR ITEMS PAID BY SELLER IN ADVANCE:			ADJUSTMENTS FOR ITEMS PAID BY SELLER IN ADVANCE:		
106. City/town taxes 01/01/04 to 06/30/04		400.00	406. City/town taxes 01/01/04 to 06/30/04		400.00
107. County taxes to			407. County taxes to		
108. Assessments to			408. Assessments to		
109.			409.		
110.			410.		
111.			411.		
112.			412.		
120. GROSS AMOUNT DUE FROM BORROWER:		219,335.76	**420. GROSS AMOUNT DUE TO SELLER:** ▶		210,400.00
200. AMOUNTS PAID BY OR IN BEHALF OF BORROWER:			**500. REDUCTION IN AMOUNT DUE TO SELLER:**		
201. Deposit or earnest money		2,100.00	501. Excess deposit (see instructions)		
202. Principal amount of new loan(s)		189,000.00	502. Settlement charges to seller (line 1400)		8,700.00
203. Existing loan(s) taken subject to			503. Existing loan(s) taken subject to		
204.			504. Payoff of first mortgage loan		
205.			505. Payoff of second mortgage loan		
206.			506.		
207.			507.		
208.			508.		
209.			509.		
ADJUSTMENTS FOR ITEMS UNPAID BY SELLER:			ADJUSTMENTS FOR ITEMS UNPAID BY SELLER:		
210. City/town taxes to			510. City/town taxes to		
211. County taxes 01/01/04 to 06/30/04		300.00	511. County taxes 01/01/04 to 06/30/04		300.00
212. Assessments to			512. Assessments to		
213.			513.		
214.			514.		
215.			515.		
216.			516.		
217.			517.		
218.			518.		
219.			519.		
220. TOTAL PAID BY/FOR BORROWER:		191,400.00	**520. TOTAL REDUCTIONS IN AMOUNT DUE SELLER:** ▶		9,000.00
300. CASH AT SETTLEMENT FROM/TO BORROWER:			**600. CASH AT SETTLEMENT TO/FROM SELLER:**		
301. Gross amount due from borrower (line 120)		219,335.76	601. Gross amount due to seller (line 420)		210,400.00
302. Less amount paid by/for borrower (line 220)		(191,400.00)	602. Less total reductions in amount due seller (line 520)		(9,000.00)
303. CASH (☒ FROM) (☐ TO) BORROWER:		27,935.76	603. CASH (☒ TO) (☐ FROM) SELLER: ▶		201,400.00

SUBSTITUTE 1099-S: This form may be used as the written statement to the Transferor. This is important tax information and is being furnished to the Internal Revenue Service. If you are required to file a return, a negligence penalty will be imposed on you if this item is required to be reported and the IRS determines that it has not been reported. See Substitute 1099-S Information Sheet.

Previous Edition is Obsolete
ITEM 15811.0 (9511)

GREATLAND ■ To Order Call: 1-800-530-9393 ☐Fax 616-791-1131

SB-4-3538-000-1
HUD-1 (3-86)
RESPA, HB 4305.2

Exhibit 13-5 — Sample Uniform Settlement Statement (HUD1)

A. U.S. DEPARTMENT OF HOUSING AND URBAN DEVELOPMENT **SETTLEMENT STATEMENT**	B. TYPE OF LOAN	OMB No. 2502-0265

B. TYPE OF LOAN		
1. ☐ FHA	2. ☐ FMHA	3. ☐ CONV. UNINS.
4. ☐ VA	5. ☒ CONV. INS.	

6. FILE NUMBER: 100101920	7. LOAN NUMBER: 127-9500
8. MORTGAGE INS. CASE NO.:	

C. NOTE: This form is furnished to give you a statement of actual settlement costs. Amounts paid to and by the settlement agent are shown. Items marked "(p.o.c.)" were paid outside the closing; they are shown here for informational purposes and are not included in the totals.

D. NAME OF BORROWER:	Joseph F. Lynch, Margaret J. Lynch
ADDRESS OF BORROWER:	384 Katona Drive Fairfield, CT 06824
E. NAME OF SELLER:	James Williams, Sally Jefferson Williams
ADDRESS OF SELLER:	89 Harvester Road Fairfield, CT 06825
F. NAME OF LENDER:	Fairfield Savings Association
ADDRESS OF LENDER:	252 Main Street Fairfield, CT 06824
G. PROPERTY LOCATION:	89 Harvester Road Fairfield, CT 06825
H. SETTLEMENT AGENT: PLACE OF SETTLEMENT:	SEDENSKY & MYERS 100 CAPITAL AVENUE Bridgeport, CT 06601
I. SETTLEMENT DATE:	02/13/04

J. SUMMARY OF BORROWER'S TRANSACTION		K. SUMMARY OF SELLER'S TRANSACTION	
100. GROSS AMOUNT DUE FROM BORROWER:		**400. GROSS AMOUNT DUE TO SELLER:**	
101. Contract sales price	210,000.00	401. Contract sales price	210,000.00
102. Personal property		402. Personal property	
103. Settlement charges to borrower (from line 1400)	8,935.76	403.	
104.		404.	
105.		405.	
ADJUSTMENTS FOR ITEMS PAID BY SELLER IN ADVANCE:		ADJUSTMENTS FOR ITEMS PAID BY SELLER IN ADVANCE:	
106. City/town taxes 01/01/04 to 06/30/04	400.00	406. City/town taxes 01/01/04 to 06/30/04	400.00
107. County taxes to		407. County taxes to	
108. Assessments to		408. Assessments to	
109.		409.	
110.		410.	
111.		411.	
112.		412.	
120. GROSS AMOUNT DUE FROM BORROWER:	219,335.76	**420. GROSS AMOUNT DUE TO SELLER:** ▶	210,400.00
200. AMOUNTS PAID BY OR IN BEHALF OF BORROWER:		**500. REDUCTION IN AMOUNT DUE TO SELLER:**	
201. Deposit or earnest money	2,100.00	501. Excess deposit (see instructions)	
202. Principal amount of new loan(s)	189,000.00	502. Settlement charges to seller (line 1400)	8,700.00
203. Existing loan(s) taken subject to		503. Existing loan(s) taken subject to	
204.		504. Payoff of first mortgage loan	
205.		505. Payoff of second mortgage loan	
206.		506.	
207.		507.	
208.		508.	
209.		509.	
ADJUSTMENTS FOR ITEMS UNPAID BY SELLER:		ADJUSTMENTS FOR ITEMS UNPAID BY SELLER:	
210. City/town taxes to		510. City/town taxes to	
211. County taxes 01/01/04 to 06/30/04	300.00	511. County taxes 01/01/04 to 06/30/04	300.00
212. Assessments to		512. Assessments to	
213.		513.	
214.		514.	
215.		515.	
216.		516.	
217.		517.	
218.		518.	
219.		519.	
220. TOTAL PAID BY/FOR BORROWER:	191,400.00	**520. TOTAL REDUCTIONS IN AMOUNT DUE SELLER:** ▶	9,000.00
300. CASH AT SETTLEMENT FROM/TO BORROWER:		**600. CASH AT SETTLEMENT TO/FROM SELLER:**	
301. Gross amount due from borrower (line 120)	219,335.76	601. Gross amount due to seller (line 420)	210,400.00
302. Less amount paid by/for borrower (line 220)	(191,400.00)	602. Less total reductions in amount due seller (line 520)	(9,000.00)
303. CASH ☒ FROM ☐ TO BORROWER:	27,935.76	603. CASH ☒ TO ☐ FROM SELLER: ▶	201,400.00

SUBSTITUTE 1099-S: This form may be used as the written statement to the Transferor. This is important tax information and is being furnished to the Internal Revenue Service. If you are required to file a return, a negligence penalty will be imposed on you if this item is required to be reported and the IRS determines that it has not been reported. See Substitute 1099-S Information Sheet.

Previous Edition is Obsolete
ITEM 1581L0 (9511)

GREATLAND ■ To Order Call: 1-800-530-9393 ☐ Fax 616-791-1131

SB-4-3538-000-1
HUD-1 (3-86)
RESPA,HB 4305.2

Exhibit 13-6 Closed First Mortgage File Contents

CLOSED FIRST MORTGAGE FILE CONTENTS

There are no specific requirements from investors on *exactly* how a closed loan file must be organized. Still, industry practice follows a general order for organizing loan file documents. Because lending and closing customs differ with each state and loan transaction, lenders will make minor changes to this universal format based on what makes sense to their organization.

The LEFT side of the file is for REQUIRED/LEGAL DOCUMENTS, mostly for closing and servicing. The RIGHT side of the file is for CREDIT DOCUMENTS, mostly for loan application and approval/denial/counteroffer. For first mortgage loan s underwritten and closed for sale on the secondary market, make sure you include the following documents in the closed loan file.

REQUIRED DOCUMENT CHECKLIST (Left Side)

Name _____ Loan Number _____

___	Automatic Payment Form	(If applicable)
___	Loan Servicing Setup Sheet	
___	Construction Transfer Sheet	(If applicable)
___	Construction Advance Breakdown	(If applicable)
___	Note + 1 Copy)	
___	Mortgage and All Applicable Riders + 1 Copy	
___	Mortgage Assignment	(If applicable)
___	Subordination Agreement	(If applicable)
___	Insurance Policy for Hazard and Flood	(If applicable)
___	Life Of Loan Flood Zone Certification	
___	Original HUD-1 or HUD 1-A Settlement Statement	
___	Final Truth-In-Lending	
___	Notice of Right of Rescission	(If applicable)
___	Initial Escrow Statement/Disclosure	
___	Escrow Waiver Agreement (If applicable)	
___	Name Affidavits	
___	Compliance/Clerical Error Agreement	
___	Title Policy and All Endorsements	
___	PMI, VA, or FHA Certificate	(If applicable)
___	Signed, Complete Commitment Letter and Rate Lock Agreement	
___	Final (Typed) Application Signed at Closing	
___	Certificate of Occupancy and Lien Waivers	(If applicable)
___	Construction Advances	(If applicable)

Exhibit 13-6	Closed First Mortgage File Contents

___ **Survey** (If applicable)
___ **Closing Agent Loan Disbursement Sheet**
___ **Loan Disbursement Documentation (to PMI, required payoffs, etc.)**
___ **First Payment Letter**

Reviewed By/Date _____

REQUIRED DOCUMENT CHECKLIST (Right Side)

Name _____ Loan Number _____

___ **Instructions to Closing Agent**
___ **Preliminary Title Search/ Title Policy**
___ **Rate Lock-In and Investor Commitment Sheet** (If applicable)
___ **Commitment Letter**
___ **Fannie Mae Transmittal Sheet (Form 1008) or Equivalent**
___ **Automated Underwriting Feedback Sheet (AU or LP or other)**
___ **PMI/VA/FHA Applic. for Insurance/Endorsement** (If applicable)
___ **Original Application (Handwritten or computer generated)**
___ **Credit Report**
___ **Verification of Mortgage, Rent, Loan, Utilities** (If applicable)
___ **Other Supporting Credit Documentation** (If applicable)
___ **Delinquent Credit Explanation** (If applicable)
___ **Verif. of Alimony/Child Support Paid/Received** (If applicable)
___ **Verification of Employment, W-2s, Paystubs, Employer Letter**
___ **IRS Personal/Corporate Returns with All Schedules** (If applicable)
___ **Verification of Other Sources of Income** (If applicable)
___ **Verification of Deposits, Bank Statements, Gift Letter, Reloc. Pkg.**
___ **Verification of Other Funds Needed to Close** (If applicable)
___ **Fully Executed Sales Contract and all Addendae** (If applicable)
___ **Termite/Water/Other Property Inspection Reports** (If applicable)
___ **Appraisal**
___ **Survey** (If applicable)
___ **Condo/PUD Project Approval or Warranty Letter** (If applicable)
___ **Initial Truth-In-Lending**
___ **Good Faith Estimate**
___ **RESPA Servicing Transfer Disclosure**
___ **Initial ARM Disclosures** (If applicable)
___ **Other Disclosures (ECOA, Fair Housing, Appraisal, PMI, etc.)**
___ **IRS Form 4506 – Request for Copy of Tax Return**
___ **IRS W-9 Form**

Reviewed By/Date _____

Income Tax Reporting

If the mortgage transaction is a purchase money mortgage, the Internal Revenue Code now requires real estate brokers (defined as the person or company responsible for closing the transaction) to file an informational return showing the gross sales proceeds of transaction in which they are involved. The return (1099-B) is sent to the IRS and a copy is provided for the seller. If the seller does not provide the necessary Social Security or taxpayer identification number, the broker is required to deduct and withhold 20 percent of the amount of money due the seller.

Quality Control

Poor documentation in lending is as serious a situation as inaccurate information for management. Depending on the error, improper or incorrect documentation can cripple a mortgage lender in several ways:

- Invalidate the lien
- Jeopardize repayment of the note
- Incur financial loss by delaying or canceling sale of the loan
- Create consumer compliance fines and/or penalties
- Cause regulatory suspension or termination of mortgage-lending activities

It is imperative that the mortgage lender perform a structured quality control review of the loan file to evaluate documentation quality, underwriting decisions, compliance requirements, and service to the applicants. Many lenders perform a quality control review immediately after the loan has closed. The primary reasons for performing this important step immediately after loan closing is that the transaction is still recent in the parties' memories, and, normally, it is easiest to correct any errors at this time. (Consumers should be required to sign a compliance agreement at closing in which they agree to correct any errors in the mortgage transaction whenever they are discovered.) Quality review is also required by Fannie Mae, Freddie Mac, other investors, and government agencies and is strongly recommended by regulators. Lenders find value in reviewing the results to improve efficiency and workflow, evaluate (and reward) employee performance, and benchmark service standards for mortgage applicants.

Discussion Points

1. Identify the reasons why residential loan closings are so important to the parties involved.

2. What are the steps in closing a residential mortgage loan? Who normally handles the closing?

3. Why is a commitment letter so important to proper mortgage lending?

4. What is the purpose of title insurance? Who is protected by title insurance?

5. Why does the Internal Revenue Service need to be informed about a loan closing?

Mortgage Loan Servicing and Administration

Introduction

After closing a mortgage loan, the next step in the residential lending process involves servicing (or as it is sometimes known, loan administration). **Servicing** includes the responsibilities, functions, and day-to-day operations an organization performs over the term or repayment of that loan. These must be completed in accordance with the terms of the commitment letter, note, mortgage or deed of trust, mortgage riders, and other closing documents. (Many forget that both the borrower and the lender make several covenants and have ongoing fiduciary responsibilities, as itemized in these documents.)

All residential mortgage loans require servicing. Performing these functions can be quite complex and expensive. Servicing departments are organized differently, depending on a number of factors, including the types of mortgages serviced. Typically, all handle the following activities for mortgage loans:

- Borrower inquiries
- Billing and repayment
- Tax and insurance escrows
- Adjustments and changes
- Delinquency and collections
- Pay-off and release
- Internal accounting and management reporting

Loan administration describes a mortgage-servicing department that plays a larger, more sophisticated role in the lender's overall strategy—one that includes servicing loans for secondary market investors. This could be a passive role, in which the lender handles only those loans it originates and sells, or it could be a role in which the lender actively sells and buys servicing portfolios from mortgage lenders.

Fannie Mae and Freddie Mac as well as other investors set the standards by which the loan servicer agrees to perform this function, which is formalized in a **servicing contract**. Loan administration includes the functions described earlier in the typical servicing department, but may also add the following functions:

- Investor accounting and management reporting
- Servicing portfolio pricing, selling, and acquisition
- Delivery and quality control

If performed correctly, loan administration should result in the following:

- Rendering of all required services to the mortgagor
- Protecting the security interest of the mortgagee (or an investor)
- Producing a profit for the servicer

The originating lender is not required to service the mortgage, regardless of whether the particular loan is sold to an investor or held in portfolio. Mortgage bankers usually sell their loans and their servicing to different entities—especially to Fannie Mae or Freddie Mac, which purchase more loans than any other investor but *never* service loans. The issue of who will service the loans is generally more significant for those lenders, typically depository institutions, who rely more on a relationship business strategy than a transactional one.

Loan administration can be the most difficult of all the steps to perform in the residential lending process. On the other hand, it can also be the most profitable. The difficulty in performing this function stems from two general areas: the broad scope of operations it entails and its duration. A myriad of problems can develop when dealing with the different tasks performed, computers, servicing systems, communications, people, and their problems. The longer the servicing relationship, the more likely an issue can develop as the result of human error, implementation of new procedures and technology, change in operation or ownership, or cyclical changes in the economy. These problems are discussed in greater detail in the following sections.

If an organization handles these problems correctly and maintains sufficient loan volume, servicing produces meaningful revenue. Servicing revenue may be the primary business reason the lender is in residential mortgage lending, since it can offset other production-related losses to make a profit.

Organization of a Mortgage-Servicing Department

The organization of the mortgage-servicing department varies. It must support the overall strategy of that institution and the manner in which other departments operate. The department's organization depends on a combination of its size, scope, and complexity, as measured by the number of loans (volume), loan programs and investor(s) (scope), and responsibilities (complexity). As these elements change, so can the department structure. A change in operation, or addition of technology, or the election to outsource a function impacts all areas of servicing.

Most departments use either the function system or the unit system. The *function system* assigns each employee to a specific servicing function, such as real estate taxes, payments, or assumptions. This system allows for specialization, a higher level of service, and, if done correctly, speed of operation. The main drawback is that that function will not be performed when that person is absent. The *unit system* assigns small teams of employees to a group of loans for which they perform all of the related tasks. All employees can perform each function to cover for each other when one is absent. The benefit is a more consistent operation. The drawback is no one person is an expert on any one function.

Most large servicers use the function system because speed, accuracy, and efficiency are critical to their economies of scale. Their loan volume requires several peo-

Organization of Mortgage-Servicing Departments	TABLE 14-1

Functional	Unit
Payment processing	ARM
Escrow administration	Fixed
Rate/payment adjustments	FHA/VA
Customer service	Delinquent/Foreclosure
Payoff and release	Fannie Mae

ple to perform the same function, which alleviates the negative effects of absenteeism. Smaller servicers with limited resources use the unit system in order to have more coverage of all functions at all times to maintain high customer service levels.

The actual loan programs serviced and/or the investor for whom the loans are serviced in large part influences the servicing department organization (and functions, discussed next). For example, a servicer with adjustable-rate loans requires a function for rate review and notification, whereas a servicer dealing with only fixed-rate loans does not; a servicer with tax or insurance escrows requires an escrow administration function, whereas a servicer of loans without escrows does not. A medium-sized servicer with few functions may need to reorganize from the unit to function system if a change in loan programs requires specialized functions.

Servicing Responsibilities and Functions

Similarly, the servicing responsibilities and functions performed are a result of the loan programs, investor requirements, and state and federal regulations for that servicer. A small servicer with 2,000 mortgage loans may be complex as a result of the many loan programs it offers, each of which require different functions. A large servicer with 400,000 may service only fixed-rate, nonescrow loans for its own portfolio, requiring only four functions.

Servicing responsibilities refers to the more global fiduciary responsibility the servicer assumes as agent for the following parties:

- Borrower
- Lender/investor
- Insurer/guarantor
- Regulator

Servicing functions refers to the operations involved in meeting these responsibilities.

Setting Up the Loan File

The first step in mortgage servicing is to establish a servicing file. The objective is to put all the right documents in all the right places, following a similar format so anyone reviewing the file can quickly find the needed information. The servicer then adds the new loan to its servicing software system, based on the specific features of the mortgage. Care must be exercised in this effort to ensure that the loan is inputted correctly. This will prevent mistakes in the future. The servicer should perform loan setup immediately after closing for two reasons: quality control and customer service.

Postclosing Review

Most lenders use the loan setup step as a type of quality control. During a normal postclosing review, the servicer compares the list of required documents to the list of documents actually in the loan file. Loan setup is probably the last convenient time for the lender to cure any defects, such as missing documents or other financial or documentation errors. Resolving these defects may take time, especially if the error involves the legal documents, but it should not delay the servicer from performing the customer service aspect of loan setup.

Welcoming Letter

The next step is to mail a welcoming letter to establish a correct relationship with a borrower. Think of it this way: this is the start of what is potentially a 30-year relationship with the borrower, involving what is for most people their largest financial commitment and their most important asset—their home. Few services can have a more significant impact, so it is critical the servicer begin this relationship properly. The welcoming letter is the servicer's first contact with the borrower. It should be mailed soon after closing—the sooner the better! It should clearly explain three areas: servicing contacts and assistance, borrower obligations, and repayment.

The welcoming letter should introduce the servicing people and provide contact information, such as locations, telephone numbers, e-mail and regular mail addresses, and hours of operation. It should also explain what is expected of the borrower as a mortgagor and restate the significant covenants contained in the closing documents regarding insurance, taxes, property damage, and so forth. Finally, the letter should provide clear instruction for the first and subsequent payments by the borrower and should help the borrower realize how important it is to make the mortgage payments on time.

Mortgage Payment Methods

Most mortgages are paid monthly, some biweekly. The method of payment varies according to the mortgage product and lender, but the most common are these:

- *Coupons.* Provided in one-year supply; mortgagor submits one with each payment. The coupon includes the loan number, due date, and payment amount (often, this information can be encoded on the coupon for rapid and efficient processing).
- *Monthly billing.* Servicer mails a bill to the borrower each month. Its main advantage is as a reminder that the payment is due, but the drawback is the mailing cost. Cross-selling other services by including advertising on the bill can offset this drawback.
- *Preauthorized automatic payment.* Mortgage payment is automatically deducted from the mortgagor's checking or share draft account. This method assures prompt payments on the due date. This is a requirement for biweekly mortgages.

For many borrowers, payment notification is the only correspondence they receive from the servicer. Depending on the mortgage terms, the servicer may notify the borrower for these other common, functional, events as well:

- An annual escrow statement
- An increase (decrease) in taxes or insurance
- A notice of interest rate and monthly payment change
- A late notice
- Annual IRS reporting for interest paid/interest received

Servicing Functions

To fulfill these responsibilities successfully, a mortgage loan servicer must have either well-trained people or separate departments to perform five essential functions.

- The payment processing department has the daily responsibility of applying all payments received and balancing the accounts. It receives payments and deposits, applies them to the individual mortgage loan, and transmits this information to loan accounting. This area may also produce and screen bills sent to borrowers and, on the other end, handle payoff requests from other lenders or their closing agents and send mortgage releases once the loan is paid off.

  Activity in this area is cyclical and can be frenetic, depending on the situation. For example, most mortgages are due on the first of the month, so most payments arrive at the beginning of each month. Changes in payments from tax escrows or adjustable-rate mortgages result in many payment issues. In times of heavy refinancing waves, payoff and release requests explode, even if the lender is refinancing its own mortgage.

- The loan accounting department reconciles loan payments to funds received, notifies investors of deposits made to their account, and draws a check (if funds not paid through a custodial account) to distribute principal and interest less the servicing fee. Today, many investors require that all funds due them (principal and interest) be collected by the investor debiting a custodial account established for their benefit. Some investors also require that excess reserves be deposited with them and not in the custodial account. This area also produces management reports to assist with investor and portfolio management.

  Activity in this area somewhat mirrors the payment-processing area but is one step away from individual mortgage loan accounts, instead dealing with the summary of activity. Loan accounting must balance investor loans daily and remit payment according to each investors' specific schedules.

- The customer service department handles all borrower inquiries and requests, resolves errors and disputes, and processes other changes that may occur. This area may also handle assumptions, payoffs, modifications, any cross-selling of other products, and any other services offered by the company.

  Activity in this area is cyclical as well. Customer service must field numerous telephone calls and requests for information at year-end and after any mass mailing to borrowers. To alleviate these waves of inquiries, many servicers now provide information online, allowing borrowers to access their loan account anytime over the Internet.

- The escrow administration department ensures the protection of the security interest by determining whether adequate coverage is in place and is current with a mortgagee-payable clause for required insurances or credit guarantees. This may include the following: hazard, flood, private mortgage, FHA, VA, or other state/federal housing agency insurance or credit guarantee. It monitors in a similar manner the status of real estate tax payments for all towns in which the servicer has loans.

  The escrow administration accomplishes this in one of three ways: it either collects funds from the borrower and disburses payments for all required taxes and policies; or it monitors the status of tax payments and required policies, "force-placing" them if it receives notification of cancellation; or it takes out a blanket or umbrella insurance policy—a mortgage impairment policy—to cover any losses sustained as a result of individual loan tax liens or insurance lapses of coverage. This department also inspects property repairs (if the damage was large and affects the actual structure of the security) before releasing an insurance claim payment to the mortgagor.

- The collection department handles past-due loan accounts. In many ways, this is the most difficult function, but it is also the most essential for a successful servicing operation. Those involved in this function must be familiar with the Fair Debt Collection Practices Act that prohibits certain collection practices. When attempts at collection fail, then this function is also responsible for initiating foreclosure proceedings.

  Ideally, this area is not as active as other departments and handles fewer loan accounts (around 1 percent of all loans), but the complexity and level of knowledge is substantial and requires an enormous amount of time for each loan account. Since it involves legal issues and court proceedings, most lenders hire outside attorneys to manage each loan that becomes severely delinquent. It is critical for this area to minimize the substantial expenses and losses that occur when a loan goes to foreclosure. Normally, it is most active in the worst economic times.

  Depending on the number or severity of delinquencies in a servicing portfolio, a separate department related to collections, a real estate owned (REO) department, may be required to handle foreclosed property.

Servicing Contract

A servicing contract establishes the servicing relationship when a mortgage loan is sold to an investor and the servicing is retained by the loan originator. This contractual relationship continues for the life of the mortgage loans sold to that investor, but it can be terminated. Termination can be either for cause (some failure to perform on the part of the servicer) or, in some cases, without cause. If servicing is withdrawn without cause, then it is common for an investor to pay a fee, typically 1 or 2 percent of the amount serviced, as compensation.

The servicing contract or the servicing manual supplied by an investor describes in detail the servicing responsibilities. These responsibilities typically include the following:

- Monthly collection and allocation of principal and interest
- Disbursement of funds to the investor
- Collection and periodic payment of real estate taxes and insurance premiums
- Handling of assumption, partial release, and modification of lien requests
- Annual review of loans involving, among other tasks, ARM adjustments, current insurance policy, taxes paid, and **escrow analysis**
- Any other activity necessary to protect the investor's security interest, including, if necessary, collection activity and foreclosure proceedings

Managing Delinquencies and Foreclosures

Of all of the functions performed by the loan administration department, the most important is managing delinquencies (defaults). Default occurs when a mortgagor breaches any of the covenants in a mortgage. Most commonly, default is the result of nonpayment of principal and interest, but also could result from a failure to pay taxes, provide hazard insurance, or maintain the premises. A residential mortgage loan is generally classified as delinquent if it is 30 days past due. (Technically, a residential loan is delinquent after the first of the month since that is when the payment is due.) Uniform instruments allow for payment until the 15th of the month with no late fee added and, of course, no additional interest due. If the payment is received on the 16th or later, the lender may impose a late fee of up to 5 percent of the payment due.

Successful delinquency management can keep servicing expenses under control and therefore enhance servicing profits. For sold loans, the investor or servicing contract outlines the steps required of servicers in managing delinquencies, especially when a loan is seriously delinquent. For portfolio loans, the lender may have more flexibility.

Mortgagee Options

The mortgagee usually has certain options in the event of a default. One option (provided by the mortgage instrument) is to accelerate all future payments immediately, but seldom does the instrument require immediate acceleration. Accelerating the entire debt may not be the best choice for a mortgagee and is certainly not the best alternative for a mortgagor. Accelerating the entire debt and suing for the total most likely will lead to foreclosure, since most consumers do not have the funds on hand to pay off their mortgage.

In practically all situations, a mortgagee does not want to proceed to foreclosure if it can be prevented. Although the average consumer may not believe it, mortgagees not only dislike foreclosure, but generally lose money if they must foreclose. Most mortgagees are in the business of lending money, not owning or managing real property. The mortgagee may have other options, depending on the reasons for the default and "work-out" possibilities. GSEs and other private investors have developed loss mitigation techniques that enable the borrower to work out of the delinquent situation and avoid foreclosure.

Reasons for Default

There are many reasons why a mortgagor defaults on mortgage obligations. They mirror the different categories of delinquent credit discussed in Chapter 7, "Underwriting the Residential Mortgage Loan." Some delinquencies are purely honest mistakes on the part of a mortgagor. People occasionally miss a mortgage payment because of vacation, forgetfulness, or some other logical, nonrecurring reason. On the other hand, the more common reasons for residential mortgage defaults read like a list of personal tragedies:

- Financial problems
- Loss of employment
- Layoff or strike
- Death of a wage earner
- Credit overextension or bankruptcy
- Illness of a wage earner or mounting family medical expenses
- Loss of wage as a result of accident
- Marital problems

Collection Procedures

The collection activity should bring the delinquent mortgage current as quickly as possible for the benefit of both the mortgagor and mortgagee. The lender's servicing system must quickly identify a loan as delinquent. Time is of the essence when dealing with delinquent borrowers. The sooner the contact, the sooner it can be resolved or a repayment plan put in place.

The first step is usually a payment reminder notice sent to the borrower 7 to 10 days after the payment was due. This notice simply reminds the mortgagor that the payment was due on the 1st and that if not paid by the 15th a late fee will be assessed. If payment is not received by the 16th, the servicer sends a second notice informing the mortgagor that a late fee is now due in addition to the scheduled payment. Some coupons may already have this information printed on the form.

Telephone Contact

Telephone calling is a very effective and inexpensive method for contacting delinquent mortgagors. Some lenders use it for habitually delinquent borrowers who, once reminded, pay by the 7th or 10th day after the due date. Other lenders use the telephone to contact a mortgagor if the scheduled payment and late fee are not received by the 20th of the first month. Of course, if a lender prefers, a personalized letter sent around the 20th of the first month could be a very effective way of explaining the difficulties caused by not bringing the loan current.

Two Months Delinquent

The critical point is when a mortgage loan reaches two payments past due. The chances of the loan going to foreclosure increase dramatically if the delinquency is not cured during this second month. Shortly after the 1st of the second month past due, the lender should perform one or all of the following actions:

- Have an extended telephone conversation with the borrower with a plan for repayment (no voicemail)
- Schedule and conduct a face-to-face meeting with the borrowers
- Send a strongly worded letter informing the mortgagor that unless the loan is brought current, the mortgagor may be seriously jeopardizing his/her credit rating

Once a loan is 60 days past due, the lender should insist on a face-to-face interview with the mortgagor. This meeting should clearly establish the reason for delinquency and what the mortgagor intends to do about it. Based on the reason or reasons for the default, the lender may be able to suggest ways to cure the default.

Mortgage lenders should report delinquent mortgagors to credit bureaus. They are required by the secondary market players to report all 90-day delinquencies. Most lenders report 30- and 60-day delinquencies as well.

Curing Delinquencies

The important concept to realize is that most mortgage delinquencies are cured. Only a small percentage of delinquent mortgages ever reach foreclosure. Often a mortgagee and mortgagor resolve the problem that led to the delinquency. In assessing a delinquency, a lender should determine why the loan became delinquent, whether the delinquency reflects a temporary or permanent situation, and the mortgagor's attitude toward the mortgage debt.

Loss mitigation options available to mortgage lenders for handling delinquencies include the following:

- Accepting partial payments
- Collecting just a portion of the past-due amount immediately
- Making a second mortgage to bring the loan current
- Extending the term
- Providing temporary indulgence
- Looking to other solutions tailored to the needs of both parties that will rectify the problem

The servicer/lender may need investor approval of one of these options if the loan has been sold. Since all parties lose in the event of foreclosure, the secondary market has become more open to avoiding this and exploring the previously listed options.

For a discussion of the various methods of foreclosure and the right of redemption, see Chapter 15, "Real Estate Law and Security Instruments."

Portfolio Management and Loan Administration

The following sections describe loan servicing and portfolio management for lenders.

Evolution of Loan Servicing

Historically, the servicing department was considered a cost center for a depository lender. Performing these functions was a necessary expense to get back the lender's money from the borrowers. More progressive depository lenders realized that servicing provides an opportunity to strengthen their customer relationship, and they implemented strategies to capitalize on that, but servicing was still accepted as an operational cost.

An even more sophisticated view of mortgage servicing developed with the expansion of the secondary market. Many investors provide funds to buy loans, but do not know how to collect them. Both investors and GSEs realize the crucial role a properly run servicing department plays in maintaining the marketability and value of the under-lying loan itself. Reliable and regular collection and transfer of money from borrower to investor is the basic foundation on which the secondary market rests. GSEs led the way in establishing servicing standards and developing quicker, more efficient methods of funds transfer from servicer to investor. Since the GSEs and many investors who purchase loans do not want the responsibility of servicing them, they pay others a servicing fee to do it. The GSEs require that investors pay a servicer a minimum of 25 basis points (0.25 percent) of the outstanding loan balances, which the servicer retains each month before forwarding the payments collected to the investor. This represents substantial servicing income from a large servicing portfolio.

In the 1980s, the technology was not available to manage large portfolios; however, as computer capacity grew and software programs handled more functions, servicing portfolios grew 10-fold in size during the 1990s. Today, the largest single servicing port-folio is almost $500 billion—approximately 4 million mortgage loans! Equally stagger-ing, the 10 largest servicers handle 50 percent of all mortgages serviced in the United States, double the percentage the largest 10 handled less than a decade earlier in 1995. The top 20 servicers handle 60 percent of all outstanding mortgage debt.

Improved computer and software technology enabled this dramatic increase in market share concentration, but the underlying explanation is a change in business strategy adopted by larger firms in loan administration. These firms want to service as many loans as possible to maximize their operational efficiency. Proper use of this technology lowers the cost per loan serviced. This strategy and the activities of just 20 companies have a dominating effect on the entire mortgage industry.

TABLE 14-2 Largest Servicers of Residential Mortgage Debt, 1993 versus 2001 (dollars in billions)

Servicer	1993 Servicing Volume
1. Countrywide Funding	$80.0
2. Fleet Mortgage	70.0
3. Prudential Home Mortgage	68.0
4. General Electric Capital	64.0
5. Citibank	47.0

Source: American Banker.

Servicer	2001 Servicing Volume
1. Washington Mutual	$496.7
2. Wells Fargo Mortgage	487.8
3. Chase Manhattan Mortgage	429.8
4. Countrywide Credit Industries	336.6
5. Bank of America	320.9

Source: National Mortgage News.

FASB Rules

In addition to the role of technology, several major accounting changes have shaped today's mortgage-servicing industry. Because of these Financial Accounting Standards Board (FASB) rulings, many servicers calculate the value of their portfolios differently than before. This process began with the adoption of FAS 65 in 1982, followed with FAS 122 in 1995, FAS 125 in 1996, and finally, FAS 133 in 1998 (see http://www.fasb.org). Each accounting change fundamentally impacted the profitability and financial structure of all mortgage servicers. They impact the manner in which a servicer values its portfolio, how it categorizes the loan for sale or to be held in portfolio, and how it can offset the interest rate and value risk present as a result of these changes. The value of a servicing portfolio is no longer "fixed" (based on what it cost a lender to obtain it). Instead, the value changes with market interest rates. And a servicer must decide at origination if it intends to keep the loan or sell it.

For example, the exact same portfolio would be valued higher if interest rates rose overnight from 7.0 percent to 7.5 percent. Why? Fewer loans refinance when rates rise, so the loans in this portfolio will generate servicing income for a longer period of time than if rates fell (or remained unchanged). Since the servicer will receive more income in this interest rate environment, the value of this portfolio increases. In this way, the day-to-day value of the servicing portfolio is more volatile and subject to factors beyond the servicer's control. This offers the potential for significant gains when rates rise. Price volatility also means increased risk from potential losses when rates drop. In any event, the result of these related FASB rulings is a strategic change in how servicers manage their portfolios.

Servicing Strategies

Today, medium to large servicers view their servicing portfolios much like a stockbroker views a stock portfolio. Some servicers buy and trade parts of their larger portfolio in different economic climates. Others specialize in certain types of loans to service, similar to stockbrokers who trade and specialize in certain stocks. The active management of the servicing portfolio led to the development and more common use of the term *loan administration*. Since servicing is an asset that can provide income to an organization that specializes in this business, a lender must answer the following question, Who will service the loan?

Several options exist. A lender that sells a loan to an investor may also sell the servicing of that loan to another entity. Some originators (usually mortgage bankers and brokers) sell the loan and servicing before it closes. Others sell it after closing the loan, or sell the loan servicing released, or enter into a subservicing arrangement. The point is the valuing and selling of mortgage servicing have grown to where these aspects of mortgage lending are more significant sources of income than the original sale of the loan.

Servicing: The Reason Some Lenders Are in Residential Lending

For some mortgage lenders, such as mortgage bankers, servicing profits are the primary reason for engaging in mortgage lending. Other mortgage lenders, who were almost exclusively portfolio lenders in the past (such as thrifts or credit unions), now sell a major portion of their originations and place a greater emphasis on loan administration. This shift in emphasis adds to the concentration of the servicing we see today, as larger organizations attempt to maximize operational efficiencies.

Servicing also plays a major role in the recent emergence of the so-called nontraditional mortgage lenders. Many of these players, such as General Motors Acceptance Corporation (GMAC), enter the residential mortgage-lending competition by buying large servicing portfolios. These large servicing portfolios give new entrants immediate economies of scale and thus enhance profit potential. GMAC bought two servicing portfolios totaling nearly $19 billion. Overnight, GMAC became one of the largest servicers of mortgage debt in the world and today is the sixth largest, servicing almost $192 billion in mortgage debt.

Servicing Income

As stated previously, originating lenders earn a fee from the investor to whom they transfer servicing. This fee, called a servicing release fee or premium, recognizes the value of that servicing operation. The servicing release premium/fee provides practically all of the mortgage servicer's revenue. Additional sources of income may include interest rate spread, origination fees, possible warehousing and marketing profits, late charges, and escrow float.

Collection of monthly mortgage payments generates the servicing income a servicer retains. The servicing fee is earned only when the payment is collected, and it is based on the agreed-upon percentage of loan principal outstanding. After receiving the monthly payment of principal and interest, a servicer forwards that amount less the servicing fee to the investor. Today, the servicing fee ranges from 0.25 percent to 0.50 percent of the outstanding balance of the loan. The amount varies depending on volume of loans serviced and also by the type of mortgage (e.g., an ARM could require a servicing fee as high as 50 basis points). The average for all residential mortgage loans today is probably closer to 25 basis points.

In the current mortgage market, many mortgage lenders are unable to generate a profit from the origination function. These mortgage lenders must look to servicing income to offset origination losses, and sometimes marketing losses, to produce a net profit from mortgage lending.

Servicing Profitability

In the early 1980s, a period of such high inflation caused the wisdom of servicing profitability to come into serious question. Servicing expense was expected to increase each year with overall inflation, while the servicing income from a mortgage loan was expected to decrease each year over the life of the loan (as the loan balance amortizes). Two fundamental factors prevented this scenario: the overall level of interest rates and inflation declined to record lows to keep costs stable; dramatic improvements in technology enabled larger servicing portfolios and increased operational efficiencies.

A Profitability Squeeze with Each Refinancing Wave

Unfortunately, the sustained decline in the overall level of interest rates throughout the 1990s presented an entirely different challenge to the profitability of mortgage servicing. With each significant decline in mortgage interest rates came the expectation of consumers that "This was it!"—the bottom of the interest rate trough. Other consumers simply realized the rate was low enough to recoup the expense of refinancing quickly. The combination was literally termed a "refinance wave" by industry professionals since a record number of borrowers refinanced at the same time. The effect was devastating to many servicers, who saw their portfolios evaporate in just a few months.

So many borrowers refinanced during these waves that lenders were unable to service the old loans long enough to make a profit on servicing. Regrettably from the servicers' viewpoint, many mortgagors refinanced their mortgage with another lender; thus, the servicing was lost to the other lender. For those lenders that counted on the servicing income to offset initial and ongoing lending expenses, the impact of the lost servicing income was painful—and even more severe for those servicers who purchased servicing rights from other lenders. These servicers not only didn't make a profit on the servicing they purchased, they did not recoup their purchase price. As a result of these losses, many medium to large servicers went out of business.

Despite these challenges, many mortgage servicers earn record profits in most years. Not all profitable servicers are the largest ones. As with most lines of business, it's not what a lender does (or plans), it's how the lender executes it. The same is true with servicing, for which loan administration plays a key role in year-end results.

The annual *Cost of Servicing Study* by the Mortgage Bankers Association of America (http://mbaa.org) and the KPMG consulting group, now Bearing Point (http://kpmgconsulting.com), analyzes a variety of servicing organizations and several important areas that impact mortgage servicing: the cost of servicing and the characteristics of profitable and unprofitable servicers. Lenders and servicers eagerly await the results to find out what the average per loan servicing cost is and what organizations and strategies were successful in the previous year.

Industry pundits assume that the largest servicers are always the most profitable, but the study shows how significant profitability in recent years depends in large part on the economic activity and interest rate behavior for that time period. Refinance waves affect profitability by not allowing acquirers of servicing enough time to recoup their acquisition costs, as discussed earlier.

A surprising result that emerged a few years ago was the success of "niche" servicers—organizations that specialize in a particular loan product or type. The study shows that those that do well in their specialty are very profitable, regardless of size. Some examples of niche servicers include FHA/VA loans, subprime or B and C credit loans, adjustable-rate loans, jumbo loans, and construction/permanent loans. While these lenders are not the lowest-cost servicers, they offset their additional expense by either earning a higher servicing fee or by successfully generating income from other areas.

Other Income

The servicer of loans for investors benefits from float income. Float exists as a result of the unequal timing between loan payment collections and remittance of those payments to the investors. The float period can be for as much as four to six weeks in some cases and potentially involves millions of dollars. The float depends on the date a payment is received by a mortgage lender. Other remittance plans, such as FNMA's actual/actual option, require remittance whenever the servicer has collected $2,500, which shortens float time tremendously.

Often overlooked by institutions just beginning servicing is the importance of other fee income generated by the loan administration department. These fees include the following, among others:

- Late charges
- Processing an assumption or novation
- Preparation of discharge and release
- Reinstatement after default (if different from late fees)
- Substitution of hazard insurance policies other than on the renewal or annual premium rate
- Insurance commissions from accident, health, mortgagor life, and other casualty policies
- Prepayment penalty fees
- Bad check fees and other miscellaneous fees

Escrow Administration

An important source of servicing income is derived from the value of funds held in escrow for the payment of real estate taxes, hazard insurance, or other insurance. (In certain parts of the country, these monthly payments are called impounds.) Many lenders require that mortgagors escrow one-twelfth of the annual real estate taxes and hazard insurance each month, while paying their mortgage principal and interest. The secondary mortgage market requires escrows when a mortgage has a loan-to-value ratio over 80 percent.

Requiring a tax or insurance escrow assures the lender that no loss will occur as a result of nonpayment. If real estate taxes are not paid, the local government could have a superior claim or position in the real estate that is securing the mortgage debt. It can eventually sell the real estate for the back taxes. Some lenders will advance funds to pay real estate taxes to avoid this situation, recovering the amount by increasing the **escrow payments** for the next year or by adding that amount to the principal.

The same risk exists if the federal government places a tax lien on the real estate securing the mortgage for failure to pay income or other federal taxes. Additionally, if a loss occurs on the real estate securing the loan and the insurance premium is not paid, the lender could suffer because its security, the real estate, was not insured and now is in need of repair.

Use of Escrow Funds

Escrows can serve, if needed by the servicer, as the compensating balance required for a line of credit from a commercial bank. The existence of these funds not only allows for this line of credit but also keeps the interest rate on that line lower than it would be without the compensating balances. Mortgagors benefit from this arrangement because a lender is then able to offer lower mortgage rates. In addition to this benefit, mortgage lenders benefit from the float period on these funds since they are collected monthly but are only disbursed semi-annually or annually. As a result, mortgage servicers can invest these funds during the interim. This can be a meaningful source of low- or no-cost funds to the servicer, the benefit of which can be passed on to borrowers by lower rates on their mortgages.

Exhibit 14-1 Sample Initial Escrow Account Disclosure Statement

FAIRFIELD SAVINGS ASSOCIATION
FIRST MORTGAGE LOAN INFORMATION

Initial Escrow Account Disclosure Statement

Date	02/13/04	**Application:** 100101920
Borrowers:	Joseph F. Lynch	**Property:** 89 Harvester Road
	Margaret J. Lynch	Fairfield CT 06825

This is an estimate of activity in your escrow account during the coming year based on payments anticipated to be made from your account.

Date	Description	Payments To Escrow	Payments From Escrow	Escrow Account Balance
	Initial Deposit:			$1,100.00
Jul 01, 2004	Monthly escrow payment	300.00		$1,400.00
Jul 01, 2004	Taxes		600.00	
Jul 01, 2004	Hazard Insurance		150.00	
Jul 01, 2004	Mtg Insurance		50.00	$600.00
Aug 01, 2004	Monthly escrow payment	300.00		$900.00
Aug 01, 2004	Mtg Insurance		50.00	$850.00
Sep 01, 2004	Monthly escrow payment	300.00		$1,150.00
Sep 01, 2004	Mtg Insurance		50.00	$1,100.00
Oct 01, 2004	Monthly escrow payment	300.00		$1,400.00
Oct 01, 2004	Mtg Insurance		50.00	
Oct 01, 2004	Taxes		600.00	
Oct 01, 2004	Hazard Insurance		150.00	$600.00
Nov 01, 2004	Monthly escrow payment	300.00		$900.00
Nov 01, 2004	Mtg Insurance		50.00	$850.00
Dec 01, 2004	Monthly escrow payment	300.00		$1,150.00
Dec 01, 2004	Mtg Insurance		50.00	$1,100.00
Jan 01, 2005	Monthly escrow payment	300.00		$1,400.00
Jan 01, 2005	Hazard Insurance		150.00	
Jan 01, 2005	Taxes		600.00	
Jan 01, 2005	Mtg Insurance		50.00	$600.00
Feb 01, 2005	Monthly escrow payment	300.00		$900.00
Feb 01, 2005	Mtg Insurance		50.00	$850.00
Mar 01, 2005	Monthly escrow payment	300.00		$1,150.00
Mar 01, 2005	Mtg Insurance		50.00	$1,100.00
Apr 01, 2005	Monthly escrow payment	300.00		$1,400.00
Apr 01, 2005	Taxes		600.00	
Apr 01, 2005	Hazard Insurance		150.00	
Apr 01, 2005	Mtg Insurance		50.00	$600.00
May 01, 2005	Monthly escrow payment	300.00		$900.00
May 01, 2005	Mtg Insurance		50.00	$850.00
Jun 01, 2005	Monthly escrow payment	300.00		$1,150.00
Jun 01, 2005	Mtg Insurance		50.00	$1,100.00

(Please keep this statement for comparison with the actual activity in your account at the end of the escrow accounting computation year.)

Cushion selected by servicer: $600.00

Your monthly mortgage payment for the coming year will be $1,433.16 of which $1,133.16 will be for principal and interest and $300.00 will go into your escrow account.

Joseph F. Lynch
Joseph F. Lynch

Margaret J. Lynch
Margaret J. Lynch

During the 1980s, many states passed laws requiring lenders to pay interest on escrows. The federal government has also considered whether a federal law is needed that would require all lenders to pay interest on escrowed funds. The amount of interest that must be paid varies from state to state. Currently, in those states where interest is required, the minimum rates generally fall between 2 percent and 4 percent per annum, while a few require interest as high as 5.5 percent. Even when lenders must pay interest on escrow, these funds are still low-cost funds and enhance profitability. A few lenders, usually thrifts, have decided not to escrow funds for taxes and insurance because they do not believe they benefit enough from these funds when the cost of collecting and disbursing the funds are calculated. This would appear to be the case only when the servicing volume is low and the cost of additional personnel outweighs the investment income that would be earned.

When viewed from the mortgagors' side, many prefer the convenience of budgeting these expenses on a monthly basis. The additional income received from the interest paid on escrows is a benefit but generally is not very important, especially since mortgagors must pay income taxes on the interest paid on escrows.

Limits on Escrows

Many lenders believe that escrows help lower the number of delinquencies and foreclosures. Most consumers like the idea of escrows because escrow allows them to budget their insurance and tax payments. In the past, some lenders have abused the purpose of escrowing funds to profit on the float. They required much more money in the **escrow account** than was needed.

RESPA now requires that servicers analyze the escrow payment amounts annually and requires that servicers limit the payment amount to sufficient funds to pay the next annual installment, plus a two-month cushion. Further, a servicer is required to send an analysis of the escrows collected over the past year to mortgagors within 30 days of the conclusion of each escrow account year. The servicer is also required to make payments for taxes and insurance from the escrow account in a timely manner.

Cost of Servicing

It is generally assumed that in today's market a mortgage lender must be servicing about $50 million of loans sold to investors **servicing retained** before the cost of servicing those loans is offset by the servicing income. This is down from the $100 million level of the late 1980s. The reason the cost has come down is the increased use of technology and the increase in the average loan size. The approximately $50 million breakeven point may vary somewhat for different lenders, but as a general rule, appears to be a sound assumption based upon the annual *Cost of Servicing Study* produced by the Mortgage Bankers Association of America.

As the servicing portfolio of a mortgage lender increases, economies of scale develop. That average annual cost can drop to approximately $100 per loan when the portfolio reaches $1 billion (or about 10,000 loans) and may get as low as $50 when the portfolio reaches $2 billion or $3 billion. The largest servicer of residential debt, Washington Mutual, services $500 billion, representing over 4 million loans. Because of this evident economy of scale, some lenders with large servicing operations purchase servicing from other lenders.

Purchasing Servicing

At certain points in the economic cycle, the purchase of servicing may be a cheaper strategy to grow the servicing portfolio than by increasing originations. During these periods of time, the lenders active in servicing attempt to buy servicing from other mortgage lenders. These other lenders may be mortgage brokers, other originators, or other servicers. The price paid for servicing varies, but can range from 100 to 250 basis points of the amount serviced. Thus, if one servicer desires to purchase $100 million of servicing from another, the price, depending on the market, could be in the $1.0 million to $2.5 million range.

The price one servicer would pay for servicing purchased from another servicer can be better calculated by equating the purchase price to the actual cash flow generated by the portfolio. For example, all other aspects being equal, a servicer would pay less for a cash flow generated by a 25-basis-point servicing fee than one generated by a 375-basis-point fee. In determining the price that a servicer will pay for another's servicing portfolio, the following items are reviewed:

- Average loan balance
- Weighted-average servicing fee
- Weighted-average remaining maturity
- Weighted-average coupon rate
- Type of loan
  - Fixed rate
  - Adjustable rate
  - Biweekly
- Average escrow amounts
- Interest to be paid on reserves
- Delinquency and foreclosure experience
- Geographic makeup of the loans
- Investors (determines float)
- Assumption and prepayment provisions
- Remaining life expectations of the loans
- Ancillary income and other miscellaneous items

Depending on a number of variables (e.g., type and size of loan, interest rate, expected life of the loan, and the volume of loans transferred), the broker could receive as much as 75 to 150 basis points from the investor for the servicing transferred. If the volume of loans is very low, the broker may receive less or nothing at all. This servicing strategy is discussed next.

Selling Servicing

It has been estimated by the Mortgage Bankers Association that as much as $500 billion in mortgage servicing changes hands yearly. This number is higher some years than others, but servicing today is often viewed as a marketable asset by many mortgage lenders. If a mortgage lender wants to sell servicing, the selling servicer—called the transferor—must (according to RESPA) provide the mortgagor with at least 15 days before the effective date of the transfer a Notice of Assignment, Sale, or Transfer of

Servicing Rights. This notice from the transferor (sometimes called a "goodbye letter") informs the mortgagor of the effective date of the transfer, provides a toll-free or collect phone number of the transferee, and provides the name of someone at the transferor's place of business who can answer questions. The purchasing servicer—called the transferee—must send a similar notice (a "hello letter") to the mortgagor within 15 days of the transfer. This notice states that no late fee will be charged for 60 days after the servicing is transferred if the borrower sends the payment to the wrong servicer.

A mortgagor is advised at the time a residential mortgage application is submitted what the mortgagee's loan-transferring practices have been based on actual transfers over the past three years. This disclosure should be signed by all applicants and must be retained in the loan file.

One of the key components to the decision to buy another lender's servicing portfolio is establishing the purchaser's cost of servicing. Many lenders have a difficult time establishing a figure for cost of servicing. When a mortgage lender calculates its cost of loan servicing, the following expenses should be included:

- Personnel expenses (including fringe benefits)
- Occupancy
- Data processing
- Other direct operating expenses
  - Equipment rentals
  - Postage
  - Telephone
  - Office supplies
  - Travel and entertainment
  - Automobiles
  - Advertising
  - Legal and auditing fees
  - Other operating expenses
- Provision for loan losses

Alternatives to Servicing Residential Mortgage Loans

For various reasons, usually involving the issue of whether a lender can service profitably, many residential mortgage lenders have decided not to service the loans they originate. Other lenders realize that they simply don't have the talent to do servicing well. For these mortgage lenders, alternative strategies exist. They include selling the mortgage loans servicing released or entering into a subservicing arrangement.

Servicing Released

As has been mentioned, servicing residential loans sold to an investor has great value to some large servicers. The reason servicing has value to these large servicers is because these servicers can service the loan for less money than they receive as a servicing fee. For that reason, some of these servicers will pay other lenders for the right

right to service loans the other lender originated. The large servicers acquire the servicing rights by purchasing a mortgage loan or loans for a premium, and then selling (normally, but not always) the mortgage loans into the secondary mortgage market, while retaining the servicing. The amount of servicing released premium servicers pay to originating lenders depends on a number of factors including the volume of mortgages sold, where interest rates are, prepayment assumptions, and so forth. For example, if one lender can sell $5 million of mortgages a month, the acquiring lender may pay as much as 100 basis points as a premium for the servicing. The acquiring lender/servicer is simply buying the right to the future stream of income associated with servicing that loan for a number of years. If the loan prepays early, the servicer loses. This situation is exactly what happened to many purchasers of servicing in the early 1990s.

Subservicing

In order to make residential mortgage lending profitable as soon as possible, some new mortgage lenders, such as credit unions, have opted not to establish a servicing department for the mortgages they have sold into the secondary mortgage market. As a general rule, they make this decision because they don't have sufficient volume to perform the function profitably or don't have a staff that is qualified. In addition, there are some mortgage lenders who don't want to sell loans servicing released (as described earlier) because they don't want another financial institution in contact with their customers. Instead, these mortgage lenders contract with another mortgage lender or servicing company to conduct all of the servicing responsibilities for them.

These lenders pay the subservicer a servicing fee (usually between $80 and $125 per loan per year) based on the total number of loans serviced. The originating lender is still responsible to ensure the loans are serviced properly, but by using another qualified servicer, the originating lender can have the servicing function performed profitably. For example, if one of these lenders sells a $100,000 mortgage to Fannie Mae and receives a 25-basis-point servicing fee ($250 a year), it can contract with a subservicer to service the loan for, say, $125. The difference between the two fees is profit to the originating lender. Many of these originating lenders will put into the servicing contract with the subservicer the right to pull servicing when sufficient volume is reached to make the function profitable.

Discussion Points

1. Discuss the difference between mortgage loan servicing and mortgage loan administration and how this difference impacts the lender.

2. Explain the benefits and drawbacks to a unit versus functional form of organization for a loan servicing/administration department.

3. What are the various mortgage-servicing strategies implemented by lenders?

4. List and explain mortgage-servicing functions and responsibilities.

5. How do refinance waves affect servicing departments (and lenders)?

6. How does a lender determine its cost of servicing and why is this important?

7. How are servicing fees calculated? When does a servicer earn these fees?

Real Estate Law and Security Instruments

Introduction

This chapter deals with real estate and mortgage law and how it developed under the common law and, finally, in the United States. This chapter is designed to provide reference material for the other chapters of the book. In addition, the second half of the chapter deals with the various forms of security instruments common to residential mortgage lending. These instruments are reviewed in order to better understand the purpose of the instruments, how they are constructed, and what legal rights and duties the various clauses contained therein create.

Possibly no other segment of the U.S. socioeconomic system is more involved with law than real estate and mortgage lending. Whether as a homeowner, a developer, or a financier, those involved with real estate and mortgage lending must understand the legal framework upon which real estate is defined and the interests therein protected.

Law and real estate have been inseparable since the early days of the development of Anglo-American jurisprudence. This close relationship continues because of custom and the perception that real estate is normally an owner's most precious possession. However, this also has hindered the changes in real estate and mortgage lending concepts that are needed in an evolving society.

A fundamental review of how this relationship between law and real estate developed and a discussion of the interests a person can have in real estate appear in the following sections. Nonlegal terminology is used as often as possible where the meaning or concept is not altered or affected in any way.

In light of broad differences in state law, this review covers only the general principles of real estate law with no discussion of the unique features of any one state's law. In those situations in which there is a basic conflict in the general principles, the majority position is reviewed. Nevertheless, the laws of individual jurisdictions should be carefully determined. This is best accomplished by consulting a competent local attorney.

English Common Law

Real estate law throughout the United States, with few exceptions, is based almost entirely on the English common law, as it existed at the time of the American Revolutionary War. This common background has been modified as each jurisdiction legislated changes or as courts interpreted the law differently. Developments in real estate finance since 1776 have required new indigenous laws, but the fact still remains that most of our real estate law is derived from the common law. As a result, the chief problem facing contemporary American real estate law is the existence of 51 jurisdictions (including the District of Columbia) with separate real estate laws based on an archaic system of law. This problem is compounded by the fact that this archaic system uses language hundreds of years old and is based on a socioeconomic environment entirely different from that of the modern-day United States. A short review of the development of the common law is vital to an understanding of current real estate law.

Feudal System of Land Tenure

Before the Norman invasion of England in 1066, there was no well-developed system of land ownership in England. The family unit rather than the individual owned land, and when the head of the household died, the new head of the household represented the ownership of the family in a particular piece of land. In 1066, when William the Conqueror invaded England, he imposed a European concept of land ownership on the English called the feudal system of land tenure, an economic, military, and political system of government that held that the king exclusively owned all land. The most valuable and important commodity in such a society was land. Land represented wealth, and all wealth came from the land. Money hardly existed and barter was the means of exchange. Since the king owned all land, he had complete control over the country and the economy.

A king, of course, needed arms for protection of the realm. For this he depended on the loyalty, fidelity, and allegiance of the lords. In return for their allegiance and military service, the king allowed the lords to use the land, although no ownership was conveyed. The lords, in turn, allowed lesser lords to use portions of this land in return for a share of the profits and for swearing allegiance to them. Finally, these lesser lords allowed serfs, who were nothing more than slaves indentured to the land, to use the land in return for a promise of military service. In this pyramid of military allegiance, the serfs owed military service to the lesser lords, who in turn owed service to the lords, who swore allegiance to the king.

The right to own land didn't exist for many years, but one of the incidents of ownership, the ability to pass the use of land to heirs, produced a confrontation with King John in 1215. The result was the Magna Carta, which provided greater rights for the lords, including the right to pass the use of the land on to their sons. Land was passed on to sons only as a result of the doctrine of primogeniture, which dictated that the oldest male child had the right to inherit the land. This was desirable at the time, since it prevented estates from being broken up into smaller tracts and allowed for the development of landed gentry, which eventually developed the English society. Out of this society evolved the common law and, eventually, English real estate law. Although modified over the years, the feudal system survived until 1660, when it was abolished by law.

Allodial System

As contrasted with the feudal system, the allodial system recognizes that an owner of real estate has title irrespective of the sovereign and thus owes no duty, such as rent or the rendering of military service, to the sovereign. This system developed throughout the world with the exception of western Europe and certain other areas where the feudal system remained.

The feudal system was an early part of the American land-ownership system in a few locations such as New York and Maryland. With those exceptions, the allodial system was paramount in America based on conquest, discovery, or purchase.

Principles of Real Estate Law

The first step in understanding the principles of real estate law is to define terms. *Real property* is land and everything permanently attached to it. Under the common law, and as a general rule today, this included ownership from the center of the earth, the surface, and up to the heavens. All other property is personal property. Real estate denotes both real property and the business of real estate, including financing.

Property can change from one classification to another fairly rapidly. For example, a tree standing in a forest is real property. When it is felled, it becomes personal property and, finally, after being made into lumber and becoming part of a house, it is real property again. The term *fixture* is used to describe a piece of personal property that has been attached in such a manner that it is now considered real property. This distinction is important, since title to real property is normally transferred by a deed, while personal property is transferred by a bill of sale.

Estate

Today, when people talk about their ownership of land, they are legally talking about the type of estate they have in real estate. This is as true in the United States as it was in England 500 years ago. An estate is defined as an interest in real property that is measured by its potential duration. There are two recognized classifications of estate in real property: freehold and leasehold, sometimes referred to as nonfreehold. The classification *freehold estate* is the highest form of interest possible in real property, as it involves all the rights in real property including use, passing the property to one's heirs, or selecting who is going to take it in a transfer. It is an estate of infinite duration, in that the **chain of title** could theoretically last forever. An example of a freehold estate would be a fee simple absolute.

On the other hand, the classification *leasehold estate* is an inferior interest in real property, because the owner of a leasehold interest has only the right of possession for a period of time. The owner of this interest does not have *seisin*, which is defined as the ability to pass title to one's heirs or assigns. An example of a leasehold estate would be a tenant's interest in leased property.

Fee Simple Absolute

There has never been nor will there ever be complete ownership of land. Examples of the restraints or limitations on ownership of land include, among others, eminent domain, adverse possession, and easements. The greatest interest a person can have in real property is known as a **fee simple** absolute. Any owner of real property, whether it is a large corporation or John Doe, has a fee simple absolute if all possible rights to that piece of real property are possessed.

In order to explain a fee simple absolute, legal pedagogues use the bundle of rights concept. For example, assume that all rights (such as the right to sell, mortgage, and build on a piece of real property) are represented by "sticks" and are contained in this bundle of rights. If all of the sticks are present and the owner has all possible rights to the real property, then the bundle of rights is complete and is called a fee simple absolute. If a stick is missing, such as the right to use the property the way one wants, then the interest is less than a fee simple absolute.

Defeasible or Conditional Fee

A freehold estate, which is similar to a fee simple absolute but minus a stick (or a right) from the bundle of rights, is the defeasible fee simple. This is a freehold estate that could but will not necessarily last forever. An example of a defeasible fee simple occurs when conditions are placed on how the property may be used. Grantors of land may put any restrictions they desire on how the land is to be used after it has been conveyed. There are, of course, a few exceptions, such as those that are racially oriented. Grantors can always give less than the full interests they own in conveying land, but never more. They can give possession for any desired period of time, or for any specific use—for use only as a church, for example. If so conveyed, a defeasible fee simple is created that could last forever, but it could also be terminated.

An example of a defeasible fee simple that would automatically end if a certain event occurs is when Adam grants land to an Anglican church on condition that the premises are used only for church purposes. The church has a defeasible fee simple that could last forever but will automatically end if the property ceases to be used for church purposes. When that happens, the title automatically reverts to Adam or Adam's heirs. This interest is classified as a fee simple since it could last forever if the property is always used for church purposes.

A distinction is made legally between two types of defeasible fee simple. They are a fee simple subject to a condition subsequent and a fee simple determinable. The typical person involved in real estate does not need to know the distinction, but counsel for that person should. An example of a fee simple subject to a condition subsequent would occur when John conveys property to Janice as long as liquor is never sold on the premises. In this situation, the grantee Janice (the person to whom the land has been conveyed) has a fee simple, but it is subject to a condition subsequent in that if liquor is ever sold on the premises, the land will revert to the grantor (the one making the conveyances). The grantor must make an affirmative action for the property to revert, that is, reenter the property and sue to terminate the estate.

The fee simple determinable has been described. Most courts lump these together as being basically the same. If forced to distinguish, courts attempt to find a fee on a condition subsequent in order that the grantor must reenter to terminate rather than have the estate terminate automatically.

Fee Tail

This type of estate came into being from a desire in feudal England to keep land in whole parcels within the family. A *fee tail* is an estate of potentially infinite duration, but is inheritable only by the grantee's lineal descendants, such as children or grandchildren. For a fee tail to be created under the common law, it was necessary to state in the conveyance that the land was being transferred to Stephen and "the heirs of his body." This differed from the wording of any other common law transfer, which required only "and his heirs" to be used.

There were various types of fee tail. The fee tail general meant the property was inheritable by the issue of the grantee. A fee tail special meant the land was inheritable only by the issue of the grantee and a specifically named spouse. (A conveyance to Robert and the heirs of his body, by his wife, Mary, would be an example.) A fee tail general could specify whether the issue need be male or female, and there also was the possibility of a fee tail special, male or female. Although the fee tail is still allowed in some New England states, the practical effect of it has been abolished in all states today.

Life Estates

A *life estate* is a freehold estate like the fee simple absolute and others already mentioned, but it is not inheritable. Life estates can be either conventional (created by the grantor) or legal (created by operation of law). The creation of a life estate is a tool often used in estate planning and is a fairly common interest in real estate. By the creation of a life estate, the life tenant (the one granted the right) has the use of real estate for a period of time measured by a human life. The human life used to measure the duration of the life estate may be that of another human life, but is most commonly measured by the life of the life tenant. An example is Jennifer conveys a life estate to Benjamin for life, and as long as Benjamin is alive, Benjamin has the right to use the real estate, with certain exceptions, as if he owned it. The only incident of ownership that Benjamin lacks is the power to pass on a fee simple absolute. The right to sell or mortgage the interest is not expressly given, but a person could acquire only that which Benjamin had, which is the use of the land for a period measured by a life.

When Jennifer created this life estate, only a part of the complete interest was transferred. In other words, someone else was allowed to use the land for a period of time. However, at the expiration of that period of time, the remaining rights to the real estate are with the grantor. In the example given, in which Jennifer conveyed land to Benjamin for the duration of Benjamin's life, the land will revert to Jennifer (the grantor) or Jennifer's heirs upon the death of Benjamin (the life tenant) since no other conveyance was made.

When Jennifer created the life estate in Benjamin, the remainder could have been transferred in this way: Jennifer to Benjamin for life, and then to Neil. In this situation, Neil is the vested remainderman, because the grantor has transferred the remaining interest to Neil. The rights of Neil are vested irrespective of whether he survives the life tenant or not. If a vested remainderman does die before a life tenant, then the vested remainderman's heirs would inherit the fee interest.

On the other hand, a life estate could be created this way: Jennifer to Benjamin for Benjamin's life, and then to Neil if Neil is alive, in which case Neil must survive Benjamin to acquire any rights to the land. If Neil dies before Benjamin, the land reverts to the original owner. If it is impossible to determine at the time of the creation of the life estate who definitely will take the fee simple after the death of the life tenant, the remainderman is referred to as a contingent remainderman.

Another common example of this situation would be: Jennifer to Benjamin for life, and then to Benjamin's children. Benjamin may not have any children; therefore, their interest is contingent upon their being born. To complicate it even further, the conveyance could read Jennifer to Benjamin for Benjamin's life, and then to Benjamin's surviving children. The children, if any, must survive Benjamin before they can acquire any interest.

In summary, a conventional life estate is an interest, which an individual has in real estate providing most of the incidences of ownership, with the exception of the ability to pass a fee simple absolute. The person who takes possession after the life tenant dies could be either the grantor, if the grantor did not convey the remainder, or it could be a third person who would be classified as either a contingent or a vested remainderman, depending on whether the identity can be determined precisely at the time of the creation of the life estate.

Legal Life Estates

In contrast with the conventional life estate, created intentionally by the grantor, a legal life estate is created by operation of the law. An example of a legal life estate is the right of dower. Dower was originally conceived to prevent a widow from being penniless during a period of English history when life insurance, welfare, and social security were unknown. Dower is a common law right of a widow still present in many jurisdictions. The equivalent right of the husband is curtesy, which has either been abolished or merged with dower in nearly all states.

Basically, the right of **dower** gives a wife, at her husband's death, a life estate in one-third of the real estate owned by her husband during marriage. Generally, the widow has a choice of which real estate will be subject to her dower right, and this right is applicable to all real estate owned by the husband during the marriage, even if he had transferred it before death. In those states where this right exists, a wife's potential dower interest is extinguished if she executes a deed with her husband transferring the land to another.

Currently, in some states, the right of dower has been abolished as unnecessary. This is because the need for a right such as dower has been eliminated in most states by the creation of a statutory right of each spouse to a minimum one-third share of the decedent's estate, and because of life insurance, social security, and other benefits.

Leasehold Estates (Nonfreehold Estates)

As mentioned earlier, the leasehold estate gives the owner the right to possession of real estate for a period of time. The actual duration may or may not be ascertainable at the beginning, but it does not carry with it the ability to pass title to the real estate. The owner of the land (the fee) has given up possession for a period of time, but retains the legal title to the real estate, and the owner (or heirs or assigns) will eventually retake possession. The legal term to describe the missing element in a leasehold estate is *seisin*.

Although the use of leases can be traced to the beginning of written history, the leasehold estate in England was originally used to circumvent the prohibition against lending money for interest since any interest was usury under early church law. The person borrowing money would allow the lender to use some or all of the land for a period of time in lieu of interest. Therefore, under the common law, a leasehold was considered personal property, but now is considered an estate in real estate. A lease, which creates the leasehold estate, is a peculiar instrument in that it is both a conveyance giving the tenant possession for a period of time and a contract establishing rights and duties for the parties. The essential elements for a lease are these:

- Name of landlord and tenant
- Agreement to lease
- Description of leased property
- Duration of lease
- Rental agreement
- Rights and duties of the parties
- Signature

A lease for a year or less may be verbal or in writing, but one for more than a year must be in writing. For the safety of both the landlord and tenant, all leases should be in writing. Most states have a 99-year limitation on a lease, although the vast majority of leases are for less than 10 years. The degree of complexity in leases increases from the relatively simple residential lease to the very complex shopping center lease. The type of tenancy acquired from a lease depends on whether the term is renewable and whether notice to terminate must be given by either party.

Additional Interests in Real Estate

In addition to the freehold and leasehold estates in real estate, there are certain other limited interests or rights to real estate. These include easements, profits, and covenants. The effect of these interests is to create a limited right to the real estate of another, although the fact that a piece of real property is subject to an easement, for instance, does not prevent it from being owned in fee simple absolute.

Easements

An *easement* is a nonpossessory interest in the real estate of another, giving the holder the right to a limited use of real estate. An example is the right to drive across the real estate of another to reach a highway. An easement is either in gross (a personal right) or appurtenant (belonging to whoever owns the benefited real estate). Although most easements are expressed in writing, they can be simply implied. The right of a gas company to install a gas line on a back property line is an example of an expressed easement appurtenant.

Covenants

Like the previous interests discussed, this interest is in the real estate of another. The difference between a covenant, or a promise to do or not to do something, and other interests is that the former restricts or limits how the owner can use the real estate.

An example of a covenant is the requirement a farmer may put on the part of a farm being sold that the grantee use the real estate only for residential purposes. This interest is of benefit to the grantor because it allows control of the use of the real estate.

Therefore, it is an interest in the real estate of another. This interest can be either in gross or appurtenant, although the term often used with covenants is running with the land. This interest should not be confused with a defeasible fee simple since title cannot be lost if a covenant is breached—only damages or an injunction can be sought.

Joint or Concurrent Ownership

There are several types of joint ownership, as the following sections describe.

Joint Tenancy

Ownership in land can be and usually is held by more than one person. The most common type of joint or concurrent ownership is **joint tenancy**, which can exist between any two or more persons. Although joint tenants share a single title to the real estate, each owns an equal share of the whole. Joint tenancies are quite common, but a few states have abolished or limited them for reasons that are discussed later. Most states will allow the creation of a joint tenancy by simply referring to John and Sally as joint tenants. But other jurisdictions require reference to John and Sally as joint tenants with the right of survivorship. This interest can be created only by affirmative action of the grantor, not by operation of law.

The right of survivorship is the key concept of a joint tenancy. Upon the death of one of the joint tenants, all the decedent's interests in the real property terminate and the surviving joint tenant or tenants retain the ownership in the land. In other words, a joint tenancy is not an inheritable estate. Therefore, it does not pass through the estate of the decedent and does not pass to the heirs. Instead, it passes to or is possessed automatically by the surviving joint tenant. For this reason, some states have abolished joint tenancy, and most courts disfavor joint tenancy because it automatically prevents property from flowing through the estate of an individual to the heirs. Therefore, if one wishes to create a joint tenancy, it is mandatory to follow the strict statutory requirements of the respective state. To avoid the possibility that a court could misunderstand a grantor's intention, a joint tenancy should be created by using this phrase: to John and Sally as joint tenants with right of survivorship and not as tenants in common.

During the time a joint tenancy is in existence, the portion of the whole belonging to any one of the joint tenants usually may be attached to satisfy that individual's legal debts. But the portion belonging to the other joint tenant(s) may not. Some states have laws that modify this approach if the joint tenants are husband and wife and the property in question is their home.

Although any joint tenant may sell or mortgage his or her interest (with some exceptions for married joint tenants), the effect is a termination of the joint tenancy by either a voluntary or involuntary transfer. It is also terminated by the death of one of two joint tenants, but not by the death of one of more than two. The survivors in that case still have a joint tenancy among themselves.

Under the common law, if both parties did not acquire ownership to real estate at the same time, a joint tenancy could not exist. Consequently, a husband owning property before marriage could not create a joint tenancy with his wife. One method devised to circumvent this requirement was the usage of a "straw man." For instance, the husband would convey title to his real estate to a friend or relative (the so-called straw man), who would then transfer the title back to the husband and wife as joint tenants, and the unit of time requirement would be satisfied.

Tenancy by the Entirety

A form of concurrent ownership much like joint tenancy is tenancy by the entirety, which is allowed in 20 states. The reason for its existence is because of a vestige from the common law of some technical requirement for a joint tenancy, such as the unity of time, or because the state had abolished joint tenancy. The primary difference between this form of ownership and the joint tenancy is that a tenancy by the entirety can exist only between a legally married husband and wife, while a joint tenancy can exist between any two or more persons.

Another important feature of a tenancy by the entirety is that the interest of one of the parties cannot be attached for the legal debts of that person. Only if the debts are of both parties can an attachment be made. For this reason, both a husband and wife in some states will be asked to sign the mortgage note if the form of ownership of the real estate is to be as tenants by the entirety, even if only one has income. Many states allowing tenancy by the entirety presume that a conveyance to a husband and wife, silent as to the type of ownership, will be a tenancy by the entirety.

The surviving tenant becomes the sole owner like the surviving joint tenant, but this survivorship right stems from the concept that the husband and wife were one, so ownership was already with the survivor. Divorce or annulment will terminate this tenancy.

Tenants in Common

Tenancy in common is a concurrent estate with no right of survivorship. Therefore, when a person dies, the interest held in the real property passes through the estate. This interest can exist between any two or more individuals and, in effect, jointly gives them the rights and duties of a sole owner. Each of the cotenants is considered an owner of an undivided interest (not necessarily equal) in the whole property, and each has separate legal title, unlike joint tenants who share a single title. Courts of law look with favor on a tenancy in common, because a cotenant's share of ownership passes upon death to the heirs and is not forfeited. As contrasted with a joint tenancy or a tenancy by the entirety, a tenancy in common can arise by operation of law; for example, when a person dies intestate (without a will), heirs automatically inherit as tenants in common.

Any tenant in common can sell his or her interest, mortgage it, or have it attached for debts without destroying the joint interest. A grantee of a tenancy in common acquires only the percentage of the whole owned by the grantor. A tenancy in common is terminated by agreement between the parties or upon a petition to a court.

Community Property

Another form of concurrent ownership is community property, which is the law primarily in those states located in the western part of the United States. Basically, the concept is that half of all property, personal and real, created during marriage belongs to each spouse. The underlying theory of this concept is that both have contributed to the creation of the family's wealth, whether or not both were gainfully employed. There are three exceptions to this rule:

- Property acquired from separate funds, such as a trust account
- Property acquired individually before the marriage
- Property inherited from another's estate

With these exceptions, if the necessity of terminating the marriage occurs, each should receive a one-half share. Since each has equal interests, both must sign a mortgage note and security agreement.

Tenancy in Partnership

The last form of concurrent ownership is tenancy in partnership. Under the common law, a partnership could not own real estate in its partnership name. Therefore, one of the partners had to own the real estate in his or her own name. This presented the possibility of fraud. The Uniform Partnership Act, as adopted by many states, provides that a partnership can own real property in its firm's name. Upon the death of a partner in a partnership, the surviving partners are vested with the share of the decedent or a percentage ownership of all property owned by the partnership. One partner's share of ownership may not necessarily be equal to that of another. It is quite common for partnerships to provide for a means of compensation for a deceased partner's estate, usually by insurance or a buy–sell agreement.

Transfer of Land

All title to real estate in the United States can be traced to one of three origins: conquest, discovery, or purchase. Today, title to real property can be transferred either voluntarily or involuntarily.

Voluntary Transfers

Most transfers of land are voluntary in that a grantor usually intends to transfer title to land to a grantee by the use of a deed or possibly a will. A **deed** is a legal instrument that purports to transfer a grantor's interest. If a grantor had no actual interest in a particular piece of real estate, an executed deed would transfer nothing. In addition, a properly executed deed from a grantor who did have title but lacked legal capacity (the grantor was legally insane, for example) would also transfer nothing. Abstracting or checking the chain of title for defects can determine the validity of the title of the grantor.

All states have a law known as a statute of frauds requiring written transfers of real estate. Today, technical words are not needed in a deed, since any words that clearly show the grantor's intention to transfer are sufficient.

There are eight essential elements of a modern deed:

- Grantor's name
- Grantee's name
- Description of real estate to be conveyed
- Consideration (does not have to be actual amount paid)

- Words of conveyance
- Signature of grantor
- Delivery and acceptances
- Proper execution

Three basic types of deeds are used, each having a specific purpose and function to perform. The least complicated is a *quitclaim deed*, which is used to clear title to real estate. A person signing this deed makes no title guarantee. Instead, a grantor is simply transferring whatever interest is owned, if any. This deed can be used to clear a cloud on the title caused by a widow having a potential right of dower. She would be requested to execute the deed, possibly for a fee, whereby she transferred whatever interest she had (in this case, dower), thus clearing the title.

A *general warranty deed* is the most common deed used to transfer interest in real estate. With this deed, a grantor guarantees to a grantee that the title transferred is good against the whole world. This guarantee extends past the grantor to those in the chain of title. If a grantor refuses to use this deed, it may be an indication that the title is defective.

The *special warranty deed* is a relatively rare deed used in situations when a grantor wants to limit the guarantee. An executor of an estate would use this instrument to convey real estate to those specified in a will. By this deed, the grantor only guarantees that nothing was done to interfere with the title to the real estate while under the grantor's control and makes no guarantee about a decedent's claim to the real estate.

Real estate that passes according to a will is also a voluntary conveyance, since it passes as the testator or the one making the will intended.

Involuntary Transfers

An involuntary conveyance occurs when a legal owner of real estate loses title contrary to the owner's intention. An example of this would be eminent domain. Any sovereign in the United States (federal, state, city, or county) and some quasi-public entities (such as the telephone company or gas line company) can exercise the right of eminent domain. This right is inherent in a sovereign and is not granted by a constitution, although it is limited by it. The key elements are that it must be exercised for a valid public purpose or use and that it requires compensation to be paid to the legal owner.

Another example of involuntary transfer of title is adverse possession. The public policy behind the doctrine of adverse possession is the encouragement of the usage of land, in addition to settling old claims to real property. Normally, a person possessing the real property of another holds that real estate for the legal owner's benefit. But if certain requirements are satisfied, the one occupying the real property could acquire legal title.

To claim title to real property by adverse possession, in most states the one occupying the real property must prove the following:

- Actual possession
- Hostile intent (to the possession of others)
- Notorious and open possession
- Exclusive and continuous possession
- Possession for a statutory period (ranges from 5 to 20 years)

Some states also require that the party claiming title by adverse possession base the claim on some written instrument—even if the instrument is not valid. Other states require the claimant to pay real estate taxes for the statutory period.

Other examples of the possibility of involuntary transfer would include foreclosure and subsequent sale if an owner of real estate does not pay the mortgage, real estate tax, or other encumbrances.

When a person dies intestate, the title to real property along with the personal property passes, not according to the dictates of the owner, but according to the statutes of that particular state. If the individual had no discernible heirs, the property would escheat (pass) to the state.

Recording

Any time an interest in real estate is being created, transferred, or encumbered, that transaction should be recorded. As in England centuries ago, the reason for recording is to prevent fraud. For example, situations existed in which the owner of land would sell, possibly inadvertently, the same real estate to two or more innocent purchasers. Therefore, it was necessary to develop a system by which fraudulent transactions could be prevented. This was accomplished by devising a system of recording transactions affecting real estate. In order to protect a buyer's interest, recording statutes require purchasers of real estate to record the instrument by which they acquired the interest. If recorded, any subsequent purchaser will have either actual knowledge of the prior interest (because he or she checked the record) or constructive notice (because if he or she did check, the purchaser would have discovered the interest).

If the party (the prior purchaser, for instance) who could have prevented a subsequent fraud by recording does not record, then that party will suffer the loss. An individual who wants to purchase real property has an obligation to check the record, usually in a county courthouse, to determine whether there have been any transactions involving that particular real estate. Recording gives constructive notice to the whole world that a party has acquired an interest in a particular real property. Therefore, any subsequent purchaser could not acquire the same interest. If no transaction appears, an innocent purchaser acquiring an interest will be protected against the whole world, even against a prior purchaser.

In summary, a prior purchaser is protected if a record is made, whether or not a subsequent purchaser checks the record. The same is true if there is actual notice. If A sold land to B, and B failed to record, and C, knowing of that transaction, buys the same land and records, B will be protected since C had actual notice of the transaction between A and B. If C did not have actual notice and recorded before B, C would be protected in any dispute between B and C.

All states have a "race statute" that dictates that the first of two innocent parties to record will be protected.

Security Instruments

In all segments of our economy, a lender will normally require some security or collateral to protect itself against nonperformance of a borrower. This protection may take the form of a conditional sales contract, an installment sales contract, or some other form. In real estate transactions it takes the form of either a mortgage or a deed of trust.

A mortgage and a deed of trust (sometimes called a trust deed or trust indenture) are alternate forms of real estate finance security instruments used throughout the United States. The purpose of each is to provide an instrument whereby a mortgage lender can obtain a security interest in the real estate that is securing a debt. As used in the United States today, the mortgage is unique in many features, but its fundamentals are based on the common law as it has developed in England over the past 900 years.

Historical Development

The classic common law mortgage, which evolved in England after the Norman invasion in 1066, was well developed and established by 1400. Basically, it was an actual conveyance—a title transfer—of real estate serving as security for a debt. For a conveyance to be effective under the common law, possession of that real estate actually had to pass, putting the mortgagee in possession of the real estate.

The instrument conveying the real estate title to the mortgagee contained a defeasance clause whereby the mortgagee's title was defeated if payment was made on the due date, called the law day. Originally, when title and possession were in the hands of the mortgagee, the mortgagee could retain all rents and profits generated by the land. This practice was established because a mortgagee could not charge interest on a loan; any interest was usury, which was illegal at this time. After this law changed and interest could be charged, the mortgagee was forced to credit all rents and profits to the mortgagor.

Early common law mortgages did not require any action on behalf of mortgagees to protect their rights if a mortgagor failed to perform. Since a conveyance had already been made, the mortgagee had title and possession and thus the only effect of the mortgagor's nonperformance was the termination of the possibility of reversion through the defeasance clause.

Equity of Redemption

The harsh result of a mortgagor not performing after the due date, even when not personally at fault, led mortgagors to petition the king for redress from an inequitable practice. Eventually, the courts of equity gave relief to mortgagors by allowing them to redeem their real estate through payment with interest of past-due debts. This was called the equity of redemption. By 1625, this practice had become so widespread that mortgagees were reluctant to lend money with real estate as security since they never knew when a mortgagor might elect to redeem the real estate. Mortgagees attempted to change this by inserting a clause in mortgages whereby the mortgagor agreed not to seek this redress. But courts of equity refused to allow the practice and would not enforce the clause. In order to restore an equitable balance, the courts began to decree that a mortgagor had a certain amount of time after default, usually six months, in which to redeem the real estate. If this were not done, the mortgagor's equity of redemption would be cancelled or foreclosed. This action soon became known as a foreclosure suit and is still used in some states today.

The equity of redemption should be contrasted with the statutory right of redemption, which is discussed in the next section dealing with American mortgage law.

U.S. Mortgage Law

In U.S. law, the most important change from the common law relates to the concept of who actually owns the real estate that is serving as security for the performance of an obligation. The common law held that the mortgagee was the legal owner of the real estate while it served as security. This was called the title theory; the mortgagee held title. Shortly after the Revolutionary War, a New Jersey court held that a mortgagor did not lose title to real estate serving as security. The court's reasoning was that since the law already recognized the right of a mortgagor to redeem the real estate after default, the law had to accept a continuing ownership interest in the mortgagor. The court held that a mortgage created only a security interest for the mortgagee and that title should therefore remain with the mortgagor. This is the law in 28 states today and is called the lien theory. Although 23 states still classify themselves as either intermediate or title theory states, all states recognize the mortgagor as the legal owner of the real estate. The principal difference between these two theories is in the manner of foreclosure. Currently, mortgagors are able to do as they please with mortgaged real estate as long as the activity does not interfere with the security interest of a mortgagee.

According to current law, any interest in real estate that can be sold can be mortgaged, including a fee simple, a life estate, or a lease. The determining factor is whether a mortgagee can be found willing to lend money with that particular interest as security.

The Security Interest

When a mortgage lender agrees to grant a loan secured by real estate, that lender acquires a security interest in the real estate. The process of acquiring that interest is discussed in the following section.

The Note: Mortgage Debt

Either a promissory note or a bond evidences the debt secured by a mortgage. The **note** is the promise to pay. Normally, the mortgage and the note are separate documents, but in some jurisdictions they are combined. The note should be negotiable so that the originating mortgagee can assign it. This is the normal practice today for most mortgage lenders. Both Fannie Mae and Freddie Mac use the same uniform note, which meets all legal requirements for each of the states. These uniform notes are the ones that all mortgage lenders should use since they contain well-conceived and tested language that protects the rights of both the borrower and lender.

The mortgage instrument, discussed later, must in one way or another acknowledge and identify the debt it secures. When the entire debt is paid (satisfied), the note and the mortgage, which secures the debt, lose their effectiveness and no longer create a valid lien. A notice of satisfaction, or notice of full payment of a note and mortgage, should be recorded when the debt is paid. This recording is done to clear the cloud on the title created by the mortgage.

Provisions of the Note

As mentioned, the uniform note provides protection for the various parties and also establishes important provisions such as what the interest rate is and how repayment will be made. For example, the note should state that the first payment is due on the first of the month following a full month after closing (if a loan closed on May 15, the first payment would be due on July 1st).

Other items that are important include the following:

- Original signatures of the borrowers must be included.
- All blanks must be filled and any corrections must be initialed (no whiteouts).
- Interest rate, payment schedule, and due dates must be clear.
- Date of note and mortgage must match.
- Appropriate uniform note must be used for each loan type.

The Mortgage Instrument

The mortgage instrument, which creates the security interest in the real estate for the lender, does not have to appear in any particular legal form. There are no set requirements except that a mortgage instrument is in writing. Any wording that clearly indicates the purpose of the instrument, which is to create a security interest in described real estate for the benefit of a mortgagee, is sufficient. Today, most mortgage lenders have adopted the Fannie Mae and Freddie Mac uniform mortgage instrument used in their particular state.

Requirements for a Mortgage

If a conveyance is made to a mortgagee that appears to be a deed absolute but is actually intended to be a conveyance as security for a debt, all state courts have uniformly held that transaction to be a mortgage even if the defeasance clause is missing. On the other hand, if the parties agree in writing that money will be advanced, with the debt for those funds secured by a later mortgage, and a mortgage is not executed, the law holds that a creditor has a security interest in the real estate. This interest is called an equitable mortgage.

A valid mortgage instrument should include the following:

- Names of the mortgagor and mortgagee
- Words of conveyance or a mortgaging clause
- Amount of the debt
- Interest rate and terms of payment
- A repeat of the provisions of the promissory note or bond in some jurisdictions
- Description of the real estate securing the debt
- Clauses to protect the rights of the parties
- Date (same date as note)
- Signature of the mortgagor (and notarized, if required)
- Any requirements particular to that jurisdiction

Clauses to Protect the Rights of the Parties

The elements mentioned are the framework upon which a complete mortgage instrument is built. A mortgage instrument, such as the Fannie Mae and Freddie Mac uniform mortgage or deed of trust, contains clauses to solve all foreseeable problems. Of course, there are many types of mortgage clauses, but the most typical and important ones are the acceleration clause, the prepayment clause, and the payment clause.

Acceleration Clause

The **acceleration clause** is the most important clause in the entire mortgage for the protection of the mortgagee. This clause is generally found in both the mortgage and the instrument that evidences the debt. It states that the entire amount of the debt can be accelerated at the mortgagee's election if the mortgagor defaults or breaches any stated covenant. (In some states, automatic acceleration clauses are allowed, but these should be avoided, if possible, because other options for curing defaults or breaches are available to the mortgagee and may be more beneficial.)

Default

The most common defaults or breaches of covenants by a mortgagor that could trigger acceleration are these:

- Failure to pay principal and interest when due
- Failure to pay taxes or insurance when due
- Failure to maintain the property
- Committing waste (destructive use of property)

Recently, some mortgagees have inserted clauses providing for acceleration if a mortgagor either further mortgages the secured real estate or sells the real estate with the mortgage still attached. This clause ostensibly protects the mortgagee from a change in risk.

Foreclosure

After all attempts to cure a default fail, a mortgagee must move to foreclose and protect its investment. It is important for a lender to realize that when it forecloses a defaulted mortgage, it is fulfilling the covenants in the mortgage and performing its fiduciary responsibility to protect the funds loaned, which may be individual savings or investor funds.

Equitable Right of Redemption

Any time before a foreclosure sale or other disposition, a mortgagor or anyone claiming through the mortgagor, such as a spouse or junior lien holders, may exercise the equitable right of redemption. This right is exercised by paying the mortgagee the outstanding balance plus interest and costs.

The first judicial method of cutting off a mortgagor's equity of redemption was known as strict foreclosure. If not redeemed within a set time, a court decree transferred the mortgagor's interest in the real estate to the mortgagee irrespective of any equity of the mortgagor in the property. This result was grossly unfair to the mortgagor. Therefore, a more balanced approach followed, which provided for selling the property to secure the debt. The proceeds of the sale went first to satisfy the mortgagee, then to other lien holders, and then to the mortgagor.

Methods of Foreclosure

The four modern methods of foreclosure, depending on the law of a state, are as follows:

- Judicial proceeding
- Power of sale
- Strict foreclosure
- Entry and possession

Judicial Proceeding

Most states provide for mortgage foreclosure through a court proceeding. This method best protects the interests of the various parties. The action is much like any other civil suit in that the case must be brought in a court with jurisdiction, either a circuit or district court of the state, where the real estate is located. This procedure requires a complaint naming the borrower, who is now the defendant, alleging that the defendant executed a mortgage, with described real estate as security for a loan, and that a default has occurred. Further, the complaint alleges that the mortgagee has had to accelerate. The complaint will request foreclosure.

The defendant always has an opportunity to answer the allegations with any defenses available. For example, the defendant may attempt to prove one of the following:

- No mortgage existed.
- The mortgage was satisfied.
- No default occurred.
- The interest rate was usurious.

If the decision of the court is in favor of a mortgagee, the decree of foreclosure terminates the equitable right of redemption at the time of sale. A mortgagor loses all rights to the real property except the right to any excess proceeds from the sale after secured parties are paid. The exception is if a state has a statutory right of redemption. The court decree will order a sale and the manner for its execution. Many courts will include an upset price in the decree that is the acceptable minimum bid at the sale. The court usually designates the officer, such as a sheriff or referee, who will conduct the sale after giving the statutory notice of the sale. To encourage purchasers, a successful bidder acquires title to the property unencumbered by any interest except that of the mortgagor's statutory right of redemption, if allowed.

With one possible exception, anyone who can enter into a contract can purchase property at a foreclosure sale. Some states prevent a defaulting mortgagor from purchasing the real estate since the unencumbered title would cut off the rights of junior lien holders. Other states allow a mortgagor to repurchase at a foreclosure sale, but if the mortgagor does repurchase the property, all liens on the real estate prior to foreclosure reattach.

The key element in this form of foreclosure is that the sale must be accepted or confirmed by the court retaining jurisdiction. This requirement is for the protection of both the mortgagor and junior lien holders since a court will not approve a price that is unconscionably low.

Power of Sale

This method is sometimes called foreclosure by advertisement, since the clause creating a power of sale calls for an advertisement to give notice of the sale. This method is used primarily with deeds of trust, but it can be used with mortgages. The power to use this method rather than the more cumbersome judicial proceeding comes from a clause that is part of the securing instrument. The clause specifically explains how the sale will be carried out. This foreclosure method does not preclude a mortgagor's statutory right of redemption if it exists. Some states do not allow the right of redemption if the instrument is a deed of trust.

Foreclosure by advertisement requires procedures that vary among the states. Therefore, extreme care should be taken to ensure that proper notice is given and that other requirements are fulfilled. The proceeds from the sale are distributed in the same way as those in a judicial proceeding.

Strict Foreclosure

As mentioned earlier, this was the original method of foreclosure. It is still used in some states that classify themselves as title theory states. The action involves a court of equity and requests a decree giving a mortgagor a period of time to exercise the equitable right of redemption or lose all rights to the property, with title vesting irrevocably in the mortgagee. When requesting this type of relief, a mortgagee must be able to prove all allegations just as it must in judicial proceedings.

Entry and Possession

Entry and possession is used only in Maine, Massachusetts, New Hampshire, and Rhode Island. After default, a mortgagee gives the mortgagor notice that possession will be taken. If the mortgagor does not agree peacefully to relinquish possession, the mortgagee will have to use a judicial method. This "peaceful possession" needs to be witnessed and recorded. If the mortgagor does not redeem in the statutory period, title vests with the mortgagee.

Deed in Lieu

An alternative to foreclosure, which can be of benefit to both the mortgagor and mortgagee, is the execution of a deed transferring the secured real estate to the mortgagee in lieu of foreclosure. The benefits to a mortgagor include not being subject to the embarrassment of a foreclosure suit or possibly being liable for a deficiency judgment. A mortgagee benefits by immediately acquiring title to the real estate for a quick sale, minimizing collection costs.

For a deed in lieu to be effective in transferring title, the existing mortgage liability of the mortgagor must be extinguished. If not, the transaction and deed will be considered as nothing more than a new security agreement.

The mortgagee must carefully consider the consequences of this alternative. If a mortgagee decides to take a deed in lieu of foreclosure, the rights of junior lien holders will not be extinguished. On the other hand, if a mortgagee forecloses, junior lien holders' rights are extinguished if not satisfied by the proceeds of the sale, but the mortgagor has the right of redemption, which can be of serious consequence to a mortgagee.

Redemption

In addition to the equity of redemption discussed previously, about half the states provide another form of redemption right that begins to accrue to a mortgagor (or those claiming through the mortgagor) after foreclosure and sale. This right is called the statutory right of redemption because it only exists if created by statute. This redemption period ranges from six months to two years, depending on the state. Basically, this right allows a mortgagor who has had property sold at a foreclosure sale to "buy" back the property by paying to the purchaser the price the purchaser paid for the property plus back interest and all costs.

There are two reasons for a statutory right of redemption: (1) to provide a mortgagor with a chance to keep the real estate, and (2) to encourage bidders at foreclosure sales to bid the market value. The first is more important in agricultural states where a bad growing season can be followed by bumper crops. This right would provide a method for a mortgagor to keep the farm. This same reasoning applies in some income-property situations, but rarely in a residential case. The second reason is equally important for all types of real estate since a bidder at a forced sale would more likely bid the true market value rather than chance later divestiture by the mortgagor.

The right of redemption currently has a limited impact on single-family transactions since most of these transactions are a trust deed rather than a mortgage. The difference is that many states do not allow the statutory right of redemption with a trust deed, since a grantor had conveyed all interest to the trustee at the creation of the transaction and consequently had nothing on which to base the redemption. Other states allow it, regardless of what the transaction is called, because if real estate secures a debt, then the transaction is a mortgage and all rights attach. Further, even when the redemption right exists, it is seldom exercised since a mortgagor is more likely to sell the property before foreclosure if there is equity to protect.

Deficiency Judgments

A *deficiency judgment* is a court determination that the mortgagor, who has lost property by foreclosure, is liable for the difference between the sale price of the property at foreclosure and the amount owed (principal, interest, and foreclosure costs). Although most states still allow for deficiency judgments for residential mortgage loans, seldom do the courts render this judgment today. In about a dozen states the ability to get a deficiency judgment has been taken away by legislation. In other states the deficiency judgment is limited to the difference between what the property sold for and the fair market value of the foreclosed property.

Prepayment Clause

Since 1979, residential mortgage loans sold to Fannie Mae or Freddie Mac may not have a prepayment penalty. Before that date, these clauses existed and were enforceable. A few portfolio lenders still use prepayment clauses, and such clauses are enforceable if allowed under state law.

Payment Clause

The most obvious clause in a mortgage is the one by which a mortgagor agrees to pay the obligation in an agreed-upon manner. Reference usually is made to the note or bond whereby a mortgagor was obligated to pay a certain amount of money. A separate clause may stipulate a covenant to pay taxes and hazard insurance (with a mortgage-payable clause) as they become due. However, this often is a part of the payment clause. A mortgagee may require taxes and insurance to be placed in escrow and collected monthly as part of the mortgage payment.

Deeds of Trust

Before deeds of trust can be used in any state, special enabling legislation must be enacted. This is required since the deed of trust was not known in the common law. One of the basic legal differences between a mortgage and a deed of trust is that a mortgage is a two-party instrument between a mortgagor and a mortgagee, while a deed of trust is a three-party instrument between a borrower, a lender, and a third party, called a trustee. If a deed of trust is used, a borrower conveys title to a trustee who holds it until the obligation is satisfied, at which time title is conveyed back to the borrower. The title is held for the benefit of the lender.

Another theoretical difference is the necessity of a mortgagee foreclosing on a mortgage if there has been a default. On the other hand, in most states there is no requirement for a foreclosure, with its time-consuming court proceedings if a deed of trust is used. Instead, the trustee has the power of sale to satisfy the debt. Some states, however, require a foreclosure even if the financing vehicle is a deed of trust. Regardless of the situation, there is always a requirement for a public notice of sale.

In using a deed of trust there is generally no statutory right of redemption, as there is with a mortgage. This is one of the more important reasons why a mortgagee would use a deed of trust rather than a mortgage. In many jurisdictions, a mortgagor has a period of time to redeem the property after default and foreclosure. If the right to redeem exists, this period varies from six months to two years, depending on state law. To a mortgagor, the advantage of a deed of trust is that a mortgagee does not have the right to a deficiency judgment. A deficiency judgment is the result of a lawsuit to make up the difference between the amount obtained at a foreclosure sale and the mortgage obligation.

Transfers of Mortgaged Real Estate

In all jurisdictions, whether the title or lien theory is followed, the mortgagor has the ability to transfer real estate that is serving as security for a debt and has options on the method of transfer.

Free and Clear

The grantor (the one transferring) could transfer the land free and clear. This would occur if a mortgagor satisfied the obligation secured by the real estate and presumes that the mortgage could be prepaid. In such an event, a prepayment penalty might be required. Much mortgaged real estate sold today is transferred in this manner, with the new owner obtaining new financing. The reason for this is inflation, which has produced increased equity in real estate. The value of this equity is more than a purchaser would want to buy for cash. Therefore, a new purchaser normally would rather finance the purchase price than assume the mortgage and pay cash for the equity. During periods of exceedingly high interest rates, as occurred in 1979–1981, purchasers may desire to assume an existing lower interest rate mortgage and pay cash or use another financing technique for the equity.

Subject to the Mortgage

The grantor could transfer the real estate subject to the mortgage, with the grantee (the one to whom the property is transferred) paying the grantor for any equity. If this occurs, the original mortgage remains effective and the personal liability of the original mortgagor to pay the mortgage continues, although the mortgage payment most likely will be made by the grantee from that point on. The grantee becomes the legal owner of the real estate after the sale, although it continues to serve as security for the original mortgage. The grantee assumes no personal liability for the original mortgage payment and could decide to abandon the real estate with no danger of contingent liability. If the grantee stops the mortgage payment and the mortgagee forecloses, the grantee loses only equity in the real estate, while the original mortgagor is liable for any amount of the obligation not satisfied by the sale of the mortgaged real estate.

Assumption of the Mortgage

The real estate could be transferred to the grantee, who would buy the grantor's equity and assume the mortgage. This is the most common manner in which real estate is transferred in those cases in which the existing mortgage remains intact. In this situation, the grantee assumes personal liability for satisfying the mortgage debt, while the original mortgagor retains only secondary liability.

Recently, some mortgagees have inserted clauses into conventional mortgages to either prohibit the transfer of the mortgage or make the transfer conditional on the approval of the mortgagee. Other mortgagees, especially savings and loan institutions, have inserted due-on-sale clauses in conventional mortgages, which accelerate the entire debt if the real estate is sold with the mortgage still intact. The stated rationale for such a clause is to protect the mortgagee's security interest by forcing the new mortgagor to meet the mortgagee's underwriting requirements. Often, however, the real reason is to force the grantee to assume an increase in the interest rate from the rate on the assumed mortgage to the higher current rate. The validity of these clauses evolved to the point at which many courts enforced the mortgagee's right to accelerate. Today, some states allow due-on-sale clauses while other states do not.

Many mortgagors, after selling the real estate to the grantee who assumes the mortgage, have requested that the mortgagee sign a novation contract that would end any secondary liability on the part of the original mortgagor. Many mortgagees have agreed to sign, but normally they require that the assuming grantee agree to an increase in the interest rate to the level of the prevailing rate.

TABLE 15-1   State-by-state Comparison of Selected Aspects of Foreclosre

State	Nature of Mortgage	Customary Security Instrument	Predominant Method of Foreclosure	Redemption Period (months)	Possession during Redemption
Alabama	Title	Mortgage	Power of sale	12	Purchaser
Alaska	Lien	Trust deed	Power of sale	None	N.A.
Arizona	Lien	Trust deed	Judicial	None	N.A.
Arkansas	Intermediate	Mortgage	Power of sale	12	Purchaser
California	Lien	Trust deed	Power of sale	None	N.A.
Colorado	Lien	Trust deed	Power of sale	2	Mortgagor
Connecticut	Intermediate	Mortgage	Strict foreclosure	None	N.A.
Delaware	Intermediate	Mortgage	Judicial	None	N.A.
Dist. of Columbia	Intermediate	Trust deed	Power of sale	None	N.A.
Florida	Lien	Mortgage	Judicial	None	N.A.
Georgia	Title	Security deed	Power of sale	None	N.A.
Hawaii	Title	Trust deed	Power of sale	None	N.A.
Idaho	Lien	Trust deed	Power of sale	None	N.A.
Illinois	Intermediate	Mortgage	Judicial	12	Mortgagor
Indiana	Lien	Mortgage	Judicial	3	Mortgagor
Iowa	Lien	Mortgage	Judicial	6	Mortgagor
Kansas	Lien	Mortgage	Judicial	12	Mortgagor
Kentucky	Lien	Mortgage	Judicial	None	N.A.
Louisiana	Lien	Mortgage	Judicial	None	N.A.
Maine	Title	Mortgage	Entry and possession	12	Mortgagor
Maryland	Title	Trust deed	Power of sale	None	N.A.
Massachusetts	Intermediate	Mortgage	Power of sale	None	N.A.
Michigan	Lien	Mortgage	Power of sale	6	Mortgagor
Minnesota	Lien	Mortgage	Power of sale	12	Mortgagor
Mississippi	Intermediate	Trust deed	Power of sale	None	N.A.
Missouri	Intermediate	Trust deed	Power of sale	12	Mortgagor
Montana	Lien	Mortgage	Judicial	12	Mortgagor
Nebraska	Lien	Mortgage	Judicial	None	N.A.
Nevada	Title	Mortgage	Power of sale	None	N.A.
New Hampshire	Intermediate	Mortgage	Power of sale	None	N.A.
New Jersey	Intermediate	Mortgage	Judicial	None	N.A.
New Mexico	Lien	Mortgage	Judicial	1	Purchaser

TABLE 15-1   State-by-state Comparison of Selected Aspects of Foreclosre

State	Nature of Mortgage	Customary Security Instrument	Predominant Method of Foreclosure	Redemption Period (months)	Possession during Redemption
New York	Lien	Mortgage	Judicial	None	N.A.
North Carolina	Intermediate	Trust deed	Power of sale	None	N.A.
North Dakota	Lien	Mortgage	Judicial	12	Mortgagor
Ohio	Intermediate	Mortgage	Judicial	None	N.A.
Oklahoma	Lien	Mortgage	Judicial	None	N.A.
Oregon	Lien	Trust deed	Power of sale	None	N.A.
Pennsylvania	Title	Mortgage	Judicial	None	N.A.
Rhode Island	Title	Mortgage	Power of sale	None	N.A.
South Dakota	Lien	Mortgage	Power of sale	12	Mortgagor
Tennessee	Title	Trust deed	Power of sale	None	N.A.
Texas	Lien	Trust deed	Power of sale	None	N.A.
Utah	Lien	Mortgage	Judicial	6	Mortgagor
Vermont	Intermediate	Mortgage	Strict foreclosure	6	Mortgagor
Virginia	Intermediate	Trust deed	Power of sale	None	N.A.
Washington	Lien	Mortgage	Judicial	12	Purchaser
West Virginia	Intermediate	Trust deed	Power of sale	None	N.A.
Wisconsin	Lien	Mortgage	Power of sale	None	N.A.
Wyoming	Lien	Mortgage	Power of sale	6	Mortgagor

Caveat. This chart lists only the customary form of security instrument used in each state and not all the forms that could be used. Therefore, the method of foreclosure and period of redemption (if allowed) are listed only for the customary form and not for all possible security instruments. The reader is further cautioned that many states have extensive qualifications and limitations on the period of redemption and for obtaining a delinquency judgment. Consult a local attorney for details.

Assignment of Mortgages

Many originators of mortgage loans, such as mortgage bankers, originate loans for sale to other investors. Any mortgage lender has the right to assign a mortgage even if the mortgagor is unaware of the **assignment**.

The instrument by which mortgages are assigned should be in writing and the assignment should be recorded immediately to protect the investor from another assignment. At the time of assignment, the mortgagor may be required to sign an estoppel certificate. This is a statement by a mortgagor stating that there is a binding obligation not yet satisfied and that the mortgagor has no defenses against the mortgagee. An assigned mortgage has full effect and the mortgage payments may be made directly to the assignee or through the original mortgagee.

Discussion Points

1. What is the term that is used in law to describe "the greatest interest a person can have in real estate"? Why is this interest not an absolute interest?

2. What is a conditional fee? Give an example of how this transaction could occur.

3. What is a legal life estate? Do these types of estates exist today?

4. What is the most common form of joint ownership today in the United States?

5. What are the essential elements of a deed that will allow for a valid transfer of real estate?

6. Identify the various means of mortgage foreclosure. Which exists in your state?

Compliance

Introduction

All mortgage lenders must be careful that they are aware of and follow the various federal and state laws and regulations or court rulings affecting residential mortgage lending. These regulations can be as complex as calculating the annual percentage rate as required by truth in lending or as simple as determining which disclosures must be given to a borrower and when. Mortgage lenders are encouraged to understand the various compliance requirements to avoid penalties for noncompliance but, more important, so that they do not discriminate against a protected class of borrowers. In short, this chapter will assist mortgage lenders in lending legally.

This chapter provides the mortgage professional with a general overview of the purpose of each law or regulation, which transactions are covered, and the specifics of what is required. Because this chapter is an overview of these federal laws and regulations, it is important that mortgage professionals have resources (compliance manuals, software references, or compliance experts on staff) to check the specifics of any compliance question or issue they may have. Further, specific state laws and regulations cannot be covered, and it is the responsibility of mortgage professionals to understand what their state may require.

This chapter covers the following rules and regulations:

- Fair Housing Act
- Equal Credit Opportunity Act (ECOA)
- Truth in Lending Act (TIL)
- Real Estate Settlement Procedures Act (RESPA)
- Home Mortgage Disclosure Act (HMDA)
- Fair Credit Reporting Act (FCRA)
- Flood Disaster Protection Act (FDPA)
- Community Reinvestment Act (CRA)
- Fair Debt Collection Practices Act
- Home Equity Consumer Loan Protection Act
- Homeowners Protection Act of 1996 (HPA)

Fair Lending

The first discussion of residential mortgage lending must start with the concept of fair lending. Two separate acts make up fair lending:

- Fair Housing Act
- Equal Credit Opportunity Act

Both of these fair-lending laws as amended and as interpreted by the courts are designed to accomplish the following:

- Prohibit discrimination in housing-related transactions
- Prohibit discrimination against credit applicants
- Cover all mortgage, construction, and home improvement loans
- Apply to all lenders

These fair-lending laws and regulations have penalties for noncompliance, including liability (fines and penalties) for the financial institution and for individuals and the possibility of criminal charges.

Fair Housing Act

The Fair Housing Act was the first of the fair-lending regulations, enacted as a part of the Civil Rights Act of 1968. The primary purpose is to prohibit discrimination in all phases of housing sales, financing, or rental on the basis of race, color, national origin, religion, sex, disability, or familial status.

Redlining

Although not specifically mentioned in the act, other practices have been held by various courts to be covered by this act. The other practices include "redlining." This practice involves a mortgage lender stating that it does not lend in certain geographic areas (drawing a red line around a particular neighborhood or section of a city) primarily inhabited by a protected class (e.g., racial minorities).

The courts have ruled that other practices fall under the Fair Housing Act, including a prohibition against the use of excessively low appraisals. This occurs when a lender uses appraisers that undervalue real estate in a defined geographical area. Further, setting a minimum mortgage loan amount that exceeds purchase price of a meaningful amount of the housing stock in a defined geographical area is prohibited. Additionally, using only one race or color in advertisements is illegal since it creates the impression that the lender lends only to that group. The use of more onerous terms or conditions on members of one class, race, or group is also prohibited by this epic legislation.

Equal Housing Opportunity Logo

An important requirement that all lenders must adhere to calls for the posting of the Equal Housing Opportunity logo and poster in any branch where mortgage loans are made. When advertising mortgage loan products, mortgage lenders must use the Equal

Figure 16-1 The Equal Housing Opportunity Logo

Figure 16-1 The Equal Housing Opportunity Logo

Housing Opportunity logo in the advertisement. If the advertisement is over the air (radio, television, or the Internet), the term *equal housing lender* must be used.

Equal Credit Opportunity Act

The second of the fair-lending laws is the Equal Credit Opportunity Act (ECOA). ECOA became federal law as part of the federal Consumer Protection Act when it became effective in 1974. (ECOA is often referred to as "Regulation B.")

Today, the ECOA applies to the following:

- Advertising
- Inquiries
- Taking and evaluating applications
- Discouragement
- Credit decisions and notification
- Administration of accounts
- Treatment of delinquent or slow accounts
- Collections and default remedies

The original ECOA was limited to prohibiting discrimination on the basis of sex or marital status. Through the years, various amendments to ECOA have expended the act to include more prohibited bases. These prohibited bases (so-called Nifty Nine) include these:

- Sex
- Marital status
- Age
- Race
- Color
- Religion
- National origin

- Receipt of income from a public assistance program
- Good faith exercise of any right the applicant has under the Consumer Credit Protection Act (or applicable state law)

(Note: The Fair Housing Act also adds to the preceding list disability and familial status. In some states, additional protected classes have been added, such as sexual orientation.)

Taking the Application

No mortgage lender may discourage any consumer from applying for a mortgage loan. In fact, the best approach for a mortgage lender is to always encourage consumers to apply. Note: ECOA applies to both written and oral applications. If a mortgage lender's policy is to accept only written applications for mortgage loans, the lender could be held to have made a credit decision based on an "oral" application *if* it gives an "opinion" (such as "you will not qualify") rather than "facts" ("our ratio for total debt is 40 percent").

It is important that mortgage lenders realize that ECOA is not prohibiting a lender from considering information that is not barred by ECOA. For example, if a person does not have sufficient income to qualify for a loan, the lender is completely justified in declining the mortgage application. But the lender may not discount the following when making these decisions:

- Part-time income
- Pensions
- Welfare
- Alimony, child support, or separate maintenance (if voluntarily given after appropriate warning)

However, the mortgage lender *can* consider the likely duration of the income.

Marital Status

It is important that a mortgage lender be able to establish the marital status of the mortgage applicant(s). Many reasons exist for establishing the status, but the most important reason is identifying whether a nonapplicant spouse will be required to sign the security agreement. For instance, if a woman qualifies for a mortgage loan, a lender must grant her the mortgage loan. But, if she is married, depending on the state (e.g., community property states), the lender may require her husband to sign the security agreement but not the promissory note. This is done so that the husband's ownership in the community property securing the mortgage loan is subject to the security interest of the lender. If the applicant defaults on the loan, the lender will be able to foreclose not only on the woman's interest but also on that of her husband, thus getting clear title to the real estate. On the other hand, by not signing the promissory note, the nonapplicant spouse has no obligation to make any payments.

Therefore, mortgage lenders can ask about marital status, but may only ask: "Are you married, unmarried, or separated?" Further, a lender should not ask for courtesy titles (Mrs., Miss, Ms., Mr., Dr., or any other title).

Cosigner

A mortgage lender cannot require an applicant to get a cosigner or guarantor if the applicant qualifies independently. If a cosigner is required, a mortgage lender cannot stipulate who that person will be, but instead should say, "Anyone that qualifies is acceptable."

Mortgage lenders may not request information regarding the applicant's spouse, unless

- Spouse will be a user of the account
- Applicants reside in a community property state
- Applicant relies on the spouse's income to support the credit
- Applicant relies on alimony, child support, or separate maintenance as a basis for repayment

As discussed, if real estate will be taken as collateral for a loan, the mortgage lender can require a nonapplicant spouse to sign the security instrument (but not the promissory note). On the other hand, if a nonworking spouse wants to sign the note (to build up a credit history), a mortgage lender should not deny that request.

Copy of the Appraisal

ECOA requires that a mortgage lender must supply the mortgage applicant with a copy of the real estate appraisal if a copy is requested. Most lenders routinely provide a copy of the appraisal today, while other lenders do so only when requested (after the applicant is informed of right to the appraisal). A mortgage lender can charge a fee to copy the appraisal, but usually it does not.

Notice of Status of the Application

A mortgage lender must notify the applicant if the application has been *denied*, application is *incomplete*, or a *counteroffer* is being made. If the application has multiple applicants, a lender needs to give notice to only one. A lender must give notice to the applicant of action taken within 30 calendar days after a complete application has been received. A mortgage application is considered complete when all required information has been received by the lender. If the application is incomplete, a lender may send either a notice of incomplete application or adverse action within 30 days. The notice should state by what date information must be received and that if the information is not received by then, the lender will consider the application withdrawn.

Adverse Action

If the adverse action taken is because of information obtained from a credit report, the lender must give the name, address, and telephone number of the consumer reporting agency; in addition, the ECOA Notice must be given.

It is important to realize that the term *adverse action* applies to the situation in which a lender does not accept a loan request as submitted but the loan is offered at terms different than requested. In this situation, adverse action occurs if the applicant

Figure 16-2   Sample Statement of Credit Denial, Termination, or Change

NORTHLAND COMMUNITY BANK

STATEMENT OF CREDIT DENIAL, TERMINATION, OR CHANGE

Applicant(s)	Mike J. Smith and Sally Smith	First-Mortgage Loan Request #334
	123 Main St.	Date: July 3, 2003
	Anytown, USA	

Part I. Principal reason(s) for credit denial, termination, or other action taken concerning credit. In compliance with Regulation "B" (Equal Credit Opportunity Act), you are advised that your recent application for an extension or renewal of credit has been declined. The decision to deny your application is based on the following reason(s): (1) excessive obligations in relation to income, (2) delinquent past or present credit obligations with others.

Part II. Disclosure of use of information obtained from an outside source. Our credit decision is based in whole or in part on information obtained in a report from the consumer reporting agency listed below. You have a right under the Fair Credit Reporting Act to know the information contained in your credit file at the consumer reporting agency.

Name: XYZ Credit Agency

Address: 85 Fifth St.   Phone: 555-121-3434

The federal Equal Credit Opportunity Act prohibits creditors from discriminating against credit applicants on the basis of race, color, religion, national origin, sex, marital status, age (provided that the applicant has the capacity to enter into a binding contract); because all or part of the applicant's income derives from any public assistance program; or because the applicant has in good faith exercised any right under the Consumer Credit Protection Act. The federal agency that administers compliance with this law concerning this creditor is the:

FDIC

Region 1, Albany, NY   Phone: 123-321-4545

Should you have any additional information that might assist us in evaluating your creditworthiness, please let us know. Thank you for applying.

Notice mailed on _____

_____   _____
        Loan Officer   Date

does not accept the revised offer. The form used to provide this information is called a Statement of Credit Denial, Termination, or Change.

Government Monitoring

Mortgage lenders are required (for government-monitoring of discrimination purposes) to ask applicants to provide the following information:

- Race or national origin using the following categories: American Indian, Alaskan Native, Asian, Pacific Islander, Black, White, Hispanic, or other (specify)
- Sex

The mortgage lender must inform applicants that the federal government requires this information. Lenders can ask for this information only if it will be reported to the government (thus, lenders should be careful not to use a first-mortgage application for a second mortgage unless the lender also reports on seconds). If an applicant decides not to provide this information, a lender must, to the best of its ability based on visual observation or surname, provide the information. If the mortgage application is mailed to a lender or received through the Internet and the applicant did not provide the required information, the lender is not in violation of this requirement if the completed application does not have this information.

Mortgage lenders must retain the mortgage application, monitoring information, and any notice of adverse action for at least 25 months.

Effects Test

The effects test applies when a practice that is not discriminatory on its face results in an adverse impact on protected applicants. Put another way, if a practice has a "disparate impact" on a protected class, that practice is discriminatory and must be avoided.

Truth-in-Lending (TIL)

The Consumer Credit Protection Act of 1968 (as amended) contained Title I, known as the Truth-in-Lending Act (or as it is often called, Regulation Z). The basic purpose of this legislation was to provide consumers with an easily understandable means of comparing the credit offerings of various lenders. The desired result is that consumers would then have an opportunity to shop for the most favorable credit terms.

Today, TIL covers consumer purpose loans in amounts less than or equal to $25,000, or any consumer purpose loan, regardless of size, if secured by a 1–4 family dwelling or real property (e.g., vacant land). Business loans are *not* included in this regulation. Agricultural or loans to "nonnatural persons" are *not* included in this regulation.

TIL requires mortgage lenders to disclose the Annual Percentage Rate (APR) and provide information in terms of finance charges. With today's advanced technology, many lenders are able to provide this and other disclosures at the time of application. If a lender is not able to provide this disclosure at the application stage, it must be provided within three business days after receiving the mortgage loan application. Whenever the terms *finance charge* and *APR* are used, they must be more conspicuous than any other term.

Finance Charge

The finance charge that must be disclosed is the cost of consumer credit expressed as a dollar amount. Charges that are included in the finance charge are as follows:

- Interest adjustments (odd day's interest)
- Loan discounts
- Origination fee
- Mortgage insurance premiums
- Underwriting fee

- Fees for determining current tax lien status
- Fees for determining flood insurance requirements
- Borrower-paid mortgage broker fees
- Any other service, transaction, activity, or carrying charge

Typical charges not included (generally, third-party fees) are as follows:

- Appraisal fees
- Credit reports
- Title examination fees
- Loan document preparation fees
- Property survey fees
- Amounts required to be paid into escrow

The finance charge must include error tolerance for the real estate transaction within $100 of the actual finance charge.

Annual Percentage Rate (APR)

Probably no other disclosure is so baffling to the average consumer as the Annual Percentage Rate. Few understand how the APR can be higher than the interest rate. The APR is the finance charge expressed as a numerical percentage, which is an expression of the annualized finance charge. Thus, the APR includes the interest rate plus all of those items that are included in the finance charge.

Although few mortgage lenders actually do it, lenders are required to disclose the APR when inquiries are made orally. The APR disclosures must include error tolerances:

- To nearest $1/_8$ percent (for regular transactions)
- To nearest $1/_4$ percent (for irregular transactions such as variable-rate loans)

Refinancings

A mortgage lender is required to give a new TIL disclosure for a loan that is refinanced. Further, a mortgage lender must give a new TIL disclosure if the lender expressly agrees to allow a subsequent mortgagor (who is assuming the existing mortgage) to become the primary obligor on an existing loan.

A mortgage lender does not have to provide a new TIL disclosure if the mortgage payment changes and there is a reduction in the APR. Further, a mortgage lender is not required to provide a new TIL if a change in the payment schedule occurs as the result of the borrower's default.

Variable-Rate First Mortgages (ARMs)

If the mortgage loan requested is an ARM, the mortgage lender must disclose a composite APR that reflects the initial discount and full indexed rate for the remaining term. The mortgage lender must provide an ARM applicant with the CHARM (*Consumer Handbook on Adjustable Rate Mortgages*) booklet at the time an application is provided to the applicant. In addition, TIL requires that a loan program disclosure be given when the application is requested. This disclosure explains how this particular type of ARM loan will adjust in the future. Finally, a historical example of a $10,000 loan,

Exhibit 16-1   Sample Truth-in-Lending Disclosure Form

TRUTH-IN-LENDING DISCLOSURE FOR REAL ESTATE MORTGAGE LOANS

LENDER	BORROWER
Fairfield Savings Association 252 Main Street Fairfield, CT 06824	**Joseph F. Lynch** **Margaret J. Lynch** **384 Katona Drive** **Fairfield, CT 06824**

APPLICATION # **100101920**   DATE OF DISCLOSURE **02/17/04**

(In this disclosure statement, the words "I," "me," "my," and "mine" refer to each consumer listed above. The words "you," "your," and "creditor" refer to **Fairfield Savings Association**

The figures set forth below are for illustrative purposes only. They reflect the rate now in effect, NOT necessarily the rate you will pay at closing which will be established as indicated in our Commitment.

Words, numbers or phrases preceded by a ☐ are applicable only if the ☐ is marked.

ANNUAL PERCENTAGE RATE The cost of my credit as a yearly rate.	FINANCE CHARGE The dollar amount the credit will cost me.	Amount Financed The amount of credit provided to me or on my behalf.	Total of Payments The amount I will have paid after I have made all payments as scheduled, based on the current annual percentage rate.
6.715 (e) %	$ **241,885.52 (e)**	$ **183,996.24 (e)**	$ **425,881.76 (e)**

My payment schedule will be:

Number of Payments	Amount of Payments	When Payments Are Due
106	1197.54	1ST OF EACH MONTH BEGINNING 07/01/2004 (e)
74	1222.74	1ST OF EACH MONTH BEGINNING 05/01/2013 (e)
179	1158.16	1ST OF EACH MONTH BEGINNING 07/01/2019 (e)
1	1149.12	PAYMENT IS DUE ON 06/01/2034 (e)

106 PAYMENTS CONTAIN $39.38 AND 74 PAYMENTS CONTAIN $64.58 PMI.

☐ **Construction Loan:** Interest on the amount of credit outstanding during the construction period will be payable based on the outstanding balance. After the construction period I will pay payments as shown above.

☐ **Variable Rate:** THIS LOAN HAS AN ADJUSTABLE RATE FEATURE. DISCLOSURES SHOWING HOW YOUR INTEREST RATE AND PAYMENT AMOUNT CAN VARY HAVE BEEN PROVIDED EARLIER.

Security: I am giving you a mortgage on real estate located at
89 Harvester Road, Fairfield, CT 06825

Late Charge:
If payment is more than **15** days late, I will be charged **5.000** % of the interest and principal payment.

Assumption:

[X] Someone buying my principal dwelling may, subject to conditions, be allowed to assume the remainder of the mortgage on the original terms.

☐ Someone buying my principal dwelling cannot assume the remainder of the mortgage on the original terms.

Prepayment: If I pay off early, I **MAY** have to pay a penalty, and I will not be entitled to a refund of any part of the finance charge.

[XX] All above numerical disclosures except for the late charge are estimates.

See your contract documents for any additional information about nonpayment, default, any required repayment in full before the scheduled date, prepayment refunds and penalties and creditor's policy regarding assumption of the obligation.

"e" means an estimate.

Initials ___ Initials ___

"By initialing, the Borrower(s) acknowledge(s) that this page is 1 of 2 of the Truth-In-Lending Disclosure For Real Estate Mortgage Loans."

ITEM 6006L1 (9511) Page 1 of 2   GREATLAND ■ To Order Call: 1-800-530-9393 ☐ Fax 616-791-1131

Exhibit 16-1   Sample Truth-in-Lending Disclosure Form (continued)

TRUTH-IN-LENDING DISCLOSURE FOR REAL ESTATE MORTGAGE LOANS

L E N D E R	Fairfield Savings Association 252 Main Street Fairfield, CT 06824	B O R R O W E R	Joseph F. Lynch Margaret J. Lynch 384 Katona Drive Fairfield, CT 06824

APPLICATION # 100101920   DATE OF DISCLOSURE **02/17/04**

(In this disclosure statement, the words "I," "me," "my," and "mine" refer to each consumer listed above. The words "you," "your," and "creditor" refer to **Fairfield Savings Association**

The figures set forth below are for illustrative purposes only. They reflect the rate now in effect, NOT necessarily the rate you will pay at closing which will be established as indicated in our Commitment.

Words, numbers or phrases preceded by a ☐ are applicable only if the ☐ is marked.

Recording Fees: $ 50.00

Insurance: I may obtain all required property insurance (including flood hazard insurance) from anyone I want that is acceptable to creditor.

Itemization of Amount Financed of $ 183996.24   (C minus D)

A. $	189000.00	Amount given to me directly
B. $		Amount paid on my account(s) with creditor
C. $	189000.00	Principal amount of loan
D. $	5003.76	Prepaid finance charge (itemized below)

$	3780.00	for "points" paid by me
$	472.50	for 15(e) days prepaid interest
$	472.50	for **INITIAL PMI PREMIUM**
$	78.76	for **INITIAL PMI ESCROW**
$	150.00	for **INSPECTION FEE**
$	50.00	for **TAX SERVICE FEE**

Insurance: Credit life and credit disability insurance are not required to obtain credit and will not be provided unless I agree to pay the additional cost by signing below. No requested insurance will be in force until I have completed an application, an insurance company has issued a policy, the effective date of that policy has arrived and the premium called for has been paid.

TYPE	PREMIUM	SIGNATURE
Credit Life	47.25	I apply for Credit Life Insurance
Credit Disability	13.50	I apply for Disability Insurance
Credit Life & Credit Disability	60.75	I apply for Credit Life and Disability Insurance

I understand that this is not a contract and does not reflect all of the terms and conditions of the mortgage transaction to which the disclosures reflected on this form relate.

All parties signing below acknowledge receiving a filled-in copy of this disclosure statement.

02/19/04	Joseph F. Lynch		
DATE	SIGNATURE	DATE	SIGNATURE

JDL		"By initialing, the Borrower(s) acknowledge(s) that this page is 2 of 2 of the
Initials	Initials	Truth-In-Lending Disclosure For Real Estate Mortgage Loans."

ITEM 6006L2 (9511) Page 2 of 2   GREATLAND ■ To Order Call: 1-800-530-9393 ☐Fax 616-791-1131

Exhibit 16-1	Sample Truth-in-Lending Disclosure Form

QUESTIONS AND ANSWERS ABOUT "TRUTH-IN-LENDING" STATEMENT

Federal law provides that you receive a "Truth-in-Lending Disclosure Statement." Study it carefully as well as other information about your loan we gave you. Your loan is an important transaction. Following are some of the most frequently asked questions about the Truth-in-Lending Statement and their answers.

Q. What is a Truth-in-Lending disclosure Statement and Why Do I Receive It?
A. Your Disclosure Statement provides information which Federal law requires us to give you. The purpose of the statement is to give you information about your loan and help you shop for credit.

Q. What is the ANNUAL PERCENTAGE RATE?
A. The Annual Percentage Rate, or A.P.R., is the cost of your credit expressed in terms of an annual rate. Because you may be paying "points" and other closing costs, the A.P.R. disclosed is often higher than the interest rate on your loan. The A.P.R. can be compared to other loans for which you may have applied and give you a fair method of comparing price.

Q. What is the AMOUNT FINANCED?
A. The amount financed is the mortgage amount applied for MINUS prepaid finance charges and any required deposit balance. Prepaid finance charges include items such as loan origination fees, commitment or placement fee (points), adjusted interest, and initial mortgage insurance premium. The Amount Financed represents a NET figure used to allow you to accurately assess the amount of credit actually provided.

Q. Does this mean I will get a lower mortgage than I applied for?
A. No, if your loan is approved for the amount you applied for, that's how much will be credited toward your home purchase or refinance at settlement.

Q. Why is the ANNUAL PERCENTAGE RATE different from the interest rate for which I applied?
Why is the AMOUNT FINANCED different?
A. The Amount Financed is lower than the amount you applied for because it represents a NET figure. If someone applied for a mortgage of $50,000 and their prepaid finance charges total $2,000, the amount financed would be shown as $48,000, or $50,000 minus $2,000.

The A.P.R. is computed from this LOWER figure, based on what your proposed payments would be. In a $50,000 loan with $2,000 in prepaid finance charges, and an interest rate of 14%, the payments would be $592.44 (principal and interest) on a loan with a thirty year loan term. Since the A.P.R. is based on the NET amount financed, rather than on the actual mortgage amount, and since the payment amount remains the same, the A.P.R. is higher than the interest rate. It would be 14.62%. If this applicant's loan were approved he would still receive a $50,000 loan for thirty years with monthly payments @ 14% or $592.44.

Q. How will my payments be affected by the Disclosure Statement?
A. The Disclosure Statement only discloses your estimated payments. The interest rate determines what your monthly principal and interest payment will be.

Q. What is the FINANCE CHARGE?
A. The Finance Charge is the cost of credit. It is the total amount of interest calculated at the interest rate over the life of the loan, plus prepaid finance charges and the total amount of mortgage insurance charged over the life of the loan. This figure is ESTIMATED on the disclosure statement given with your application.

Q. What is the TOTAL OF PAYMENTS?
A. This figure indicates the total amount you will have paid, including principal, interest, prepaid finance charges, and mortgage insurance if you make the minimum required payments for the entire term of the loan. This figure is ESTIMATED on the Disclosure Statement and is estimated in any adjustable rate transaction.

Q. My statement says that if I pay the loan off early, I will not be entitled to a refund of part of the finance charge. What does this mean?
A. This means that you will be charged interest for the period of time in which you used the money loaned to you. Your PREPAID finance charges are not refundable. Neither is any interest which has already been paid. If you pay the loan off early, you should not have to pay the full amount of the "finance charges" shown on the disclosure. This charge represents an estimate of the full amount the loan would cost you if the minimum required payments were made each month through the life of the loan.

Q. Why must I sign the Disclosure Statement?
A. Lenders are required by law to provide the information on this statement to you in a timely manner. Your signature merely indicates that you have received this information, and does not obligate either you or the Lender in any way.

illustrating how payments and a loan balance would have been affected by interest rate changes over the past 15 years, must be provided to the applicant.

Variable-Rate Adjustment Notice

TIL requires that servicers of ARM loans provide the consumer with rate-adjustment notices 25 to 120 days before a payment at a new level is due. The notice must contain the current and prior interest rate, the index used to calculate the rate, and the new payment rate. The new payment rate is based on the new interest rate and the unpaid principal balance at the time of the adjustment.

Home Equity Lines of Credit (HELOCs)

The Home Equity Loan Consumer Protection Act of 1988 was an amendment to TIL that further extended TIL into HELOCs. TIL requires that whenever a consumer requests an application for a HELOC, a mortgage lender must provide a disclosure explaining how that lender's HELOC works. (This disclosure is similar to an "early" TIL.) A lender is also required to give the consumer the booklet *When Your Home Is on the Line* at the time of providing the application. In addition, TIL requires that a lender must mail at the end of each billing cycle a periodic statement for all HELOC loans. This requirement and other details about HELOC are examined extensively in Chapter 18, "Home Equity Loans."

Billing Rights

TIL requires consumers be notified about their billing rights concerning mortgage loans. Basically, the consumer has 60 days after receiving a billing statement to give the creditor written notice of an error in the billing. The creditor must resolve any alleged billing errors within 90 days of the error notice.

Right to Rescind

TIL provides consumers with a very important right to cancel certain real estate financial transactions if they change their mind about wanting to put up their primary residence as security for a debt. At the closing of certain mortgage loans, a mortgage lender must give the Notice of the Right of Rescission (or, as it is sometimes called, the right to cancel) to all parties with a legal interest in the property. The material disclosure must clearly state that the lender is taking a security interest in the applicant's principal residence (can be a mobile home or trailer), that the applicant has the right to cancel the transaction, how to cancel, the effects of canceling, and the date the right to cancel expires.

At the loan closing, the mortgage lender must give two copies of the written notice of the right to cancel to each person with an interest in the real estate (whether that person's name is on the note or not) and one copy of material disclosures.

The right of rescission applies to the following types of loans:

- Loans to purchase (or construct) new principal residence if that loan is secured by existing principal residence (otherwise, does not apply to purchase money mortgages)
- Any added principal as part of refinancing (otherwise, does not apply to refinancing)
- Closed-end seconds and HELOCs, and to all increases in the credit line (but does not apply to advances)

Exhibit 16-2	Sample Right to Rescission or Cancel Statement

RIGHT TO CANCEL

To: Joseph F. Lynch
    Margaret J. Lynch

Re: application: 100101920
Property: 89 Harvester Road
             Fairfield, CT 06825

Date of Notice: 02/13/04

YOUR RIGHT TO CANCEL

You are entering into a transaction that will result in a mortgage, lien or security interest on/in your home. You have a legal right under federal law to cancel this transaction, without cost, within three (3) business days from whichever of the following events occurs last:

      (1) the date of the transaction which is ; or
      (2) the date you received your Truth in Lending disclosures; or
      (3) the date you received this notice of your right to cancel.

If you cancel this transaction, the mortgage, lien or security interest is also cancelled. Within twenty (20) calendar days after we receive your notice, we must take the steps necessary to reflect the fact that the mortgage, lien or security interest on/in you home has been cancelled, and we must return to you any money or property you have given to us or to anyone else in connection with this transaction.

You may keep any money or property we have given you until we have done the things mentioned above, but you must then offer to return the money or property. If it is impractical or unfair to you to return the property, you must offer its reasonable value. You may offer to return the property at your home or at the location of the property. Money must be returned to the address below. If we do not take possession of the money or property within twenty (20) calendar days of your offer, you may keep it without further obligation.

HOW TO CANCEL

If you decide to cancel this transaction, you may do so by notifying us in writing at:

      Fairfield Savings Association
      252 Main Street
      Fairfield, CT 06824

You may use any written statement that is signed and dated by you and states your intention to cancel, or you may use this notice by dating and signing below. Keep one copy of this notice because it contains important information about your rights.

If you cancel by mail or telegram, you must send this notice no later than midnight of (or midnight of the third business day following the latest of the three events listed above). If you send or deliver your written notice to cancel some other way, it must be delivered to the above address no later than that time.

I WISH TO CANCEL:

_____   _____   _____   _____
Borrower   Date   Coborrower   Date

_____

CONFIRMATION

More than three business days have elapsed since the date of the new transaction and we received this Notice and Truth-in-Lending disclosures with regard to the new transaction. We certify that the new transaction has not been rescinded.

I herewith acknowledge receipt of two copies of this notice:

Joseph F. Lynch   *03/19/04*   *Margaret J. Lynch*   *03/19/04*
Borrower   Date   Coborrower   Date

Canceling the Transaction

This right to cancel the transaction must be exercised within three business days of the closing of the loan. For example, if the loan closed on Monday, the clock for rescission begins at midnight on Monday, and the consumer has until midnight on Thursday to exercise the right to cancel the transaction. Sundays and legal holidays are not business days, but all other days are considered business days whether or not the lender is open for business.

Notice of cancellation may be given by mail, telegram, or other written communications (notice is considered given when mailed). Any one borrower can cancel, and that cancels the transaction for all parties.

Confirmation of Noncancellation

Mortgage lenders should (but are not required to) use a Notice of Right to Rescission (or Cancel) form that has a section for the consumers to confirm that they have not exercised their right to cancel. A lender should not disburse any funds until consumers sign the form confirming they have not exercised the right to cancel. If this form is not signed, a lender should wait a reasonable period of time for the mail to be delivered before disbursing any funds.

Until the three-day period expires, the creditor may not

- Disburse any funds
- Permit any services to be performed
- Permit any materials to be delivered

If the transaction is rescinded, the creditor must

- Cancel the transaction
- Not charge any interest or other finance charge
- Return any money received

In rare situations, the right of rescission can be waived so that monies can be disbursed immediately if any of the following conditions are met:

Figure 16-3   Sample Notice of Right to Rescission

DO NOT SIGN UNTIL THREE BUSINESS DAYS HAVE ELAPSED

Three business days have elapsed since the undersigned have received two copies of this document. The undersigned hereby certify and warrant that they have not exercised any right that they may have to rescind the transaction, that they do not desire to do so, and that they ratify and confirm the transaction in all respects.

_____   _____   _____   _____
Borrower   Date   Borrower   Date

- A personally handwritten note is delivered to the lender explaining a bona fide, personal or financial emergency.
- A letter specifically waives the right to rescind.
- A letter containing the signatures of *all* persons having the right to rescind is delivered to the lender.
- Printed forms for these purposes are prohibited except when allowed by the Federal Reserve (e.g., natural disaster).

If the mortgagor is not given the proper right of rescission notice, the right to rescind shall extend to the earliest of the following times:

- Three years from closing
- Transfer of consumer's interest in the property
- Sale of the property

The TIL amendments of 1995 provided special rescission rules for borrowers in *foreclosure*:

- Mortgagor can rescind any time after foreclosure if mortgage broker fee is not included in finance charge.
- Rescission notice did not follow FRB's prescribed form.
- Three-year time limit still applies.

TIL has been modified for high-rate, high-fee mortgages (so-called Section 32 loans). This applies whenever a closed-end loan is secured by the applicant's principal dwelling and the APR is more than 10 percentage points above the yield on a Treasury security with a similar maturity or when the total points and fees the customer paid at or before closing exceed the greater of 8 percent of the loan amount or $400. A creditor of a Section 32 loan must provide the following disclosure at least three days before the transaction is consummated (in addition to APR and amount of payment): "You are not required to complete this agreement merely because you have received these disclosures or have signed a loan application. If you obtain this loan, the lender will have a mortgage on your home. You could lose your home, and any money you have put into it, if you do not meet your obligation under the loan."

Real Estate Settlement Procedures Act (Regulation X)

This regulation was enacted to ensure that consumers are provided with full disclosure of the costs involved in the real estate settlement process. RESPA applies to federally related mortgage loans, which basically means all residential mortgage loans. Since 1994, the coverage of RESPA has been expanded to include subordinate liens.

RESPA does not apply to the following transactions:

- Construction loans
- Loans on 25 acres or more
- Business loans, unless security is residence
- Vacant land
- Bona fide secondary market transactions

RESPA also prohibits such practices as these:

- Illegal kickbacks
- Referral fees
- Excessive escrow requirements

RESPA requires that mortgage lenders *must* provide the following disclosures to mortgagors:

- Notice of Transfer of Servicing Disclosure Statement
- Good Faith Estimate of Closing Costs
- Special Information Booklet (for loans to *purchase homes* only)
- HUD-1 or HUD-1A Settlement Statement
- Initial Escrow Statement
- Annual Escrow Statement

Servicing Disclosure Statement

RESPA, as amended in 1990, requires mortgage lenders to provide applicants with a Notice of Transfer of Servicing of Mortgage Loans at the time of application. The applicant must acknowledge receipt of this disclosure at the time the application is completed (or the disclosure is mailed to the applicant within three business days if the application is not taken face to face). The disclosure declares the lender's ability to service loans and what its history of selling servicing has been over the past three years.

	RESPA Disclosure Requirements Summarized		TABLE 16-1
Forms	First Liens	Equity (Closed-End)	Equity (Open-End)
Servicing disclosure	Yes	No	No
Good Faith Estimate	Yes	Yes	No
Closing Cost Booklet	Yes— Purchase only	No— Unless to purchase	No
HUD-1 or HUD-1A	Yes	Yes	No
Notice of Transfer of Servicing	Yes	No	No

Exhibit 16-3 / Sample Loan Servicing Disclosure Statement

FAIRFIELD SAVINGS ASSOCIATION
FIRST MORTGAGE LOAN INFORMATION

SERVICING DISCLOSURE STATEMENT

NOTICE TO MORTGAGE LOAN APPLICANTS: THE RIGHT TO COLLECT YOUR MORTGAGE LOAN PAYMENTS MAY BE TRANSFERRED. FEDERAL LAW GIVES YOU CERTAIN RELATED RIGHTS. IF YOUR LOAN IS MADE, SAVE THIS STATEMENT WITH YOUR LOAN DOCUMENTS. SIGN THE ACKNOWLEDGEMENT AT THE END OF THIS STATEMENT ONLY IF YOU UNDERSTAND ITS CONTENTS.

Borrower:	Joseph F. Lynch
	Margaret J. Lynch
Property:	89 Harvester Road
	Fairfield, CT 06825

Because you are applying for a mortgage loan covered by the Real Estate Settlement Procedures Act (RESPA) (12 USC 2601 et seq.), you have certain rights under that federal law. This statement tells you about those rights. It also tells you what the chances are that the servicing for this loan may be transferred to a different loan servicer. "Servicing" refers to collecting your principal, interest and escrow account payments, if any. If your loan servicer changes, there are certain procedures that must be followed. This statement generally explains those procedures.

TRANSFER PRACTICES AND REQUIREMENTS

If the servicing of your loan is assigned, sold or transferred to a new servicer, you must be given written notice of that transfer. The present servicer must send you notice in writing of the assign- ment, sale or transfer of the servicing not less than 15 days before the effective date of the transfer. The new loan servicer must also send you notice within 15 days after the effective date of the transfer. The present servicer and the new servicer may combine this information in one notice, so long as the notice is sent to you 15 days before the effective date of transfer. The 15 day period is not applicable if a notice of prospective transfer is provided to you at settlement. The law allows a delay in the time (not more than 30 days after a transfer) for servicers to notify you, upon the occurrence of certain business emergencies.

Notices must contain certain information. They must contain the effective date of the transfer of the servicing of your loan to the new servicer, the name, address, and toll-free or collect-call tele- phone number of the new servicer, and the toll-free or collect-call telephone numbers of a person or department for both your present servicer and your new servicer to answer your questions. During the the 60-day period following the effective date of the transfer of the loan servicing, a loan payment received by your old servicer before its due date may not be treated by the new loan servicer as late, and a late fee may not be imposed on you.

COMPLAINT RESOLUTION

Section 6 of RESPA (12 USC 2605) gives you certain consumer rights, WHETHER OR NOT YOUR LOAN SERVICING IS TRANSFERRED. If you send a "qualified written request" to your servicer, your servicer must provide you with a written acknowledgement within 20 Business Days of receipt of your request. A "qualified written request" is a written correspondence, other than notice on a payment coupon or other pay- ment medium supplied by the servicer, which includes your name and account number, and the information regarding your request. Not later than 60 Business Days after receiving your request, your servicer must make any appropriate corrections to your account, or must provide you with a written clarification regarding any dispute. During this 60-Business Day period, your servicer may not provide information to a consumer reporting agency concerning any overdue payment related to such period or qualified written request.

A Business Day is any day in which the offices of the business entity are open to the public for carrying on substantially all of its business functions.

Exhibit 16-3 Sample Loan Servicing Disclosure Statement (continued)

DAMAGES AND COSTS

Section 6 of RESPA also provides for damages and costs for individuals or classes of individuals in circumstances where servicers are shown to have violated the requirements of that section.

SERVICING TRANSFER ESTIMATES

1. The following is the best estimate of what will happen to the servicing of your mortgage loan:

We may assign, sell or transfer the servicing of your mortgage loan sometime while the loan is outstanding. We are able to service your loan, and we will service your loan.

2. For all the first lien mortgage loans that we make in the 12 month period after your mortgage loan is funded, we estimate that the percentage of such loans for which we will transfer the servicing is between 15 and 30 percent.

This is only our best estimate and it is not binding. Business conditions or other circumstances may affect our future transferring decisions.

3. We have previously assigned, sold or transferred the servicing of first lien mortgage loans.

Fairfield Savings Association

Craig Carragan
Craig S. Carragan
President

ACKNOWLEDGEMENT MORTGAGE LOAN APPLICANT

I/we have read this disclosure form, and understand its contents, as evidenced by my/our signature(s) below. I/We understand that this acknowledgement is a required part of the mortgage loan application.

Joseph F. Lynch   Date: __02|15|04__
Joseph F. Lynch

Margaret J. Lynch   Date: __02/15/04__
Margaret J. Lynch

Notice of Transfer of Servicing

The existing servicer, as required by RESPA, must give this notice to the consumer 15 days before any transfer of servicing occurs. The new servicer must provide the notice within 15 days of when the transfer actually occurs. For a more extensive discussion of the transfer of servicing, see Chapter 14, "Mortgage Loan Servicing and Administration."

Good Faith Estimate of Closing Costs

RESPA requires mortgage lenders to provide to the applicant a Good Faith Estimate of Settlement Charges (sometimes referred to as closing costs) either at the time of application or within three business days. The Good Faith Estimate is intended to provide a clear and concise estimate of the dollar amount of each settlement charge that the applicant is expected to incur. The estimate must be a reasonable or a good faith estimate of each charge.

The items that must be disclosed are as follows:

- Items payable in connection with the loan, such as origination fee and discount points
- Items required to be paid in advance, such as prepaid interest or mortgage insurance premiums
- Title charges, such as examination fees and insurance premiums
- Government recording and transfer charges
- Additional settlement charges, such as surveys
- The name of the provider, the type of service provided, and whether a business relationship exists with the lender, if a particular provider or group of providers is required by the lender to be used

Special Information Booklet

RESPA requires that the Special Information Booklet (called *Settlement Costs* on the cover) be provided by the mortgage lender to the applicant if the loan is to purchase a home. The booklet is provided at the time of application or within three business days. The purpose of this booklet is to provide mortgage loan applicants with an overview of the process of purchasing real estate from a seller. Included in this booklet is an explanation of the process that occurs after the applicant has found a home to purchase. It explains the roles the real estate broker, the lender, the appraiser, the attorney, and others play in this process. In addition, the buyer's rights, including the various compliance disclosures, are discussed in the booklet.

The second part of the booklet explains the HUD-1 Settlement Statement and the fees that are disclosed on that form. See an example in Chapter 13, "Closing the Residential Loan."

HUD-1 Uniform Settlement Statement

The Uniform Settlement Statement (either a HUD-1 if a buyer and seller are involved, or a HUD-1A if only a mortgagor is involved) must be prepared by the mortgage lender or other organization that will conduct the loan closing (or, as it is called, settlement). The settlement statement itemizes all settlement charges that are the responsibilities of the buyer and the seller.

If a mortgage applicant requests it, the Settlement Statement must be available for review during the business day immediately preceding the day of settlement. The settlement statement should be provided to the mortgage lender and retained in the loan file. RESPA prohibits the charging of any fees for the preparation of the Settlement Statement.

Escrow Statement

RESPA, as amended, requires that all mortgage lenders who require the establishment of escrow accounts (or, as they are called in California, impounds) follow certain

---

Exhibit 16-4   Sample Good Faith Estimate of Settlement and Closing Costs Statement

FAIRFIELD SAVINGS ASSOCIATION
FIRST MORTGAGE LOAN INFORMATION

GOOD FAITH ESTIMATE OF SETTLEMENT AND CLOSING COSTS

The information provided below reflects estimates of the charges which you are likely to incur at the settlement of your loan. The fees listed are estimates -- the actual charges may be more or less. Your transaction may not involve a fee for every item listed. The numbers listed beside the estimates generally correspond to the numbered lines contained in the HUD-1 settlement statement which you will be receiving at settlement. The HUD-1 settlement statement will show you the actual cost for items paid at settlement.

TITLE OF MORTGAGE:	Joseph F. and Margaret J. Lynch	DATE:	02/17/04
LOAN AMOUNT:	$189,000.00	APPLICATION #:	100101920

800	ITEMS PAYABLE IN CONNECTION WITH LOAN:		
801	LOAN ORIGINATION FEE	$	1,890.00
802	LOAN DISCOUNT FEE	$	1,890.00
803	APPRAISAL FEE	$	300.00
804	CREDIT REPORT FEE	$	65.00
805	INSPECTION FEE	$	150.00
806	MORTGAGE INSURANCE APPLICATION FEE	$	50.00
808	APPLICATION FEE	$	300.00
809	TAX SERVICE FEE	$	50.00
900	ITEMS REQUIRED BY LENDER TO BE PAID IN ADVANCE:		
901	PREPAID INTEREST	$	472.50
902	MORTGAGE INSURANCE PREMIUM	$	472.50
1000	RESERVES DEPOSITED WITH LENDER:		
1002	MORTGAGE INSURANCE INITIAL ESCROW	$	78.76
1003	CITY PROPERTY TAX RESERVES	$	250.00
1100	TITLE CHARGES:		
1105	DOCUMENT PREPARATION FEE	$	200.00
1106	NOTARY FEE	$	25.00
1107	ATTORNEY'S FEE	$	200.00
1108	TITLE INSURANCE	$	567.00
1111	LEGAL REVIEW FEE	$	100.00*
1200	GOVERNMENT RECORDING AND TRANSFER CHARGES:		
1201	MORTGAGE RECORDING FEE	$	50.00
1300	ADDITIONAL SETTLEMENT CHARGES		
1301	SURVEY FEE	$	250.00
1302	PEST INSPECTION FEE	$	50.00
1400	TOTAL ESTIMATED CLOSING COSTS	$	7,310.76

(Items followed by an asterisk "*" are P.O.C.)

These estimates are provided pursuant to the Real Estate Settlement Procedures Act of 1974, as amended (RESPA). Additional information can be found in the HUD Special Information Booklet, which is to be provided to you by your mortgage broker or lender, if your application is to purchase residential real property and the lender will take a first lien on the property.

Exhibit 16-4	Sample Good Faith Estimate of Settlement and Closing Costs Statement

GOOD FAITH ESTIMATE OF SETTLEMENT AND CLOSING COSTS

We, the lender, will require the services of the particular persons or entities listed below, and the applicable estimated charges listed above are based on the charges of these designated providers.

This lender maintains a controlled list of 10 providers, and a particular provider has not been chosen at this time. Generally, appraisal service providers charge between $200.00 and $300.00 for their services. The fees for appraisal services above represent an estimate of the actual fees you will be charged.

Provider: BOWLEY MOORE APPRAISAL SERVICES
Address:OLD BLACK ROCK TPKE
Address:FALL RIVER, VA 19293
Phone: 234-678-6758
The provider is an associate of the lender.

Provider:
Address:
Address:
Phone:
The provider is an associate of the lender.

Provider:BOWLEY MOORE APPRAISAL SERVICES
Address:OLD BLACK ROCK TPKE
Address:FALL RIVER, VA 19293
Phone:234-678-6758
In the past twelve months, the provider has maintained a deposit account or loan or credit arrangement with the lender.

Provider: BOWLEY MOORE APPRAISAL SERVICES
Address: OLD BLACK ROCK TPKE
Address: FALL RIVER, VA 19293
Phone: 234-678-6758
In the past twelve months, the provider has maintained a deposit account or loan or credit arrangement with the lender.

Provider:
Address:
Address:
Phone:
The lender has within the past twelve months repeatedly used or required the borrower to use this provider to provide services.

By signing below, you acknowledge that you have received a copy of the HUD special information booklet "Settlement Costs", unless the loan you have applied for is a refinancing of your property.

Joseph F Lynch
Joseph F. Lynch

_02/19/04_
date

Margaret J Lynch
Margaret J. Lynch

_02/19/04_
date

---

escrow rules. *Escrow accounts* mean any account that a servicer establishes or controls on behalf of a borrower to pay any of the following:

- Mortgage insurance
- Hazard/flood insurance
- Taxes or other charges (e.g., credit life, mortgage insurance)

The intent of the RESPA amendment is to put an end to excessive escrow practices and, therefore, put more money in consumers' hands. HUD now requires lenders to use a standard accounting method known as aggregate accounting. *Aggregate accounting* means using the escrow account as a whole in analyzing sufficiency of escrow funds.

RESPA now limits the charges to the borrower when a lender creates an escrow account and limits the cushion permitted to build up in the escrow account to one-sixth (thus, a two-month cushion) of the total annual payments from the account (but excludes monthly charges such as for private mortgage insurance). A mortgage servicer is allowed to charge a monthly sum equal to one-twelfth of total annual escrow payments anticipated (plus the cushion).

This escrow change requires lenders to provide a borrower with an initial escrow statement at closing (or within 45 calendar days for accounts that are established as a condition of the loan) and an annual escrow account statement (within 30 days of the end of the computation year).

Escrow Surplus and Deficit

If a lender requires an escrow account, disbursements from the account must be timely. An escrow account analysis must be conducted on establishing the escrow account and at least annually thereafter. If an analysis disclosed a surplus, the servicer must, within 30 days, refund the surplus to the borrower if the surplus is in excess of $50. If the surplus is less than $50, it may be refunded or credited to the escrow account.

If a loan is more than 30 days delinquent, the surplus may be applied in accordance with the terms of the loan. If there is a shortage, the servicer may do any of the following:

- Do nothing and allow the shortage to exist
- Allow the borrower to pay a shortage that is less than a one-month shortage in 30 days
- Allow the borrower to pay a shortage of more than one month over a 12-month period

If there is a deficit (an actual negative balance), the servicer may do the following:

- If it is an under 30-day deficit, the servicer may collect in 30 days.
- If it is more than a 30-day deficit, the servicer may collect in 2 to 12 months, lender's choice.

Records on escrows must be kept for five years.

Home Mortgage Disclosure Act (HMDA)

The Home Mortgage Disclosure Act (Regulation C) is intended to permit regulators and the public to determine whether certain depository institutions and mortgage companies are meeting the housing needs of their communities by reviewing lending registers. The mortgage lenders that are required by HMDA to collect data include those that meet the following conditions:

- Have assets of $32 million (for year 2002, changes each year-end) or more
- Do business in a metropolitan statistical area (MSA)
- Made at least one 1–4 family first mortgage in the preceding calendar year

In order to determine whether these lenders are servicing their communities, they are required to collect data on applicants, including the following:

- Gross annual income of applicants
- Race or national origin of applicants
- Sex of loan applicants
- Both approved and denied applications

Mortgage lenders are also required to collect data on the property, including the following:

- Property location by census tract number, MSA, state and county codes
- Whether owner-occupied as principal residence

Additionally, starting in January 2003, mortgage lenders must also report the spread between the loan Annual Percentage Rate and the yield on the comparable Treasury security when the APR exceeds the Treasury yield by a certain amount:

- 3 percentage points for first liens
- 5 percentage points for subordinate liens

HMDA Loan Activity Register (HMDA-LAR)

The data must be maintained in a log or register of all applications for home loans. This register is sent to the lender's regulator by March 1 of the year following the calendar year of data collection. Types of loans included in the register are as follows:

- Home purchase
- Home improvement
- Refinancing
- Subordinate financing
- Purchased, broker, or correspondent loans (if approved and subsequently acquired according to a preclosing arrangement)

Mortgage applications for loans not covered include these:

- Loans on unimproved land
- Construction loans
- Purchase of an interest in a pool of mortgages or purchase of servicing rights

In addition to the information mentioned here, the following information must be reported on the HMDA-LAR:

- Identifying number
- Date the application was received
- Type of loan (conventional, government insured, etc.)
- Purpose of loan
- Action taken and date
- Loan amount
- Type of entity that purchased loan if it was originated, or purchased and then sold within same calendar year
- Reason for denial (optional)

Fair Credit Reporting Act

The purpose of this act is to regulate the activities of consumer reporting agencies and users of consumer credit reports. If a lender denies a loan because of information on a credit report, it must notify the consumer of that fact and supply the consumer with the name, street address, and telephone number of the consumer reporting agency supplying the report.

Consumer credit reports cannot contain information regarding bankruptcies over 10 years old. Credit reports cannot contain adverse information over seven years old unless it was in connection with a credit of $50,000 or more. Consumer reporting agencies must provide free of charge a credit report if a consumer was turned down for a loan because of a credit report.

A mortgage lender may share the contents of a credit report with a mortgage applicant. This, however, does not make the lender a consumer reporting agency.

Generally, credit reports can be obtained only to determine whether the applicant has acceptable credit for a deposit or credit account. This report can also be obtained to prescreen a list of customers to be solicited for credit services.

Flood Disaster Protection Act (FDPA)

The National Flood Insurance Act of 1968, as amended in 1973 and 1994, was passed to reduce flood relief assistance expenditures made by government. All mortgage lenders are covered by FDPA. FDPA applies to all loans *(first or second mortgages) made, increased, renewed, or extended* (regardless of purpose) that are secured by improved real property (this includes manufactured homes, condominiums, and cooperatives).

A mortgage lender is required to determine whether the community in which the improved real property is located participates in the National Flood Insurance Program (NFIP). The lender is also required to determine whether any portion of the improved real property is located in a special flood hazard area. This determination can be done using maps produced by FEMA or by using vendors or appraisers. Mortgage lenders should realize that the use of an outside vendor does *not* release the lender from responsibility for any errors committed by the vendor.

If property is in a special flood hazard area, a lender must require the borrower to purchase flood insurance. A lender must notify the borrower at least 10 days before closing whether flood insurance is available and requires the borrower to acknowledge in writing that the borrower realizes the property is in a flood hazard area.

The amount of flood insurance required is the loan principal minus the value of the land or the maximum available amount (under the program). Mortgage lenders must ensure that the insurance is in effect for the *life of the loan*. If the property is later classified as existing in a special flood hazard area, the lender must notify the mortgagor of that fact and require flood insurance to be purchased within 45 days; if flood insurance is not purchased within 45 days, the lender must force-place it.

Exhibit 16-5 Sample Flood Hazard Determination Form

FEDERAL EMERGENCY MANAGEMENT AGENCY STANDARD FLOOD HAZARD DETERMINATION	O.M.B. No. 30670264 Expires October 31, 2001

SECTION 1 – LOAN INFORMATION

1. LENDER NAME AND ADDRESS

ACME Investments
123 Anystreet
STE 100
Anytown, CT 10000

Phone: 999-999-9999

Contact: Susan Smith

2. COLLATERAL (Building/Mobile Home/Personal Property)
PROPERTY ADDRESS (Legal Description may be attached)

Certified Location:
51 GOODNOW LN
FRAMINGHAM, MA 017025575

Originally Submitted (or AKA) Address:
51 GOODNOW LANE
FRAMINGHAM, MA 01702

Borrower(s) Names:
John Doe

APN:

3. LENDER ID. NO. 29950	4. LOAN IDENTIFIER	5. AMOUNT OF FLOOD INSURANCE REQUIRED

SECTION II

A. NATIONAL FLOOD INSURANCE PROGRAM (NFIP) COMMUNITY JURISDICTION

NFIP Community Name	County	State	NFIP Community Number
Framingham, Town	MIDDLESEX COUNTY	MA	250193

B. NATIONAL FLOOD INSURANCE PROGRAM (NFIP) DATA AFFECTING BUILDING/MOBILE HOME

NFIP Map Number/Community-Panel Number (Community name, if not the same as "A")	NFIP Map Panel Effective/Revised Date	LOMA/LOMR	Flood Zone	No NFIP Map
250193-0007B	2/3/82		C	

C. NATIONAL FLOOD INSURANCE AVAILABILITY (Check all that apply)

[X] Federal Flood Insurance is available (community participates in NFIP) [X] Regular Program   [ ] Emergency Program of NFIP
Date: 2/3/82

[ ] Federal Flood Insurance is NOT available because community is not participating in the NFIP

[ ] Building/Mobile Home is in a Coastal Barrier Resources Area (CBRA), Federal Flood Insurance may not be available.
CBRA Designation Date:

D. DETERMINATION

IS BUILDING/MOBILE HOME IN SPECIAL FLOOD HAZARD AREA (ZONED BEGINNING WITH LETTERS "A" OR "V")?

If yes, flood insurance is required by the Flood Disaster Protection Act of 1973.
If no, flood insurance is not required by the Flood Disaster Protection Act of 1973.

[ ] Yes [X] No

E. COMMENTS   **LIFE OF LOAN DETERMINATION**

HMDA CENSUS - State: 25 County: 017 MSA: 1120 Tract/Group: 3840.00-3

This determination is based on examining the NFIP map, and Federal Emergency Management Agency revisions to it, and any other information needed to locate the building/mobile home on the NFIP map.

F. PREPARER'S INFORMATION

NAME, ADDRESS, TELEPHONE NUMBER	DATE OF DETERMINATION
Integrated Loan Services 31 Inwood Rd Rocky Hill, CT 06067 Phone: (800)842-8423	6/7/02 10:42:39 AM **CERTIFICATE NUMBER** 253014

FEMA Form 81-93, OCT 98

Exhibit 16-5   Sample Flood Hazard Determination Form (continued)

NOTICE TO BORROWER

Notice Is Given To: John Doe
Subject Property: 51 GOODNOW LN
                      FRAMINGHAM, MA 017025575
NFIP Community: 250193 - Framingham, Town

Date: 6/7/02 10:42:39 AM
Certificate #: 253014
Loan #:

THE LEGAL REQUIREMENT: The Flood Disaster Protection Act of 1973, and amendments, state that Federally regulated lending institutions shall not make, increase, extend, or renew any loan secured by improved real estate, or a mobile home located or to be located, in an area that has been identified by the Director of the Federal Emergency Management Agency (FEMA) as an area having special flood hazards and in which flood insurance has been made available under the National Flood Insurance Act of 1968, through the National Flood Insurance Program (NFIP), unless the building or mobile home and any personal property securing such loan is covered for the term of the loan by flood insurance in an amount at least equal to the outstanding principal balance of the loan or the maximum limit of coverage made available under the Act with respect to the particular type of property, whichever is less.

NOTICE OF SPECIAL FLOOD HAZARD AREA STATUS

☐ **Notice of Property in Special Flood Hazard Area (SFHA)**
The building or mobile home securing the loan for which you have applied is or will be located in an area with special flood hazards. The area has been identified by the Director of FEMA as a SFHA using FEMA's Flood Insurance Rate Map or the Flood Hazard Boundary Map. This area has at least a one percent (1%) chance of a flood equal to or exceeding the base flood elevation (a 100-year flood) in any given year. During the life of a 30-year mortgage loan, the risk of a 100-year flood in a SFHA is 26 percent (26%). Federal law allows a lender and borrower to jointly request the Director of FEMA to review the determination of whether the property securing the loan is located in a SFHA. If you would like to make such a request, please contact us for further information.

☒ **Notice of Property Not in Special Flood Hazard Area (SFHA)**
The building or mobile home securing the loan for which you have applied is not currently located in an area designated by the Director of FEMA as a SFHA. NFIP flood insurance is not required; however, a preferred rate (lower hazard risk) policy is available if your community "participates" (see below). During the term of this loan, if the subject property is identified as being in a SFHA, you may be required to purchase and maintain flood insurance at your expense.

NOTICE REGARDING FEDERAL FLOOD DISASTER ASSISTANCE

☒ **Notice in Participating Communities**
The community in which the property securing the loan is located participates in the NFIP. If the property is or will be located in a SFHA (see section above), federal law will not allow us to make you the loan that you have applied for unless you purchase flood insurance. The flood insurance must be maintained for the life of the loan. If you fail to purchase or renew flood insurance on the property, Federal law authorizes and requires us to purchase the flood insurance at your expense.

Flood insurance coverage under the NFIP may be purchased through an insurance agent who will obtain the policy either directly through the NFIP or through an insurance company that participates in the NFIP. Flood insurance also may be available from private insurers that do not participate in the NFIP. At a minimum, flood insurance purchased must cover the lesser of:

1. The outstanding principal balance of the loan; or
2. The maximum amount of coverage allowed for the type of property under the NFIP.

Flood insurance coverage under the NFIP is limited to the overall value of the property securing the loan minus the value of the land on which the property is located. Federal disaster relief assistance (usually in the form of a low-interest loan) may be available for damages incurred in excess of your flood insurance if your community's participation in the NFIP is in accordance with NFIP requirements.

☐ **Notice in Non-Participating Communities**
Flood insurance coverage under the NFIP is not available for the property securing the loan because the community in which the property is located does not participate in the NFIP. In addition, if the non-participating community has been identified for at least one year as containing a SFHA, properties located in the community will not be eligible for Federal disaster relief assistance in the event of a Federally-declared flood disaster.

John Doe 6/10/02	
Borrower's Signature **Date**	**Co-Borrower's Signature** **Date**
[signature]	*J. L. Smith* 6/10/02
Lending Institution *ACME INVESTMENTS*	**Lending Institution Authorized Signature** **Date**

Community Reinvestment Act (CRA)

The purpose of CRA is to encourage commercial banks, savings banks, and saving associations to meet the borrowing needs of their local community (but it does not apply to credit unions). Regulators of those depository institutions covered by CRA will review the lending records of that institution to determine whether they are meeting the credit needs of the community and will grade that lender accordingly. CRA requires each institution to have available to the general public a CRA statement, which delineates the characteristics of the local community, lists the types of credit the institution is prepared to extend in that community, and includes a copy of the CRA notice. The statement must be readily available for public inspection at the institution's main office and all its branches within the community.

Fair Debt Collection Practices Act

The Fair Debt Collection Practices Act was enacted to eliminate abusive, deceptive, and unfair debt collection practices. It applies only to the collection of consumer debt (including real estate). Any person (or financial institution) who regularly collects or attempts to collect consumer debts for another person or institution is classified as a debt collector. A financial institution that collects only its own debts is not a debt collector.

Home Equity Loan Consumer Protection Act

The Home Equity Loan Consumer Protection Act of 1988 is a revision of Truth-in-Lending (Regulation Z), thus the Federal Reserve Board provides commentary and enforcement. This act covers open-end lines of credit, *not* closed-end seconds. It reenforces that the Right to Rescission applies to HELOCs and requires that lenders provide consumers at application the brochure "When Your Home Is On the Line" and the early disclosure of the terms of the lender's HELOC.

Truth-in-Lending requires a lender to establish a draw and a repayment period. A *draw period* is the period during which the borrower may draw against the line. The *repayment period* is the period during which any balance at the end of the draw period is fully repaid. The combination of the two cannot exceed the maximum term for a mortgage loan in that state. A few lenders let the two periods run concurrently—this could result in a balloon payment and is probably not competitive in today's market.

Homeowners Protection Act (HPA) of 1998

The HPA's cancellation/termination provisions apply to loans originated on or after July 29, 1999, with borrower-paid mortgage insurance (MI). Mortgage loans entered into before that date may also have the mortgage insurance cancelled, but the process is different. Both situations are discussed in the following sections. HPA applies to owner-occupied, residential mortgage loans regardless of lien priority, but excludes FHA insurance. The disclosure provisions of HPA depend on the type of loan (i.e., when it was originated, whether the loan is high risk, whether MI is borrower- or lender-paid).

Automatic Cancellation of Mortgage Insurance

A mortgage lender must automatically terminate MI when a borrower is current on payments and LTV is first scheduled (based on an amortization schedule) to reach 78 percent. Equity based on property appreciation is not a factor. Automatic termination is not limited by decline in property value or existence of a subordinate lien.

Borrower Cancellation of Mortgage Insurance

A borrower can request that a lender cancel MI when the principal balance of the loan reaches 80 percent of the mortgaged property's original value (lesser of sales price or appraised value). A lender does not need to take into account increases in property value in determining when a borrower may cancel. The LTV calculation may be based on either the initial amortization schedule of the loan or actual loan payments. Upon reaching 80 percent, the borrower must do the following:

- Request cancellation in writing from the servicer
- Have a good payment history, which means no 60-day lates within 24 months of reaching 80 percent and no 30-day lates within 12 months before that time
- Satisfy any lender requirements for proof that property values have not declined below the original value and/or there is not a subordinate lien

Other Termination

If the borrower is current on payments, a lender may not require MI beyond the midpoint date of the amortization period of the loan (e.g., 15 years on a 30-year loan). In all situations, any unearned premiums must be returned to the borrower within 45 days.

Disclosure Requirements

If the lender is paying for the MI at the time of commitment, that lender must disclose to the applicant information comparing lender- and borrower-paid MI. If the borrower pays for the MI (and the loan is not a high-risk loan), the lender must disclose at consummation of the transaction that the borrower has the following rights:

- For a fixed-rate mortgage—to request MI cancellation once the LTV reaches 80 percent and to request MI automatic termination once the LTV reaches 78 percent
- For an adjustable-rate mortgage—to request MI cancellation once the LTV reaches 80 percent and that the lender notify the borrower when that date is reached and to request automatic termination once the LTV reaches 78 percent

Annual Notice

If the borrower paid for the MI for loans made on or after July 29, 1999, the lender must advise the borrower of cancellation rights and provide the address and telephone number of the servicer. For loans made prior to July 29, 1999, the lender must advise the borrower that MI may, under certain circumstances, be canceled by the borrower and must provide the address and telephone number of the servicer.

The servicer must notify the borrower of termination or cancellation of MI within 30 days. Upon determination that the borrower does not meet the requirements for cancellation or termination, the servicer must inform the borrower of grounds for its determination.

Discussion Points

1. ECOA (Regulation B) prohibits discrimination based on which factors?

2. If a mortgage lender declines an application for a mortgage loan, what must the lender do? How is it done?

3. Are business loans covered by Truth In Lending? What is covered?

4. What items are included in the annual percentage rate? What is excluded?

5. What is the Right of Rescission (Right to Cancel)? What is required of a mortgage lender?

6. What does "life of loan coverage" mean? Why is this important to a mortgage lender?

Construction Lending

Introduction

This chapter provides an overview on the financing of residential 1–4 family home construction, the special risks associated with this line of business, who provides this type of financing, and how it is done. This chapter cannot discuss in detail all the specific local and state regulatory issues, zoning requirements, building codes, legal documentation, and title insurance requirements, but it does point out when these items require special consideration compared to conventional mortgage financing.

As discussed in Chapter 2, "Role of Residential Mortgage Lending in the Economy," single-family residential construction comprises one of the most significant elements of the U.S. economy, directly accounting for approximately $230 billion, or 4 percent, of the economy. Over 6 million people are directly involved in construction, materials, and other construction resources. Millions more are involved in jobs related to construction. Construction of 100 homes generates approximately 244 construction and construction-related jobs, almost $8 million in wages, and over $4 million in local, state, and federal fees and tax revenue. Despite these large numbers, the majority of firms producing new homes is family owned and produces fewer than 25 homes per year. (See the National Association of Home Builders [NAHB] **www.nahb.com**.)

Housing Starts

Each month the financial markets watch closely the numbers released for annual housing starts—a leading indicator for the economy. There are over 100 million housing units in the United States, valued at approximately $12 trillion. For the past 10 years, approximately 1.0 to 1.3 million new single-family housing starts and 160,000 to 345,000 multifamily starts occurred each year. During the recessions of 1980–1982 and 1990–1992, total housing starts dipped below 900,000.

As can be seen from the U.S. Census Bureau 2000 Census information, residential construction involves more than single-family units. Multifamily units and mobile homes account for almost 34 percent of all housing. It is also important to recognize that U.S. housing stock is replenished at approximately 15 to 20 percent per decade. As one might imagine, the age of housing stock varies significantly from older, colonial states along the East Coast to recent "boom" areas, such as Phoenix, Arizona. Although each year has significant swings in production, residential construction proceeds at a fairly steady pace over time, driving the U.S. economy.

Multiplier Effect

It's not only actual home construction that impacts the economy to such a large degree, but it is also the multiplier effect housing has on the economy. Purchases associated with new home construction comprise a significant amount of consumer spending, which is the largest single element of the U.S. economy. Buyers of newly built homes on average spend $8,900 in housing-related purchases within 12 months—twice the amount spent by buyers of existing homes. This means that many consumers fill their homes with durable and nondurable goods: furnishings, alterations, appliances, lighting fixtures, cabinets and woodworking, plumbing, flooring, lawn and garden items, and so forth. One trip through a Home Depot or WalMart demonstrates the full economic impact building and moving into a new home have. See Chapter 2, "Role of Residential Mortgage Lending in the Economy."

Who Does Construction Loans?

All types of mortgage lenders participate in construction lending: commercial and national banks, thrifts and community banks, credit unions, and mortgage companies. Precise figures are not available because 1–4 family construction lending is not reported as a separate category and is excluded from HMDA data, but, in 2001, residential construction lending totaled approximately $260 billion for those lenders regulated by the FDIC and the OTS. FDIC-regulated lenders extended the majority of the money, with almost $232 billion in residential construction and land development loans provided.

Almost 86 percent of 436 community banks that completed a 1997 survey by America's Community Bankers (**www.acbanker.org**) reported participating in residential construction lending. The highest percentage group was the local lenders that had between $100 million and $500 million in assets. Why does it appear that more residential construction lending takes place in small to medium-sized institutions rather than nationwide lenders?

Unlike conventional mortgage financing, construction lending is extremely specific to the area, so it is less of a commodity. Lenders must develop their operations to match the restrictions, limitations, and procedures imposed by the state, county, city/town, neighborhood, and even parcel in their lending areas. Large lenders would lose their advantage in lower production costs if they had to set up numerous local branches to serve the residential construction markets.

Developing a large secondary market for residential construction loans has been very difficult. This is partly a result of the dynamic of the residential construction project and partly a result of the lack of uniformity in process and procedure, since so many smaller lenders perform construction lending in an independent fashion tailored to their specific regions.

Why Lenders Do Construction Loans

Despite the difficulties and risks involved, construction lending provides several benefits to a lender and the communities it serves. Construction loans

• Earn a higher interest rate and provide excellent fee income, which, given the short maturity of one year or less, are usually reflective of current market rates and result in a significantly higher yield than first-mortgage lending.

- Fill a product and market niche and reach different segments within an institution's marketing area, such as small builders and other individuals who will build the home.
- Facilitate the expansion, renewal, and renovation of local housing stock. This increases the number and condition of homes, which increases the market for mortgage loans and produces economic growth.

A secondary benefit derived from construction lending is the economic stimulus to local suppliers, businesses, and industries whose products and services are tied directly to home construction—the multiplier effect described previously. This includes professionals and laborers throughout the process: architect, surveyer, excavator and landscaper, concrete pourer, carpenter, framer, roofer, drywaller, electrician and plumber, floorer, appliance supplier, interior decorator, and all the materials these people use during construction.

Finally, construction lending enables the relationship-oriented lender (typically, the small bank, thrift, or credit union) to solidify its connection to the customer and compete more effectively against the transaction-oriented lender (typically, regional or national lenders or mortgage bankers). Transaction-oriented lenders usually avoid very involved or "hands-on" loan products, and mortgage bankers cannot fund loans for long construction periods before selling them on the secondary market.

An exception to this general statement are larger mortgage bankers, who now offer correspondent construction programs. These are nationwide lenders (such as GMAC) that, because of their large size, offer programs in most states and can fund the construction period before selling the loan on the secondary market. A Fannie Mae program helped develop and standardize the secondary market for the construction-permanent loan product.

Construction Lending Basics

Construction lending differs from permanent financing in two basic ways: funding and collateral. As a result, a construction lender's policies, programs, and practices reflect the procedural changes and unique risks associated with this type of lending.

The most obvious situation in which a borrower would request construction financing is for building a new home on a vacant building lot. Although building a new home is a complicated and time-consuming project, consumers can save thousands of dollars and at the same time tailor the design to their specific taste by building.

Advances

Unlike a normal first-mortgage purchase or refinance transaction, at a construction loan closing the lender disburses to the borrower only a portion of the loan funds. Each disbursement is called an advance. After closing, the borrowers receive additional construction advances according to a schedule that is determined ahead of time by the lender. The timing and amount of these advances vary with each lender, but in general each advance matches the progress on the home. The lender makes the final advance, thereby disbursing the full loan amount, only upon completion of construction. As a result, the borrower must rely more on liquid assets (cash) to keep the project going between these advances.

Collateral

The second way in which construction and permanent lending differ is that for construction lending only a portion of the loan collateral exists at the time of closing. This poses a challenge for the lender. If the borrower defaults with insufficient collateral securing the loan, the lender faces an enormous risk. The lender may need to contribute additional funds to complete the project before selling it to recover the defaulted loan amount. Lender and borrower must work together—and share the risk—to complete the project on which the loan is based. Managing this relationship successfully is the key to construction lending.

Construction lending involves other questions and issues: What if the borrower needs additional funds to complete the project? Can the borrower afford to build and pay for the project? What if the house is not worth the projected value? What if the house is not built correctly or does not conform to zoning? How good is the builder? What if something else goes wrong?

Construction Loan versus Permanent Loan

Construction lending requires special loan products that match the dynamics of these transactions. Loan structure differs from conventional loan products in three ways: term, repayment, and disbursement.

Term

The loan term is the first decision a lender must make when developing its construction loan program and product. *Term*, in this context, does not mean "time," but "phase." A lender must first determine exactly what it wants to finance in home construction: only the construction phase, or the construction phase and the amortized repayment phase (the payback) of the loan.

A typical construction period generally lasts 6 to 12 months, depending on the type of house being built, overall construction activity, and weather. If the lender also finances the permanent financing phase of the loan, that phase is normally 15 to 30 years.

Phases of Disbursements

The second area in which a construction loan differs from permanent financing is in the phases of disbursement of funds. Many construction lenders advance less than 20 percent of the total loan amount at closing, with additional funds disbursed later in the construction phase. After the borrower completes a stage of construction, the lender (or an agent) inspects the property, then disburses an amount that reflects the work completed. To avoid daily, small disbursements, the lender allows up to four or five construction advances.

All construction loans, whether they end at the construction phase or continue through repayment of the permanent financing, have this disbursement schedule in common. This differs from first-mortgage loans, which advance the full loan amount at closing to either purchase or refinance the subject property.

Schedule of Disbursements

No universal schedule would apply to all areas of the country, since construction differs widely as a result of geography and climate, zoning, economic factors, and the laborers' work schedules. But notice how the schedule of disbursements mirrors the construction activity on the house and matches funding to the expenses involved.

The use of an advance schedule allows the lender to monitor the progress of construction and its risk exposure. For administrative consistency, a lender assigns each advance a percentage of the total loan amount. Within that advance, each specific stage of construction is also assigned a percentage, allowing lenders to "mix and match" the funds disbursed to the actual level of completion the lender sees when inspecting the property for an advance.

Figure 17-1	Sample Construction Loan Advance Schedule

Construction Disbursement Schedule

Each line item should be completed and inspected before issuing funds:

1. First Advance—33%
   - 10%   Foundation
   - 23%   Frame, Sheathing, and Roof
2. Second Advance—33%
   - 3%   Rough grading
   - 3%   Rough plumbing
   - 2%   Rough electric
   - 4%   Rough heating
   - 5%   Exterior walls and trim, windows, and doors installed
   - 1%   Exterior prime coat of paint
   - 5%   Interior walls complete
   - 3%   Water supply connected
   - 3%   Sewer system connected
   - 4%   Cellar floor installed
3. Third Advance—34%
   - 4%   Plumbing complete
   - 2%   Electrical complete
   - 4%   Heating complete
   - 1%   Exterior paint complete
   - 2%   Bathroom(s) complete
   - 8%   Interior trim complete
   - 5%   Floors complete
   - 4%   Interior painting complete
   - 4%   Kitchen cabinets complete
4. Final Advance—2% of loan amount or minimum of $2,000

The Final Advance is disbursed after the lender receives a satisfactory Certificate of Occupancy, final survey, and as is appraisal inspection.

The previous figure is a sample advance schedule showing a typical format in which loan funds are disbursed to the borrower. Many lenders follow a similar schedule, but their particular advance schedule mirrors the manner in which residential construction occurs in that area.

Repayment

The final area in which a construction loan differs from permanent financing is in its repayment. As discussed earlier, the borrower receives funds over time, so the principal balance changes during the construction phase. During this time, the lender normally requires interest-only payments on the advanced loan amount, instead of requiring a principal and interest payment based on the full loan amount as in conventional financing. In this way, the borrower pays interest only on the money used. Interest-only payments lower the borrower's debt burden during the construction phase so the borrower can dedicate more liquid assets to the construction of the home.

Who Is the General Contractor: Builder or Borrower?

Before developing the actual loan program, lenders must first decide who they will allow to perform the construction: an individual borrower or a builder. This is a critical decision for a lender, since project management falls squarely in the hands of the person responsible for the construction and directly affects loan repayment.

In building a new home, many consumers wish to manage the construction project themselves. They become the **general contractor** (**GC**) and are then responsible for seeing the work gets done according to code and is approved by the town. The general contractor deals with all workers, town, zoning, material providers, and so forth, and must manage the schedule and order of work and delivery of materials on-site. This is an enormous responsibility for the average consumer, who may have other obligations such as work and family.

Not all lenders will allow an "amateur" consumer to be the GC. Some lenders require a licensed builder to be the GC. Normally, lenders with this policy will not select the builder or officially recommend a particular builder for the consumer. But as a result of past experience, a lender may decide to make it a policy to not work with certain builders.

Construction Loan Programs

Lenders active in residential construction lending often develop different programs. Which program is best for the situation depends on how each suits the particular transaction, borrower preference, and the lender's business strategy. Residential construction lending programs fall into three main categories, depending on the product or the borrower:

- Construction only (with two closings)
- Construction/permanent (with one closing)
- Builder speculative construction

As stated earlier, construction loans are not as uniform from lender to lender as is permanent financing developed by the secondary market. According to data from FDIC, the following is true of lenders participating in single-family construction:

- 80 percent use a variable-rate feature based on prime.
- 48 percent require more than 10 percent in cash available.
- 97 percent require an LTV of less than 85 percent.

The following FDIC limits apply to LTV for those institutions regulated by that agency:

- Raw land: 65 percent
- Land development: 75 percent
- Commercial development: 80 percent
- 1–4 family residential development: 85 percent

Construction Only (With Two Closings)

In this program, the lender finances only the construction phase, so financing is for one purpose only: to complete the home. There is no extended repayment feature for the permanent financing. Typically, the loan term is 6 to 12 months and calls for monthly interest-only payments on the loan amount outstanding (not the full loan amount). The loan then repays with one balloon payment for the full outstanding balance and interest due at the end of construction or in one year, whichever occurs first.

Since the full amount of the loan is due with that one balloon payment, it is not an amortizing loan. The borrower must obtain separate financing, if needed, to pay off the loan amount in monthly payments (permanent financing). It is the borrower's responsibility either to have sufficient liquid assets or to find other financing to pay off the construction loan.

This program places more emphasis on the short-term aspects of the project—the value of the finished collateral (the house) and the present financial condition of the borrower—rather than on the ongoing repayment ability of the borrower.

Construction/Permanent (With One Closing)

This program begins like the preceding one, but then adds a repayment phase similar to permanent financing, with principal and interest amortization over a 15- to 30-year term. As described previously, the borrower receives principal advances during the construction phase, but then the loan automatically converts to the permanent loan phase. This phase begins when the loan is fully advanced or at the end of the construction phase, again usually within 6 to 12 months.

In this loan program, the borrowers go through the application, processing, approval, and closing process only once. Like the construction-only program, funds are advanced according to a predetermined schedule. Then once the home is complete, the documents detail the manner in which the repayment of the loan occurs: interest rate on the loan, monthly payment, start date of loan, and maturity date. The terms of repayment may be set before the loan closes, or the rate, payment, and start date may be set upon completion of the construction phase.

Since only one application, processing, approval, and closing covers everything, both lenders and consumers find this loan program more convenient. However, it presents additional underwriting and financial risks for both the lender and consumer. Unlike the construction-only program, with construction/permanent financing more emphasis is placed on the long-term aspects of the financial transaction. These include the present financial condition of the borrower, the ongoing ability of the borrower to repay the loan, and the value of the collateral.

Builder Speculation Homes

A third construction lending program involves lending to a builder and not to the occupant of the new home. This home is being built on "speculation" (or as it is sometimes called, **spec home**) to be sold upon completion. The builder may or may not have a signed contract of sale for the home when construction financing begins.

Like the construction-only program, this program finances only the construction phase, has a loan term of 6 to 12 months, and requires monthly interest-only payments on the loan amount outstanding. The loan repays with one balloon payment.

The difference here is the source of repayment. The borrower (and lender) relies on proceeds from the sale of the house to pay the debt, not ongoing cash flow or profit of the builder–borrower. The reality is that the lender is somewhat an investor in the home, as is the builder. Like the construction-only program, the short-term aspects of the project, the value of the finished collateral (the house), are more significant than the repayment ability of any particular borrower.

Construction Loans for Rehabilitation

Construction loans also finance the extensive rehabilitation of older or damaged homes. These projects can be riskier and more complicated than building a new home, partly because of the amount and the difficult nature of the work involved. In addition, the total cost and time can change dramatically once the project begins (and everyone has committed resources).

Rather than "starting from scratch," as in new-home construction, rehab projects must first demolish or expose significant sections of the existing dwelling. This may either cause more damage in the process or uncover new areas needing rehabilitation—either way, it means more work and, therefore, more (unbudgeted) time, money, or financing to complete the project.

Normally, it is more difficult to assess and rehab an existing dwelling than it is to build a new one. Also, the type of work required is often of a higher or specialized level of craftsmanship, so fewer people possess the skills or experience required for the project.

As a result of these difficulties, the borrower embarking on the rehabilitation project faces more difficult challenges in budgeting and cash flow, as well as more constraints on time, material, and labor. Simpler remodeling or home improvement projects do not require the involved financing structure of a construction loan. Less-involved projects that require less time and work, such as adding a room or remodeling a kitchen, are better financed by a second mortgage or home equity line of credit.

Construction Lending Drawbacks for the Leader

Lenders may earn a higher return on construction loans, but they also incur higher costs. This type of lending requires additional time and training for originators, processors, underwriters, and closers. After closing, the loans require constant management until final disbursement of all funds. During this time, lenders must monitor exposure on each account, inspect construction progress, and calculate the amount of each disbursement.

If a default and foreclosure occur, the lender is in an extremely difficult position. A partly built home cannot be sold "as is." It requires that the lender provide additional time and funds to complete the project. Once completed, the house must appraise for what it cost to build and must be sold in a housing market that is as favorable as when the loan was made. If the project has many unique or custom features, it may not be as valued by others as the original borrowers.

Construction Loan Management

For these reasons, it is imperative that lenders manage their residential construction lending program by monitoring the status of each loan regularly. A prudent practice is to review weekly the following for each loan:

- Repayment history
- Stage of construction
- Mechanic's lien waiver documentation
- Percent of total loan advanced
- Advance history
- Date and amount of the last advance
- Time remaining in the construction phase of the loan

In addition to this "office" review, it would be ideal (but impractical) for a lender to visit on-site all construction projects weekly. Instead, in practice, each construction advance request provides the lender an opportunity to inspect the collateral and compare the level of construction to the loan amount remaining. In most situations, this level of inspection ensures that the loan has sufficient collateral and that the project progresses in a satisfactory manner.

Another source of concern is when the lender receives no construction advance requests on a loan for a period of time. This may indicate simply that the borrower is using cash to avoid paying interest, or it may indicate a serious problem that will result in default. Perhaps the builder has encountered a major problem, or work has otherwise been delayed because of shortages, materials, zoning issues, or nonpayment of subcontractors. Whatever the reason, when a project falls behind schedule, the lender must determine quickly a resolution to the situation since the construction period is set at loan closing and may end before the borrower completes the project. Depending on the situation, the lender may extend the construction period, provide additional financing, or foreclose and take possession of the property and all materials on it.

Mechanic's Liens

One can imagine the complications that arise in the preceding worst-case scenario. Anyone who performs work on that property who is not paid has the right to place a lien on that property. This **mechanic's lien** in most states takes priority over the first mortgage—even if it is filed after loan closing—putting the lender in second or third position, if more than one party is not paid.

Operational Issues

Aside from program design, pricing, and underwriting considerations, when designing a construction lending program, the lender must consider the following operational items separately from conventional financing:

- Creation of closing documents since standard secondary market documents alone do not work for this type of lending
- Selection of closing attorneys/agents based on their construction expertise, particularly when using customized documents
- Selection of appraisers based on their construction experience
- Selection or updating of the loan-servicing system to handle construction advances and other manual transactions
- Determination of whether the same area will handle the construction, conversion, and permanent phase of the loan
- Development of an in-house loan-tracking system or purchase of an outside system
- Development of policies and procedures for all areas of origination, servicing, and collections
- Training of origination, servicing, and collection staff

Origination of Construction Loans

The origination or application process for a construction loan is more involved than for permanent loan financing for both the lender and the applicant. These differences are significant and must be fully understood by both the lender and the applicant.

Application

Prior to actual application for a construction loan, the loan officer often must educate applicants by informing them of the difficulty and unpredictability of the construction process—even if the applicants hire a builder as general contractor. At application, lenders can use the standard secondary market forms for the application and verifications, but they will need nonstandard forms and to provide more information as well.

The loan officer should obtain as much information as possible on the actual construction of the home. Many lenders have a checklist for consumers who plan to build a home that details what is needed, depending on the type of house, property, and local zoning and building codes. This information includes any and all of the following items (some of which may not be available at application):

- Building plans and specifications
- Plot plan and site survey
- **Building permit**
- Builder's license and liability insurance
- Inspections for water, well, perk, and so forth
- Material list and cost estimates
- Contracts for materials and work to be performed
- Payment receipts for materials purchased and work performed

From what is usually a sizeable package of documentation, the construction loan officer must make a reasonable estimate of what it will cost to construct the home, including all large items such as labor, cement, lumber, roofing, windows, floors, down to the cost of paint, nails, and duct tape. The construction loan officer is able to do this based on experience/understanding of what it costs to build a particular type of house in that geographical location. Normally, builders have this information better organized than consumers acting as the general contractor do.

Instead of using the term *purchase price*, which implies one set, known amount, construction lending may use the term *acquisition cost* if the applicants need to purchase the lot, or **cost to construct** if the applicants already own the land. In any event, once this cost is determined, the loan officer can then concentrate on qualifying the applicants.

Cash Flow Analysis

Of particular importance in qualifying applicants for construction lending is the cash flow analysis. Some applicants may have a satisfactory credit history and earn enough income to support repayment of the debt, but may not have enough savings required to meet the demands of home construction. The construction loan officer will then match the lender's advance schedule to the construction project. This means calculating the timing and amount of funds needed for each phase of construction, then reviewing when the lender will advance funds to replenish the borrower's liquid assets.

Another area the loan officer should assess is how well prepared the applicants appear to be to handle such a complicated project. Construction delays and unanticipated problems arise over the course of the project, resulting in additional expense. Lenders typically require applicants to have an additional 10 percent of the projected cost to construct in reserve to meet cost overruns.

Lenders should at this time also provide a detailed description of their particular construction loan program(s). This description should cover the following:

- Required documentation to be supplied by applicants
- Interest rate, points, and fees
- Loan terms—construction period and repayment period
- Loan payment—timing and amount
- Loan advance schedule—manner and requirements
- Underwriting guidelines
- Property requirements
- Acquisition cost/cost to construct
- Construction and builder documentation

| **Figure 17-2** | Sample Construction Program Description Letter |

Construction Program Information

Thank you for choosing us for your construction financing needs. We provide the following information to assist you in understanding our program and to answer questions you may have. Please contact a loan officer for additional information or to set up an appointment.

1. The Application Process—What do I need to do?

We need the following information to begin processing your construction loan application:

    A. Completed mortgage application

    B. Construction contract

    C. Building plans and specifications

    D. Lender's builder questionnaire

    E. Lender's construction cash flow worksheet

    F. Lender's advance schedule

    G. Application and origination fee

    H. Supplemental construction cost estimate

    I. Construction program information

    J. Verification of income, assets, and liabilities

2. Inspections and Construction Loan Advances—How do they work?

    A. Land advances

We will advance part of the land value at the closing under the following conditions:

1. For land that you own free and clear for over 1 year, up to 50 percent of the appraised value, but no more than the lesser of $100,000.00 or 40 percent of the loan amount.

2. For land that you are purchasing, up to 75 percent of the lesser of the sales price or appraised value, but no more than the lesser of $100,000.00 or 40 percent of the loan amount.

    B. Construction advances

      At application you will receive a Construction Loan Advance Schedule that breaks down your advances into percentages. You should budget your funds since the money provided in the mortgage will be only a percentage of the funds required for each advance.

      You should discuss the advance schedule with your builder to avoid any misunderstandings or delays in the construction. If any funds are advanced against the land, the remaining funds of loan amount are computed against the reduced amount. You should demonstrate that sufficient funds are available to complete the construction with this schedule.

    C. Inspections

      Lender employees or a fee inspector will inspect the property before authorizing an advance. All inspections should be scheduled 5 days prior to the advance.

      Please note that inspectors are neither engineers nor architects and should not be relied on to evaluate material or workmanship.

    D. Final inspection

      Lender will hold back at the greater of $2,000.00 or 2 percent of the loan amount. These funds will be advanced on completion of the property and receipt of lien waivers, final inspection report, final survey, and Certificate of Occupancy.

3. Contractor Requirements

You should select an established contractor to build your home. The Lender will require the completion and review of a Builder Questionnaire, but it is up to you to check the builder's references and reputation. Lender takes no responsibility for the builder's ability or reputation.

4. Closing Requirements—What will I need?

    A. All required building permits

    B. Builder's risk insurance

    C. Flood insurance, if applicable

    D. Certified survey with proposed foundation, well, septic, driveway, and other improvements

Please sign and date below acknowledging that you have received and understand our requirements.

_____   _____

Name   Date

While lending regulations do not require all these items, it is critical that the lender and applicants understand how the process works and what is needed. Following is a sample construction program description letter.

Depending on how the loan product is structured, adjustable-rate mortgage regulations may apply. If the interest rate can change at any time during the construction period, at conversion, or during the repayment period, the loan officer may need to provide ARM disclosures.

Processing

From a lender's perspective, the differences between conventional first-mortgage lending and construction lending processing occur mainly relating to the cost to construct, appraisal, and deposit verifications. Often the loan officer does not receive complete cost estimates for all phases of construction. It is the processor's job to help follow up and track down the remaining pieces of information to develop a complete construction estimate. Once this is complete, the processor can order an appraisal report.

The processor sends along with the appraisal request all information collected for the cost to construct to give the appraiser the most accurate picture of what the house will look like. Since there is no house yet (or it is partially complete), the appraiser must work from plans and specs (and whatever else he or she can find to estimate the value of the property). Instead of completing the appraisal report as is, the appraiser will complete it "subject to plans and specifications." Upon completion of the house at a later date, the appraiser must return to determine whether the actual property built is what was appraised originally and certify its value.

Because cash flow is such an important element in construction, the processor must be careful to obtain an accurate snapshot of the applicants' deposits. Verifications and deposit statements must be closely dated, since applicants often move funds around to consolidate them for the project. Some lenders also obtain information on the builder or the applicant, if he or she is the general contractor. This would verify whether that person is licensed to perform this function and has insurance for people working on the site, and it may include personal or business financial statements for the builder.

Underwriting

As mentioned previously, residential construction lending differs from conventional first-mortgage lending in liquidity risk and collateral risk, where underwriters must place special consideration. In addition to the prudent guidelines discussed in Chapter 7, "Underwriting the Residential Mortgage Loan," construction loan underwriters require additional skills in the following areas: determining the cost to construct, cash flow analysis, and reviewing property appraisals.

Cost to Construct

For an underwriter to successfully review a construction loan application, he or she must be familiar with all stages of construction and relative costs involved for typical houses in the area. Land and labor costs vary widely across the United States, and certain areas present unique construction challenges, such as ledges or swamps. An experienced underwriter knows the area's general costs from reviewing many applications and will review the present applicants' estimates with this store of knowledge as a reference. The underwriter must be able to determine whether the cost estimate prepared by the applicants is realistic or whether it has omitted any significant items. Many lenders request actual signed estimates from suppliers and laborers to verify actual costs.

To assist in this step, lenders develop a checklist of items that mirrors their advance schedule, but includes more specific information at each step of the construction process—estimates for labor, materials, appliances, and so forth. Some construction lenders require labor and material costs to be separated. A sample cost projection worksheet follows.

Cash Flow Analysis

Once the underwriter verifies the actual cost to construct, the next step is to compare the costs to the construction loan advance schedule. This calculation determines the actual construction cost from loan advance to loan advance. Finally, the underwriter compares the amounts needed to how much verified cash the applicants have on deposit.

This analysis is critical to the success of the construction project. The essence of cash flow analysis is to ensure the applicants are the main supporters of the construction project and the lender is not. Do the applicants have enough liquid assets to get them through all stages of construction? What happens if excavation runs over or the contractor must dig several wells before one passes inspection? Are there sufficient funds—between the applicant's funds and the construction advances—to allow the project to progress from construction advance to advance even with some additional costs?

Although the applicants may have excellent debt/income ratios, they may have insufficient funds to complete the next stage in construction. This undermines the entire project and would leave the lender in a difficult position. For this reason, many lenders require applicants to have an extra 10 to 15 percent above the estimated cost to construct to allow for unanticipated cost overruns and upgrades.

Property Appraisal

When reviewing the appraisal report, the underwriter's main concerns are as follows:

- Is the subject property appraised the same lot and structure as detailed in the construction cost estimates submitted to the lender?
- How will the market value and market appeal support the cost to construct and the proposed property?

As stated earlier, appraisals for new construction are completed using plans and specifications. This sometimes makes locating the subject property difficult, as well as projecting what it will look like once built. Appraisers use standard values for estimating construction costs usually obtained from cost estimates, such as Marshall and Swift, local builders, and the appraiser's prior files. The appraiser must explain in the appraisal report any substantial changes to these objective reference sources.

Ideally, the appraiser will include at least one newly constructed home to establish the current value of new construction in that area. If the proposed home is a modular home, or log cabin, or other structure that may be somewhat unique to the neighborhood, the appraiser must try to use a comparable of similar type.

| Figure 17-3 | Sample Cost Projection Worksheet |

Construction Cost Projection Worksheet

Estimate

1. Land acquisition
2. Land clearing
3. Excavation
4. Concrete—labor and materials
5. Waterproofing
6. Drains
7. Driveway—labor and materials
8. Septic—design, labor, and materials
9. Water hookup/well drilling
10. Pump and installation
11. Modular home sales price
12. Framing and trim—labor and materials
13. Doors—labor and materials
14. Windows—labor and materials
15. Siding—labor and materias
16. Roofing—labor and materials
17. Gutters and leaders
18. Interior stairs and railings
19. Fireplace and chimney—labor and materials
20. Flashing
21. Electrical Hookup and temporary service
22. Electrical—labor and materials
23. Telephone—prewire and jacks
24. Plumbing—labor and materials
25. Insulation—labor and materials
26. Plasterboard and taping—labor and materials
27. Heating—labor and materials
28. Deck/Porch—labor and materials
29. Flooring—labor and materials
30. Linoleum and tile—labor and materials
31. Carpeting—labor and materials
32. Exterior walls, walks, steps—labor and materials
33. Painting—Exterior
34. Painting—Interior
35. Garage and cellar doors
36. Appliances
37. Electrical fixtures
38. Bathroom accessories
39. Cabinets, vanities, amenities
40. Mirrors
41. Landscaping
42. Upgrades—Interior
43. Upgrades—Exterior
44. Upgrades—Fixtures
45. Upgrades—Other

Total Projected Costs $

10% Cost Overrun Estimate $

Total Needed $

The underwriter must compare the dimensions and characteristics of the house described in the appraisal to the information submitted in the loan application file. Another consideration is how well the proposed property conforms to the neighborhood. Finally, the underwriter should note how the change in land use and built-up rate may affect property value, especially if the subject property is part of a larger development.

The appraiser completes the report "per plans and specifications," and the loan closes with this appraisal report. After closing—but before the final construction loan advance—the appraiser must recertify the property value on an "as is" basis. This recertification of value requires the appraiser to reinspect the property upon completion of the house and after the town issues a **Certificate of Occupancy**.

Closing

As stated previously, unlike conventional mortgage financing, in construction lending not all loan funds are advanced at closing. The underwriter determines the amount disbursed at closing, based on total loan amount, LTV, the stage of construction, and what has been paid to date.

Either prior to or at closing, the lender should require the following documents unique to a newly constructed house:

- Survey
- Building permit
- Builder license
- Builder liability/builder's risk insurance
- Mechanic's lien waivers for all completed work
- Applicable town inspections/approval for all completed work
- Title insurance endorsements for construction

Application Process—Builder

If the applicant is a builder, then the lender may require the following documents for a commercial application package:

- Dunn & Bradstreet report (equivalent to a business credit report)
- Tax returns
- Recent personal and corporate financial statements
- Complete schedule of all real estate work in progress
- Trade references/suppliers

To evaluate the builder, the lender really performs more of a commercial loan analysis than a consumer analysis. Briefly, the lender evaluates the following characteristics of the builder:

- *Capacity*: Does the builder have the experience, management expertise, staffing, and finances to handle this project? A builder questionnaire asks a series of questions to help evaluate this.
- *Credit*: What has the builder's repayment history been? The lender builds a main credit file that includes references from

- Dunn & Bradstreet
- Credit reports
- Trade creditors/suppliers
- Local building supply organizations
- Bonding company
- Building departments
- Other lenders
- *Experience*: In addition, the lender may do the following:
  - Visit past and current projects/historical experience
  - Talk to prior customers

While lending directly to a builder is more of a commercial loan transaction, many small to medium-sized lenders handle these applications in the residential mortgage area since it is most familiar with real estate.

Loan Administration and Funding

Once a residential construction loan closes, the lender must pay particular attention to its administration during the construction phase. Usually, a separate department or person handles these loans. It is imperative that the lender constantly communicate with the borrower and builder and serve their funding needs by processing advance requests promptly.

In order to advance funds, the lender must inspect the property using either a qualified employee or an outside appraiser and document the exact stage of construction. Once this has been established, the applicant must provide the applicable mechanic's lien waivers and receipts for payment to contractors, suppliers, and others. The lender determines the amount of the advance based on the loan amount and the preceding documentation.

As mentioned previously, the lender must notify the borrower of loan expiration dates and track progress of construction with this date in mind. A lender (or borrower or builder) cannot always control construction delays, as unfortunate events are part of the risk of lending. But it is critical that the lender keep accurate documentation during the construction phase in case a problem occurs and the lender needs to evaluate this situation for modification, delinquency, and so forth.

Before issuing the final advance, the lender must obtain the following documents:

- Completion certificate
- Recertification of value
- Certificate of Occupancy/temporary Certificate of Occupancy
- Complete mechanic's lien waivers

At that time, the loan either matures or goes into repayment, depending on the loan documents.

Discussion Points

1. Why do lenders participate in residential construction lending?

2. How are construction loans structured?

3. What are the benefits and drawbacks for both the lender and borrower in using "two-closing" loan products? What are the benefits and drawbacks of "one-closing" products?

4. How do construction loans differ from first-mortgage, home improvement, or home equity loans?

5. What should a lender review when managing a construction loan portfolio?

6. Explain the construction and funding process.

Chapter 18

Home Equity Loans

Introduction

This chapter examines in detail the various types of equity loans that consumers can obtain using their home as security. These loans are becoming very popular with the American consumer, with nearly 30 percent of homeowners having one of these loans. Mortgage lenders are very interested in these loans because they are typically made to the best credits in our society and these loans are often variable rate.

Nomenclature

Equity loans are referred to by many names. Often they are referred to as second mortgages because they are commonly in a secondary lien position. On the other hand, some people have one of these loans but do not have a first mortgage; thus, the equity loan is in a first-lien position. These loans can be either closed end (the traditional second mortgage) or open end (home equity lines of credit). A home improvement loan is another type of loan secured by a person's home that is usually in a second-lien position.

One type of mortgage loan that is not discussed in this chapter is the loan that is for more than 100 percent of appraised value of a person's home. These loans are often workout loans used by a creditor to convert unsecured consumer loans into secured real estate loans. Most traditional mortgage lenders do not engage in this type of mortgage lending, leaving it to finance companies. Another related loan is an automobile loan that is also recorded as a mortgage loan so that the borrower can deduct the interest on his or her tax return. This type of loan is not a true mortgage loan and is not discussed in this chapter.

Consumer Loans or Mortgage Loans?

Some lenders treat equity loans as consumer loans because, to a great extent, they have replaced many types of consumer loans. Other lenders consider these loans to be mortgage loans because they are secured by real estate. Although it does not make a great deal of difference which department handles these loans, as long as they are administered correctly, traditionally they have been considered mortgage loans.

How Important Are Equity Loans to Lenders?

Many lenders consider these loans as important—if not more so—as first-mortgage loans. One of the reasons for the importance of equity loans is the high credit standard of borrowers using them. The Consumer Bankers Association (*2001 Home Equity*

Study) has found that the average FICO score for equity borrowers is a high 715. Another startling fact about equity loans is that nearly 60 percent of all consumer credit (excluding credit cards) granted in the United States each year is in the form of equity loans.

Many lenders consider equity loans excellent tools for asset/liability management primarily because many of these loans are variable rate. Finally, these loans are the safest loans a lender can make. Of all the major types of loans a mortgage lender can make, the loan with the lowest rate of delinquency is the home equity line of credit. This is discussed in greater detail later in this chapter.

For the reasons mentioned, many lenders consider equity loans to be quite important to them. As a result, the competition for equity loans is quite intense. If sufficient equity exists, some mortgage lenders will automatically approve a borrower for an equity loan when they approve that borrower for a first-mortgage loan. This is a strategy that all mortgage lenders should consider since it allows for the equity loan to be made at little or no additional expense.

Consumers' Choice

Equity loans are very popular with consumers for a number of reasons. Probably the most important reason is that the interest on the loan (with some limitations) can be deducted on the borrower's income tax return. In fact, the modern equity loan market really began to thrive after the 1986 tax law change, which phased out the deduction of interest for consumer loans. Basically (with a few limitations), the interest of an equity loan up to $100,000 can be deducted as long as the loan does not exceed the original purchase price of the home.

Consumers are also attracted to equity loans, especially the home equity line of credit, because they can write themselves a loan (up to the maximum line) at any time. This takes away the uncertainty that many consumers feel when applying for a loan.

After the cyclical low interest rates of 2002–2003, when 30-year fixed-rate mortgages were offered for as low as 5.50 percent, equity loans should experience dramatic growth in future years. The reason is that once consumers have locked in a low rate on their first mortgage, they are hesitant to refinance it when they need additional funds. Instead, they will turn to an equity loan for those additional funds.

Types of Collateral

Both the closed-end and open-end lines of credit are usually secured by a person's single-family dwelling. Initially, all equity loans were so secured. Recently, the type of collateral that lenders accept has begun to evolve. Many lenders today will accept condominiums and cooperatives as well as second and vacation homes as collateral. A few lenders will also allow the use of residential rental property as collateral, but if rental property is used as collateral, it will usually be at a higher interest rate.

Closing Equity Loans

These loans are typically closed by the lender. By closing these loans internally, a lender saves the cost of paying an attorney or title company. The documentation for equity loans is not extensive, and a competent loan officer, with minimal training, can handle the closing of these loans.

Underwriting Equity Loans

Both types of equity loans can be underwritten using the same procedures and ratios. The only real difference between the two loan types should be that one is a closed-end and the other is an open-end line of credit. Of course, the payment method is different for the two loans, as is discussed later. But most lenders use the same debt-to-income ratio for both loans. The average debt-to-income ratio (for all debts, including the equity loan) used by most lenders is 42 percent. Some lenders will allow this ratio to be as high as 50 percent. When calculating the ratio for the HELOC loan, it is based on a payment necessary to repay the maximum draw on the line. The debt-to-income ratio used for both of these loans is higher than the one used for first mortgages, but the use of this higher ratio is justified by the credit standards of the typical equity borrower and the very low delinquency rates for these equity loans.

When lenders underwrite equity loans, they use a different approach than that used for first-mortgage loans, for which many of the requirements are dictated by the secondary mortgage market. Although equity loans can be sold in the secondary market, few are because lenders very much prefer to keep these loans in their own portfolios. As a result, most lenders do not attempt to follow secondary market requirements when making these loans. For example, instead of using the Verification of Employment to verify income and employment, many lenders use the consumer's pay stub (covering 30 days) for such verification. The credit report used for these loans is a typical consumer credit report (costing a dollar or two) and is not the more expensive Residential Mortgage Credit Report. Other verifications, such as a valuation method and title searches, are discussed in the following sections.

In order to underwrite and process equity loans quickly, most mortgage lenders use credit scores or a combination of credit scores and personal judgments to approve loan applications. The ever-growing popularity of credit scores has led some lenders to use them as a shortcut for approving applicants with high scores.

Depending on the size of a mortgage lender, equity applications can be approved at the main office, a regional office, or a branch. Because these are relatively simple loans to underwrite and process, it appears that the strategy producing results the fastest is to allow the branches, if they are properly staffed, to handle these loans.

Documentation

Unlike first-mortgage loans, for which most of the loan documents are derived from the secondary market, lenders normally develop equity loan documents themselves. The secondary market does have a security form and note that can be used for closed-end second mortgages, but the secondary market does not have a form for open-end loans. Many mortgage forms companies can supply the required documents or a lender can request these documents from a local attorney. It is critical that a lender be very careful in developing these documents since each state has unique laws governing equity loans.

	Closed-End Loans	Open-End Lines of Credit	TABLE 18-1

List of Documents Typically Required for Closed-End and Open-End Lines of Credit — **TABLE 18-1**

	Closed-End Loans	Open-End Lines of Credit
Any state disclosures	x	x
Application	x	x
ARM disclosures	x	
Closed-end mortgage	x	
Closed-end note	x	
Commitment letter	x	x
Credit report	x	x
Final TIL	x	
First mortgagee letter		x
Good Faith Estimate of Closing Costs	x	
Hazard insurance with loss payee	x	x
HUD-1A	x	
Initial HELOC disclosure		x
Notice of Right to Appraisal	x	x
Notice of Right to Rescission	x	x
Open-end mortgage		x
Open-end note		x
Payoff letters (if needed)	x	x
Pay stub (income verification)	x	x
Some form of valuation	x	x
Standard flood determination	x	x
Title search (or title insurance)	x	x
Underwriting worksheet	x	x
When Your Home Is on the Line		x

Keys to Success

Because the competition for equity loans is so intense, lenders must be aggressive in two areas if they want to attract consumers for their loans. The two keys to success for a lender's equity loans are product design and marketing. *Product design* refers to how the loan product is structured, including the interest rate and fees. *Marketing* simply means that lenders have to use as many means as practical to communicate why their equity loans are better than the competition's. Both areas (discussed in more detail later) are equally important, and usually one without the other leads to low acceptance by consumers.

Closed-End Second Mortgages

The so-called traditional equity loan, often called a second mortgage, is a closed-end loan whereby the borrower is approved for a certain dollar amount that is advanced all at once and is repaid on an amortized basis over a fixed term. This loan is called closed-end because, as payments are made, those funds cannot automatically be borrowed again. These loans have been around for centuries, although not all depositary institutions could make these loans until fairly recently. For many years, the largest supplier of these loans was finance companies. During the Great Depression, many of the real estate loans that became delinquent were second mortgages. Because of the high delinquency rate on these early second mortgages, lenders were very hesitant to grant these loans for many years.

All Mortgage Lenders Now Offer Closed-End Loans

The market for these loans changed dramatically after the 1986 tax law change that phased out consumer credit deductions. Today, all classifications of mortgage lenders offer this loan. In today's society, when consumers want to buy an automobile, take an extended vacation, or repay outstanding credit card debt, they often turn to equity loans. For many consumers, that equity loan is a closed-end mortgage. Such loans are attractive to a segment of society that wants the discipline of being required to make a principal and interest payment every month and to others who want the security of a fixed interest rate. For these consumers, the closed-end second mortgage is the type of equity loan that is most attractive.

Closed-End Second as a Fixed-Rate Product

A closed-end second mortgage can be either fixed rate or variable rate. Most lenders (approximately 75 percent) offer the loan as a fixed-rate product to distinguish it from the variable-rate home equity line of credit. Since a line of credit is usually variable rate, the closed-end loan is to serve those consumers who want a fixed-rate product.

Product Design

Because the closed-end loan has been around for a long time, the product is well developed. Most lenders offer basically the same product as other lenders, the only difference being the interest rate, loan to value, or the type of real estate offered as security. To repeat, the characteristics of this loan are as follows:

- It is a closed-end loan.
- The entire loan is advanced at one time.
- It is for a fixed period of time.
- Payment is sufficient for the loan to be self-amortizing.

All lenders offer these loans with 5- and 10-year terms, and a few extend the term to 15 years. Of course, these loans legally can be for any period of time up to the maximum term for a mortgage under state law. Many lenders charge consumers closing costs for this loan, although some lenders are starting to pick up some or all of these costs.

Home Equity Line of Credit

In direct contrast to the closed-end equity loan, which varies little from one lender to another, the home equity line of credit (HELOC) gives a lender the opportunity to be inventive. Because the competition for HELOC loans is so intense, a lender should review the terms and features of its HELOC at least annually to ensure that the loan product is still attractive to consumers.

Some mortgage lenders have recently tried to entice consumers to their HELOC by offering various incentives, such as free airline tickets or no closing costs, and a few lenders were even "buying" balances ("transfer $20,000, get a 50-basis-point bonus, which equals $100 paid at closing"). The features that a lender can vary to make its loan product different from other lenders is discussed later. But some features should not be changed.

HELOCs Should Use Variable Rates

Some features of a HELOC, such as the type of interest calculation, should not differ from one lender to another. Practically all lenders offer the HELOC with a variable rate. It really does not make sense for a lender to allow consumers to borrow funds in the future at a rate that is fixed today. Interest rates in general could skyrocket two or three years in the future, and to allow a consumer to borrower money at that time at rates set two or three years in the past is not advisable.

Some mortgage lenders have devised a means for letting part of the line of credit carry a fixed rate. These lenders allow the consumer to lock in at a fixed rate a portion of the line that is tied directly to a single advance. For example, if a consumer with a $50,000 line of credit buys a $25,000 automobile and uses the HELOC to pay for it, the lender could allow that particular $25,000 advance to carry a fixed rate, while the rest of the line remains variable rate. Treating part of the line at one rate while the remainder of the line is variable requires a sophisticated data-processing system.

Index and Margin

Similar to other variable-rate loans, the interest rate for a HELOC is calculated by adding the index and margin together. The index that most lenders use (over 85 per-cent) is the average prime rate as reported in the *Wall Street Journal* and other news-papers. Other indices used include the three- and six-month Treasury bill yields. A lender should not use its own internal cost of funds as an index; in fact, many lenders are prohibited from using this index.

Some lenders have considered other indices because they believe the prime rate is too volatile, as evidenced by its progression from a high of 9.50 percent in December 2000 to a low of 4.50 percent in December 2001. The prime rate can indeed be volatile, although it has also been stable for years at a time. Despite its volatility, the general public is accus-tomed to using it as the index for HELOCs, so lenders should continue to do so.

The amount of the margin used to calculate the interest rate depends on what the lender wants the interest rate to be. For many lenders, the margin today is a negative figure. If a lender wants to advertise that its HELOC has a rate of 50 basis points below prime, the doc-umentation for the loan will have to state that the margin is minus 50 basis points.

Introductory Rate

The vast majority of mortgage lenders believe they must offer the consumer a low introductory rate, or, as it is sometimes called, a "teaser rate," to initially attract them. This rate, which should be 50 to 100 basis points below the regular or fully adjusted rate, can be offered for 30, 60, 90, or 120 days. A few lenders actually apply the introductory rate for a full year. A review of local competitors can help determine how long the introductory rate should last to be attractive in the local market.

Tier Rates

The interest rate for a HELOC loan is often the same for loans up to a 90 percent loan to value. But the rate may be different for loans with higher loan to value. Other features that can produce a different, or tier, interest rate include the following:

- Type of collateral
- Credit risk
- Amount of the loan

An example of how a tier rate would be applied is when a consumer uses rental property as collateral, many lenders will charge at least a 1 percent higher rate for this type of collateral.

Maximum Loan to Value

When HELOCs first became popular after the 1986 tax law change, most lenders offered this loan with a maximum loan to value (LTV) of 80 percent, meaning that the maximum LTV for all mortgage debt secured by the real estate could not exceed 80 percent. Thus, if a property was appraised at $100,000 and had a $60,000 first mortgage, the maximum HELOC could be only $20,000.

As competition for these loans increased, lenders began offering higher and higher maximum LTV. At the present time, practically all lenders will lend up to 90 percent of appraised value. These lenders will probably suffer little increased risk of delinquency with this higher LTV unless the nation experiences a serious economic event that depresses real estate values.

On the other hand, those lenders that are willing to lend up to 100 percent of value are taking a much greater risk. To address this risk but still be able to advertise that they will lend up to 100 percent of appraised value, many of these lenders limit the dollar amount of the HELOC loan if the LTV is 100 percent. For example, the lender may limit the dollar amount of a 100 percent LTV loan to $60,000. Since the vast majority of houses appraise for much more than that, the actual LTV is not 100 percent.

Term

Practically all HELOCs consist of two periods: a draw period and a repayment period. A few lenders offer these two periods as one concurrent period, but this type of HELOC is disappearing fast as consumers select loans with the two separate periods. The *draw period* is that time within which a consumer can draw on the line of credit. This draw period usually ranges from 5 to 10 years, although it can be for any period up to the maximum period for a mortgage loan in a particular state. During this period,

Figure 18-1 / Sample Home Equity Line of Credit Disclosure Statement

HOME EQUITY LINE OF CREDIT DISCLOSURE

This disclosure contains important information about our **Home Equity Line of Credit (EQUITY LOAN)**. You should read it carefully and keep a copy for your records.

Availability of Terms: All of the terms described below are subject to change. If these terms change (other than the ANNUAL PERCENTAGE RATE) and you decide, as a result, not to enter into an agreement with us, you are entitled to a refund of any fees that you paid to us or anyone else in connection with your application.

Security Interest: We will take a mortgage on your home. You could lose your home if you do not meet the obligations in your agreement with us.

Possible Actions: We can terminate your line, require you to pay us the entire outstanding balance on payment, and charge you certain fees, if:

(1) you engage in fraud or material misrepresentation in connection with the plan; (2) you do not meet the repayment terms of this plan; or (3) your action or inaction adversely affects the collateral or our rights in the collateral.

We can refuse to make additional extensions of credit or reduce your credit line for:

(1) any reasons mentioned above; (2) the value of the dwelling securing the line declines significantly below its appraised value for purposes of the line; (3) we reasonably believe that you will not be able to meet the repayment requirements due to a material change in your financial circumstances; (4) you are in default of a material obligation of the plan; (5) government action prevents us from imposing the **ANNUAL PERCENTAGE RATE** provided for under this plan; (6) the priority of our security interest is adversely affected by government action to the extent that the value of the security interest is less than 120% of the credit line; (7) a regulatory agency has notified us that continued advances would constitute an unsafe and unsound business practice; or (8) the maximum **ANNUAL PERCENTAGE RATE** is reached.

Minimum Payment Requirements: You can obtain advances for 10 years. This period is called the "draw period." During the draw period, you can repay interest only; however, **principal payments in any amount can be made at any time.** Your required minimum monthly payment will be 1% of the interest accrued on the outstanding balance as of the last business day of the previous month.

After the draw period ends, you will no longer be able to obtain credit advances and must pay the outstanding balance over 180 monthly statement periods (the "repayment period"). During the repayment period, payments will be due monthly. Your minimum monthly payment will equal 1/180th of the balance that was outstanding at the end of the draw period PLUS all the financial charges that have accrued on the remaining balance.

Minimum Payment Example: If you made the minimum payments (of interest only) over a 10-year period (the draw period) on an original advance of $10,000, at an annual rate of 10.00%, you would make 120 (estimated) monthly payments of $84.93 (interest only—estimated) leaving a (principal) balance of $10,000 (estimated at the end) of the draw period.

If that $10,000 is outstanding at the beginning of the repayment period (the end of the draw period), then the monthly payment during the repayment period would be 1/180th of the initial balance plus monthly accrued interest (assuming a 10% **ANNUAL PERCENTAGE RATE**) resulting in monthly payments between $137.75 (estimated) and $56.02 (estimated).

| Figure 18-1 | Sample Home Equity Line of Credit Disclosure Statement |

Fees and Charges: We do not charge any fees to open and maintain a line of credit.

To open and maintain a line of credit, you must carry hazard insurance and flood insurance, if applicable, on the property that secures your loan. The insurance coverage must be a least equal to the maximum amount available under your credit limit, plus the amount of any prior mortgage on the property at the time your line of credit is opened.

You may have to pay certain fees to third parties (unless these fees are paid for by the credit union) to open a line of credit. If you ask, we will provide you with an itemization of the fees you will have to pay to third parties.

Refundability of Fees: If you decide not to enter into this plan within three days of receiving this disclosure and the Home Equity brochure, you are entitled to a refund of any fee you may have already paid.

Transaction Limitations: The minimum credit advance that you can receive is $500.

Tax Deductibility: You should consult a tax advisor regarding the deductibility of interest and charges for the plan.

Variable Rate Features: This plan has a variable rate feature and the **ANNUAL PERCENTAGE RATE** (corresponding to the periodic rate) and the minimum payment can change as a result. The **ANNUAL PERCENTAGE RATE** includes interest and no other costs.

The **ANNUAL PERCENTAGE RATE** is based on the value of an index. The index is the Prime Rate published in the *Wall Street Journal*. When a range of rates has been published, the highest rate is used. We then add a margin to the value of the index.

Ask us for the current index value, margin, and **ANNUAL PERCENTAGE RATE**. After you open a plan, rate information will be provided on periodic statements that we send you.

Rate Changes: The **ANNUAL PERCENTAGE RATE** can change monthly. There is no limit on the amount by which the rate changes in any one-year period. The maximum **ANNUAL PERCENTAGE RATE** that can apply during the plan is 18%. There is no minimum rate.

Maximum Rate and Payment Examples: If you had an outstanding balance of $10,000, the minimum monthly payment at the maximum **ANNUAL PERCENTAGE RATE** of 18% would be $147.95. The maximum **ANNUAL PERCENTAGE RATE** could be reached during the first month. If $10,000 was outstanding at the beginning of the repayment period, the maximum monthly payment during the repayment period would be 1/180th of the balance plus accrued interest (assuming an 18% APR) resulting in payments between $203.50 and $56.38.

Historical Examples: The following table shows how the **ANNUAL PERCENTAGE RATE** and the minimum payments for a single $10,000 credit advance would have changed based on changes in the index over the last 15 years. The index values are from January of each year. While only on payment amount per year is shown, payments would have varied during each year of the draw period. The table assumes that no additional credit advances were taken, that only the minimum payments were made and that the rate remained constant during each year. It does not necessarily indicate how the index of your payment(s) would change in the future.

Figure 18-1	Sample Home Equity Line of Credit Disclosure Statement (continued)

☐ Draw Period   ☐ Repayment Period   **Int. Only H.E.L.P.**

Year	Index (%)	Margin* (%)	Annual Percentage Rate	Minimum Monthly Payment
1987	7.50	1.00	8.500	69.86
1988	8.75	1.00	9.750	80.14
1989	10.50	1.00	11.500	94.52
1990	10.00	1.00	11.000	90.41
1991	9.50	1.00	10.500	86.30
1992	6.50	1.00	7.500	61.64
1993	6.00	1.00	7.000	57.53
1994	6.00	1.00	7.000	57.53
1995	8.50	1.00	9.500	78.08
1996	8.50	1.00	9.500	78.08
1997	8.25	0	8.250	97.04
1998	8.50	0	8.250	97.04
1999	7.75	−.50	8.250	97.04
2000	9.00	−.50	8.250	97.04
2001	9.00	−.50	8.250	97.04

I acknowledge receipt of the booklet *When Your Home Is On The Line*, and the specific disclosures of the bank's HELOC.

_____ Date_____

© REMOC ASSOCIATES, LTD.

consumers can draw on their lines up to the amount they are approved for and, as they repay that advance, they can draw that amount again and any unused amount in their line. When the draw period ends, the ability to draw on the line ends. Any amount that is owed at this point is either due as a balloon payment or, more commonly, is repaid in the repayment period.

The *repayment period* is that period of time, usually 10 to 15 years, when the borrower must repay all money owed at the end of the draw period. The payment during the repayment period is principal and interest, thus is a fully amortized loan. The interest rate during the repayment period can be either fixed rate or variable rate. Thus, if a borrower owes $10,000 at the end of the draw period and the repayment period is 15 years, the $10,000 would be divided by 180 repay periods and the principal payment would be $55.56 per period. The interest payment that is combined with the principal payment would depend on whether the HELOC is fixed or variable and what the interest rate is at the time the payment is calculated.

Payment Method

Lenders have many options for how to establish the consumer's minimum monthly payment during the draw period. It is important to realize that consumers can make any payment they choose as long as it is at least the minimum. A consumer can pay off the entire balance with their first payment if they so select. The major decision a lender has to make is the amount it will require as a minimum payment: principal and interest or interest only. For many years, the majority of lenders believed they had to require some principal reduction each month to prevent default. This belief has changed dramatically with the development of interest-only payments.

Interest-Only Payments

The vast majority of lenders (over 75 percent) today offer interest-only payments. This interest-only payment is, of course, used only during the draw period. During the repayment period, the loan is a self-amortizing loan with principal and interest due each month.

The reason so many lenders have converted to interest only is the substantial difference between an interest-only payment and one that requires principal payments during the draw period. Many lenders have an 18 percent maximum interest rate on their HELOCs; thus, to avoid the possibility of negative amortization, they require a monthly payment that produces enough to add up to 18 percent interest if necessary. For example, if a borrower owes $10,000, the monthly payment with a principal reduction requires a minimum payment of 1 and $^1/_2$ percent of the loan amount, or, in this case, $150, to always collect enough money to meet an interest rate of 18 percent ($10,000 × 18 percent = $1,800, and 12 monthly payments of $150 = $1,800).

If a competing lender offers interest-only payments, and the interest rate on its HELOC is 6 percent, the difference of $100 in the minimum monthly payment ($10,000 × 6 percent = $600 divided by 12 months = $50 monthly payment) is so obvious that most consumers will go to the competitor.

Other Payment Methods

Some lenders amortize the amount owed over the remaining life of the loan (draw period and repayment period) to establish the minimum payment. A few lenders use a payment calculation method whereby the amount of the payment is established by a range of outstanding debt. For example, if the balance is between $1,000 and $3,000, the minimum payment is $75. Consumers no longer are attracted to this type of payment calculation.

Whichever way a lender establishes the payment, it should establish a minimum payment plus whatever else it wants to collect. For example, the minimum payment may be $50 or interest only, whichever is greater.

Adjustment Periods

The *adjustment period* refers to how often the interest rate could change. Most lenders have a monthly adjustment period, with a few using a daily period. Lenders should strive to use an adjustment period that is at least monthly. If the adjustment period is longer than one month, the asset/liability advantage of a variable-rate loan is diminished.

Methods of Access

Mortgage lenders have devised many ways for consumers to access their lines of credit. Today, the most common way is by check, and it is the way that 90 percent of consumers access their lines of credit. On the other hand, the method that is increasing in use very rapidly is for consumers to access their line by plastic, either credit card or debit card. It appears clear that this way could be the major access method in the future since it is so convenient for the consumer. A little over a third of lenders already offer this access method, but only about 10 percent of consumers are currently using this method.

Other access methods for HELOC include the following:

- Overdraft for regular checking
- Telephone transfer to regular checking
- Personal withdrawal
- Automated teller machines (ATMs)

Closing Costs and Other Fees

Offering to pay all the closing costs is one of the devices that lenders use to get consumers to consider a HELOC loan rather than some other loan. This practice has become so common that the lender that tries to pass on some of the closing costs to the consumer has a hard time in the marketplace. Depending on the state, closing costs for a HELOC loan generally run between $200 and $300. Of course, if a state or locality charges a mortgage tax, the cost is much higher.

Appraisals

The way lenders keep the closing costs so low is that they use alternative methods to document or close the loan. For instance, rather than use a full-blown appraisal, lenders will use tax assessments, existing appraisals if not dated, and a drive-by appraisal, if any new appraisal is actually needed. Some lenders may even make the loan without an appraisal if the loan to value is perceived to be low (say, below 60 percent).

Title Insurance or Title Search?

Many lenders do not require title insurance for a HELOC if the first mortgage has title insurance. In this case, the lender simply has a "title update" or search done, which involves a professional checking the public record to see whether any additional security interest has been filed. Other lenders require title insurance only if the HELOC is in a first-lien position or if the HELOC is for more than a certain dollar amount (say, $50,000).

Other fees that a lender has to absorb include a consumer credit report, flood determination, and recording fees. Again, for most lenders, these fees add up to $200 or $300. Many lenders protect themselves against consumers who refinance often by requiring the consumer sign an affidavit at closing that states the consumer will pay back the closing costs paid by the lender if he or she refinances the loan with another lender within two years.

Annual Fee

The only other fee that lenders sometimes charge consumers is an annual fee for keeping the line open. This annual fee can be $25 or $50 per year. The basic concept behind these fees is that if a consumer is not going to use the line, the consumer will not pay the fee, and thus the lender can close the line.

Traditional Home Equity Line of Credit Product — TABLE 18-2

Feature	Typical Arrangement
Index for interest calculation	Average prime rate
Margin for interest calculation	Zero to minus 50 basis points
Introductory rate	Minus 100 basis points below fully adjusted rate
Frequency of adjustment	Monthly
Draw period	5 or 10 years
Repayment period	10 or 15 years
Closing fees	$0
Annual fees	$50
Maximum loan to value	90 percent in most markets; 100 percent in some markets
Caps on annual increases	None
Maximum line	$100,000 is average, but some lenders have no limits
Minimum line	$10,000
Payment (monthly)	Draw period: $50 or interest only, whichever is greater Repayment period: $50 or principal and interest, whichever is greater
Access method	Check or credit card
Security	Primary residence; some lenders have added second homes and rentals
Underwriting	
• Debt ratio	40–45 percent
• Employment/income	Pay stub (tax returns if self-employed)
• Credit report	Consumer credit report
• Data to establish value	Tax assessment, existing appraisal, drive-by appraisal
• Title	Title search usually; insurance if needed
• Flood determination	Always
• Hazard insurance	Always
Payment due date	Anytime, often twentieth of month

Periodic Statement

Truth in Lending requires mortgage lenders with a HELOC product to send out a periodic statement to each HELOC borrower. Basically, the statement looks like a credit card statement many consumers receive in the mail each month. The statement must be mailed or delivered for each billing cycle (but at least quarterly) that a loan has a balance of more than $1 or on which a finance charge has been imposed.

This statement must be mailed at least 14 days prior to any payment date or the end of any time period required to be disclosed in order for the consumer to avoid an additional finance or other charge. For this reason, many lenders have decided to make the payment date for HELOC different from other mortgage loans. Often the day selected is the twentieth of the month.

The periodic statement must contain the following information:

- Balance outstanding at the beginning of the billing cycle
- Identification of each credit transaction, including amount, date, and so forth
- Any credit to the account during the billing cycle, including the amount and date
- The periodic rate used to compute the finance charge, along with the range of balances to which it applies and the corresponding APR
- Balance to which a periodic rate was applied and any explanation as to how that balance was determined
- Amount of any finance charge added to an account during the billing cycle, using the term *finance charge* and itemizing the components of the finance charge
- APR equivalent to the total finance charge imposed during the billing cycle
- Amounts, itemized and identified by type, of any charge other than finance charges debited to the account
- Closing date of the billing cycle and the outstanding balance on that date
- Date by which the new balance may be paid to avoid additional finance charges
- Address for notification of billing errors

Marketing Equity Loans

As mentioned earlier in this chapter, the two keys for success in equity lending are the loan product design and marketing. This section discusses some of the techniques and tools that mortgage lenders have used that have resulted in successful marketing of these loans.

Marketing Plan

Probably the first requirement for successful marketing of any loan product is that the lender has a marketing plan for the loan product. One part of this plan should examine the medium to be used for advertising the product, while another part will provide a realistic budget to allow for success. The Consumer Bankers Association, in its yearly home equity study, concludes that lenders spend between $50 and $90 in marketing and advertising costs per equity loan actually made.

Understanding Your Market

An essential part of a marketing plan for an equity loan product is to understand what the competition is offering. Many lenders make the mistake of assuming they have to be concerned only with what local lenders are offering as equity loans. Of course, that is important, but these lenders must also consider what the national lenders are offering. Because these loans are so attractive, many of the national lenders (GMAC, General Electric Capital, Bank of America, Merrill Lynch) have attractive home equity products that are offered across the United States. In any locality, the best credits are going to be receiving solicitations for equity loans from these national lenders. Local lenders must understand what the national lenders are offering and have a loan product that is comparable.

Types of Media Used

Mortgage lenders have many options for getting the story of their equity loans out to the public. Most lenders use some combination of the following media:

- Statement stuffers
- Newspapers
- Direct mail
- Radio
- Telemarketing
- Television
- Outside billboards
- Magazines

Lenders often find that the effectiveness of the various media falls approximately in the order of this list. It is interesting to note that statement stuffers are one of the most effective but also one of the least expensive media. Newspapers are also effective but are quite expensive. Direct-mail pieces are effective for many lenders but are also quite expensive. Billboards are not generally effective except in some specific geographical areas where a large volume of traffic passes the billboard location.

Other tools that lenders use for marketing inside their places of business include the following:

- Banners in the branch offices
- "Tents" at teller windows
- Displays at loan officer desks
- Video displays
- Brochures

Discussion Points

1. Why are equity loans so popular with consumers?

2. Identify and discuss the keys for success from a mortgage lender's perceptive.

3. What are the important differences between a closed-end equity loan and a home equity line of credit (HELOC)?

4. What is the most popular method of repaying a HELOC? Why is this payment method so popular?

5. What is the periodic statement that is used with a HELOC? What information is contained in this statement?

A

Acceleration clause A clause in a security instrument that gives the lender the right to demand payment of the entire principal balance if a monthly payment is missed.

Acquisition cost In FHA lending, the total amount needed to complete the purchase of a home. Calculated by adding the sales price to the allowable closing costs, as determined by FHA. In construction lending, it is the cost to construct plus the amount to purchase the land (instead of land value). *See* Cost to construct.

Actual/actual (A/A) A type of remittance requiring the lender to remit to an investor only principal and interest payments actually collected from borrowers. *Compare with* Scheduled/Actual (S/A) and Scheduled/ Scheduled (S/S).

Adjustment date The date on which the interest rate changes for an ARM loan.

Adjustment period The period between adjustments for an ARM loan.

Advance commitment A written promise to make an investment or buy a loan or loans at some time in the future if specified conditions are met.

Amortization Repayment of a debt in equal installments of principal and interest, rather than interest-only payments.

Amortization schedule A timetable for the payment of a mortgage loan that shows the amount of each payment applied to interest and principal and shows the remaining balance after each payment is made.

Annual Percentage Rate (APR) The cost of a mortgage stated as a yearly rate. The APR includes interest, loan origination points, discount points, prepaid fees, mortgage insurance, and other fees that are required to be paid for credit to be granted. APR does not include appraisal fee, credit report costs, and some other third-party fees.

Appraisal A written analysis of the estimated value of a property prepared by a qualified appraiser.

Appraised value An opinion of value reached by a qualified appraiser on property to serve as security for a mortgage loan.

Assignment The transfer of a mortgage from one person to another.

Assumable mortgage A mortgage that can be assumed (i.e., taken over) by a buyer when a home is purchased.

AUS Automated underwriting system.

Automated valuation (AV) A method for determining the value of a property that relies on a statistical model, which analyzes various data. Not a traditional appraisal, AVs do not use the income or sales comparable approach and may or may not meet USPAP standards. They are sometimes used in conjunction with a property inspection to verify the condition of the property.

B

Balloon mortgage A mortgage that has level monthly payments that amortize the loan over a stated term (e.g., 30 years) but that provides for a lump sum payment to be due at the end of an earlier specified term (e.g., 5 years).

Basis point A basis point is one-hundredth of 1 percent interest; thus, 50 basis points equals one-half of 1 percent.

Best efforts A secondary mortgage market transaction for which a seller is obligated to deliver only those loans that actually close.

Biweekly payment mortgage A mortgage loan that requires payment of principal and interest every two weeks that equals half of a regular monthly payment. The resulting 26 (or 27) payments a year produce the equivalent of an additional month's payment each year, which greatly speeds the repayment of the loan.

Bridge loan A second mortgage that is secured by the borrower's present home (which is usually for sale) in a manner that allows the proceeds to be used for closing on a new house before the present home is sold.

Building permit   A document issued by the local government housing authority that certifies that proposed construction is legally acceptable according to the plans and specifications submitted.

Buydown   Money advanced by an individual (builder, seller, or borrower) to reduce the monthly payments for a home mortgage either during the entire term or for an initial period of years.

C

Cap   A provision of an ARM loan that limits how much an interest rate or payment can increase or decrease.

Capital market security   A financial instrument, including both debt and equity securities, with a maturity greater than one year. Those instruments with maturities of less than a year are traded in the money markets.

Capital markets   Markets (including informal markets as well as organized markets and exchanges) in which long-term funds in the form of mortgages, stocks, and bonds are bought and sold.

Cash delivery   The submission of a whole mortgage or a participation to an investor in exchange for cash rather than a mortgage-backed security.

Cash-out refinance   A refinance transaction in which the borrower obtains a loan for more than the amount owed on the existing mortgage (including the mortgage, subordinate financing, closing costs, points, etc.).

Certificate of Eligibility   A document issued by the federal government certifying a veteran's eligibility for a VA mortgage.

Certificate of Occupancy   A document issued by the local government housing authority that certifies a dwelling has been built according to local housing code and is legally ready for residential occupancy.

Chain of title   The history of all of the documents that transfer title to a specific piece of real property. A history starting with the earliest existing document and ending with the most recent.

Charge-off   The write-off of the portion of principal and interest due on a loan that is determined to be uncollectible.

Commitment   A written promise to make, insure, or buy a mortgage loan for a specified amount and on specified terms.

Commitment fee   Any fee paid by a borrower to a lender for the lender's promise to lend money at a specified date in the future. The lender may or may not expect to fund the commitment.

Condominium   Real estate in which individual owners own title to a part of the whole (e.g., a unit in a building) and an undivided interest in the common areas.

Conduits   Entities that issue mortgage-backed securities backed by mortgages, which were originated by another, probably one or more of the traditional originators.

Construction loan   A short-term, interim loan for financing the cost of construction.

Construction loan advance   A partial disbursement of mortgage loan funds by a lender to the borrower after verifying a portion of the home construction has been completed. Borrower and lender normally agree to an advance schedule beforehand to formalize the amounts and requirements for each advance.

Construction/permanent loan   A type of mortgage loan that includes terms and conditions for both a construction phase (to build the proposed house) and a repayment phase (to amortize the loan to the maturity date).

Conventional loan   A mortgage loan neither insured by FHA nor guaranteed by VA.

Correspondent   A mortgage banker who services mortgage loans as a representative or agent for the owner of the mortgage or for the investor. Also applies to the mortgage banker's role as originator of mortgage loans for an investor.

Cost of Funds Index   An index that is used to determine interest rate changes for some ARMs. It represents the weighted-average cost of savings, borrowings, and advances of members of the 11th District of the Federal Home Loan Bank of San Francisco.

Cost to construct   The amount needed to complete the construction of a home. Calculated by adding documented values for the land, labor, materials, permits, fees, and all other aspects of home construction.

Coupon rate   The annual interest rate on a debt. The coupon rate on a mortgage is the contract rate stated in the mortgage note. The coupon rate on a mortgage security is the rate stated on the face of the security, not the rate of the mortgages in the pool that backs the security.

Credit report   A record of a person's open and repaid debts.

Credit score   A numerical value that summarizes a borrower's credit risk at a given point in time. Credit scores are calculated using statistical methods that evaluate certain information that has proved to be indicative of loan performance.

Custodial account   A bank account that the servicer of a mortgage must establish to hold funds on behalf of the borrower and investor.

Custodian   Usually a commercial bank that holds for safekeeping mortgages and related documents backing an MBS. A custodian may be required to examine and certify documents.

D

Debt/income ratios   Underwriting ratios used to qualify mortgage applicants. Three common ratios used are for housing expense, total debt, and owner-occupant. These monthly amounts are divided by the monthly income used for qualification.

Deed   A legal document that conveys title to real estate.

Default   Failure to make mortgage payments when due or to comply with other requirements of a security agreement.

Delinquency   An instance in which payment on a mortgage loan has not been made by the due date.

Delivery   The sending of the loan documents to an investor.

Discount   In loan obligations, it refers to an amount withheld from loan proceeds by a lender. In secondary market sales, it is the amount by which the sale price of a note is less than its face value. In both instances, the purpose of a discount is to adjust the yield upward, either in lieu of interest or in addition to interest. The rate or amount of discount depends on money market conditions, the credit of the borrower, and the rate and terms of the note.

Discount point   *See* Point.

Dower   The rights of a widow in the property of her husband at his death.

Downpayment   The difference between the sales price of real estate and the mortgage amount.

E

Equity   A homeowner's financial interest in real estate established by the difference between the market value of the property and the amount owed on its mortgage.

Escrow account   Funds held in a separate account by a legally agreed upon party that will be used to pay a third party at a later date. Mortgage lending uses escrow accounts for construction, property tax, and hazard, flood, or mortgage insurance.

Escrow analysis   The periodic examination of escrow accounts to determine whether current monthly deposits will provide sufficient funds to pay taxes, insurance, and other bills when due.

Escrow payment   That portion of a mortgagor's monthly payment held by the lender to pay for taxes, hazard insurance, mortgage insurance, lease payments, and other items as they become due. Known as *impounds* or *reserves* in some states.

F

Fallout   Loans that fail to close because the borrower decides not to take the loan (borrower fallout); also loans that fail to sell in the secondary market because an investor reneges on a commitment (investor fallout).

Fallout risk   The risk incurred by the lender that a borrower will not close on a loan after filing an application or that an investor will back out on a contract to purchase the loan.

Fannie Mae   *See* Federal National Mortgage Association (FNMA).

Federal Home Loan Mortgage Corporation (FHLMC)   A private corporation originally authorized by Congress to provide secondary mortgage market support for conventional mortgages. It can buy all types of mortgage loans today. It holds loans in its portfolio and also sells participation certificates secured by pools of conventional mortgage loans. Popularly known as Freddie Mac.

Federal Housing Administration (FHA) A division of HUD. Its main activity is the insuring of residential mortgage loans made by private lenders. It sets standards for construction and underwriting. FHA does not lend money or plan or construct housing.

Federal National Mortgage Association (FNMA) A privately owned corporation created by Congress to support the secondary mortgage market. It purchases and sells residential mortgages insured by the FHA or guaranteed by the VA as well as conventional home mortgages; also issues mortgage-backed securities. Popularly known as Fannie Mae.

Fee option An option allowing lenders to pay a one-time commitment fee in exchange for a reduction in Fannie Mae's required yield. Also called *fee/yield tradeoff*.

Fee simple The greatest possible interest a person can have in real estate.

Fixed-rate mortgage A mortgage in which the interest rate does not change during the entire term of the loan.

FHLMC *See* Federal Home Loan Mortgage Corporation (FHLMC).

Float The time between a lender's collection of payments from borrowers and the remittance of those funds to an investor.

FNMA *See* Federal National Mortgage Association (FNMA).

Forbearance The act of refraining from taking legal action despite the fact that a mortgage is in arrears. It is usually granted only when a mortgagor makes a satisfactory arrangement by which the arrears will be paid at a future date.

Foreclosure An authorized procedure taken by a mortgagee or lender under the terms of a mortgage or deed of trust for the purpose of having the property sold and the proceeds applied to the payment of a defaulted debt.

Forward delivery The delivery of mortgages or mortgage-backed securities to satisfy cash or future market transactions of an earlier date.

Forward sale An agreement in which a lender agrees to sell to an investor a specified amount of mortgages or securities at an agreed-upon price at a specified future date. A mandatory delivery commitment is a type of forward sale.

Freddie Mac *See* Federal Home Loan Mortgage Corporation (FHLMC).

Funding The disbursement of funds to complete a transaction. In mortgage finance, it occurs when the lender provides money to close a real estate sale and when an investor transfers funds to the lender to purchase a mortgage loan.

Futures contract A contract purchased on an organized market (e.g., Chicago Board of Trade) either for the purchase of a GNMA certificate at a specified price on a specified future date or for the sale of the certificate at a specified future date.

G

General contractor (GC) The person (or entity) legally responsible for the proposed construction on a residential property. Can perform all the work or use subcontractors to complete it.

GNMA-backed bond A mortgage-backed bond using GNMA Certificates as the collateral rather than the individual mortgages.

GNMA Futures Market A regulated central market in which standardized contracts for the future delivery of GNMA securities are traded.

GNMA mortgage-backed securities Securities guaranteed by GNMA that are issued by mortgage bankers, commercial banks, savings and loan associations, savings banks, and other institutions. The GNMA security holder is protected by the "full faith and credit of the U.S. government." GNMA securities are backed by FHA, VA, or FmHA mortgages.

Government National Mortgage Association (GNMA) On September 1, 1968, Congress enacted legislation to partition FNMA into two continuing corporate entities. GNMA assumed responsibility for the special assistance loan program and the management and liquidation function of the older FNMA. Also, GNMA administers the mortgage-backed securities program, which channels new sources of funds into residential financing through the sale of privately issued securities carrying a GNMA guaranty. Popularly known as Ginnie Mae.

GSEs Government-sponsored enterprises (e.g., Fannie Mae and Freddie Mac).

Guaranty fee A guarantor's fee for guaranteeing to an investor the timely payment of principal and interest from all mortgages underlying a mortgage-backed security.

H

Hazard insurance Insurance coverage on real estate that compensates the owner for physical damage to a property from fire, wind, or other hazards.

Home equity line of credit (HELOC) A mortgage loan, often in a second position, that allows the borrower to obtain multiple advances of funds up to an approved amount. As the funds are repaid, they can be advanced again during the draw period.

I

Index A number used to compute the interest rate on a variable-rate mortgage (ARM loan or HELOC). The index is added to a margin to obtain the interest rate.

Initial interest rate The original interest rate on a variable-rate mortgage. Sometimes referred to as a *teaser rate*.

Inventory The loans a lender has closed but has not yet delivered to an investor.

Investor The holder of a mortgage or the permanent lender for whom a mortgage lender services the loan. Any person or institution investing in mortgages.

J

Joint tenancy A form of co-ownership that gives each tenant equal interest and equal rights in the property.

Judicial foreclosure A type of foreclosure proceeding used in some states that is handled as a civil lawsuit.

Jumbo loan A loan that exceeds the secondary mortgage market's mortgage amount limits. Also called a *nonconforming loan*.

L

Late charge The penalty (usually 5 percent) a mortgagor must pay when a payment is made a stated number of days (usually 25) after a due date.

Legal description A property description that is sufficient to locate and identify real estate.

Lien A legally enforceable claim against real estate that must be paid when the property is sold.

Loan A sum of money borrowed that is expected to be repaid at a stated rate of interest.

Loan constant The yearly percentage of interest that remains the same over the life of an amortized loan based on the monthly payment in relation to the principal originally loaned.

Loan submission A package of pertinent papers and documents regarding specific property or properties. It is delivered to a prospective lender for review and consideration for the purpose of making a mortgage loan.

Lock-in A written agreement between a lender and an applicant in which the lender guarantees a specified interest rate if the loan closes within a specified period of time.

M

Mandatory delivery commitment An agreement that a lender will deliver loans or securities to an investor by a certain date at an agreed-upon price and yield. *Compare with* Optional commitment.

Margin The number of basis points a lender adds to an index to determine the interest rate of an adjustable-rate mortgage.

Marketable title A title that may not be completely clear, but has only minor objections that a well-informed and prudent seller would accept.

Mechanic's lien A lien placed on the property by someone who has performed work on it and who has not been paid. Like a mortgage lien, it is recorded. In most states, this lien will take priority over a prior mortgage lien if recorded within a certain time from when the work was performed on the property.

Modification The act of changing any of the terms of a mortgage.

MORNET Fannie Mae's communications network that enables customers to use a data terminal, personal computer, or mainframe to send and receive documents and reports electronically.

Mortgage   A conveyance of an interest in real property given as security for the payment of a debt.

Mortgage-backed securities (MBSs)   Bond-type investment securities representing an undivided interest in a pool of mortgages or trust deeds. Income from the underlying mortgage is used to pay off the securities. *See* GNMA mortgage-backed securities.

Mortgage banker   A firm or individual active in the field of mortgage banking. Mortgage bankers, as local representatives of regional or national institutional lenders, act as correspondents between lenders and borrowers. Mortgage bankers need to borrow the funds they lend out.

Mortgage banking   The packaging of mortgage loans secured by real property to be sold to a permanent investor with servicing retained for the life of the loan for a fee. The origination, sale, and servicing of mortgage loans by a firm or individual. The investor-correspondent system is the foundation of the mortgage-banking industry.

Mortgage broker   A firm or individual bringing the borrower and lender together and receiving a commission. A mortgage broker does not retain servicing.

Mortgage company   A private corporation (sometimes called a mortgage banker) whose principal activity is the origination and servicing of mortgage loans that are sold to other financial institutions.

Mortgage discount   The difference between the principal amount of a mortgage and the amount for which it actually sells. Sometimes called *points*, *loan brokerage fee*, or *new loan fee*. The discount is computed on the amount of the loan, not the sale price.

Mortgage insurance (MI)   Default insurance for the lender for a certain percentage of the original loan amount. Mortgage insurance premiums are usually paid by the borrower with monthly payments, although other arrangements are used. Most common forms are FHA, private mortgage insurance, and self-insurance by the lender.

Mortgagee   The lender in a transaction whereby real estate is being taken as security for the debt.

Mortgagor   The borrower in a transaction whereby real estate is being taken as security for the debt.

N

Negative amortization   An increase in mortgage debt that occurs when the monthly payment is not large enough to cover the entire principal and interest due. The amount of the shortfall (usually interest) is added to the remaining balance to create the negative amortization. *See* Amortization.

Negotiated transaction   A secondary market transaction in which the terms and conditions are negotiated between the lender and the investor. These transactions do not fall under any of the investor's standard loan programs.

Note   A legal document that obligates a mortgagor to repay a mortgage loan at a stated interest rate during a specified period of time.

O

Optional commitment   A commitment that gives the lender the option to sell loans to an investor under specified terms. The lender pays a nonrefundable fee to obtain the commitment but, because delivery is not mandatory, suffers no penalty for not fulfilling the commitment. *Compare with* Mandatory delivery commitment.

Origination   The process of originating mortgages. Solicitation may be from individual borrowers, builders, or brokers. Origination is the process by which the mortgage lender brings into being a mortgage secured by real property.

Origination fee   A fee or charge for the work involved in the evaluation, preparation, and submission of a proposed mortgage loan.

Originator   A person who solicits builders, brokers, and others to obtain applications for mortgage loans.

P

Pair-off   A transaction whereby an investor allows a lender to "buy back" the mortgages it previously agreed to sell by means of a mandatory delivery commitment.

Par   The principal amount of a mortgage with no premium or discount.

Partial payment   A payment that is less than the scheduled monthly mortgage payment.

Participation certificate (PC)   Mortgage-backed security issued by FHLMC that consists of mortgages purchased from eligible sellers. Called a PC because seller retains some interest (5 or 10 percent) in the mortgages sold to FHLMC.

Participations   A mortgage made by one lender, known as the lead lender, in which one or more other lenders, known as participants, own a part interest, or a mortgage originated by two or more lenders.

Pass-through rate   The rate at which interest is paid to an investor for a mortgage. It is the lower of an investor's required yield or the mortgage interest rate after a minimum servicing fee has been deducted.

Pass-through security   A form of mortgage-backed bond for which the monthly collections on the mortgage pool are "passed through" to the investor.

Piggyback loans   A residential mortgage loan featuring a 75 or 80 percent LTV first mortgage and a 10, 15, or 20 percent LTV second mortgage that are both closed at the same time. As a result of this structure, the down-payment may be only 5 or 10 percent of the loan amount. This loan is structured this way so as to not require mortgage insurance.

Pipeline   The aggregate of loans in process for eventual sale in the secondary market. The term encompasses both loans that are in production and those that have been closed but have not yet been delivered to an investor.

PITI   Stands for principal, interest, taxes, and insurance.

Point   An amount equal to 1 percent of the principal amount of an investment or note. Loan discount points are a one-time charge assessed at closing by the lender to increase the yield on the mortgage loan to a competitive position with other types of investments.

Pool insurance   Mortgage insurance for the investor for a percentage of the original amount of a group (pool) of mortgage loans. The pool is usually securitized and sold in the secondary market.

Portfolio   Investments (including mortgages and mortgage securities) held by an individual or institution. In mortgage lending, the term variously refers to mortgages held by a lender prior to their sale in the secondary market, to MBSs held by lenders for investment purposes, and to loans that a lender continues to service for investors.

Portfolio mortgage   A loan that an originator places in its portfolio or that an investor purchases for cash and holds as an asset.

Preapproval   A formal commitment by a lender to an applicant for a period of time for a maximum loan amount. Usually provided to assist the applicant in searching for a property to purchase and may contain other conditions. Preapprovals are subject to essentially the same compliance regulations as formal (written) applications.

Premium   The amount, often stated as a percentage, paid in addition to the face value of a note or bond.

Prequalification   An informal meeting during which a lender provides a consumer with information on mortgage loan products, procedures, and underwriting guidelines. The lender may do limited financial counseling as well, but does not discourage a formal application from being completed or make a credit decision on a specific loan request (or give such an impression to the consumer).

Primary mortgage market   The market in which lenders originate mortgages by making direct loans to homebuyers. *See also* Secondary mortgage market.

Principal   The amount borrowed or remaining to be repaid.

Private mortgage insurance (PMI)   Mortgage insurance provided by a private mortgage insurance company that protects the lender against loss if a borrower defaults. Usually obtained if the initial loan to value exceeds 80 percent.

Promissory note   *See* Note.

Q

Quality control   A system of safeguards to ensure that all loans are originated, processed, underwritten, closed, and serviced according to the lender's and an investor's standards.

R

Rate lock   *See* Lock-in.

Recording   The recording of the details of a property transfer at the registrar's office.

Recourse   An originating lender's acceptance, assumption, or retention of some or all of the risk of loss generally associated with ownership of an asset, whether or not the lender owns or has ever owned the asset.

REMIC   A security that represents a beneficial interest in a trust having multiple classes of securities. The securities of each class entitle investors to cash flows structured differently from the payments on the underlying mortgages.

Required yield   An investor's required yield. It is quoted on a net basis—that is, it does not include the lender's servicing fee.

Reverse price risk   Exposure to the risk of falling interest rates that occurs when a lender makes a commitment to sell a loan to an investor before making a loan commitment to the borrower.

S

Seasoned loan   A loan on which a borrower has made payments for more than one year, as compared to newly originated or current production loans. For some investors, a loan may require two or more years before it is considered seasoned.

Scheduled/Actual (S/A)   A type of remittance requiring the lender to remit to Fannie Mae the scheduled interest due (whether or not it is collected from borrowers) and the actual principal payments collected.

Scheduled/Scheduled (S/S)   A type of remittance requiring the lender to remit to Fannie Mae the scheduled interest due and the scheduled principal due (whether or not payments are collected from borrowers).

Secondary mortgage market   A market in which existing mortgages are bought and sold. It contrasts with the primary mortgage market, in which mortgages are originated. *See also* Primary mortgage market.

Seller/servicer   A term for an approved corporation that sells and services mortgages for either FNMA or FHLMC.

Servicing   The duties of the mortgage lender as a loan correspondent as specified in the servicing agreement for which a fee is received. The collection for an investor of payments, interest, principal, and trust items such as hazard insurance and taxes on a note by the borrower in accordance with the terms of the note. Servicing also consists of operational procedures covering accounting, bookkeeping, insurance, tax records, loan payment follow-up, delinquency loan follow-up, and loan analysis.

Servicing contract   A written contract between an investor of mortgages and an organization that will perform the servicing responsibilities for those loans for the investor.

Servicing fee   The compensation a lender receives from an investor each month for servicing loans on its behalf.

Servicing released   Sale of the rights to service a loan when the loan is sold in the secondary market.

Servicing retained   Retention of the rights to service a loan when the loan is sold in the secondary market.

Spec home   A proposed house built by a builder without a contract for sale with a consumer. Usually financed by a lender and built on the "speculation" by the builder that someone will purchase the property at a later date.

Standard commitment   An agreement to sell or swap loans based on an investor's posted yields, rather than on negotiated terms.

Standby commitment   A commitment to purchase a loan or loans with specified terms, when both parties understand that delivery is not likely unless circumstances warrant. The commitment is issued for a fee with willingness to fund in the event that a permanent loan is not obtained. Such commitments are typically used to enable the borrower to obtain construction financing at a lower cost on the assumption that permanent financing of the project will be available on more favorable terms when the improvements are completed and the project is generating income.

Standby fees   The fees charged by an investor for a standby commitment. The fees are earned upon issuance and acceptance of the commitment.

T

Table funding A financing technique that occurs when a broker closes a mortgage loan with funds belonging to an acquiring lender and immediately assigns the loan to that lender. This activity gives the mortgage broker the opportunity to say it is a direct lender since it can close loans with its own funds.

Takeout commitment A promise to make a loan at a future specified time. It is commonly used to designate a higher cost, shorter term, backup commitment as a support for construction financing until a suitable permanent loan can be secured.

Title A legal document evidencing a person's right to ownership in real estate.

Title insurance Insurance that protects the lender (or borrower, if separate policy) against loss arising from disputes over ownership of real estate.

U

Underwriting The process of evaluating a loan application to determine the risk involved for the lender. Establishing whether the risk is worth taking.

V

VA mortgage A mortgage that is guaranteed by the Department of Veterans Affairs (VA).

W

Warehousing The holding of a mortgage on a short-term basis pending either a sale to an investor or other long-term financing. These mortgages may be used as collateral security with a bank to borrow additional funds. A builder warehouses mortgages when it takes back a mortgage from a homebuyer and holds the mortgage for a time period.

Whole loan A loan in which an investor purchases a 100 percent interest.

Y

Yield In real estate, the effective annual amount of income that is being accrued on an investment. Expressed as a percentage of the price originally paid.

Yield spread premium Basically, incentives paid by lenders to mortgage brokers for getting a client to accept a higher-interest-rate loan than the client qualifies for. Sometimes they are useful tools for borrowers to pay less closing costs upfront.

Index